10/18/90

To M.J.
SON who wants
To be a lawyer
Someday
Love, Dad.

1395

The
DOUGLAS
LETTERS

The DOUGLAS LETTERS

Selections
from the Private Papers of
Justice William O. Douglas

Edited with an Introduction by
MELVIN I. UROFSKY
with the assistance of
Philip E. Urofsky

ADLER&ADLER

Published in the United States in 1987 by
Adler & Adler, Publishers, Inc.
4550 Montgomery Avenue
Bethesda, Maryland 20814

Library of Congress Cataloging-in-Publication Data

Douglas, William O. (William Orville), 1898–1980
  The Douglas Letters

  Includes bibliographical references and index.
  1. Douglas, William O. (William Orville), 1898–1980
2. Judges—United States—Correspondence. I. Urofsky,
Melvin I. II. Urofsky, Philip E. III. Title.
KF8745.D6A4 1987 347.73'2634 87–1273
ISBN 0-917561-46-5 347.3073534

Printed in the United States of America
First Edition

For
Ronne and Cecil Jacobs
and
Sylvia and David Fine

Good food and good times with good friends

Contents

Introduction

William O. Douglas, 1898–1980

A BRIEF OUTLINE of William Douglas's life would strike some as totally implausible, akin to the luck-and-pluck Horatio Alger stories of the late nineteenth century—born into a poor but loving family, the widowed mother raising her brood in the near frontier conditions of the Pacific Northwest; a bout of polio, with determined self-rehabilitation by constantly pushing himself on long hikes in the Cascade Mountains; attendance at a small local college, followed by a brief stint at schoolteaching; riding the rails across the country to New York; working his way through Columbia Law School by tutoring; marriage to a hometown sweetheart; a brief interlude at a Wall Street firm; appointment as a professor at Columbia, where he soon became a member of the reform faction; after resignation over a matter of principle, joining the Yale Law School faculty, where he gained a reputation as one of the leaders of the new Legal Realism; consulting with New Deal agencies; appointment first as a member and then as chairman of the Securities and Exchange Commission; and finally nomination as the youngest person ever to sit on the United States Supreme Court.

If this were not enough, he participated in some of the great constitutional revolutions of the century, including civil rights and civil liberties; fulfilled the yen to travel with trips to nearly every corner of the world, resulting in books and articles making his a household name; almost died in a spectacular riding accident in the mountains; championed environmental protection and saved the historic C & O Canal from "development" as a road. There was romance as well, his first marriage breaking up, two more unsuccessful efforts, and then happiness with his fourth wife. Suspense was added by efforts to impeach him for his liberal judicial and political views and unorthodox life-style. In the end, death came as it must to all persons, but true to form, he did not go gently into that good night.

The scenario is there, but such a recounting hardly does justice to the man; it is too simple and straightforward. For all that he liked to portray himself as a simple country boy, Douglas was hardly that. In his memoirs he claimed that he never sought any appointment or advancement, yet as his letters show, he frequently maneuvered himself into the right position at the right time. He idolized and idealized his mother, a fact that at least two of his wives believed undermined his ability to develop an intimate adult relationship with other women. He could write eloquently about the sanctity of marriage, yet his womanizing was one of the poorest kept secrets in Washington. A man whom some considered a genius, he could never focus his energies in any one area and became intellectually lazy in his Court work. He wrote his opinions quickly—some would say in a slapdash manner—and they lacked the rigorous analysis and logical coherence which could have formed the basis for a lasting jurisprudence. He and Hugo Black gained reputations as absolutist interpreters of First Amendment protections, but the more stolid and plodding Black, not Douglas, wrote the opinions that created and sustained the preferred position doctrine.

Douglas's life and work, though, are important because of his involvement in many of the important legal and political developments of the middle fifty years of this century. How historians will ultimately evaluate his contribution is difficult to predict; it is unlikely that he will ever share the pantheon of Holmes, Brandeis, and Cardozo, or perhaps even the second level of Black or Frankfurter. But Douglas will continue to fascinate laypersons and scholars for many years to come, for few members of the nation's highest court have ever led such colorful and controversial lives.

Born in northwestern Minnesota on October 16, 1898, to the Reverend William and Mrs. Julia Douglas, the man who championed a rugged outdoors life barely survived a sickly childhood. He contracted infantile paralysis, and a doctor gave him little chance of survival. His mother spent hours administering the only remedy the local physician could suggest, frequent bathing and rubbing of his legs with warm salt water. The family moved to the state of Washington for the benefit of the Reverend Douglas's health, but when the pastor died of complications following surgery in 1904, the Douglas family stayed on in Yakima, a small commercial city in central Washington. There the widow Douglas raised her three children, Martha, William, and Arthur. And there Bill fought to regain full use of his legs.

He began to hike in the nearby Cascade Mountains, pushing himself to go a little farther and a little faster each time, until he overcame the lingering effects of the bout with polio. The frequent trips into the mountains also laid a foundation for Douglas's lifelong romance with nature. He learned all he could about plants and animals and watched with wonder the great seasonal changes. He learned to fish and hunt, but perhaps most important, he found peace in the mountains, tranquility which existed no place else for him and to which he would return time and again, an Anteus restoring his strength.

The drive to build himself up physically carried over into other areas of his life. The Yakima High School yearbook of 1916 noted that its valedictorian that year had been "born for success," and in his class oration he spoke of "concentration of mind and self-control." That fall Douglas enrolled in Whitman College in Walla Walla on a full-tuition scholarship, and continued the pattern of studying hard and working hard, although now free of his mother's protective eye, he began to play hard as well. Professors such as Benjamin H. Brown and William R. Davis also opened his eyes to the excitement of ideas and literature, which Douglas had only partially begun to grasp during his earlier solitary forays into the mountains.

After graduation he returned to Yakima, tried his hand at a few jobs, and taught in the local high school, but in his spare time he kept wandering over to the courthouse to sit in on the proceedings. He applied to law school, and both Harvard and Columbia accepted him. A friend advised him that a young man without money would never last three years in Cambridge; New York, however, provided opportunities to work one's way through law school. In the summer of 1922, with seventy-five dollars in his pocket, Douglas began the trek to New York as guardian of two thousand sheep bound for Minnesota. The adventures he encountered on the cross-country trip seemed to grow with the telling over the years, but there is no doubt that few of Douglas's classmates who entered Kent Hall with him that September had ever spent time in the company of hoboes and tramps or running from the "bulls" who policed the railroad yards. For Douglas, the experience not only introduced him to a new class of people, but also reinforced the mistrust and disdain of the "establishment" which the family's earlier poverty had engendered.

At the time Columbia, under the leadership of Dean Harlan Fiske Stone, had begun to explore new areas of legal research along lines which eventually coalesced into "Legal Realism." In the 1870s, Christopher Columbus Langdell had revolutionized legal education with the case method, in which students learned legal principles by studying their evolution through the leading cases. Although this marked a radical advance over the earlier method of rote memorization of rules, a significant weakness of the case method involved a near total ignorance of nonlegal events or conditions. Progressives such as Oliver Wendell Holmes, Roscoe Pound, and Ernst Freund had called for judicial cognizance of social conditions, and Louis Brandeis had brilliantly exemplified that idea in his famous "sociological" brief in *Muller* v. *Oregon* (1908).

By the 1920s, the new social science disciplines promised to provide legal scholars with the tools by which one could measure social conditions objectively and draw scientific conclusions regarding their impact on law. Underhill Moore, for example, whom Douglas regarded as perhaps his greatest teacher at Columbia, had been dipping into economics, anthropology, and psychology to discover why certain legal institutions behaved as they did. Moore soon picked the bright young Douglas to be his research assistant and invited him to his home in nearby New Jersey to discuss new and troubling ideas.

At Columbia Douglas again worked hard to earn his keep and played when he could, but law took up much of his time. He did well, won election to the *Columbia Law Review,* and graduated second in his class. The failure to rank first robbed him of the opportunity to serve as law clerk to Stone, who had just been appointed to the Supreme Court. He would later complain the choice had been unfair, but despite this setback, the world looked rosy in the summer of 1925. He had married Mildred Riddle (whom he had met while teaching in Yakima) in the summer between his second and third years of law school, and his scholastic accomplishments brought an offer from one of the outstanding Wall Street offices, the Cravath firm.

Douglas stayed in private practice for two years and hated the drudge work he did there. He spent much of his time doing the tedious research involved in the reorganization of the Chicago, Milwaukee, and St. Paul Railroad, which had gone into receivership. Douglas later claimed that he had learned all about Wall Street greed in those two years, as he watched dozens of banking houses and their lawyers pick up large fees for the reorganization work (Cravath put in a bill for $450,000), which should have gone to the bond and shareholders. At the time, however, Douglas complained not about the system but of the unexciting work he did as a junior associate, albeit as a well-paid one. He began looking for an alternative, even returning to Yakima with the idea of opening a private practice there. He found what he wanted when Columbia, where he had been teaching a few courses on a part-time basis, offered him a regular appointment as an assistant professor in the law school.

Douglas soon allied himself with the reformers, for his experience with Cravath had confirmed what Moore and others had taught him earlier—that economic, social, political, and psychological factors played as important a role in the law as legal principles. Within a short time after his arrival, however, the faculty split between reform-minded and more traditional members over who would become the new dean. The autocratic president of Columbia, Nicholas Murray Butler, named Young B. Smith to the post without consulting the faculty. Although opposed by the reformers, Smith did not stand against change; he could well be described as a moderate, but for Douglas he personified stand-pat conservatism.

In his autobiography, Douglas paints the struggle in far more dramatic terms than it deserves; although more than the usual bickering among disparate faculty interests, it hardly amounted to an apocalyptic struggle between the forces of light and darkness. Douglas resigned, supposedly in protest against Butler's high-handedness; what he fails to mention is that he already had an offer from the Yale Law School. Moreover, the departure of a junior faculty member, even one as promising as Douglas, attracted little attention at the time.

Yale then constituted *the* center for Legal Realism. Under the leadership of a young and brilliant dean, Robert M. Hutchins, the once-staid school led the way in exploring how nonlegal events and ideas affected the law. The presence of economist Walton Hamilton and political scientist Walter Dodd proclaimed Yale's willingness to learn from the social sciences. Hutchins hired Douglas and Underhill Moore from Columbia, and over the next few years, before he left to become president of the University of Chicago, he added other faculty members who made Yale the most exciting law school in the country for the next two decades.

His tenure at Yale may have been the most peaceful and happiest years of William Douglas's life. There is a note of contentment in his letters of that period which would not be heard afterwards. Happily married, the father of two children, enjoying his work, and recognized by his peers as a rising academic star, Douglas seemed to have found his place. A good but not a great teacher, he seemed popular among both students and colleagues. He pioneered in establishing a joint program between Yale Law and the Harvard Business School and published several important articles on business failures, an important subject in the Depression years. The Douglases themselves suffered little from the general economic collapse; Douglas earned a good salary, as well as royalties from his four casebooks. Within a few years after arriving in New Haven, he had been promoted to Sterling Professor of Law at the princely salary of $15,000, and he turned down an offer to go to Chicago which carried an even higher remuneration. What more could he want?

Evidently, a good deal. Despite the outward calm, Douglas often appeared restless and suffered from frequent migraine headaches. He entered into analysis with Dr. George Draper of Columbia and gradually rid himself of some anxieties. If a fear could only be brought into the open, Douglas believed, it could be conquered. Despite his fear of water, due to a near drowning in early childhood, Douglas forced himself into the Yale pool five days a week until he learned to swim. He never enjoyed the water, but at least he no longer feared it.

With the advent of the New Deal, Douglas yearned to get involved in the great reform work under way in Washington. It was well enough to do academic studies—even important ones— but the hordes of young lawyers who descended on Washington had the opportunity, or so they believed, of actively remaking society. In 1934, Douglas secured an assignment from the Securities and Exchange Commission (SEC), the agency stockholders used during bankruptcy reorganizations to protect their interests, to undertake a study of protective committees. Douglas began commuting from New Haven to Washington and gradually began spending more time in the capital than at school. He came to the attention of Joseph P. Kennedy, the first chairman of the SEC, who introduced the young professor to other movers and shakers in Washington politics.

Kennedy had agreed to head the SEC only until it could get its feet on the ground, and true to his word, he resigned in 1935. President Franklin D. Roosevelt promoted one of the SEC commissioners, former Harvard Law professor James M. Landis, to replace Kennedy, and then named the thirty-seven-year-old Douglas to the Commission. Where the conservative Landis focused most of his attention on administrative details and tried to avoid confrontation with the financial community, his new colleague seemed to court it. He told a group of stockbrokers that they were little more than money-grubbing salesmen who served little or no social purpose. In March 1937 Commissioner Douglas spoke at the Bond Club in New York, at a meeting attended by nearly every major investment banker on Wall Street. In tones many of them had never heard before from a government official, he castigated their predatory practices and called for reforms in the stock market which would have significantly limited their power and influence.

When Landis returned to Harvard to become dean of the law school in the summer of 1937, speculation on his successor soon centered on Douglas. Wall Street waged a desperate campaign to prevent the appointment, but Douglas had caught Roosevelt's attention; the President liked the way Douglas had told off the bankers and also enjoyed the young westerner's jokes at the private poker parties in the White House. Moreover, powerful political allies such as Kennedy, Benjamin V. Cohen, and others backed Douglas. In September, the President sent his name to the Senate for confirmation as the new SEC chairman.

If Wall Streeters expected Douglas to turn conservative with this added responsibility, as Landis had supposedly done, they soon learned otherwise. Douglas would be more than willing to cooperate with the banking and investment houses provided that they lived up to both the letter and spirit of the law. Where Landis had avoided conflict, Douglas seemed eager to butt heads. He had no desire, he told the press, to do away with the stock exchange, or to impose unreasonable rules; investors had to take their chances in the market, and if they lost, they lost. But the game had to be played fairly, which meant the stock exchange would have to reform itself; if not, the sec would do the job.

Few people expected Douglas to succeed, but backed by the President and his fellow sec commissioners, Douglas plowed ahead. The governors of the New York Stock Exchange resisted, but their opposition collapsed with the disclosure of embezzlement by one of their own, Richard Whitney, who had diverted funds from a trust account to cover his company's stock losses and then could not repay the amount. This proved too much for his fellow governors and for the public. Whitney, a former president of the Exchange, had personified Wall Street; he had constantly assured the public that the market operated honestly and therefore needed no government supervision. With his exposure as a common crook and his subsequent arrest, the governors of the Exchange soon agreed to the reform measures proposed by Douglas.

With this victory in hand, Douglas turned the sec into a crusading investigative body that searched out and exposed financial wrongdoing, even among influential and important banks and brokerage houses. At a time when many other New Deal agencies seemed unable to fulfill their early promise, the sec succeeded brilliantly. Douglas's name became known not only on Wall Street but also on Main Street, and Democratic Party leaders began to consider him as a potential candidate for elected office. But Douglas had already tired of the game, and when Yale offered him the deanship of the law school, he thought it would be a good time to leave Washington.

Douglas anticipated that Roosevelt would not like this idea and would try to keep him in the administration. On March 19, 1939, a messenger interrupted a golf game to inform Douglas that the President wanted to see him immediately at the White House. Roosevelt teased Douglas for a few minutes, implying that he wanted him to leave the sec and take over the troubled Federal Communications Commission; he then broke into a broad smile and told him that he had decided to name Douglas to replace Louis D. Brandeis on the Supreme Court.

He later alleged that the nomination came as a total surprise, a claim Felix Frankfurter also made about his own appointment. In fact, both men had had their friends busily at work promoting their candidacies; one might not be able to lobby openly for an appointment to the nation's highest tribunal, but other ways existed. Their greatest assets consisted of quick minds, loyalty to the New Deal, and the personal friendship of the President of the United States.

Douglas, the youngest man ever appointed to the Supreme Court, would establish a record for longevity of service before illness finally forced him to retire in late 1975. Moreover, no other justice ever engaged in so extensive and public a nonjudicial life. Douglas always claimed that the work of the Court never took more than three or four days a week; he read petitions rapidly, rarely agonized over decisions, could get to the heart of an issue instantly, and wrote his opinions quickly. This left him time for other activities, such as travel, lecturing, writing, climbing mountains, and, as some critics claimed, getting into trouble.

It would be impossible to treat Douglas's judicial career within the confines of a few pages. It is not that he developed a complex jurisprudence so much as that in thirty-six years he participated in thousands of cases and wrote hundreds of opinions on an enormous variety of topics. He gave the Court's opinion in *Ex parte Endo* (1944), which marked the Court's first objection to the internment of Japanese Americans in World War Two; in *Williamson* v. *Lee Optical Co.* (1955), his decision put an end for all practical purposes to judicial scrutiny of economic regulation; he established the basis for a modern constitutional right to privacy in *Griswold* v. *Connecticut* (1965), his most innovative and often-cited opinion; and he spoke for the Court in striking down the poll tax in *Harper* v. *Virginia Board of Elections* (1966).

He wrote many others, of course, and joined with Hugo L. Black in expanding the protections guaranteed by the Constitution. Douglas gladly deferred to Black in the latter's unsought role as leader of the libertarian wing of the Court. But like Black, he believed government should interfere as little as possible in a person's life. He wanted, he often said, to keep government off the backs of the people. Douglas could be just as eloquent as his Alabama friend in espousing the preferred position of First Amendment rights. The Constitution said Congress shall make *no* law abridging freedom of speech, and that meant just what it said—there could be no interference with the right of expression.

Critics complained that Douglas wanted the Court to be too active, that he ignored the inherent conservatism of the judicial role.

He agreed; at least in the area of civil liberties and civil rights, the judiciary should be active. Courts ought to defend constitutional rights in a positive manner and not just put restraints on executive or legislative actions. As for precedent, Douglas could pull them out with a law professor's facility when it suited his purpose; but as he said on more than one occasion, he would rather create a precedent than cite one.

Douglas's record, however, is far from consistent. In the Japanese internment cases, for example, he voted with the majority in the two major decisions validating the program. He spent several pages in his memoirs extolling his efforts to prevent the execution of Julius and Ethel Rosenberg, but he did not mention that on five separate occasions he had voted against the Court's accepting their petition for review. Several scholars have noted his reflexive vote against the Internal Revenue Service in tax cases, although even in dissent he rarely explained why he voted as he did.

To emphasize these inconsistencies, however, is to overlook Douglas's very real commitment to a libertarian jurisprudence. Very few people can review a lifetime's work and find no inconsistency, no regrets for opportunities missed, no errors of judgment or betrayal of principle. One can ignore Douglas's bravado and the self-congratulatory tone of his autobiographical writings because, for the most part, he did stand up for civil liberties both on and off the Court. During the 1960s, for example, he often differed with Black, and proved willing to give more protection to activists arrested in protests against racial discrimination and the war in Vietnam. One need not love the man—and he certainly had his share of unlovable characteristics—to concede that in most instances, William O. Douglas could be counted upon to stand for free speech, civil rights, and individual freedoms. To those who held these things dear, Douglas could be forgiven much.

Many scholars, and his colleagues on the bench, believe Douglas might have been more effective if he had tried to be a team player. He enjoyed his role as the great dissenter, but he often made it hard for others to join him because he would insist on taking the most extreme stance. As one of his fellow justices noted, Douglas would "put two or three sentences in a dissent that were so outrageous, you just couldn't join him." Beyond that, some of Douglas's opinions are just plain sloppy. Douglas biographer James Simon suggests that after his first decade on the Court, Douglas stopped writing for lawyers and law school teachers and began aiming his opinions and dissents at the general public. He certainly had the ability to write solid technical opinions, but for the most part he chose not to do so. He could write far more clearly than most judges and lawyers, and he hoped the people would understand his pleas for religious and racial tolerance and his explanations of why civil liberties had to be protected in a democracy.

While it is true that without popular support liberty cannot be preserved, without judicial cooperation liberty cannot be protected. Douglas never tried to be a "judges' judge," one whose opinions influenced and shaped decisions not only by colleagues on the high court, but also more importantly, by lower federal and state court judges. A result-oriented jurist, he cared more for the final decision than the process and reasoning by which one arrived at the result. In the school desegregation cases, for example, Douglas thought his nemesis on the bench, Felix Frankfurter, overcautious and unconcerned about civil rights. In fact, Frankfurter wanted to strike down segregation as much as Douglas but recognized the need to hand down a unanimous opinion, one that would carry judicial weight with the federal judges who would have to implement and enforce the decision.

Every court needs a libertarian conscience such as Douglas; but it also needs the craftsman who can forge a coherent and persuasive *legal* as well as moral argument as to why a certain result is necessary. William Douglas never saw this as his role; he preferred to be the loner on the bench, the dissident voice of conscience. It no doubt proved personally satisfying, but one can lament that a person so intellectually gifted chose not to exercise his talents in a more effective and lasting manner.

Douglas, of course, had items on his agenda other than court business. He had a wanderlust, which he learned to indulge soon after World War Two. Although in his letters he often claimed to have traveled at his own expense, he rarely paid for trips directly. In most instances he would contract with a publisher or a magazine, frequently *National Geographic,* for an article or book and use the advance to cover the costs of the adventure or bill the expenses to the publisher afterward. He also took advantage of frequent speaking engagements in faraway places to explore even further into strange worlds. The results were a series of engagingly written books and articles which reflected Douglas's wide-ranging mind. He had a marvelous childlike interest in everything—plants, animals, local customs, and above all, people. When he wanted, Douglas could be exceedingly charming.

He often went places and saw things and people far off the track taken by the diplomats and professional Foreign Service officers. As a result, he learned a great deal about what the common people thought, and this frequently ran against the official governmental position. Douglas had no compunction about pointing out the fallacies of American foreign policy in his writing, often to the despair and anger of presidents and State Department officials. Too often he claimed to be an "expert" on a country just because he had spent a couple of weeks traveling around in rural areas. But there is no question that on a number of occasions his analysis of the problems proved far more prescient than the overly optimistic prognoses of the State Department officials.

One area in which Douglas remained consistent throughout his career involved protection of the environment, especially preservation of wild habitats. He had learned to love hiking in the mountains as a boy and feared the encroachment of so-called progress in the ever-shrinking wilderness areas. As in so much of what he did, Douglas went to extremes. He believed wilderness should be just that, with no accommodations made for man. He opposed cutting trails or campsites; if people wanted to get in, they should park their cars outside, strap on a backpack, and hike. People who wanted comfort should stay in motels; if they wanted to stay in the wilderness, then a tent and a bedroll would be sufficient. He recognized that this would keep many people from going in to wilderness areas, and that suited him just fine. Too many people polluted the environment and infringed upon the true outdoors type, a person like himself willing to take nature on its own terms.

Where man had already invaded nature, Douglas did not call for a retreat; but he did oppose further destruction of natural resources. His greatest victory and most publicized effort came in connection with efforts to prevent paving over the old C & O Canal next to the Potomac River, running northwest from Washington. Every year Douglas led a hike along the canal, and eventually Congress voted funds to turn it into a national park, with the towpaths devoted to hikers and bicyclists, and the canal itself reserved for canoeists. Fittingly, the park would eventually be dedicated to Douglas.

Douglas did not confine his speeches and writings to travel or to the environment or to generalized legal lectures. He believed that as a citizen he had a right to speak out on any issue which might affect him, and he saw his judicial responsibilities as limited only in that he should not make public pronouncements on a matter which might come before the Court. He resigned from several environmental groups when they began to litigate as part of their effort to protect natural resources, but he rationalized his statements on foreign policy by explaining that such issues rarely come to the Supreme Court for adjudication. Some of his other activities, however, including the liaison with the Parvin Foundation, did involve potential conflicts of interest, and a more prudent jurist would have recognized that, like Caesar's wife, a judge must be above reproach.

The effort to impeach Douglas grew out of political motivations far more than from a sense that he had done something wrong. Douglas's outspoken liberalism, his half-muted criticisms of government policy, and above all, Republican desire to name one of their own and thus transform the high court into a conservative bastion, led to the impeachment proposal, which never really had a chance of success. It exposed some of Douglas's weaknesses, but none of them could even remotely be construed as the "high crimes and misdemeanors" which the Constitution requires for the removal of a federal official. The hearings, in fact, made Gerald Ford, soon to be President of the United States, appear mean, petty, and sanctimonious.

Douglas erroneously viewed the dismissal of the charges as a vindication of his conduct; the committee properly concluded that he had not committed an impeachable offense, but to many people the exposure of his off-the-court activities raised troubling questions about his judicial conduct. Douglas certainly had no intention of behaving improperly or unethically; rather, he assumed an incorruptibility on his part which could rationalize anything he did. If Douglas had acted in a certain manner, it could not be wrong. Unfortunately, it might not have been right or proper.

An unspoken but nonetheless crucial item on the impeachment agenda involved Douglas's four marriages, the last two to women young enough to be his granddaughters. Again, conduct the public tolerates among movie stars is not the same it expects from members of the Supreme Court. One can argue that a justice or senator or president should be able to marry whom he or she pleases, and if the marriage fails, to secure a divorce and try again, and perhaps more than once. There is a double standard applied to elected officials, who are well aware of the political liability of a divorce, even today. Judges, of course, enjoy life tenure during good behavior. To many people, Douglas's well-publicized marriages and less-publicized philandering did not constitute "good behavior."

The failure of Douglas's first three marriages, as well as his poor relations with his children, is one of the more tragic aspects of his life. Whether the psychological trauma of his youth and his close ties to his mother prevented the establishment of an adult relationship with other women, whether he found his children disappointing because they could not or would not live up to his often unreasonable expectations, or whether, as some claimed, Douglas was just selfish and self-centered, his often unhappy personal life stands in stark contrast to his public accomplishments and élan. The letters that follow illustrate both the accomplishments and the failures of William O. Douglas's remarkable life and career.

A Note on the Douglas Papers

T HE LETTERS in this volume have been selected from the William O. Douglas Papers in the Manuscript Division of the Library of Congress. At the time we used them, they were closed to public research, although the staff had started the arduous task of preparing the hundreds of thousands of documents for eventual access by scholars. Those selected for this volume have been edited and annotated in a manner that allows Douglas to speak for himself through his letters. The notes have been kept to a minimum and include only information which we hope will allow the reader to better understand the documents.

There have been some questions raised about whether Douglas cleansed his files of embarrassing material in the years between his retirement from the Court and his death. We have heard conflicting stories from persons who ought to know; the evidence in the papers themselves is far from conclusive. There are gaps, especially in files dealing with his private life; one *expects* certain folders to be thicker. However, there are many letters still extant which one might have expected to have been destroyed if a purge had taken place. There does not seem to have been any systematic or wholesale destruction of documents, and beyond that one will have to wait until the library cataloging is complete to identify any large gaps in the contents, if in fact they exist.

The Justices with whom William O. Douglas Served on the United States Supreme Court 1939–1975

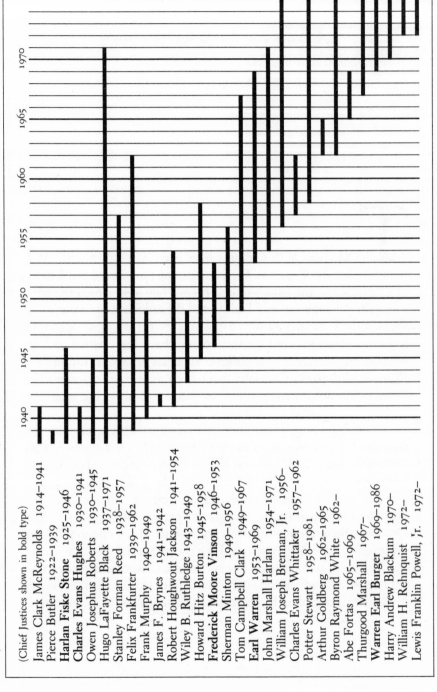

(Chief Justices shown in bold type)

James Clark McReynolds 1914–1941
Pierce Butler 1922–1939
Harlan Fiske Stone 1925–1946
Charles Evans Hughes 1930–1941
Owen Josephus Roberts 1930–1945
Hugo LaFayette Black 1937–1971
Stanley Forman Reed 1938–1957
Felix Frankfurter 1939–1962
Frank Murphy 1940–1949
James F. Brynes 1941–1942
Robert Houghwout Jackson 1941–1954
Wiley B. Ruthledge 1943–1949
Howard Hitz Burton 1945–1958
Frederick Moore Vinson 1946–1953
Sherman Minton 1949–1956
Tom Campbell Clark 1949–1967
Earl Warren 1953–1969
John Marshall Harlan 1954–1971
William Joseph Brennan, Jr. 1956–
Charles Evans Whittaker 1957–1962
Potter Stewart 1958–1981
Arthur Goldberg 1962–1965
Byron Raymond White 1962–
Abe Fortas 1965–1969
Thurgood Marshall 1967–
Warren Earl Burger 1969–1986
Harry Andrew Blackmun 1970–
William H. Rehnquist 1972–
Lewis Franklin Powell, Jr. 1972–

Chapter 1

Professor Douglas

THE YEARS AT the Yale Law School may have been among the happiest in William O. Douglas's life. For the first time, he had a good income; he doted on his wife and two young children; his research excited him intellectually and earned him a national reputation; and he found his colleagues and some of his students congenial and stimulating.

As a teacher, Douglas received mixed reviews. Although well organized, his shyness nonetheless prevented him from being a popular and dynamic teacher in the large sections. He shone, however, in the small seminars, where he won the admiration and lifelong devotion of a number of students. Robert Hutchins exaggerated when he characterized Douglas as "the nation's outstanding law professor," but in the intellectual ferment which gripped American law schools in the late twenties and thirties, there is no doubt Douglas played a leading role.

Douglas had become a law teacher at an exciting time. The so-called Realist school had begun its campaign to analyze law not only in terms of prior case decisions and so-called first principles, but also in light of economics, history, sociology, and psychology. First at Columbia and then at Yale, Douglas not only identified with the Realists, or as they were also called, Functionalists, but also became a major figure in the movement, gaining national renown for his pioneering work in commercial law, especially bankruptcy.

The Realists attacked the Conceptualists who, they claimed, tried to deduce first principles from studying prior case law. The conceptualist bastion had long been Harvard, where in the 1870s Christopher Langdell had revolutionized legal education by introducing the case method. Douglas had no particular problem with studying prior judicial decisions, but he opposed limiting the study of commercial law to just cases. He wanted his students to understand how corporations worked, what economic factors affected decision making, and what financial problems they faced. In short, he wanted them to know as much about the business end as the law segment of commercial law; this view informed his teaching and research and led to the famous joint experimental program between the Yale Law School and the Harvard Business School.

Douglas got his start at Columbia, which pioneered the functionalist approach early in the 1920s, originally with the support of its autocratic president, Nicholas Murray Butler. But well before Douglas and other Realists proved willing to admit it, some Columbia faculty recognized that the social sciences, supposed to provide the basis for the new understanding of law, had not developed to the point where they could carry that burden. At Yale the Realist movement lasted until after World War Two, but it too eventually faded. The social science insights did not prove all that useful, and nearly all law schools accepted the need to add the facts of the real world to legal theory.

To Nicholas Murray Butler[1]

April 5, 1928

My dear President:

Your decision to nominate Professor Smith[2] as Dean of the Law School disturbs me greatly. I respectfully suggest a delay and postponement in the matter for the following reasons.

In the first place, the members of the Faculty of Law have had no opportunity to canvass thoroughly the situation because they learned of Mr. Jervey's[3] decision only on receipt of your letter. And there is every reason to believe that if the members of the Faculty were given an opportunity to make a recommendation, they could get unanimity.[4]

Further, if the office of Dean required nothing but routine, secretarial, intra-University duties, the choice would be admirable.

But the office is not thus delimited. In fact more important than such duties would seem to be (1) the contacts with students; (2) the contacts with the outside world; and (3) the leadership of, and the cooperation with, the members of the Faculty on educational programs.

On the student phase his deficiencies are extremely great. I daresay the majority of those students who come into contact with him have no respect for him either as a person or as a scholar. Evidence on this point of a conclusive nature could be marshalled. Under such circumstances no *esprit de corps* among alumni could ever be secured. That respect and love for an institute which the name of Stone[5] conjures would be entirely lacking.

In regard to his contacts with the outside world, the choice is likewise quite unhappy. His lack of general culture and his uncouthness are patent. Even students in his classes are open in their comment on it. His total lack of appreciation of the general educational program which is in the making in Kent Hall,[6] makes him peculiarly unfitted to give it the generous, intelligent publicity and leadership needed to launch it and steer it over even a chartered course, let alone an unchartered one.

And finally, Mr. President, his almost total lack of imagination and his decidedly deficient intellectual equipment make it not only unlikely but impossible that he can bind together and lead and direct that group of unusually promising young men who are well launched on the new project and on whose efforts the success for the new law school depends, a law school which would eclipse the Columbia and Harvard of yesterday and which would blaze the path in legal education for the future.

On the other hand the appointment presages for legal education at Columbia mediocrity rather than excellence; recession instead of progress; disintegration rather than new life. The appointment sounds the death knell to the present promising program. And there is an incongruity in it—the man who for years has done more than any one to make impossible the present program is peculiarly unfitted to head it up.

The abundance of the evidence which can be adduced to support these assertions recommends delay. The seriousness of these charges warrants postponement.

Only my deep-rooted love for the institution and my despondency in seeing it about to miss its splendid opportunity, and to continue to be dominated in spirit by the narrow craft outlook of the practitioner, lead me to speak so frankly.

I am taking the privilege of sending a copy of this letter to the Chairman of the Committee on Education.

---

1. Butler (1862–1947) served as president of Columbia University for more than four decades and built it into a major and prestigious institution.

2. Young Berryman Smith (1889–1960) was hardly the reactionary WOD painted, but he remained quite skeptical about the claims of the Realists and their reliance on social science methods. He also opposed their desire to turn Columbia into strictly a research school and wanted to maintain its traditional mission of training practitioners.

3. Huger Wilkinson Jervey (1878–1949) had been the compromise appointment as dean, but after four years he wanted nothing else to do with the growing factionalism on the faculty.

4. There was hardly unanimity on the faculty, either on Smith's incompetence or of another candidate; moreover, the faculty had never elected the dean, which had traditionally been the prerogative of the university president.

5. Harlan Fiske Stone (1872–1946) had been dean of Columbia Law from 1910 to 1923, when Butler had forced his resignation because of his alleged un-receptiveness to new ideas. He became Coolidge's attorney general and then a member of the Supreme Court in 1925; in 1941 Franklin Roosevelt elevated the Republican Stone to be Chief Justice.

6. The home of the Law School.

To Nicholas Murray Butler

June 11, 1928

Dear Mr. President:

I hand you herewith my resignation as Assistant Professor [of] Law to become effective July 1, 1928.

The reason for this action is your nomination to the Trustees of Professor Y. B. Smith to be Dean of the Faculty of Law, without consultation with the members of said faculty.

Such action makes it impossible for me to continue to serve this institution at this time.[1]

---

1. WOD was not the only member of the faculty to resign, but there is a question of when he actually did so. According to Simon's biography, WOD was reappointed to the faculty for the following academic year, and his resignation was

not announced until the fall. Moreover, he continued to sit on faculty committees. In his autobiography, WOD claims that he resigned and was trying to decide where to practice law when he met Hutchins, who then offered him a job. It appears more likely that although he intended to resign, WOD did not do so until assured he would have a place at Yale.

To James Rowland Angell [1]

June 12, 1928

Dear Mr. President:

I have your letter of June 11th inviting me to come to Yale as an Assistant Professor of Law. I accept your invitation with pleasure.

I am delighted with the opportunity to work with your group in the further development of the Yale School of Law. I am confident that under the leadership of you and Dean Hutchins [2] it will make unprecedented progress in legal education.

---

1. Angell (1869–1949) served as president of Yale from 1921 to 1937.

2. Robert Maynard Hutchins (1899–1977) would be a lifelong friend and champion of WOD after their meeting in 1928; they reportedly got drunk together on bootleg whiskey at a country club where Hutchins, then dean of Yale Law School, had given a speech. A few days later, he offered WOD a job. Hutchins championed the Realists at Yale, and when he went to Chicago to become the country's youngest university president, he tried to lure WOD out there. Later the two men would collaborate at the Center for Democratic Institutions, which Hutchins headed after his retirement from the University of Chicago.

To Stephen Beasley Linnard Penrose [1]

December 14, 1928

Dear President Penrose:

. . . In recommending your students to eastern law schools, I wish you would keep in mind Yale. I don't know of any Whitman man who has attended Yale Law School. This school deserves at this time the attention of the entire country in view of the new methods for the study of law being undertaken here. It transcends every development in legal education in the last half century. In essence it treats law as one of the social sciences closely correlated to and coordinated with all other social sciences. Measurable improvement of both the bar and the bench seems inevitable. In addition to this peculiar advantage which this law school has there is another. It is in all respects a national law school, for men from practically every state in the country meet and live together for a period of three years. Its other advantages you are well aware of. . . .

---

1.   Penrose (1864–1947) served as president of Whitman College, WOD's alma mater, from 1894 to 1934.

To Harper Joy [1]

March 20, 1929

My dear Harper:

. . . I am glad to hear that another boy from the west has decided to come east to study law. I would give Mr. Rothrock the following advice. There are only two eastern law schools to consider, Yale and Columbia. They are the only ones that have anything progressive and unique to offer. It is not hard to choose between these two on the merits. Yale, I believe, is by far the better because of its smaller numbers, its superior location and its superior administration. Columbia has over 800, Yale has only 500. The students at Yale are highly selected and are, therefore, on the average of a higher calibre. The staff of instruction is as large as the staff at either Columbia or Harvard. Here there are not over ten students to each instructor. I am sure this will prove particularly attractive to a man who has gone through a small college and is sold on the small college idea. At the same time the Law School here is particularly well off financially, having recently received five million dollars for a new law school building and over seven million dollars for field investigation and research. This means that the best possible equipment and facilities for the study of law will be found here. The teaching staff here exceeds in quality on the whole the staff at Columbia and Harvard. So much for the merits. Since your friend will probably be under-financed when he comes east, he should know something about the prospects of being able to work his way through. He should not come to Yale unless he has $500 a year to draw upon. The total expenses for the year should run close to $1000. If his scholastic standing is high, he can get a scholarship here which will run from $100 to $400, depending largely upon his scholastic standing. If his law school record is good, this scholarship can be renewed. The chances of making money on the side while going to the Law School here are not so good. Tutoring is very very scarce, and as you can surmise that is the only highly paid work. The other work consists of tending furnaces, etc., which bring little financial return. The good jobs are hard to get because the Yale undergraduates seem to have most of them. It is hard for an outsider to break in, naturally.

The conditions at Columbia on that score are a little different. If your friend has a good scholastic standing, he can probably get a scholarship at Columbia. Application should be made before May 1st, however, and I should be glad to give any recommendation which is necessary. The scholarship at Columbia will cover most, if not all, of the tuition. The total expenses for one year would be $1000 at the minimum. The chances of making this amount on the outside are good, although not absolute. As you know, a lot depends upon breaks, but Art[2] and I did it. Each of us made from $1000 to $1500 a year tutoring. There is a lot of tutoring in New York. The most common is Latin. If your man is well versed in Latin, I should judge he would have little difficulty in making expenses. Next to Latin comes the lower mathematics and after mathematics come History and the other languages. Both Art and I know the director and the assistant-director of the Appointments Bureau at Columbia and both of us would do as much as possible to see to it that your friend got the right introduction.

The upshot of this is that if your friend has $500 a year for three years, he should head for Yale; if he hasn't he should head for Columbia. . . .

---

1.   Joy had been a classmate and close friend of WOD at Whitman College; he then became an investment banker.

2.   WOD's brother, Arthur.

To Wilbur Clayton Plummer[1]

December 7, 1929

Dear Dr. Plummer:

The clinic[2] yesterday was a great success. We got very satisfactory data on almost thirty cases. The next clinic is December 13th at the same hour. After that there will be no more clinics until the first part of January. Judge Clark[3] wants a conference with you, Dr. Hiscock, members of the field staff and me on Tuesday morning, December 17th, for the purpose of going over all the cases which we will have by then, with a view to making some tentative analysis and statement which can be given to the press. I told him that it was my impression that Tuesdays were one of your free days.

The Psychology Department here has been interested in the possibility of giving some intelligence tests to the various bankrupts. Probably all of us have the hunch that most of these men are quite dumb and perhaps morons. It is probably a good hunch but it doesn't mean very much unless it is backed up by facts. Dr. Hull[4] of the Psychology Department here selected an intelligence test devised particularly for business institutions, which has been used quite extensively and successfully throughout the country by various businesses. He went down with me yesterday and we presented the proposition to Judge Clark who thought that it might be inadvisable to give the test at the clinic because it might arouse opposition. He felt that it might be taken as an insult by these men. However, he did call Robbins into his office and suggest that as Robbins made his rounds to these various men, he might occasionally try to get the men to take one. It occurred to me that it might be a very sensible idea, if it could be worked. If lack of intelligence is a or the cause of failure, it certainly is significant. No complete analysis of causes would be complete without it. It remains to be seen whether any information can be secured. I should like to talk to you at some length about it when I see you next time.

---

1. Plummer taught at the University of Pennsylvania.

2. WOD and his staff conducted so-called clinics at bankruptcy courts. They administered questionnaires to those filing for bankruptcy and tried to pry out as much information as possible on a variety of subjects. From this data, they hoped to learn about behaviors and outcomes of those behaviors.

3. William Clark (1891–1957) served as a U.S. district court judge from 1925–1938 and was then named to the Third Circuit. It was in his Newark court that WOD conducted his clinics for nine months.

4. Clark Leonard Hull (1884–1952) was associated with the Institute of Human Relations at Yale, the focus of the social science expertise for the Law School Realists.

To Karl Nickerson Llewellyn[1]

March 17, 1930

Dear Karl:

I made a big mistake before I sent the final copy of Management[2] to the printer. I went over very carefully your casebook on Sales. I became immediately discouraged at my own feeble efforts. I realized that I should be publishing two years from now rather than now but it was too late to rescind. So off it went leaving me with a feeling that I had produced something half baked. I was not discouraged at the quality of what I had done but merely with the fact that I had gone but half the distance which I wanted to go. My stuff will look like a hybrid between your book and the typical ancient casebook.

You have really done a beautiful job and I wish to compliment you on it. . . .

---

1.   Llewellyn (1893–1962), then at Columbia Law, was perhaps the outstanding Realist scholar. His *Cases and Materials on the Law of Sales* (1930), which had just appeared, became the model for many other functionalist texts.

2.   WOD and Carroll Shanks, *Cases and Materials on the Law of Management of Business Units* (1930).

To Robert Patterson Lamont[1]

May 21, 1930

Dear Mr. Secretary:

I wish to thank you for your letter of May 17 in which you spoke of your great interest in the study of the causes of business failure. Your co-operation with us in the past has been invaluable. We are pleased to know that this co-operation will continue in the extended study to be launched in the fall. We feel that your co-operation will be indispensable to the success of such study.

With the funds which we hope to raise we will expand the study so that it will lose some of its purely local aspects and become more national in scope and importance. We feel that this project will have a great appeal to foundations and other groups in view of the fact that it will be conducted under the auspices of your Department and the two Universities.

I hope to be able to advise you in the near future that the additional funds which we are seeking have been raised.

---

1. Lamont (1867–1948) was secretary of commerce under Hoover from 1930 to 1932.

To Robert Maynard Hutchins

May 22, 1930

Dear Bob:

Upon receiving your letter of May 20th, I have about concluded that my trip to Chicago will not be worthwhile. Under the guise of a few conferences and a minor social whirl, I was going to attempt to create such a nuisance value that you would do anything to remove me from either the servants' quarters or the master bedroom. I thought (perhaps foolishly) that you might either offer me my return fare to New Haven or thrust me upon one or more of your hired men as an assistant, with possibly enough income to keep me from starving and at the same time keep me from becoming too conspicuous. . . .

If I recover from this depression, I shall probably be in Chicago May 31st and part of June 1st. If your faculty and time permit, I may try to keep you away from Church on that Sunday.

To Arthur O'Keeffe[1]

November 26, 1930

Dear O'Keeffe:

. . . Work here goes along in much the same way except that I have been extraordinarily busy. The book on Management is going to appear February first, and at the present time I am busy reading galley. A month ago we just finished the manuscript for the second book which we are calling Finance.[2] I expect to be swamped with galley on that before long. The third book is still in preparation, and I am beginning to feel that I do not care if it ever appears.[3] My desire for collecting cases is about as low as my desire for collecting postage stamps. In addition I have been giving about one-half of my time to the Federal Court Study which we are making for the National Commission on Law Observance and Enforcement. I also have a staff of four people diligently at work on the bankruptcy study which we are making in the field in Boston. I am also engaged in doing a job for the President's Committee on Social Trends. Of course, in addition to these matters is the regular teaching schedule. So you can see by this that I do not have much time to risk my fortune on games of poker or other games of chance. . . .

---

1. O'Keeffe taught law at the University of Southern California.

2. WOD and Carroll Shanks, *Cases and Materials on the Law of Financing Business Units* (1931).

3. The last of the three texts, WOD, Shanks, and James Cooper, *Cases and Materials on Business Units—Losses, Liabilities and Assets,* appeared in 1932.

To James Rowland Angell

December 19, 1930

Dear Mr. Angell:

I was very pleased to learn from Dean Clark[1] yesterday of your willingness to raise my salary to $15,000 next year. Should I decide to stay at Yale rather than accept Mr. Hutchins's most attractive offer, there would be one complicating factor in the situation. I thought it best to call it to your attention at this time. It is that I should be most embarrassed to accept a salary which would exceed the salary of Dean Clark. In fact, I really do not think I could bring myself to do it. I wish to take this occasion to thank you for your most generous offer. It is making my decision even more difficult.[2]

---

1. Charles Edward Clark (1889–1963) served as dean of Yale Law School from 1929 to 1939, when he was appointed to the Second Circuit Court of Appeals.

2. Yale had offered WOD $11,000 for the 1930–31 academic year in a letter from Dean Clark dated June 10, 1930, with a promise to raise it to $15,000 annually by the beginning of the 1933–34 year, a generous offer in light of Yale's financial difficulties during the Depression. Hutchins, trying to lure WOD to Chicago, offered him the unheard-of salary of $20,000. WOD, however, while attracted by Hutchins and the money, had a number of projects going at Yale which he did not want to abandon or have to move. He informed Dean Clark of the Chicago offer, and the Yale Corporation, in order to keep WOD, offered to promote him to full professor

and raise his salary; soon after, WOD became Sterling Professor of Law at a salary of $15,000, and he stayed at Yale until joining the SEC.

To William Clark

January 16, 1931

My dear Judge:

Commuting between here and Chicago, working for Wickersham, editing two books of my own, working on bankruptcy, plus the normal teacher's activity has consumed so much of my time that I am weeks behind in my correspondence. I was planning to write you congratulating you on your courageous stand. It was a genuine pleasure to read the opinion.[1] It was an exceedingly brilliant piece of work. Several Ph.Ds in political science should be given for it. Never has an opinion caused so much comment and discussion. I dare say even the Dred Scott decision created no more than a ripple compared with the tidal wave which has followed your decision. It is most gratifying to read an opinion dealing with principles of government so well bottomed on theories and facts. Most of them are written in vacuo with no relationship to the issues involved. All this though I have a sneaking hunch the Supreme Court will reverse.[2]

---

1. In *United States* v. *Sprague*, 44 F.2d 967 (E.D.N.J. 1930), Judge Clark had ruled the Eighteenth (Prohibition) Amendment invalid, since it had not been ratified according to strict constitutional requirements.

2. The Court did just that on February 24, 1931, at 282 U.S. 716. The same argument which Judge Clark had set forth had been heard, and rejected, by the high court in the *National Prohibition Cases*, 253 U.S. 350 (1920).

To Karl Nickerson Llewellyn

April 13, 1931

Dear Karl:

I enclose herewith a few notes I made re: Pound.[1] I am sorry I did not have the opportunity of spending more time on it. In fact I did not get at this until the small hours of this morning after a long day's work, and when I was dog tired. I have not had an opportunity to check it over but I am sending it on to you with the hope that you will not use it against me and may find one or two points therein which you may be able to use.

I had thought for a while writing you not to go ahead with the article.[2] I felt it might be purely or largely defensive, but from what you said the other day I gathered it would not be that. I have some distrust for mere battles of words. The proof of the pudding is in the eating and a couple of careful fact studies will do more to overthrow Pound than dozen articles, but I think you have persuaded me of the wisdom of going ahead. However, I think we have secured just about as much advertising as we can stand without doing some productive work along the line indicated. Contra, of course, might be cited Pound who has done a hell of a lot of talking but has never produced a first class job in the application of the things he has been talking about.

---

1.   Roscoe Pound (1870–1964) was longtime dean of the Harvard Law School and a leading opponent of the Realists. He had just published an attack on them, "The Call for a Realist Jurisprudence," 44 *Harvard Law Review* (*h.l.r.*) 697 (1931). Ironically, Pound had been one of the leaders of the so-called "Sociological Jurisprudence" just twenty years earlier; reformers had praised the call by Pound and others that judges take notice of social, economic, and political facts and not just legal principles, an idea which had much in common with Realism.

2.   Nickerson responded to Pound in "Some Realism About Realism," 44 *h.l.r.* 1234 (1931).

To Alfred McCormack[1]

October 1, 1931

Dear Al:

I am glad to know that you are contemplating an anti-Berleian[2] effusion. I too am in the same mood. In fact I am contemplating an article for the Harvard Law Review which will be an answer to his most recent article entitled "Corporate Powers as Powers in Trusts."

There is very little critical literature on minority stockholders actions. Offhand I do not recall anything particularly worth reading. However, in the next few days I will go through my notes and see if there is anything. Some of the stuff this boy Berle has been getting off is not only bum law but also very very poor theory.

I am very sorry I did not get a chance to see you and your wife at Wilton this summer. After my family returned from the west, the infantile paralysis scare drove us out of town sooner than we had expected. Since the first week in August I have been summering on the rocks in and around Triggs Island.

---

1. McCormack (1901–1956) had been a classmate of wod at Columbia Law and had barely edged him out to graduate at the top of the class. McCormack had gone on to clerk for Harlan Stone and then entered the Cravath firm.

2. Adolph Augustus Berle (1895–1971) was professor of corporation law at Columbia from 1927 to 1964, with frequent absences for government service. wod's pique at Berle was at least partially personal, for although more conservative than wod, Berle did advocate an approach to law blending large doses of economics with legal theory.

To Nathan Isaacs [1]

July 20, 1932

Dear Mr. Isaacs:

I have delayed a long time in answering your letter of a month or so ago relative to an interchange of law students between here and the Harvard Business School. On receipt of your letter I had a long talk with Dean Clark about it. He, as well as I, was very enthusiastic . . . .We have canvassed the various graduates here and do not find the proper individual to send up to you next year. By the time the men finish three years here they are very anxious to begin active practice or to get into teaching. Of course a number of them do desire to take graduate work but the stipends available in some law schools for that purpose are so attractive as to put all graduate work pretty much on a competitive basis.

Hence I am not so sure that we can expect good results by drawing on men who have received their LL.B. from the law school. It strikes me that we will have to start with the men in their first year in law school and work out a program of education which will give them part of their time here and part of their time in Boston. It might mean changing back and forth each semester or it might entail a longer stay at each place. I propose to talk to first and possibly second year men this fall to see if I cannot get some of them started on such a program. I believe it can be done, and I am convinced that it should be done. It will require considerable planning. . . .

---

1. Isaacs (1886–1941) had taught business law at the Harvard Business School since 1924; under this program he would also give occasional lectures at Yale Law School.

To William Joseph Donovan [1]

December 12, 1932

Dear Colonel Donovan:

I am taking the liberty of sending down to see you a member of our third year class who is looking for work next year. He is Mr. Abe Fortas,[2] chairman of the Yale Law Journal this year. I have no idea what your requirements for next year may be, but I wanted Mr. Fortas to have the privilege of meeting you and talking with you about law practice in New York.

I send him down because he is not merely a good man, but an outstanding man in every respect. In my seven or eight years of teaching I have seen but few men equal to him. He is an extraordinary person. My contacts with him have been very frequent and intimate during his three years here. I have seen him not only in class, but in honors and research work where he has shown great independence of thought and an unusual amount of imagination and resourcefulness.

He is not anxious to get into a big firm in New York but would prefer to work for men whom at a distance he has come to respect and admire. You are one of these men, and, irrespective of whether or not you would have a place for him, I wanted him to meet you and to talk over the whole New York situation with you.

---

1. Donovan (1883–1959) is best remembered as the founder of America's intelligence operations, but for many years he maintained a law practice in New York and had a special expertise in bankruptcy.

2. Fortas (1910–1982) would work with WOD at the SEC, be his lifelong friend, and eventually join him on the Supreme Court. See WOD's letters to Fortas in chapter 5.

To George E. Bates [1]

April 7, 1933

Dear George:

The following is a rather confidential matter about which I want to talk with you when you come down next week. I was called down to New York this week to have luncheon with Ferdinand Pecora,[2] Special Counsel to the Senate Committee on Banking and Currency—the fellow who put Mitchell[3] on the spot. He wants me to make a study for him which will be used in his investigation of the stock exchange. What I would prepare would be given publicity only by him through his Committee. As you probably know he has hopes of being able to present at the close of his investigation a regulatory bill covering stock exchange operations.

He wants my study to be done here in New Haven in connection with three or four of the biggest brokerage houses here. He suggests a rather general theme of "social and economic incidences" of stock market operations. I was quite offish to begin with, as you might well imagine. I told him that everyone knew what the dire effects of unlimited speculation were, and I did not think it would be particularly illuminating to count the number of people who had jumped off buildings, fired their maids, sold their Lincolns, or stolen their employers' money. He agreed but stated nevertheless that he wants some illustrative episodes to use in presenting various aspects of the stock exchange to the Committee. I did not have an awfully long time with him, but at that point in our conversation I asked him if he would be interested in the consequences of particular financial processes, for example, secondary distribution. He said that he clearly would. In fact he will leave pretty much up to me what should be done.

He wants one report in June and another report in September. I have not as yet cleared with the University authorities but I am sounding them out today or tomorrow. If they give their approval, then I want to examine in detail just what might be done. I do not want to turn myself into a reporter for the New York Journal or

Liberty magazine, but through the power of subpoena which we would have it might be interesting to make a little exploration in a very limited field.[4]

---

1.   George E. Bates taught at and was later dean of the Harvard Business School.

2.   Pecora (1882–1971), a New York State judge, won national attention as chief investigator for the Senate Committee on Banking in its examination of stock market practices prior to the crash. The findings ultimately led to the creation of the SEC.

3.   Charles Edwin Mitchell (1877–1955), head of the National City Bank, had admitted to Pecora that he had manipulated stock of the bank for his benefit and that of his friends. He was soon after indicted for tax evasion, but acquitted after a sensational six-week trial which brought out other questionable financial practices.

4.   WOD finally turned down Pecora's invitation because of his heavy involvement in other projects.

To Thurman Wesley Arnold[1]

June 26, 1933

Dear Partner:

In fulfillment of our bi-lateral contract (which, as I recall, contained mutually dependent covenants) I took it on myself to read your illuminating and brilliant article in the June issue of the Yale Review.[2] To get a copy of it, however, I had to spend one dollar.

I have looked over the Uniform Partnership Act rather carefully and have gone through an extremely fine book in Business Units I, and have discovered that much to my pleasure you owe me fifty cents. Uniform Partnership Act, Sections 6, 8, 9, 18, 19, 20 and 22 cover the case explicitly. Of course, it was worth more than fifty cents to me to read the article, but, on the other hand, it was worth still more than that to you to write it. . . .

---

1.   Arnold (1891–1969) taught at Yale from 1931 to 1938, when he became assistant attorney general; later he headed a prestigious Washington law firm, Arnold, Fortas & Porter. An articulate member of the Realist group, he argued their case in brilliant books such as *The Folklore of Capitalism* (1937). The reference

to partner is because WOD and Arnold collaborated on a study of criminal statistics for the Wickersham Commission.

2. Arnold and Wesley Sturges, "Progress of the New Administration," 22 *Yale Review* 656 (1933).

To A. A. Heald[1]

December 7, 1933

Dear Mr. Heald:

. . . I do not believe that there is any definite accepted procedure in using the case method. Instructors in law vary so much in their approach and analysis. This variation is particularly noticeable as the student becomes more advanced. So far as the first year goes, any generalization which could be made would be the following. An effort would be made to get the student to state the precise narrow issue which was before the particular court. This would entail discovering between whom the litigation arose, what the uncontroverted facts were, what phase of the case was before the particular court for discussion, what its decision actually was, how it justified or rationalized its decision and what it said by way of obitur [*sic*] dictum. Most of the cases studied are cases in appellate courts. Before the case has reached those courts it has passed through a trial court. The trial court may or may not have used a jury. The jury may or may not have established certain facts. The case may have come up in many different ways. For example, it may have been appealed on the basis that even if the facts were as stated as a matter of law, liability would or would not follow, or the appeal may involve a review of the facts. What the student is normally drilled in is an analysis of all of these various factors in order to arrive at a determination of what this particular case actually decides.

I might add that there is some tendency in law schools in recent years to elaborate on that method of teaching law. There is a growing tendency to look upon that form of drill as having limited utility. The change is taking two forms, neither of which involves abandonment of the case method but merely supplementing it. The first is to require additional background reading in legal materials for a particular course. This not infrequently involves an addition of treatises and records of cases as constituted in trial courts. In the second place there is being brought now more into the curriculum additional social, economic and business materials designed to show the particular institutions and problems with which the legal rules deal.

If this material is not sufficient for your purposes I would be very glad to amplify on it.

---

1.   Heald was with the YMCA in Waterville, Maine.

To Chester C. Maxey [1]

March 21, 1934

My dear Maxey:

. . . I hasten to assure you that Yale is not anti-Jewish. We are after the best men in the country, irrespective of race or creed. In our student body we have an exceptionally able group of Jewish boys who are making quite a record for themselves. So Mr. Lehrer can be assured that his case will be considered by the Admission and Scholarship Committees on its merit as it should be.[2]

I appreciate very much your kindly interest in the things which we are doing here. It is my hope and ambition that we can draw more and more from the western men. I think they will be particularly well adapted to the type of study and instruction which are available here.

---

1.   Maxey taught at and was later president of Whitman College.

2.   It is possible that Yale Law did not practice overt discrimination, but recent studies show conclusively that Yale College admissions policy definitely attempted to restrict the number of Jews.

To George E. Bates

May 3, 1934

Dear George:

I too am disappointed at the small number of men actually in line for the Combined Course. My diagnosis is somewhat as follows, though I am not sure of its validity.

(1) We rested too much on the optimism of the initial showing that 15 men were interested. I had figured that probably 5 would

change their minds. Ten men looked like an adequate group for the first time. I had that figure in mind rather than 20.

(2) No direct effort was made to keep these 15 men interested or to get more interested. No attempt at selling the idea was undertaken. It was left merely to grow as it might.

(3) No special attention was directed to these 15 men to find more particularly what their interests were; to sharpen those interests; or to direct their thinking along business-law channels. Dean Donham[1] talked to them once; but no continuing supervision was given.

(4) The men with whom these students came into contact during their first year were more concerned with teaching them the fundamentals of the law than in endeavoring to supply some picture of the intimate relationship between law and business. That type of instruction (which, by the way, I am not criticizing) is quite antithetical to the broadening influence of a law-business program. It tends to be a pretty self-sufficient and adequate system, effectively isolated from the realm of economics, business et al.

(5) The depression and the cost of one more year of professional training had some effect. How much I do not know.

(6) I sense, though I do not know, that a feeling is abroad in some of the students that they do not desire to be submitted to the diet of a regular business student. That feeling is difficult to analyze. Perhaps it has the following component parts: (a) that they need business *in relation to* law not law *and* business; (b) the first year curriculum at the business school is too far away from law to make its utility obvious; and (c) that for their purposes the first year curriculum at the business school is too elementary and/or general.

(7) The failure to advertise or promise a particular Business School degree.

The result was probably due to a combination of these factors not to one alone. My thinking on the matter has not gone very far. But I have a few suggestions to make. These are wholly personal, as I have not talked with anyone here about them.

A. The students who indicate at the beginning of the year that they are interested in the Combined Course should be segregated in at least one course or seminar and kept together throughout the year. As you know the first year class is divided into small groups the first year and seminars are conducted. This is to start individualization of work early. One unit of credit is given for this work. Segregation of this group of students might be utilized in several ways: (1) to put them under the influence of a man who is interested in breaking down the conceptual nature of law and showing it in relation to business; (2) or to have one of your men (alone or with one of ours) take these men into some adventuresome realm which would quicken their interest toward business and whet their appetites. The latter would be better in my view. It could be an introduction to a Combined Course or perhaps even a course of the kind we had planned for the third year.

In this way I think we could keep a handle on the men and do the necessary promotional work. To date it has suffered just for lack of that.

B. Effort should be made towards preparation of a special business school course for these men the second year to counteract any feeling that their diet is hap-hazard and not balanced and to emphasize that they are getting special educational treatment. This might entail condensation, substitution or new courses. Of this I am not competent to speak.

C. In lieu of B, effort might well be made to reduce the Combined Course to three years. I think that is essential for its long term growth. It may be immediately desirable. On that I have no specific suggestions now. Obviously conferences and exchange of views would be necessary.

The foregoing matters deal only with the next class not the present one. We might try right now to arouse interest. It should not be a campaign or an effort to round up men; but something more casual. I would suggest one of you (preferably Dean Donham) meeting our first year Marketing course for an hour and talking to them about the significance of studying law in relation to business. A presentation of the importance and significance of such a study rather than a plea for enrollment in the Combined Course would be in order.

---

1. Wallace Brett Donham (1877–1954) was dean of the graduate Business School at Harvard from 1919 to 1942.

2. The combined program appears to have been an idea ahead of its time, and although both Yale and Harvard attempted to keep the program going, even after WOD left, they eventually dropped it in 1938. Later on, in the 1970s, the combined law and business programs proved very popular.

To Alfred McCormack

October 29, 1935

Dear Al:

I have your letter of October 26th. The partners in the firm of Swaine, Swatland and McCormack, together with their wives and/or other ladies, are cordially invited to attend a cocktail party at my house after the Princeton-Yale football game. The house is at 286 Livingston Street. You can tell the senior partner in the above named firm that I will endeavor to have all the hostesses dressed in red for the occasion. You can also tell all the partners in the above named firm that the invitation is also good for all other football games.

To Corbey Court[1]

May 9, 1938

I'd love to accept, except
    I can't

To honor Sturges,[2] the old
    bacchant

To hear him rave and roar
    and rant;

I'd even come on an
    elephant

If I could—but I'm afraid
    I can't.

---

1. The private dining room for law students. An annual banquet was held there to honor a Yale professor or graduate, and faculty and alumni would attend.

2. Wesley A. Sturges (1893–1962) had taught at Yale since 1924 and would later return as dean in 1945. He was about to leave Yale to become executive director of the Distilled Spirits Institute, a position he left in 1940 to enter government service during the war.

To Wesley A. Sturges

October 20, 1938

Dear Wes:

This is a rather tardy letter of congratulations on your new job. I was delighted that it came your way as I felt sure from our mutual friends that it was a thing which lay very close to your heart. Since you wanted it, I was cheering on the side lines for you to get it. It may not be remiss for me to point out that I indicated to you about a year and a half ago that the job was yours for $80,000 a year. I am confident that you have once more outdone the best which I could do.

I am of course terribly sorry to see you leaving Yale. You have made such a deep imprint on the place that it will not seem to be the same institution without you. I speak feelingly and with a sense of irreparable loss. The one bright spot is the rumor that you and Myra will move down here. I hope that is true and I also hope that I will have an opportunity to extend to you personally my felicitations in the near future.

Chapter 2

Commissioner Douglas

T HE STOCK MARKET crash of October 1929 did not cause the Great Depression, but to millions of people it symbolized what had gone wrong in America. Subsequent investigations uncovered the financial manipulations of the stockbrokers and investment bankers, the same men who had claimed credit for the twenties' prosperity. When Franklin Roosevelt and the New Dealers arrived in Washington in March 1933, they determined to impose meaningful reform on the stock market.

William Douglas by 1933 had developed a national reputation in corporation law, and his bankruptcy studies tied in directly with some of the key concerns of the new administration. He set out to secure an invitation to Washington, and during the debate over the Securities Act of 1933, which established a division in the Federal Trade Commission to oversee stock issues, he wrote to Jerome Frank: "I think there is a splendid opportunity for adventurous thinking and planning in that field. I was thinking the other day that it would be a good thing to go down there for the first year or two of that division's existence and help organize it in an intelligent and efficient way." In addition to Frank, Douglas contacted other friends, such as Felix Frankfurter, who could mention his name in the right places. He also published several articles criticizing the New Deal securities legislation as too weak and ineffective. The final version of the Securities Exchange Act elated Douglas, since the new agency received a far broader grant of power than had originally been intended.

Douglas had unrealistically hoped for a seat on the Securities and Exchange Commission; instead, he received an invitation from the chairman, Joseph P. Kennedy, to direct an SEC study of manipulation of bankruptcy and receiverships by protective and reorganization committees. Theoretically, these committees existed to protect a bankrupt firm's assets for the benefit of the stockholders; in practice, lawyers who had been affiliated with the management controlled the committees and exploited their powers for their benefit and that of a few large stockholders and banks.

Utilizing the SEC's subpoena power and relying on thousands of questionnaires, Douglas (who still taught each week at Yale) and his staff began a massive investigation. One assistant described Douglas's "total preparation. During the public hearings, Douglas was always polite, but tough and unyielding. . . . By the end of the day, the witnesses were exhausted from the rigorous examination. Then Douglas and his staff would go back and prepare for the next day." In the end, the group sent in an eight-volume report to Congress, which in 1938 strengthened the SEC's role in corporate reorganization; the subsequent Trust Indenture Act also tightened standards for trustees in bankruptcy proceedings.

Kennedy, who had promised to stay at the SEC only as long as it took to get the agency into full operation, resigned in 1935, to be succeeded by James M. Landis, a former Harvard Law professor and one of the drafters of the 1933 Securities Act. Douglas, despite the opposition of Wall Street, took Landis's place on the Commission. The two men did not work well together. Landis, a Frankfurter protégé, was meticulous in preparing his work but extremely cautious; business spokesmen, who had initially feared he would be hostile to their interests, soon began praising him for his sensitivity to the needs of the securities market. Douglas, however, wanted to use the agency to force the industry to clean up its practices. "The SEC's primary concern," he declared, "is the investor, not the speculator." Throughout 1936 and 1937, Douglas put philosophical distance between himself and Landis and also made clear his full support of the President and the New Deal. When Landis returned to Harvard to become dean of the Law School in the fall of 1937, Franklin Roosevelt named Douglas chairman of the Commission.

In the year and a half he headed the SEC, Douglas utilized its powers to force the New York Stock Exchange into accepting a complete reorganization, including bringing in an outsider to be president. As Douglas himself admitted, the task had been made considerably easier by the scandal surrounding the defalcation by Richard Whitney, former president of the Exchange, on loans he had illegally secured. The sec staff kept pounding away at the illegal and/or immoral practices it found. "We were doing what had to be done," Abe Fortas later recalled, "and we weren't afraid. Nobody worried what Douglas would say if we went after somebody big. He'd say, 'Piss on em!' "

Although Douglas encouraged portrayals of himself in the press as an uncompromising, determined idealist fighting corporate greed, he had a good sense of the practical. He knew just how far he could push, and keeping in mind realistic goals, he knew when he had to compromise in order to achieve his policy. He never wanted to manage the stock exchange personally or have the sec do so; rather, he wanted the Exchange to reform itself, and then police its members to ensure future honesty. Only when the old boy club that ran the Exchange refused to reform did Douglas come down hard; once he had forced the Exchange to mend its ways, he left it alone to live up to its promises.

Despite his busy schedule at the sec, the gregarious Douglas found time to socialize and soon knew nearly everyone worth knowing in the capital. He caught the President's eye as well, and before long he had become a regular in Roosevelt's poker parties. By 1939, however, Douglas thought his days in Washington would soon be over. He had lived at a frenetic pace for six years, and while he had accomplished much and had become one of the most powerful men in government, he wanted to return to his research. An offer to become dean of the Yale Law School seemed just what Douglas wanted.

To James McCauley Landis [1]

July 18, 1934

My dear Jim:
Relative to our recent telephone conversation, may I say that I would be willing to undertake a study of protective committees for the Securities and Exchange Commission. Due to the pressure of other

work I could not begin this study until some time in September, 1934. Beginning not later than October 1, 1934 and continuing until the completion of the study I believe that I could give it substantially half of my time. However, so far as I can judge now, it would be necessary for me to work this in along with my regular duties here at the Law School.

I can arrange to come down to talk to you and the other Commissioners at your convenience. It would be preferable if I could see you some time within the next two weeks. At that time I can put before you a few of the ideas which I have relative to the scope and nature of such a study. And I will be very anxious to obtain your ideas, both as to substance and method. I look forward with pleasure toward the opportunity of discussing the various details with you. As I told you I have spent a lot of time on this subject during the last eighteen months. During the last two months I have been digging in to the New York and Chicago situations in the real estate field. The conditions which I found were most astounding. I am delighted that a study of the whole problem is going to be made under your auspices, and I shall be gratified if I can make a contribution to that end.

---

1. Landis (1899–1964) had been one of the authors of the New Deal's securities program; an original appointee to the SEC, he chaired the agency from 1935 to 1937. His later work in the field led many to call him the "dean of regulators."

To Abe Fortas

October 8, 1934

My dear Abe:
I have been wanting to have a long talk with you to bring you up to date with the various developments in the plan about which I spoke to you in February of this year on your return to Yale from the Agricultural Adjustment Administration. I was sorry not to have had the opportunity to go into the matter with you when I was in Washington last week.

You will recall that last February we had several talks relative to a study of protective committees. We thought at first we would do it in conjunction with a study for the New York Law Society and when that fell through we concluded that we would do it on our own. ... We had done considerable work on the subjects when Congress passed the Securities Exchange Act of 1934 containing Section 211, authorizing and directing the Commission to make a rather comprehensive study and investigation of protective committees. When that statute was passed, you will recall that we held our plans temporarily in abeyance to see what disposition the Securities & Exchange Commission would make of that undertaking. At that time, you were uncertain as to your summer program. Nevertheless, we had not decided to abandon the project but to go ahead on our own, if necessary.

When the Securities and Exchange Commission asked me to undertake that study for them we had some additional communication. It was agreed upon between us that if you returned to Yale you were to arrange your schedule here in such manner as to permit your participation in the study to the fullest extent possible. In fact you will recall that we had discussed plans for placing you on the commission budget for that study. We also discussed the possibility of your participation, in case you did not return to Yale. You will recall how insistent I was at all times that you participate even though you did not return here. In fact the question never arose in oral discussion as to whether you would or would not participate. It was solely a question as to the extent of your participation as affected by your decision on returning to Yale.

I mention the foregoing matters in some detail merely to emphasize to you your relationship to the study as I had conceived of it. Since February 1934 I had always thought of you as an active participant in such work and in laying plans for the official investigation for the Commission I had always counted upon your collaboration in it. In other words, I had never even thought of making the study without your assistance.

While in Washington last week I had a long talk with Jerome Frank[1] who stated to me in unequivocal terms that he would not consider your release from the Agricultural Adjustment Administration under any circumstances. He stated that there was an executive order which would not permit your release without his consent. I stated to him that in view of our long-standing arrangement and in view of the fact that by giving you an appointment in the Agricultural Adjustment Administration he had disrupted our plans the executive order was not applicable. He did not concede this point but insisted that you could not be released.

You may, in view of all that has transpired, deem it inadvisable to disassociate yourself from the A.A.A. at this time. Or you may be still so deeply interested in the subject of protective committees that you will want to discuss the whole situation with Jerome Frank to see if he will release you. At this time I want to assure you of two things, the first is that there is a place for you on this study at the Securities and Exchange Commission. If you came over, I would make you chief of the staff. The second is that if you decide you cannot under the circumstances come over, I will understand perfectly. I will know that it is due to circumstances beyond your control.[2]

---

1. Frank (1889–1957) had been one of the leaders of the Realism school and had known WOD at Yale. He came to the New Deal with the Agricultural Adjustment Administration and, like WOD, raided Yale for staff. When WOD became chairman of the SEC, Frank took his place; and when WOD went onto the Court, he urged Roosevelt to name Frank as his successor, which the President did.

2. The calm tone of this letter obscures the rather heated although friendly exchange which had taken place betwen WOD and Frank. Both men wanted Fortas badly, since they both considered him one of the best students they had had at Yale. WOD kept pushing until Frank finally capitulated, and in November 1934, Frank wrote: "Apparently you and Abe think I am like old man Barrett in the Barretts of Wimpole Street . . . . Nonsense! Bless you my children. You needn't elope. You can be married at the old homestead . . . . I told Abe to prepare his trousseau but to stay with papa for a brief time until I can get a hired girl to take his place."

To Joseph Patrick Kennedy[1]

February 4, 1936

Dear Joe:

It was very kind of you to write me your extremely generous letter of January 28th and to send me your felicitations on my appointment to the Securities and Exchange Commission.

There is one nice thing about the whole matter which transcends all others in importance, and that is the appointment was for the balance of the term of one Joseph P. Kennedy. You set such a high standard of performance down here that I realize there is tough sledding ahead for me. I fear the shoes are much too large. All I can say is that I will be in there trying all the time to live up to the high standard of performance set by you.

It is always gratifying to me to think that you are not completely out of the picture. It was most reassuring to know of your continuing interest.

I hope you will forgive me if you find me leaning on you heavily in the months that lie ahead. You see, I have suspected for some weeks that you were the one responsible for my appointment.

---

1.   Kennedy (1888–1969) had made his fortune in the 1920s in the movies and real estate. The Catholic Kennedy and WOD, however dissimilar in background, hit it off well and in the years ahead would remain close friends.

To Adolf A. Berle, Jr.

February 4, 1936

My dear Adolf:
I am deeply grateful to you for your kind letter of January 29, containing your felicitations on my appointment to the Securities and Exchange Commission. I, too, had mixed feelings about the matter and chewed it over at some length. I think the venture should prove to be interesting, exciting, and highly educational. I appreciate the great drawbacks but I believe that the long-range view is the only tenable one, provided we can build on a firm foundation as we go along. There is, of course, a tremendous job to be done immediately, but my mind is seriously engaged in the problems that lie ahead after the next cyclic term. I hope we can get together soon and explore some of these things together. The one nice thing about the appointment is that it will probably make it possible for me to see you and to get the benefit of your insight and analysis of these knotty problems more frequently.

To James W. Cooper[1]

February 18, 1936

My dear Jim:

. . . We are located in Washington at 3136 Ellicott Street, N. W., which is a small house with about an acre and a quarter of land. We have all sorts of fruit trees, grapes, raspberries (not the Bronx kind), gold fish in an outdoor pool (which Bumble[2] swears he is going to catch with flies he himself has tied, which in turn gives you some idea of the kind of fellow Bumble is), magnolia, roses —in fact, just about everything but poison ivy and statues of dogs and deer. You may get the impression that I am on the verge of bankruptcy. Such impression is absolutely correct as I have not rented my New Haven house. But in this, as in other respects, I have endeavored to enter into the spirit of the New Deal. I can see now that my budget will be added to the list of those which cannot be balanced.

The guy we rented the house from had an idea that Louis XIV had exquisite taste. As a consequence, we have a lot of very hideous things around the house which would not be there but for the fact that they are so heavy and I am so tired at the end of a day. Nevertheless, I think we will manage to survive on the cultural if not on the financial side.

Please tell Art Corbin[3] that prior to joining the Commission I had been very much impressed with his criticisms and attacks but now that I see it from the inside I cannot conclude anything but that his tirades were wholly vitriolic. Or to state it another way, I have looked through all the rules and regulations of this venerable organization and I cannot see anything in them which makes Republicans any more liable than Democrats. . . .

---

1. A friend and Connecticut neighbor.

2. woo's son, William Jr.

3. Yale's Arthur Linton Corbin (1874–1967) was one of the nation's outstanding law teachers and one of the leading experts on the law of contracts. Although he and woo differed on legal philosophy, the two remained on good terms.

To Robert Maynard Hutchins

April 29, 1936

Dear Bob:

The overstimulation of which you speak was still present in New Haven when I arrived the day after you left. I understand that your lectures[1] filled the Yale Bowl for the first time since 1929. Any such accomplishment will be not easily forgotten at Yale, so I am still hopeful for the Yale offers.

I would be very happy to come out to your University and to lecture for you, not because I like to lecture and not because I have anything to say which could be understood by the run of scholars, but because I am slowly going bankrupt. . . .

---

1. Hutchins had delivered the Storrs Lectures, which were subsequently published as *The Higher Learning in America* (1936), one of the most influential works in American higher education in this century. Hutchins charged that universities had become too involved in vocational education and had to return to their classic function of teaching people how to think and solve problems. The book generated an enormous controversy and became the "bible" of educational reformers.

To Robert Maynard Hutchins

May 6, 1936

My dear Bob:

This is a serious letter. I accept, not because I like to talk, not because I enjoy having you listening to me while I talk, not because I have any idea that more than a hand-full of your learned associates would understand what I had to say, not because I like to get my picture in the paper, but solely because I would like to reach once more that affluent state when I would be able to send some lovely flowers to your lovely wife.[1]

---

1. The speech, which woo delivered in October and entitled "The Forces of Disorder," proved a vigorous defense of the New Deal and an attack on the established financial interests. "These financial termites," he charged, "are those who practice the art of predatory or high finance. . . . High finance is interested solely in the immediate profit. Its organizations are not interested in whether our natural resources are wasted. . . [or] whether our economic machinery is getting out

of balance." The speech is included in wod's *Democracy and Finance* (1940). According to James Simon, it brought together a number of ideas and expressed a coherent economic philosophy close to that of Roosevelt and also of Louis D. Brandeis, as the next letter attests.

To Louis Dembitz Brandeis [1]

May 20, 1936

Dear Mr. Justice Brandeis:
I have your kind note of May 19th. Part IV of our report to the Congress on protective committees is the only one which has been prepared and released to date. Other parts of the series will be ready in the near future. As these come off the press I will send you copies, as I know of your great interest in the subject matter of our study and investigation.

It is needless for me to add that your own monumental work on "Other Peoples Money"[2] has been a guiding star and inspiration to all of us who have collaborated on this present project. . . .

---

1. Brandeis (1856–1941) had won fame as the "people's attorney" during the Progressive Era; Wilson named him to the high court in 1916, and throughout his tenure younger liberals such as wod looked to him as a polestar. Brandeis's very pronounced bias against bigness, especially big business, had received renewed interest from reformers following the crash.
2. Brandeis's classic statement against the big financial interests; published in 1914, it drew extensively on the findings of the Pujo Committee.

To Arlene B. Hadley [1]

May 22, 1936

Dear Arlene:
You are quite right. I am very, very important!

---

1. A secretary at the Yale Law School.

To Franklin Delano Roosevelt

July 7, 1936

Dear Mr. President:

When you honored me by appointing me to this Commission, Chairman Landis assured me that he would shortly arrange for me to meet you on one of his trips to your office so that I could have the privilege of thanking you in person for the opportunity for public service which you have afforded me. Hence I deferred writing you and expressing to you my deep appreciation of the honor which you have bestowed on me, thinking that I would have the opportunity to do it in person.[1] But due to the pressure of work and the rush of activity, that occasion never arose. So I am writing you belatedly (and with a feeling of considerable embarrassment at the long delay) to express to you my deep appreciation of this opportunity to serve you and the nation in your great constructive reform program . . . . And I want you to know that I am ever at your service in the high cause which you are serving.

---

1. Simon speculates that Landis deliberately kept WOD away from the White House. If that were the case, WOD had now reached out himself to make the contact, and in doing so he indicated that some tensions possibly existed between himself and Landis, and that as a devoted New Dealer, his loyalty lay with the man in the White House.

To John G. Forrest (Telegram)

May 18, 1938

Please convey to Mr. Gay[1] my best wishes. I cannot help but contrast the expressions of regret at his retirement from the management of the exchange with the feeling in the street that would follow an announcement that I was going back to Yale.

---

1. Charles Richard Gay (1875–1946) was president of the New York Stock Exchange from 1935 to 1938 and served as the focal point of the SEC's efforts to impose reforms on that institution. Gay actually had a most difficult time; on the one hand he was trying to fight back the SEC, and on the other was being under-

mined by Richard Whitney and his coterie, which wanted to keep the Exchange basically a private club.

To Franklin Delano Roosevelt

October 14, 1938

Memorandum: Re West Tennessee Power and Light

In pursuance of Mac's[1] suggestion, I am setting down in this memorandum some of the facts which led me to suggest that the present time seems to me extremely propitious for a satisfactory settlement of the issue between West Tennessee and t.v.a.[2]

1. As a result of your comments to the Press this morning,[3] Groesbeck will be in a decidedly favorable state of mind to reach a quick settlement.[4]

2. The rate base of the property is, I believe, around three and a half million dollars. The dollar stake is not a big one, and the situation is a small one, making possible, if necessary, even a liberal settlement.

3. Settlement of this will lead to a withdrawal of Electric Bond and Share from the pending case before the Supreme Court which is to be argued this term.[5]

4. Settlement of the West Tennessee matter would leave a single solitary issue of United States Government vs. Willkie.[6] That latter issue could then be easily dealt with on a purely personal basis.

---

1. Marvin Hunter McIntyre (1878–1943), the President's personal secretary, had been with Roosevelt since 1920.

2. Many of the private utility companies had been fighting the Tennessee Valley Authority, both on grounds of philosophy and because one of the goals of the tva was to provide a "yardstick" by which to measure the efficiency and rate fairness of private firms.

3. Roosevelt had told the press that the national government would be devoting more of its resources and energies to preparedness and expected private firms to do so as well.

4. C.E. Groesbeck, the chairman of the board of Electric Bond & Share, had in fact announced to his stockholders the previous day that the company would comply with Section 11 of the Public Utility Holding Company Act of 1935, the so-called death sentence clause which forbade pyramiding of public utility holding companies. Electric Bond and Share would cooperate with the sec, which had

enforcement power over this act, and would eliminate its holding company struc-
ture and develop an integrated power system.

5.   *Electric Bond and Share Co.* v. *SEC*, 303 U.S. 419 (1938), upheld the stock
regulation powers of the SEC.

6.   Wendell Lewis Willkie (1892–1944), an Indiana-born lawyer, headed the
giant Commonwealth and Southern utility; he would be the Republican candidate
for president in 1940 and afterwards championed international cooperation.

To Joseph P. Kennedy

October 29, 1938

Dear Joe:

. . . Things are going along very well here. We are in the process
of getting out the Whitney report,[1] the first part of which has
already been published. The second part is a honey. It will be out
in a few days. It contains the program which we have worked out
with the stock exchange. That program is really a swell one. It shows
what can be done when the real guys in the street put their shoulders
to the wheel with us 10¢ an hour birds down here in Washington.

Also, the utility boys are knocking out some home runs. The
Groesbeck statement you probably saw. It is no longer a question if
they will submit to the old death sentence. The race is on to get in
here and have it over with. And that isn't all, Joe. But I have to save
something for the next letter. . . .

---

1.   Richard Whitney (1877–1974), the scion of an old and distinguished
family, had been president of the New York Stock Exchange from 1930 to 1935
and epitomized the old guard view of the Exchange as belonging to a privileged
few, immune to any governmental regulation. Early in the year it had become
known that Whitney had illegally borrowed money from a fund of which he was
a trustee to cover his stock losses, and when the market declined, he had been
unable to pay back the $1.1 million. The SEC had used the occasion to probe the
trading activities of the insiders and had issued a devastating three-volume report,
In the Matter of Richard Whitney et al. (1938), on the immoral, if not always illegal,
activities of men like Whitney.

Part II

Mr. Justice Douglas

Chapter 3

The Business of the Supreme Court

I
N ADDITION TO deciding cases, the members of the nation's highest tribunal deal with a variety of "business" associated with the work of the Court or related to their position. Nearly all of this is minor compared to the central task of deciding constitutional issues, but it would be infinitely more difficult for the justices to accomplish that work if they neglected these other matters. The following sections give us a glimpse of some of this business. In some areas, Douglas's experiences proved fairly typical; in others, he can be considered quite exceptional. Very few other members of the Court would claim, as he did, that the bench is "underworked," and that all of the Court's business could be handled in less than four days. But whether it takes them four or seven days a week, all of these items must be handled if the work of the Court is to move along smoothly.

Appointment
In his memoirs, Douglas wrote of the Court: "I never dreamed of being there. I did dream of being Chief Forester. I dreamed of being a professor of English literature and, later, dean of the Yale Law School. I dreamed of being simultaneously a professor both at the Harvard Business School and at the Yale Law School. I dreamed of being Solicitor General. I dreamed of being an advocate like Hiram

Johnson, William Borah, Louis D. Brandeis. . . . I never had a yen for public office." When informed of rumors that he would succeed Louis Brandeis shortly after the latter retired from the bench in early February 1939, "I shrugged the whole thing off and gave no serious thought to it." He went on about his business, he claimed, and when Roosevelt called him to the White House to inform him of the appointment, he was "dumbfounded. And I walked in a daze until the following noon, when my name went to the Senate."

Douglas could not have been that "dumbfounded," since he acknowledges that friends of his were working to persuade Roosevelt to name the SEC chairman to the bench. But as James Simon writes, "Douglas was very much aware that he was in contention for the Court seat and, in fact, shrewdly worked in his own behalf." His speeches at that time not only reinforced his reputation as a Roosevelt loyalist, but also took on a very Brandeisian tone in regard to big business. He not only knew that his friends were promoting him, but gave them his cooperation as well. As he wrote, the only way to secure a Court appointment is to "stay in the stream of history, be in the forefront of events," and he made sure to follow that advice.

Douglas's responses to congratulatory messages upon his nomination are included in this chapter because they indicate his initial impressions of the Court and its work. Within a relatively short time he decided that one did not have to live a monklike existence while on the bench, and he became the most visible and accessible justice of this century.

To Louis Dembitz Brandeis

March 20, 1939

My dear Judge Brandeis:

The President has just appointed me to the Supreme Court, as your successor.

I am overwhelmed and filled with a deep sense of humility.

These feelings are due in part to my recognition of the great responsibility of one who is asked to wear your robe.

The honor of the position is itself a great one. But the honor of following in your footsteps is even greater.

If the Senate confirms, I pray God may give me power to maintain your high standards and to serve the cause of liberalism in accordance with your noble traditions. . . .[1]

---

1. A quarter-century later WOD claimed that "my predecessor, Louis D. Brandeis had recommended me to the President." It is impossible to determine if this is true, but everything we know about Brandeis and his methods would lead us to doubt the veracity of WOD's allegation.

To James Maxwell Fasett[1]

April 29, 1939

Dear Mr. Fasett:
I have your letter of April 27, in which you very kindly suggest a dinner in New York at some time convenient for me. . .
   I should add that I have adopted a policy, since coming on the Court, of not making any public addresses. I was not sure whether the dinner you had in mind would entail an address by me.

---

1. A Wall Street lawyer. The policy which initially adopted had been a hallmark of Brandeis's tenure; eventually WOD not only abandoned this enforced silence, but also came to believe it important for justices to speak to the bar.

To Elizabeth Howland

May 10, 1939

My dear Elizabeth:
. . . There is one paragraph in your letter which bothers me greatly. You speak of the fact that now that I am a member of the Court your reticence will increase. Please never let that happen as I would feel very badly. On this job one gets isolated fast enough without losing the intimacy of old friends. . . .

To Karl Nickerson Llewellyn

May 26, 1939

My dear Karl:

. . . Your message of congratulations touched me deeply. I appreciate it more than mere words can convey.

The change in tempo from the Securities and Exchange Commission is very considerable, but on the basis of previous experience I suppose that I can confidently expect to get used to it. I remember when I took and passed the bar examination in 1925 I heaved a big sigh of relief at the thought that I would never have to take another one. And now it has dawned on me with great clarity that I will be taking them from now on ad infinitum. When one takes an examination in law school he soon finds out what his grade was, but now I fear I will never know unless you promise to keep tab and to give me on appropriate occasions an adequate report. I hope you do, as there is none I would more confidently trust.

The tradition here makes one feel like a statue. Life moves by but for some reason or other one is not supposed to be a part of it. It brings to mind the old Charlie Chaplin film in the days of the silent movies where a rather animated statue gets into quite a brawl.

I always did like Charlie Chaplin.

To Earnest G. Lorenson [1]

May 26, 1939

My dear Earnest:

. . . As you know, I was headed back to Yale[2] when the President nominated me to the Court. I was looking forward with great pleasure to the opportunity to rub elbows with you again. I have not yet quite gotten over the shock which the nomination gave me. It was wholly unexpected so far as I was concerned, and it caused a major change in my whole life's work. . . . The pace here is somewhat reminiscent of the pace at Law School. Of course we don't have any examination papers to read, unless petitions for certiorari[3] be regarded as such.

---

1. A professor at the Yale Law School.
2. WOD had been offered the deanship of the law school.
3. A request for the Court to review the findings of a lower court.

To Yale Law Journal

June 16, 1939

Dear Fellow Editors:

. . . I was delighted to know that you are going to be very critical of every opinion which I write. I hope that the Yale Law Journal will hang on jealously to its appellate jurisdiction and reverse or affirm as it chooses without restraint.

Law Clerks

Although only a few justices took recent law school graduates as "clerks" at the beginning of this century, by the time Douglas went on the Court nearly all the members had one clerk, and over the years, this number increased. Clerks assist the justices in legal research, take on special projects, do summaries of petitions for certiorari, and serve as sounding boards for ideas. When the relation works well, it is a rewarding experience to the clerk and a great benefit to the justice. Not all of Douglas's clerks recalled their year with him as a pleasurable period; he could, and often was, short-tempered with them and imposed high and at times impossible standards. Unlike Brandeis, who taught his clerks a great deal, Douglas seems merely to have expected them to do their work; some got along with him very well, and others did not.

A complete list of the men and women who clerked for Douglas can be found in *The Court Years*, 415–16.

To Richard M. Biddell[1]

September 19, 1940

Dear Mr. Biddell:

... I would like to be able to consider your application but I cannot for the following reason:

I am taking each year a graduate of one of the law schools in the Ninth Circuit. There are, as you know, a number of schools in that section and each year there are a number of graduates of those schools who are interested in the position. I do not feel that I should depart from my policy by taking a graduate from one of the eastern schools, no matter how well qualified the man is. . . .

---

1. A student at Harvard Law School; through his lengthy tenure, WOD stuck, with a few exceptions, to this rule of taking clerks only from the Ninth Circuit.

To Judson P. Falknor[1]

March 24, 1943

Dear Dean Falknor:

... When you say that you have "no available graduates" whom you could recommend for appointment as my clerk, do you include women? It is possible that I may decide to take one if I can find one who is absolutely first-rate.[2]

---

1. Dean of the University of Washington Law School.

2. During the war years, many male law school graduates faced immediate induction into the armed forces. WOD did take a woman graduate from the University of Washington, Lucille Lomen, for the 1944 Term. As the following letters indicate, however, WOD had a mixed mind about woman clerks; he would take one if she were absolutely first rate, but he did not really see a woman as equal to a man. WOD, for whatever reason, did not take women clerks again until the 1972 Term.

To Max Radin[1]

May 27, 1946

Dear Max:

I wonder if I could put another burden on your shoulders?

. . . So far I have had men either from the law school at Berkeley or the law school at Seattle. It is proving to be very difficult to make the right choice. I must choose rather blindly either on the basis of paper records or on the basis of a brief interview. So I have been casting around in my mind for a better method of selection.

This is the big league. I think I have been cheated and somewhat handicapped at times. It has been particularly true this year. Perhaps I should give up my policy of getting men from law schools in the Ninth Circuit. I have seen some exceptionally good men from eastern schools this year. But I still think, as I thought originally, that the idea is a good one and that probably my mistake has been in the method in which I have gone about it.

So I have come to the conclusion that if you are willing I will ask you to find me a law clerk each year.[2] I do not want you to restrict yourself to your own graduates. . . .

I think you know exactly the kind of man I want. I need not only a bright chap, but also a hard-working fellow with a smell for facts as well as for law. I do not want a hide-bound, conservative fellow. What I want is a Max Radin—a fellow who can hold his own in these sophisticated circles and who is not going to end up as a stodgy, hide-bound lawyer. I want the kind of fellow for whom this work would be an exhilaration, who will be going into teaching or into practice of the law for the purpose of promoting the public good. I do not want to fill the big law offices of the country with my law clerks. . . .[3]

---

1. Radin (1880–1950) taught at the Berkeley Law School from 1919 until his retirement and was considered one of the leading legal scholars of his generation.

2. Felix Frankfurter had performed this function for both Oliver Wendell Holmes and Louis Brandeis.

3. Brandeis had a similar philosophy; he wanted his clerks to teach afterwards, so they could enlighten future lawyers on the idea of public service.

To Frederic Moore Vinson [1]

June 7, 1946

Dear Fred:

Here is a suggestion for a law clerk for you in case you have not already made your arrangements. This man came down to see me a month or so ago. I would have taken him without any hesitation but for the fact that I am already committed to someone else.

His name is Byron White,[2] who comes from Colorado and who is finishing at Yale Law School this summer. You have probably read of him in the sport section of newspapers. He was an All-American football player whose nickname was Whizzer White. He played professional football. He was in the service for a couple of years. He has led his class at Yale Law School for three years. Members of the faculty tell me that he is the most outstanding man they have had for a long time. As a matter of fact, he probably will have an all-time scholastic record at the Yale Law School.

He is a delightful person, of great charm and poise. I have no idea what his personal plans may be. But if you would be at all interested in him, I will see that he gets down here right away so that you may have a talk with him.

---

1. Vinson (1890–1953), after long service in the House of Representatives, had been appointed by Roosevelt to the Court of Appeals; his good friend Harry Truman named him Chief Justice of the United States in 1946.

2. White did not clerk, but in 1962 President Kennedy named him to the Court.

To Max Radin

February 18, 1947

Dear Max:

First. I have no plans to resign from the Court.

Second. On the selection of my law clerk, you have all the voting power. I don't even have a veto. That's the way I wish it.

Third. I change law clerks each year, the new one reporting in September and taking over October 1st.

To Stanley M. Sparrowe [1]

June 13, 1950

My dear Sparrowe:

. . . As you know, all of the judges have taken two law clerks, with the exception of Black and me. Black has succumbed and is taking two next year. Just the other day I finally decided to do the same. It did not seem practical to get another one from the Ninth Circuit on such short notice so I took the second man from Yale. I am not sure that the two law clerk idea will prove to be satisfactory. I am taking it merely on trial. But if it works out I will want to take both of the men from the law schools in the Ninth Circuit. So you would have two to select. But I think it would be desirable to spread them among different schools if possible.

There is this additional aspect of the matter to consider. It may be that the second law clerk should be someone who is an accomplished typist and who can [be assigned] a half or three-quarters of the time help Mrs. Allen. In this connection it might be desirable to consider getting a woman who is a graduate or is graduating from a law school, who can qualify as a lawyer and who can assist the regular law clerk for part of the time and help Mrs. Allen part of the time. If that procedure is worked out the person selected, who probably should be a woman, might stay for more than one year, say two years or perhaps even three. The regular law clerk would be changed annually as at present.

These latter suggestions are very tentative and I would like to get your reactions to them. . . .

---

1. Sparrowe, an Oakland lawyer, had clerked for WOD during the 1947 Term and shortly after establishing his practice took over the task of selecting WOD's clerks from Max Radin.

To Stanley E. Sparrowe

March 20, 1953

My dear Sparrowe:

. . . I think I would leave all of the schools in the Ninth Circuit in the competition unless they themselves voluntarily withdraw. I think over a period of time they are beginning to realize the kind of requirement needed if they are to succeed in the competition. As to women, I have nothing to say. I certainly would not give an applicant preference because she was a woman, nor would I put her at a disadvantage because she was a woman. If the best of the lot was a woman, I would take her as a law clerk. If on a scholastic basis a man and a woman would seem to be equal, I would make my judgment on the total personality and the imponderables that would make you decide whether a particular person would fit well into this very hard-working office. . . .

To Stanley E. Sparrowe

January 19, 1956

Dear Stan:

. . . As to the Harvard man, I think I would not take him no matter how good he is. I have had a number of situations of that kind. Over and again men who were raised in the Northwest and went to college there, like I did, and who plan to practice there, think they qualify by reason of those facts. But the main purpose of my present system of selection is to favor the schools in the Ninth Circuit. I felt that there are some outstanding schools in the Ninth Circuit and that they deserve recognition and that their best men over the years will compare favorably with the best of the law schools in the east. When I first came on the Court Harvard, Yale and Columbia had a monopoly on all the law clerkships. They still have the edge by reason of the fact that they are so close to Washington, D.C. that the students can come down and have personal interviews with the Justices. I have nothing against Harvard, Yale or Columbia. Columbia is my alma mater and I taught many years at Yale and I think today the best law school in the whole eastern part of the United States is Harvard. But if I start making an exception I will have difficulty in turning down strong personal requests to consider an outstanding boy from Yakima who went to Michigan, Yale, etc.

To Stanley E. Sparrowe

December 29, 1959

Dear Sparrowe:

... The boys that do not have the Public Law background have extra digging to do once they get here. But if they are of the high calibre as Duke[1] and Ares[2] they make up for it in short order, although it may take long extra hours of digging. . . .

---

1. Steven Duke, a graduate of the University of Arizona Law School, clerked for WOD during the 1959 Term. In writing a letter of recommendation for Duke in 1961, WOD declared: "Of the 25 or more law clerks I have had, he ranks among the first few in terms of a teacher's potential . . . . His fires burn brightly. He has a real dedication to the law as an instrument of justice, as an expression of the democratic idea, as a reflection of the dignity and worth of the individual."

2. Charles E. Ares, also from the University of Arizona Law School, had clerked in the 1952 Term.

To James S. Campbell[1]

March 11, 1965

The other day I gave you my desk copy of No. 307—*O'Keefe* v. *Smith Hinchman*,[2] with a rider and some suggested changes. What I specifically asked you to do was to make another addition, bringing the facts of this case into focus with the standards that Rider 3 sets out.

When I sent for my desk copy today I found it was in Goldberg's office. This is a high breach of office ethics. I was asking for your views and opinions—not for Goldberg's. I have other ways of getting that.

So I think that when you return from your present illness, you should make a response to this show cause order.

I do not like to have on my staff anyone who is working for someone else in the building.

---

1. A Stanford graduate, Campbell clerked during the 1964 Term.

2. In *O'Keefe* v. *Smith, Hinchman & Grylls Associates*, 380 U.S. 359 (1965), the Court upheld a commissioner's ruling that an accidental drowning could be

covered under workmen's compensation. wod entered a *dubitante,* a statement doubting the correctness of the decision but not dissenting. He also felt the Court should not have taken this type of case but left the determination to the lower courts.

To Peter K. Westen[1]

October 1, 1968

. . . You apparently are under the impression that the Congress at certain times can be estopped from exercising its constitutional power to make the laws. Your memorandum to me on the two *gold clause*[2] cases indicates pretty clearly your ignorance in this field, and as I wrote you yesterday, you have not yet brought into focus the other line of cases, i.e. that in the rather vague and undefined so-called "regulatory" area Congress has some leeway. We do not need to cite in this case where that line is drawn or where it should be drawn. But we do need some relevant citations that qualify the apparent absolutism of the Westen ideas as expressed in that earlier draft. In any event, I want any suggestions you may have by Thursday afternoon.

I have written you about your failure to send me the basic material I asked for over a week ago in the *Winters* case.[3] Why you have not sent this material is still a great mystery to me. I have been holding it perhaps for a week. I have no law library out here[4] and the nearest one is 250 miles away. And even though I got there I would not be able to get the papers I needed in the *Winters* case.

I do not desire to have a law clerk unless he is on the same team as I am on, and willing to run these errands for me from time to time, even though at the time they seem to him to be unimportant.

You might think these things over, because the first case we have to dispose of when I get back is the case of P.K. Westen.

1.　Westen, a graduate of the Berkeley Law School, clerked in the 1968 Term. According to another one of wod's clerks, a personality clash between the two poisoned relations from the beginning.

2.　At the start of his administration, Franklin Roosevelt took the United States off the gold monetary standard, and Congress rescinded the gold clause in public and private bonds. The Court upheld congressional power in regard to private bonds in *Norman* v. *Baltimore & Ohio Railroad,* 294 u.s. 240 (1935), but the same day in *Perry* v. *United States*, 294 U.S. 330, the Court admonished Congress for exceeding its powers. However, since the petitioner had not suffered real damages, he had no remedy.

3. There were several petitions from Winters, a Marine Corps reservist who tried to prevent the government from recalling him for active duty in Vietnam.

4. Goose Prairie, Washington.

To William H. Alsup, Richard L. Jacobson,
and Kenneth R. Reed

April 22, 1971

This is a note to you all about cert memos. The best I have had in recent years were prepared by [Thomas C.] Armitage in the 1969 Term and I suggest that you go over what he did to see the quality that they have.

The memos done in the 1970 Term were some of the poorest I have ever seen. I have asked [Dennis] Brown to preserve and show to you some of the real horribles that he, himself, perpetuated.

The purpose of the cert memo is to prepare an accurate summary of the issues in the case which can be used three months or a year from the time it is written so as to give a rather complete conception of what the case involves without going back to the original briefs and records.

The flow of cases is so great that it is difficult to carry in mind even during one Term the precise issues raised in each case. Some of the cases in which you prepare cert memos will be discussed that very week but others will go over from Conference to Conference and a final vote and discussion may not be had until some months later. In that time the case may very well become dim in the memories of everyone in the office. . . .

The cert memo need not always cover every single point raised because some of the cases are just plain frivolous. But they should contain the main points with pros and cons relevant to granting the cert petition or noting the appeal or granting the motion to dismiss or affirm. . . .

During the summer I go over the cases in the Far West and merely send back my votes attached to each numbered case. I make no separate notes. During the winter, while I am here, I go over each case separately from the law clerks' memos. But I repeat, the law clerks' memo is a very important point of reference in every Conference discussion especially those where the Conference discussion comes some weeks or even months later.

To Thomas Klitgard[1]

November 11, 1971

Dear Tom:

... The law-clerk-selection committee has informed me that my two clerks for next year are women.

That's Women's Lib with a vengeance![2]

By the way, the CJ has advised me that I can have only two next year. I wonder who needs four?

---

1. Klitgard had clerked for WOD in the 1961 Term; he took over the selection process from Sparrowe in 1967.

2. Janet Meik of the University of Southern California and Carol S. Bruch of the University of California at Berkeley. According to Bob Woodward and Scott Armstrong, *The Brethren,* (New York: Simon & Schuster, 1979), both women had a difficult time with WOD that year.

Business of the Court

How the Supreme Court goes about its business has been a subject of constant fascination to scholar and layperson alike. In other letters in this book, there are often allusions to this work; in the letters that follow, Douglas comments specifically on the daily operations of the Court and his views on it.

To Robert W. Lucas[1]

June 7, 1954

Dear Bob:

... Since 1925 the Court has had discretion to grant or deny large groups of cases. These are cases that come here by writ of certiorari. In that [1925 Jurisdiction] Act Congress merely set up certain standards for the exercise of discretion.

When I first came on the Court fifteen years ago we were taking roughly twenty-five percent of the cases. This last Term I think we took not more than ten percent. The total volume has stayed just about the same. . . . The Court has been criticized in some quarters for taking fewer and fewer cases. I suppose it is due to the change in the membership of the Court. The falling off in the number of cases taken by the Court is not due to the fact that the Court is over-worked.

How many judges would the Court need in the future? That is very difficult to say. Under Lincoln there were ten. The present number of nine was fixed under Grant. Under our Constitution the Court cannot sit in panels. The whole Court must sit in every case. It would take a Constitutional amendment to change that. Roosevelt tried to increase the number of judges to fifteen, as you know. It was not a change from nine to fifteen but an addition of one judge for every judge who was on the Court and over 70 years of age until not more than six additional judges had been appointed. Fifteen would be a very unworkable unit. Nine is about the maximum for efficiency. A group that would be larger than nine would be very difficult to work with as a team. There would be that many more views to be heard, that many more dissenting views to be expressed, etc. . . . The number of judges has fluctuated throughout our history. No evils developed from the manipulation of the number of judges. There is always the potential evil but in this case it does not seem to be a real one . . . .

Compulsory retirement at the age of 75 is likewise a rather dubious proposition. One who has served ten years consecutively and has reached 70 may retire. That is in the law and would take care of necessitous cases. There have been in the past judges who have hung on beyond the time they should have been on the Court because they had no way of making a living after they retired . . . . Compulsory retirement at 75 is hard to argue against, I suppose. But then again there is no particular need for it. Holmes served almost 15 years after he was 75 and did some of his best work then. When I came on the Court Hughes was 78 and some of his outstanding work was done in his last few years as Chief Justice. The same is true for Brandeis . . . .

---

1. Lucas was first editor of the Yakima, Washington *Daily Republic* and later of the *Hartford Times* (Connecticut).

To Emanuel Celler[1]

June 11, 1954

Dear Mannie:

. . . This Bill,[2] as you know, provides for the creation of a new Eleventh Circuit. . . . I see no reason whatsoever for the creation of that new Circuit. I do not know of any real demand for it, and I get around that Circuit quite a little bit because it is a Circuit over which I am Circuit Justice, having been assigned to it by Chief Justice Hughes in 1939.

Judge William Denman,[3] Chief Judge of the Court of Appeals for the Ninth Circuit, has been the promoter of it. He got a vote through the Ninth Circuit at the last Conference in favor of it. But I know Judges who voted for it, under pressure, and now regret it. I would think that if you wanted to get a real picture of the sentiments among the Federal Judges for the creation of a new Circuit on the West Coast, it would be desirable to get on for your hearing not only Judge Denman who has sponsored the Bill, but also the newly appointed Judge from Oregon, James Alger Fee,[4] who, I think, you will find is solidly against it. I think the sentiment among the District Judges is largely against it. . . .

---

1. Celler (1888–1981), a representative from Brooklyn, chaired the House Judiciary Committee.

2. S. 2910 would have divided the Ninth Circuit in two and created a new Eleventh Circuit. Congress did not create a new circuit until 1981, and then it cut out Alabama, Florida, and Georgia from the old Fifth Circuit.

3. Denman (1872–1959) had been a progressive politician in California before his appointment to the circuit court in 1935.

4. Fee (1888–1959) had been chief judge of the U.S. District Court in Oregon until his appointment to the Ninth Circuit in early 1954.

To Grosvenor Chapman[1]

November 8, 1955

Dear Mr. Chapman:

. . . I do not think it would be within the bounds of propriety for me to explore the periphery of that decision because we are constantly getting cases calling for its application, and I do not want to prejudice my position in cases yet to come before us. So I shall be very happy to attend but I should not speak on the subject. . . .

1. Chapman (1911–), a Washington architect, had invited WOD to address the American Institute of Architects on the Court's recent decision in *Berman* v. *Parker*, 348 U.S. 26 (1954). The ruling, delivered by WOD for a unanimous bench, upheld the power of local government to condemn property for area redevelopment.

To Jerome N. Frank

September 27, 1956

Dear Jerry:

. . . You state in your letter that you assume we are too busy to scrutinize carefully all the [petitions for] certs coming to us from State courts denying relief. I do not think that is true. We look at all these things very closely. The difficulty is that there are often persuasive grounds for believing that the State court judgment rests on an adequate State ground.[1] Some here are sticklers on that point. Others of us are more liberal in that regard. But nonetheless a lot of cases get impaled on that barrier. So we do not get to the merits. That leaves open the avenue of relief through the Federal courts. . . .

1. A decisional rule of the Supreme Court is that it will not decide a case on constitutional grounds if the state law is adequate to determine the merits.

To Chester Collins Maxey[1]

November 5, 1956

Dear Chet:

I have been looking over Mason's biography of Harlan Fiske Stone.[2] I am shocked to find freely used in the book inter-office memos that those of us on the Court with Stone wrote each other concerning the cases under argument and up for decision.

This struck me as being quite improper unless our permission was obtained, which it was not.

All my papers of every kind go to Whitman. In view of what

Mason has done with Stone's confidential files, I think I should attach a condition (or request) to my papers that the Court material not be made public as long as my colleagues are alive.[3]

---

1. President of WOD's alma mater, Whitman College, from 1948 to 1959.
2. *Harlan Fiske Stone: Pillar of the Law* (New York, 1956).
3. WOD changed his mind several times over the disposition of his papers, and finally left them in the care of the Library of Congress. He did, however, delay the opening of those papers.

To Irita Van Doren[1]

January 28, 1958

Dear Irita:

. . . I do not believe I have ever expressed an opinion on a matter which has not come before the Court. Those who know the body of decisions around which I wrote THE RIGHT OF THE PEOPLE should know that everything I state in the book I had previously stated in some dissenting or concurring opinion, or in some opinion I have written for the Court. I very carefully refrained from passing on any question that had not reached us. A person is bound to be criticized and if you try to please everybody you would end up doing nothing. At least you would not be a member of the U.S. Supreme Court.

---

1. Van Doren (1891–1966) served as literary editor of the *New York Herald-Tribune* for nearly forty years.

To Eliot Janeway[1]

January 16, 1959

Dear Eliot:

[The Supreme Court] always acts as a constitutional court even when, over my dissent, the decision seems unconstitutional.

---

1. Janeway (1913–) is a widely read economic author and columnist.

To Robert Staughton Lynd[1]

November 11, 1959

Dear Professor Lynd:

. . . I remember particularly the volatile atmosphere in Washington, D.C. at the time an application was made to me for a stay of execution for the Rosenbergs.[2] I believe there were 200 reporters, photographers and radio men outside the door here at the Courthouse and there was a picket line around the building. The atmosphere seemed to be as inflammable as that in a gasoline plant. I did get one telegram that reached my desk from some people who knew me in the Far West who promised a lynching party when I reached that part of the country. I started out by car, traveling alone on Route 40, and I stopped somewhere in Pennsylvania at a motel. I went out to dinner and when I got back a great crowd had collected and before I shut off the motor, a spokesman came up and asked if I was Justice Douglas. When I said that I was, he turned around and shouted to the crowd "It's him!"

That was the only real mob I had ever seen face-to-face and I thought surely they were going to move into action. But instead they broke forth into loud cheers and applause. It turned out they were all, or most of them, immigrants from eastern Europe working in the coal mines of Pennsylvania. The demonstration that these very simple and perhaps illiterate people put on was one of the most moving experiences of my life. . . .

---

1.   Lynd (1892–1970), along with his wife, had done the famous Middletown sociological surveys.

2.   For the controversy surrounding WOD's stay in the famed spy trial, see *The Court Years* (New York: Random House, 1980), 78–82, and Simon, *Independent Journey*, 298–311.

To Robert Estabrook[1]

December 7, 1959

Dear Bob:

. . . The alleged overwork of the Court is really and truly nonsense. Those like Hart[2] who say we have not enough time to consider important cases refer to the cases we take under the Federal Employees Liability Act. But that is a strawman. Last Term out of 229 hours of argument we spent only one hour on the FELA case. And our record for the 10-year period is shown in the enclosed opinion in the *Harris* case, written after the Hart article went to press. . . .[3]

---

1.   An editor at the *Washington Post.*

2.   Henry M. Hart, Jr., had written in "Foreword: The Time Chart of the Justices," 72 H.L.R. 77 (1959), that the Court wasted too much time on insignificant workmen's compensation cases.

3.   *Harris* v. *Pennsylvania Railroad Co.*, 361 U.S. 15 (1959). In his concurring opinion, WOD responded to criticism about the workmen's compensation cases by listing all of the FELA cases the Court had heard in the previous ten years. The fact that in *Harris* the Court had reversed a lower court decision proved, WOD maintained, that appellate review by the high court still served an important function.

To Earl Warren[1]

February 18, 1961

Dear Chief:

Johnny Wright has been with us many years. He first served on the elevator force and then for reasons of health he decided to be transferred to the outside force where he has served well and faithfully for a number of years.

He now has some injuries and his health is not as good as it was. He therefore desires to shift back to the elevator staff which will mean less exposure to outdoor conditions.

I have known Johnny ever since he was employed here and can recommend him. He is a person of fine character and ability.

---

1.   Warren (1891–1974) had been a popular governor of California; he served as Chief Justice of the United States from 1953 to 1969, and despite some of WOD's criticism of him, WOD always thought of him as "the Chief."

To Hugo LaFayette Black[1] *and Tom C. Clark*[2]

February 23, 1961

Since you represent the Court before Congressional committees in the matter of the budget, I thought you should know these facts.

Back in 1950 I set up an outside pool to take on my overflow work, particularly any books I might write. . . .

Recently my staff in utter good faith and under pressure of getting work out has sent some things to the pool in the Court. My six Baghdad Lectures were sent there. So was *A Living Bill of Rights* and *The Rule of Law in World Affairs.* There were probably others also, as they sent things up without consulting me, but only when our pool was otherwise engaged.

There is apparently the feeling that my office has abused the privilege of the pool. To avoid any controversy, no matter how petty, I have instructed my staff to send nothing whatsoever to the Court pool and I have advised Miss Helen Dwyer to that effect also. Hence in representing the need of the pool in the future you can say that it is for eight members of the Court only, not including myself.

---

1. Black (1886–1971) had been a populist Democratic senator from Alabama for two terms when Roosevelt named him to the high court in 1937. He and WOD became the chief advocates for an activist jurisprudence, especially for the preferred position of First Amendment rights.

2. Clark (1899–1977) had been Truman's attorney general from 1945 to 1949, when the President named him to the Court; he retired in 1967 when President Johnson appointed Clark's son Ramsey as attorney general.

Memorandum to the Conference

July 1, 1961

I received a letter from a man, saying his ambition had been realized. He has established contact with Tom Paine and Benjamin Franklin. Moreover, he has recorded their conversations; and the tape he sent is in my office.

You are all welcome to it. In fact, it may be more interesting than most of the certs.

To Earl Warren

October 1, 1962

Dear Chief:

This Summer a young lady working for me left the building at 11:30 PM and asked the guard if he would escort her to the street while she waited for a bus. He refused, saying "If anyone attacks you, scream real loud so I'll hear you."

This is not a complaint. But in view of the lawless nature of the environment around the neighborhood, it seemed to me that we might inaugurate a policy of having a guard, on request, escort after dark any of the ladies to their car or to a bus or taxicab.

To Edgar Wayburn[1]

October 1, 1962

Dear Ed:

I hate to write this letter, but after considerable deliberation I have thought that it is the only alternative I have.

By this letter I am resigning as a member of the Board of Directors of the Sierra Club, effective October 1, 1962.

The reason that I am resigning is that I understand from some of our mutual friends that the Sierra Club, like other conservation agencies, may be engaging in litigation in the state or federal courts on conservation matters which at least in their potential might reach this Court. During the time of my membership on the Board, no such action was taken nor, so far as I am aware, was any contemplated. But now, with the changed circumstances and the likelihood that the Sierra Club may be in litigation, I think that in fairness to the office which I hold and in fairness to the Sierra Club I should no longer serve as a member of the Board of Directors. . . .

---

1.   A California physician and head of the Sierra Club.

To James T. Brady[1]

November 2, 1962

Dear Jim:

. . . All of the petitions that are filed *In Forma Pauperis* are screened by a law clerk in the offices of the Chief Justice, who sends a synopsis of the case to each of the Justices.

These cases are not the long, involved matters that are involved in the run of litigation, but usually a few sheets which may be handwritten or maybe typed, making certain charges. Since there is only one copy, the synopsis makes the distribution easier than if each of the papers were sent through each of the offices. That is a matter of some importance because we get of the total 2300 cases a year about 900–1000 in this group. Experience has shown that 90% of them are frivolous and deal with questions which present no aspect of federal law, and it is only federal law that our Court passes on, as you know.

If any Justice has any question in his mind about any of the points covered in the synopsis he sends for the papers himself, and that is done in dozens and dozens of cases each Term.

Moreover, as a matter of routine all capital cases, whether they are frivolous on their face or not, are circulated among all the Justices. We grant on the average not more than 2% of these cases. When we grant them we put them down for oral argument, send for the record from the lower court, have it printed at our expense, and appoint a lawyer. The meritorious cases, however, are few and far between, and the screening system seems to work quite well.

---

1. A popular writer for magazines and news supplements.

To Meier Steinbrink[1]

June 5, 1963

Dear Mr. Steinbrink:

I have your ill-tempered letter of June 4. There is nothing in the dissent which I wrote in *Arizona* v. *California*[2] which breaches the proprieties. What I said from the Bench was in the dissent.

Some dissents in the past have been much more emphatic than the one I delivered this past Monday. And my brother Black, whom I admire greatly, has himself given much more vigorous ones.

That is in the tradition of the Court. You should know better than to think that any dissent from this Court is *ad hominem.*

---

1. Steinbrink (1880–1967) sat on the New York bench from 1932 to 1950 and then served as a special referee for state and federal courts.

2. 373 U.S. 546 (1963). The case involved very complicated questions of the division of water in the Boulder Canyon project. Although WOD dissented vigorously, his opinion could not be characterized in any way as astringent or disrespectful.

To Thomas Gardiner Corcoran[1]

April 17, 1964

Dear Tommy:

Your greetings on my 25th Anniversary[2] touched me deeply. I thank you for the warm sentiments you expressed.

In ten more years I could set a new record for active service on the Court, although there are more interesting things than that on which records should be set. . . .

---

1. Corcoran (1900–1981) had been a key aide to Franklin Roosevelt; among his other accomplishments, he drafted the Securities Exchange Act of 1934.

2. Of service on the Court.

To Edmond Cahn[1]

April 20, 1964

Dear Edmond:

I saw you in the Courtroom the other day and I was happy to know you were there. It seemed to me a very dreary occasion that was being conducted out of a feeling of propriety, not out of sentiment or elation.[2] So anything I had to say must have had a note of sadness in it because that was my mood.

Many thanks for your congratulations on my 25th Anniversary. The friendships I have made, such as yours, rather than work done, are the rewards for living.

---

1. Cahn (1906–1964), an old friend of wod, taught at the New York University Law School for many years.

2. wod's quarter-century on the Court had been noted at a special ceremony earlier in the day.

To the Judicial Council of California

December 14, 1964

Dear Sirs:

I congratulate you for consideration of a court rule to prevent photography and radio and TV broadcasts from courtrooms and adjoining corridors. A trial is ordeal enough without outfitting it with all the paraphernalia of the modern news media. The courtroom should be a quiet, dignified place, not under the extra tensions of a theatrical production.

Memorandum for the Files

March 21, 1966

I did not sit in these cases,[1] argued today.

Tom Corcoran came to see me last Fall and told me the Court must grant these petitions and reverse. He emphasized the importance of reversal to him—how a leading figure in a corporation he was interested in was "milking" it and how the rule of the Court of Appeals blocked effective remedy.

I said nothing to him. But I did not vote on the petitions nor participate in the hearings.

He was not offering me anything. But [he was] guilty of a gross impropriety. We all refrain from sitting in a case if (as is seldom true) we are approached on it by anyone.

---

1. *Holt* v. *Alleghany Corp.* and *Holt* v. *Kirby*, both at 384 u.s. 28 (1966). The cases involved appeals by the corporation to overturn stockholders' derivative suits instituted to recover profits fraudulently diverted by company officers. By a 4–3 vote on April 18, with both woo and Fortas recused, the Court dismissed the suit as improvidently granted.

To the Editor, the Washington Post[1]

September 27, 1968

Dear Sir:

Your editorial of September 16 criticized my stay in the Ready Reserve case,[2] from the Fourth Circuit, calling it a "shop around."

Are you aware of the number of stays granted by one Justice after another has denied it? Is the volume so great as to cause alarm?

Would you feel the same way if one Justice denied a stay in a death case and another granted it, so that the entire Court could consider the matter? In view of the high rate of fatalities, would you classify an embarkation to Vietnam with a death case?

If the entire Court must be consulted on petitions for certiorari

and four can grant one, why should not the entire Court be consulted on issuance of stays?

Are you aware of the practice of referring important stays to the
entire Court?

Do you realize that all I did in the Ready Reserve case was just
that?

It is amazing how little the press knows about Supreme Court
procedures. A country paper that we read at Goose Prairie can be
excused, but not THE WASHINGTON POST whose editors could find
someone to give them a seminar on judicial procedure any time they
choose.

---

1. The letter is marked "Did Not Send."

2. *Morse* v. *Boswell*, 393 U.S. 802 (1968), involved one of several efforts by
draftees to prevent their assignment to Vietnam. Almost alone on the bench, WOD
wanted the Court to deal with the alleged unconstitutionality of the war. The
editorial criticizing the "shop-around" had appeared on September 16.

To Warren Earl Burger[1]

October 18, 1969

Dear Chief:

This is another Saturday when everything in the building closes
down at 12:00 Noon.

I wonder if that policy can be reconsidered?

Saturday is historically a work day here, at least for many of us,
in order to get caught up with odds and ends which accumulate
during the week.

To have no telephone service, and no library after 12:00 Noon
is very disadvantageous.

---

1. Burger (1907–   ) had been named Chief Justice earlier in the year by
President Nixon after serving on the court of appeals. Personal relations between
the new Chief and WOD always remained cordial, but professionally they were at
odds from the time Burger took his seat until WOD retired.

To Alan Gordon

March 9, 1970

Dear Alan:

Holmes once said that a dissent was like "a brooding omnipresence" in the sky. It perpetuates a discussion which in time often goes the other way.[1]

---

1. Holmes said no such thing; he used the term in derision of the Legal Formalists, who believed that law consisted of eternal and immutable principles, existing as "a brooding omnipresence," and all judges had to do was seek and determine the right rule, regardless of changing circumstances.

Memorandum to the Conference

August 8, 1970

The decision of some of the Brethren to file financial statements[1] came to a head without prior notice to me or Conference discussion. I was at a disadvantage being in the State of Washington and having my financial records with the House Committee and/or my counsel.

So it took me extra time to prepare the statement. Moreover, when I saw the form, it seemed to me to be quite inadequate.

There was no disclosure of income from investments.

Nor was there disclosure of royalties paid.

These two items seemed to me necessary for full disclosure. While I always felt that the precise contents of a judge's portfolio should not be made public, lest he become prey to the vultures of the press, I thought that the size of his outside income was relevant. For the same reason I thought royalties should be added.

As I stated in the memo filed with the Clerk, there is no law requiring disclosure; and it is plainly not in the competence of judges to write such a law as I said in the *Chandler*[2] case. A law should be uniform and applicable to all federal officials—executive, legislative, and judicial. But since some Justices were filing, I thought I should do so also. But by disclosure standards I thought the form being used was quite inadequate.

I am sending this note to the Conference lest there be any misunderstanding.

---

1. A voluntary step taken by the justices in the wake of efforts to impeach WOD; see chapter 15.

2. *In Chandler v. Judicial Council of the Tenth Circuit,* 398 U.S. 74 (1970), WOD had dissented from the decision upholding the power of judicial councils to set rules for judicial conduct.

To Catherine DeNoyer[1]

October 4, 1971

Dear Catherine:

The Court gets about 4500 cases a year. They come in on the average of 80 to 100 a week. We are here in Washington, D.C. from October to July. Then I go to my home in the State of Washington, and I go over the summer cases out there as they come in. There were 815 which came in this past summer.

We do not go to school to become judges. The federal judges are named by the President and confirmed by the Senate. I have been on the Court since 1939. I was a lawyer fourteen years prior to that time.

There is no reason why a woman could not be on the Court, although none has so far been on this federal court. Women, however, have sat on the other lower federal courts and on many state courts. . . .

---

1. Ms. DeNoyer was a student in Baldwin Park, California; this letter is typical of many Douglas wrote to young people wanting to know about different aspects of the Court's work.

To Warren Earl Burger

December 6, 1971

Dear Chief:

. . . Over this last weekend a lawyer with the Department of Justice, at a social occasion, told one of my law clerks the precise vote in this case,[1] saying that Thurgood and I were the only dissenters and that the case had been assigned to Harry to write. Since there seems to have been some leak concerning the case and since the information leaked was absolutely correct, I thought I should bring it at once to your attention.

---

1. *United States* v. *Generes,* 405 u.s. 93, a tax case, had been argued on November 8, 1971; the Court did not hand down its final ruling until February 23, 1972.

To *Warren Earl Burger*

May 31, 1972

Dear Chief:

... I have been planning to bring to the attention of the Conference, for discussion, a practice which was in vogue when I took my seat under Hughes and which has been more or less in vogue since that time, although some regimes have not observed it as faithfully as others. Stone, for example, meticulously observed it. Vinson, and to an extent Warren, did not. I refer to the policy that whenever an opinion for the Court is circulated that the dissenters drop everything else and prepare their dissents. It is, I think, a good practice as it enables the case to come to a rather rapid focus.

I think as far as this Term is concerned that *Fuentes* is a good example for the need to restore that practice.[1] This is no criticism of anyone in particular. It is merely a suggestion that we try to improve the present system and I thought that *Fuentes* was perhaps a prime example.

---

1. *Fuentes* v. *Shavin,* 407 u.s. 67, upheld a Florida replevin statute defining how an owner could regain possession of goods unlawfully taken away. White, along with Burger and Blackmun, dissented. The case had been argued on November 9, 1971, but the decision did not come down until June 12, 1972.

To *Warren Earl Burger*

June 12, 1972

Dear Chief:

I understand that the NATIONAL OBSERVER has an uncomplimentary piece done by a woman by the name of Nina Tottenberg.[1]

She tried to see me a week or so ago to talk to me off-the-record about the Court.

I never talk to anyone on-the-record or off-the-record about the Court.

But I was particularly allergic about the NATIONAL OBSERVER. I had seen one of the reporters several years back who wanted to do a piece about me. I saw him and it was a friendly visit. But as I suspected, it ended up with my decapitation.

So I made it a point never to talk to NATIONAL OBSERVER reporters about things as innocuous even as fly fishing or the weather.

---

1. Currently the legal reporter for National Public Radio.

To Warren Earl Burger

June 13, 1972

Dear Chief:

I told Harry Blackmun[1] the other day I might decide to move to my old quarters, which he now occupies.

It is, as you know, a three-room suite, which is plenty large enough for me. I will never have more than two law clerks. I think, as a matter of fact, that three are a waste of the taxpayer's money. The decisions here can be made only by one person and it is for him to do most of the work. This is no reflection on anyone else, but states my own philosophy and habits of work.

Moreover, I really think that the enlargement of the offices is a waste of public money. They are plenty large enough now.

But that, of course, is not for me to decide.

I think I would be happier in my old three-office suite than I would in a new one which has been enlarged but in the enlargement loses the corner-office advantages . . . . After all, I spent 25 years in those three offices and did not seem to suffer too much.

I would add as a PS something which is unnecessary, I guess—i.e., that the stairwell on the side of that three-office suite makes it virtually impossible for anyone to enlarge it.[2]

It would help if the new lights, which you kindly arranged to put into my present office, could this summer be installed in 108 in the three rooms, because we have found that they are a great help and they do relieve the eystrain.

---

1. Harry Andrew Blackmun (1908–   ) of Minnesota had been appointed in 1969 to replace Abe Fortas. Although originally considered a conservative, Blackmun came to occupy one of the swing votes in the middle of the Court's ideological spectrum.

2. In order to accommodate larger staffs assigned to each justice, Burger had arranged for office suites to be remodeled, creating more space. WOD, who had steadfastly opposed increasing his own staff, hit upon the stratagem of taking his old suite which, as he points out, could not be remodeled. For his glee over this, see *Court Years*, p. 5.

To Irving Dilliard [1]

November 14, 1972

Dear Irving:

I am glad that you are aware of the adjudicatory court plan.[2] It would screen all the cases, telling us the ones to take.

Brandeis used to say that "what we do not do" is more important at times than what we in fact do.

There is a great illusion about our overwork. . . . Today we take no more than two per cent of the *in forma pauperis* cases and no more than six per cent of the others. Of the 900 of all types which came in last summer we took 23, which is less than three per cent. We are now down essentially to three days a week of argument. Under Hughes we had five days a week. Warren reduced it to four days. Burger is trying to reach three days. That is the case this week. Some weeks we still sit four days. It's half three and half four now, with the trend being toward three. . . .

We actually are underworked. We write about 17 opinions for the Court apiece each Term. Hugo and I used to write over 60 for the Court; and that was when our total argued caseload was greater than it is now.

The Bar is a victim of clever propaganda. There is enough hostility against the Court to give it credence.

The new adjudicatory court scheme would give the [Supreme] Court power to lift any case the other Court rejects. But that would take five votes. Since the 1925 Act it has taken only four votes to get a case here.

----

1.   Dilliard (1904–   ) has had several careers; after a lengthy stint as a newspaperman, he entered academia and wrote or edited books on Brandeis, Black, and Learned Hand.

2.   Like other proposals to "reform" the Court, this one also died. See *Court Years*, 384–86, for further comments by woD denying that the Court was overworked.

To Michael Joseph Mansfield[1]

June 3, 1974

Dear Mike:

Someone sent me a copy of your letter to the Chief Justice implying we get a four month vacation with pay and with nothing to do.

I invite you and Maureen to visit our home at Goose Prairie. Each week brings a mail bag full of certs and appeals—averaging 80 or more each week.

Goose Prairie is a busy headquarters for a Circuit Justice. I have several hearings a week on stays, habeas corpus and the like. At times 70 applicants for interim relief came in each week, though the average is about five a day.

The lawyers of the Ninth Circuit enjoy the trip to Goose Prairie. It's better than Washington, D.C. and there is a constant parade.

So if you and Maureen come, which I hope you do, I may ask you to shift for yourself in the mornings while I am locked in my study. . . .

----

1.   Mansfield (1903–   ), was the longtime senator from Montana and majority leader from 1961 to 1977; he then served as ambassador to Japan.

Chapter 4

Felix . . .

LOUIS BRANDEIS considered Felix Frankfurter (1882–1965) "the most useful lawyer in America," and many legal reformers, including William Douglas, shared that opinion. Frankfurter defended radicals during the Red Scare, helped organize the defense for Sacco and Vanzetti in the 1920s, and spoke out time and again for civil liberties. During his quarter-century of teaching at the Harvard Law School, he trained two generations of students to appreciate the dynamic interplay of law and government in the twentieth century. To younger reformers like Douglas at Yale, Frankfurter set an example of how commitment could be translated into action. There is no doubt that while a teacher at Yale and later on the SEC, Douglas looked up to Frankfurter and sought his approval.

Roosevelt named Frankfurter to the Court late in 1938; after quick confirmation by the Senate, Frankfurter took his seat in February 1939, and served until illness forced his retirement in 1962. At the time of his appointment, Douglas rejoiced, and a few months later, Frankfurter welcomed Douglas to the bench. Frankfurter saw his new colleague as an ally and expected his support. After all, they had both endorsed New Deal reforms, subscribed to the same tenets of legal reform, admired Franklin Roosevelt, and worshipped Louis Brandeis. For a while it seemed this would happen, that Frankfurter, with the support of Douglas and other Roosevelt appointees, would capture the leadership of the Court. After one of Douglas's early opinions came down, Frankfurter sent him a teasing note: "I am bound to say that it is bad for both of us that we are no longer professors. Because if you were still a professor, you would have written a different elaboration and if I were still a professor, I would get several lectures out of what you have written."

But the two friends soon parted company. Frankfurter, used to manipulating men of lesser intellect, could never admit that his colleagues had minds of their own, and they resented his treating them as first-year law students. Douglas, Black, and Murphy, whom Frankfurter labeled "the Axis," broke with him over the second flag salute case (*West Virginia Board of Education* v. *Barnette*, [1943]). But the break would have come sooner or later, for Frankfurter represented one trend of jurisprudence in the modern Court, and Douglas another.

Frankfurter's two great heroes, Holmes and Brandeis, had both advocated "judicial restraint." They believed that economic policy-making should be left to the legislatures, and courts ought not interfere merely because judges disagreed with the wisdom of the legislators. In the early decades of the century, however, the courts *had* interfered, in a wide range of cases from *Lochner* v. *New York* (1905) to the invalidation of many New Deal measures in the 1930s. Frankfurter had been the leading academic proponent of judicial restraint, and once on the bench he practiced what he had preached. If the legislature had the constitutional power, he would not examine the wisdom of the policy.

But where judicial restraint had been an argument for allowing reform in the hands of Holmes and Brandeis, it became an instrument of judicial inflexibility with Frankfurter. By the time he went on the bench, the battle to keep courts out of economic policy-making had been won. The Roosevelt appointees practically abandoned oversight of business or economic regulation. From the late 1930s on, however, the expansion of civil liberties topped the agenda of judicial concerns, and here Douglas, not Frankfurter, led the way.

Judicial restraint, as Brandeis had pointed out, did not necessarily apply in one area—civil liberties. No matter what reason to restrain speech, press, assembly, or any right protected under the Constitution, courts should never meekly accept that rationale. The judiciary had a special obligation to promote civil liberties; this, however, required judicial activism, that is, courts would have to act positively in interpreting the meaning of rights, not merely react to legislative policy. Frankfurter could not accept this idea, and many of his followers who had applauded the professor's defense of civil liberties came to denounce the justice for his failures in this area.

Douglas, however, welcomed the chance to use the Court's powers to expand civil liberties and, together with Black, became the leading proponent of an expanded Bill of Rights on the high court. The two battled with Frankfurter constantly, and personal relations, once so close, deteriorated. Douglas saw his colleague as crafty, self-serving, and power hungry, and Frankfurter in turn looked down on Douglas's allegedly inferior intellectual powers and his supposed subservience to Black. Even off the Court, Douglas found evidence of Frankfurter's evil influence, and although in his memoirs he claimed there was never any real ill feeling between the two, the following letters document the deterioration of a once-close relationship.

May 11, 1931

Dear Felix:

On Friday evening, June 5th, in Boston the Yale Law School, the Yale Institute of Human Relations and the Department of Commerce are tendering to the three Boston referees in bankruptcy a dinner as part consideration of their cooperation rendered this last year in our bankruptcy study.[1] As duly authorized representative and agent of at least two of those distinguished institutions I extend to you herewith an invitation to attend said banquet. The dinner will be formal, social and non-intellectual except for your contribution which we hope will be an answer to a discourse by one Thomas Reed Powell, entitled "The Prevention of Mental or Other Bankruptcies.". . .[2]

---

1. See Chapter 1.

2. Frankfurter (hereafter FF) responded the next day: "This is a good season of the year for a survey of mental bankruptcy, but there is no danger of moral bankruptcy in taking part in any enterprise of which the slogan is 'For God, for Country, and for Yale!'"

March 1, 1932

My dear Felix:

All those interested in improvement of the law and growth of jurisprudence in this country will always be greatly in your debt for the noble service you rendered in making known in influential places the righteousness, strength and grandeur of Judge Cardozo. It was a genuine pleasure to see his appointment finally come through.[1] I am very happy that I could contribute my small bit to it.

I have been meaning to write to you for some time about an article you wrote in the Yale Law Journal five or six years ago on the compact clause of the Constitution.[2] I came across that article a few months ago for the first time and read it with great interest. In fact I reread it two or three times. I wanted you to know that I have found a pearl and enjoyed it. Truly, Felix, there are passages in the article which for sheer beauty of content and style have seldom been equalled in legal literature.

---

1. Nearly all legal progressives had called upon President Hoover to name Benjamin Nathan Cardozo (1870–1938), the highly respected chief judge of the New York Court of Appeals, to take Holmes's seat when the latter retired in 1932.

2. FF and James M. Landis, "The Compact Clause of the Constitution—A Study in Interstate Adjustments," 34 *Yale L.J.* 701 (1925). FF's article is considered among his best pieces of writing, and he noted in his answer on March 7: "It is one of the things I am least ashamed of, and I do feel that it embodies some important considerations for the development of American public law."

June 24, 1932

My dear Felix:

I read with great joy in yesterday's Times the Governor's recommendation of you for the Supreme Judicial Court. I was happy not only because it spells the end of mediocrity of a formerly distinguished bench but also because it is such an appropriate and timely tribute to your own distinctions and accomplishments. I fully realize the great loss this would entail for the Harvard Law School and the veritable host of young men whom you inspire and stimulate in your incomparable fashion. The loss to the teaching profession would be absolutely irreparable. On the other hand, the call of public service is strong and insistent and the service you would render to your distinguished Commonwealth would be memorable. . . .[1]

---

1. Upon the advice of Louis Brandeis and because of his desire to work with Franklin Roosevelt, FF turned down the surprise appointment to the Supreme Judicial Court of Massachusetts which Governor Joseph Ely had tendered. In his

letter declining the offer, FF emphasized the obligation he felt to continue his work in legal education.

December 8, 1933

My dear Felix:

. . . During the last two months I have missed you more than I can say.[1] I have sorely needed your advice and consultation, for I have spent much time on the Securities Act[2]—a thing which I know must still be close to your heart.

As you know, a battle has been waging on these shores. It has been a bitter one. Good old Jim[3] has been maintaining a noble front against all attacks. You know where my sympathy lies. I saw just enough of the horrors of Wall Street to know that an adequate control of those practices must be uncompromising. The attacks being made on the Act were ill conceived, to say the least. And I knew that much which was emanating was merely a disguised attack on the fundamental principles of the Act. This I resented very much.

At first I decided to bring my small and insignificant battery into place and employ it to attack the citadels of high finance. But then I concluded that my small contribution (if any) might be more effective if I . . . endeavored to appraise it dispassionately in light of its ability to do the things desired. And so I degenerated into a technician, trying not to lose sight of the forest for the trees. The result is two articles. . . .[4]

But the doing of these two articles has caused me great suffering. The first is that what I said might be taken as an advocacy of the cause of the goddam bankers, who have handled their own affairs so badly as to deserve no support. In fact they have suffered more actual damage by the Pecora investigation[5] than they ever would under the Securities Act. . . . The second is that some of the things that I said might be taken as an effrontery to you and the noble cause you serve. I have not been able to free myself from either of these fears. But I write you to assure you that I have no cause except the public good and no client except the investor. . . .

As I said above I write you because I want it clear that I stand with you not against you and that no effrontery was intended. I cannot hope to convince you of my posiiton. That is an intellectual matter on which disagreement among individuals must be expected.[6] I would have been happier if I could have been in constant

touch with you during the last few months. I would have then been
sure that there were no blind spots in my reasoning and no naivete
in my assumptions. . . . It will be swell to have you back again. We
all suffer when you leave.

---

1.   FF was spending a year as Eastman Professor at Oxford.

2.   The Securities Act of 1933 was the first effort to bring the stock market
under federal regulation. It set up a special division in the Federal Trade Commission to oversee stock issues.

3.   James Landis was then serving on the Federal Trade Commission; he
would soon join the SEC and then be chairman.

4.   WOD and George E. Bates had written two articles on the Securities Act.
In them, WOD defended the purpose of the act but hammered at its technical
deficiencies which he charged would prevent achievement of those goals. The first
article, "Some Effects of the Securities Act upon Investment Banking," 1 *University
of Chicago Law Review* 283 (1933), argued that the act did not provide enough
protection for the investment banks, since the overbroad language of the act could
make bankers liable for certain securities even in cases where they ought not have
liability. This would lead investment houses to refrain from underwriting badly
needed new securities issues. The second article, "The Federal Securities Act of
1933," 43 *Yale L.J.* 171 (1933), published a month later, charged that nothing in
the act "would prevent a tyrannical management from playing fast and loose" with
stockholders' funds. The article also proposed that a separate agency be created to
deal solely with the securities market in a rigorously honest but fair and flexible
manner.

5.   The investigation into banking and investment practices headed by Ferdinand Pecora for the Senate had exposed a number of unethical and illegal practices
and had made possible the enactment of the Securities Act.

6.   FF replied on January 1, 1934: "It was a damned generous letter. But also
revealing a surprisingly foolish streak in you. That you should ever worry lest I worry
about any professional writing of yours being against *me*, 'an effrontery to you'. For
heaven's sake, Bill, are we dealing with ideas or throwing spit balls at each other?
Suppose you did disagree with me, even on a major public or legal matter. What
the hell? The friends I care about I expect to be disinterested, surely. But agreement
with what I think—that's an irrelevance."

February 19, 1934

My dear Felix:

I appreciated your letter of January 16th . . . . One would imply from
what you say that I was aligned with the bankers on the current
problems. If you can find support for that in my writings then you
may pillory me in any fashion you choose. . . . My heart would indeed

"bleed" if I thought I was inadvertently championing the cause of "the Street." Inadvertence, myopia or stupidity on my part are the only things which could cause that. I hope they are absent.

The difference between us is not in social values but in ways and means. You would call me impractical and too idealistic. I would call you conservative. I still hear Wall St. comment on my article in the December issue of the Yale Law Journal. It is not what you apparently imagine. Curiously enough they appraise it very much as you do.[1] I never thought I would find you and the bankers together in any such respect. They deplore the fact that I have gone "administrative." They would have rejoiced had I promoted specific amendments. (Thereon hangs a tale.) Have you seen Flexner's article?[2] As a legal essay it rates about a C. But as a political document it is an A. I was not writing on the public or political level. Can't you imagine me writing my article and at the same time heartily agreeing with Flexner? I think he is dead right. Any amendments should come from the Commission. To start amending now might well leave the Act toothless and clawless. . . .

I have seen too many of the horrors and intricacies of high finance and I understand them too well to be impressed with the Securities Act. It just cannot be done that way. It would be quite another thing if it were Main Street business. But it isn't and it won't be. Tighter knots than that will have to be tied. It can't be left, as you apparently would leave it, to the trading instincts of the people and to in terrorem methods.

I hate to see (even more than you do) the shift of power to Washington. If you will recall my bankruptcy ideas, you will remember that even in that minor respect I am anxious to see the states assume control. . . .

So, you see we take different roads to the same end. You fear the government's imprimatur on securities. I would not want it on. I do not think that such tradition should be established. Would you take away the I.C.C.'s powers under 20a?[3] Has the I.C.C. injured investors? . . . Before long we are going to have an I.C.C. (so to speak) for every business. Witness the governmental authorities in some of the codes.[4] Those are our beginnings. If prices, costs, expansion, competition, trade practices, etc. are in the codes, why are security issues outside? Security issues just cannot stay outside if the codes are to amount to anything. The great advance in security regulation is going to be made when we put responsibility on industry and articulate that control with requirements of the public interest. Couple that with truth about securities and I think we will be going places and seeing things. Meanwhile let's not be too antithetical in our planning.

So I end where I began . . . . So, malign and libel me as you will. I only ask that you give me at least the benefit of a small doubt. And just because I have a deep understanding of corporate finance do not infer that I am an Ivy Lee[5] for Wall St. The Securities Act will be fully justified if it drives the government into the investment banking business. I wonder how the clients you are trying to thrust upon me would like to hear that? . . .

---

1.   In his January 16, letter, FF had been rather skeptical of the act and questioned whether any administrative rules would in fact be able to curb Wall Street.

2.   Bernard Flexner (1865–1945), a friend of FF and of Louis Brandeis, was a New York attorney; the article is "Fight on the Securities Act," 153 *The Atlantic* 232 (February 1934).

3.   Sec. 20a gave the Interstate Commerce Commission some oversight on the issuance of railroad securities.

4.   The National Industrial Recovery Act of 1933, the keystone of the Roosevelt recovery program, called for each industry to adopt a code of practice, which would include provisions for ethical conduct, fair labor practices, and be subject to legal enforcement.

5.   Ivy Ledbetter Lee (1877–1934) is credited with founding the public relations business; he is best known for his rehabilitation of John D. Rockefeller's reputation.

November 6, 1934

My dear Felix:

My office is on Wall St.[1] But so is that of each member of the Yale law faculty.[2] My hair, however, is not red. Is not this long deferred frontal attack ever going to materialize? Very few country lawyers[3] like myself have ever survived one of your assaults. But I am willing to take my chances and risk such tail feathers as I have.

In any event I would like to see you[4] and would thoroughly enjoy the rattle of your glass once again.

---

1.   FF had scribbled on this letter the following comments: "This I had suspected."

2.   "but that is worse than I had possibly feared."

3. "So you're another one of those innocents in Wall Street."
4. "Now you're talking real sense."

June 10, 1936

Dear Felix:

If the pamphlet entitled "I Have No Speech, by Felix Frankfurter" were a prospectus under the Securities Act of 1933 I believe a stop order would issue, for it is a misleading statement since it reveals that you had, rather than had not, a speech.

I am very happy to have it as it partially fills the gaps between my very infrequent opportunities to chat with you.

April 1, 1937

Dear Felix:

My affection for you is so abiding that, although I have not discovered any financial skull-duggery sufficient in size and importance to warrant going to Boston, I nevertheless will arrange to come up there this month.[1]

---

1. FF had written on March 29: "It is too bad that Boston is such a small, pure city that there is no financial skulduddery [*sic*] big enough for you to attend to in person. I would like to see you one of these days."

June 30, 1937

Dear Felix:

Many thanks for your kind and generous letter of June 28.[1] I deeply cherish your praise of the protective committee reports. I think that over a period of years they will make their dent because, in the first place, the facts are there and, in the second place, the philosophy is sound. . . .

When Congress adjourns and I finally get up to New England for a vacation late this summer, I hope you are about so that I may see you, particularly to discuss some of the broad questions of policy raised not only by these reorganization reports, but other matters closer to the day to day administration of our three statutes.

---

1. FF had received the SEC Report on corporate reorganization and had written: "While I have only sniffed it—paged it here and there—one does not have

to strike all the matches on the box to know that they light. Having a little familiarity with the field, I think I appreciate the thorough preliminary analysis, the indefatigable industry, the resourcefulness in examination, and, above all, the fearless clarity that followed trails, wheresoever they led. And your report makes luminous what your examination revealed."

December 8, 1937

My dear Felix:

I appreciate very much your gracious note of the 4th on my recent statement on the Stock Exchange, coming as it did from a veteran who knows how lonely the front line trenches can be.[1]

---

1.   On November 23, WOD had warned the stock exchanges that unless they instituted more effective measures for self-regulation, they could anticipate sharper SEC curbs. In a brief note, FF had written "What a refreshing thing it is to read an official statement that is fresh in its language and wisely informed and courageous in its underlying policies. More strength to you!"

Re: No. 151 Deputy v. Du Pont[1]

December 28, 1939

I would have been glad to have undertaken to draft an opinion on the basis that the activities of respondent did not constitute a trade or business under the Act. However, as you may recall, only Stanley [Reed] and myself indicated that as a ground for the decision when we discussed the matter at Conference. Since no interest was shown in that point of view at Conference, I then decided to drop the matter. . . .

I have not had an opportunity to tell you how badly I felt over the assignment of this case to me. I thought it was one of the poorest assignments which the Chief Justice has made. After all, the respondent here has been much in the public eye as an opponent of this Administration and for the opinion to be written by one of the new judges had in it possibilities of ignition of emotions. I thought it far better that one of those who voted to reverse and who was not associated with this Administration write the opinion. Hence, when it came to me I was not entirely unhappy that the Conference decided to put the case on the very narrow ground stated, rather than on the ground which Stanley and I urged at the Conference and which you set forth in your draft. For that ground does quicken somewhat possibilities of rich man-poor man distinctions . . . .

---

1. *Deputy et al.* v. *Du Pont,* 308 u.s. 488 (1940). Pierre S. Du Pont had undertaken private borrowing to arrange for stock to be given to certain executives of the Du Pont Corporation, because it had been legally impossible for the corporation itself to arrange the transfer. He had claimed the costs of these transactions as a deductible business expense, and the commissioner of Internal Revenue had disallowed them. For the Court, woo upheld the government because the expenses had resulted not from the respondent's own business, but from what he did to help the corporation. ff, joined by Stanley Reed, concurred but wanted the decision based on a more precise definition of what constituted a trade or business.

June 14, 1940

Dear Felix:

I told you before you left that I was going to the Texas Bar meeting July 4th. . . .

You will remember how Stone took on the corporate bar at Michigan three or four years ago.[1] What would you think of me developing a talk around the country lawyer, the general practitioner—his citizenship and responsibilities at times like this, propogation of democratic faith, civil liberties, etc.?[2]

---

1. Harlan F. Stone, "Public Influence of the Bar," 48 *H.L.R.* 1 (1934).

2. wod's speech is [Bar no.] *Texas Law Review* 81 (1940). ff applauded the idea, "for in your sly, innocent way you will be able to get in a good deal of innuendo."

April 4, 1944

In your opinion in the *General Trading Company* case,[1] you state at the bottom of page 2 and the top of page 3, "No state can tax the doing of interstate business or go against the gross receipts from it." I agree to the former but the latter goes much further, I feel, than you or I would ever agree to go. The *Berwind-White* tax also impinges on the proceeds of an interstate transaction. The Indiana gross receipts tax, in many of its applications sustained here (*Allied*

Mills, Wood Preserving) likewise has such an impact. And then there are the cases involving proration, etc.

But for that clause, I agree with your opinion which I thought handled the problem nicely. I hope you can rephrase the sentence so that I can join in the opinion.[2]

---

1. *General Trading Co.* v. *State Tax Commissioner of Iowa,* 322 U.S. 335 (1944). FF, for a 7–2 Court, upheld a state tax on goods solicited by traveling salesmen for an out-of-state firm and shipped from out of state; the salesmen were deemed to have a place of business within the state.

2. FF accepted the suggestion and deleted the phrase.

November 14, 1947

If we reached the constitutional question in No. 49, *Shapiro* v. *United States*,[1] there might be no major disagreement between us on the facts of this case. But I do not see why it is either necessary or appropriate to squint the opinion against the constitutionality of the regulation. It would seem to me much better Court policy to make a reservation that is wholly neutral.

---

1. *Shapiro* v. *United States,* 335 U.S. 1 (1948). WOD joined the majority in upholding the government's contention that Congress had intended to include in the Emergency Price Control Act the immunity provisions of the Compulsory Testimony Act. FF joined Jackson, Rutledge, and Murphy in dissent.

February 25, 1948

Dear Felix:

The issue of whether or not there is a cause of action is for me the starting point, as I think it must be for every lawyer.[1] The Hepburn Act problem is reached only after a cause of action is found. That has seemed to me so elemental as not to necessitate repetition. But the added importance of the problem here is indicated by the divergent views as to the interpretation of Utah law. Under one view, which found support in the *Halling* case,[2] the defendant would not have, as against the heirs, the same defenses that it would have had against the defendant had he lived and sued.

In this case it is at the very threshold necessary to determine whether or not Utah law creates that kind of a cause of action. . . .

It was to resolve that question that I cast the fourth vote for certiorari in this case. Whether the other three who voted for certiorari voted for that reason, or because they wanted to reexamine the free pass cases under the Hepburn Act I do not know. . . .

I strongly believe that the four vote rule[3] should be preserved in all of its integrity. If those who vote to deny cert adhere to their position that the case is one which the Court should not bother with and hence, after argument, vote to dismiss as improvidently granted, then I repeat the four vote rule in the certiorari cases has been seriously undermined. We had this out once at conference when Chief Justice Stone was presiding, and I dislike very much to see the problem appear under this new disguise.

---

1. *Francis et al.* v. *Southern Pacific Co.*, 333 U.S. 445 (1948). An employee of the railroad, while not at work, had been killed in an accident while riding on a free pass. The Hepburn Act forbade such passes, and WOD, for a 6–3 Court, ruled that a federal law took precedence over a state statute in determining whether negligence constituted a cause of action.

2. *Halling* v. *Industrial Commission of Utah*, 71 Utah 112 (1927), expressed state law on railroad negligence.

3. If four members of the Court believed a petition raised serious constitutional issues or had other reasons why they thought the Court should hear it, then the Court would grant certiorari, that is, it would accept the petition for review.

May 29, 1954

Today at Conference I asked you a question concerning your memorandum opinion in Nos. 480 & 481.[1] The question was not answered. An answer was refused, rather insolently. This was so far as I recall the first time one member of the Conference refused to answer another member on a matter of Court business.

We all know what a great burden your long discourses are. So I am not complaining. But I do register a protest at your degradation of the Conference and its deliberations.

---

1. The combined cases, *Secretary of Agriculture* v. *United States* and *Florida Citrus Commission* v. *United States*, 347 U.S. 645 (1954), involved an ICC ruling which FF, for a 5–3 Court, upheld; WOD dissented along with Black and Chief Justice Warren.

March 11, 1955

Dear Felix:

The majority vote on this case, as I understood it, concerned solely and simply a question of statutory construction.[1] The opinion that you circulated has many due process emanations. The opinion, as I understand it, rests on the statute, only by force of the major constitutional issues raised if the contrary result is envisaged.

I do not share the doubts on the constitutional issues, and I stated as much to the Conference. My vote is necessary, as I recall, for a Court opinion.[2] But I cannot join a Court opinion that pushes me to the result for fear of constitutional difficulties. . . .[3]

---

1. *Granville-Smith* v. *Granville-Smith,* 349 U.S. 1 (1955), involved an interpretation of a Virgin Islands statute and a congressional law over what constituted the minimum stay necessary to establish domicile for a divorce.

2. Justice Harlan did not take part, and three other justices dissented from FF's opinion; without WOD's vote an evenly divided Court would have upheld the lower court ruling.

3. FF struck the offending passages, and WOD joined him in a straightforward statutory construction opinion.

December 16, 1957

Dear Felix:

. . . I am afraid you misunderstood what I said earlier about Lambert[1] when it was in process of being discussed at the table.

I preferred, as I think you know, to go on the ground of "vagueness," and I wrote the opinion that way to begin with. What I said was that this other ground of "lack of notice" was less desirable and not as clear as the other ground. I still have a preference for the other ground, but that did not get any vote in the conference except Hugo's.

The reason that I asked you for some statute which would run afoul of Lambert other than the ordinance involved in Lambert was your statement on the bench that it would make a dissent much, much too long to list the statutes which would fall as a result of Lambert.

We made a fairly exhaustive search in this office, and we have not been able to find any others that would have this defect.

In view of the fact that you had found so many that would suffer from the same infirmity, I thought you might be willing to disclose their identity—at least the identity of a single one.

---

1.   In *Lambert* v. *California*, 355 U.S. 225 (1957), WOD for a 5–4 Court struck down a Los Angeles ordinance requiring the registration of convicted felons when it applied to persons who had no knowledge of their duty to register. In a bitter dissent FF wrote "I feel confident that the present decision will turn out to be an isolated deviation from the strong current of precedents—a derelict on the waters of the law."

The next day WOD wrote to Hugo Black that he had handed down Black's opinions in several cases the day before.

"The Green case [355 U.S. 184, involving a problem of double jeopardy] got our friend from Harvard extremely excited. He went to great lengths on the bench to denounce it, departing from his printed dissent.

"When he got around to Lambert he also went hogwild. He said it would take a book to list all the criminal statutes which this decision held unconstitutional. Therefore, he did not want to clutter up the law books with all these hundreds or thousands of citations.

"Since the announcement of his dissent, I have been writing him asking him to give us just one citation of one other statute which would be held unconstitutional.

"It is now 11:40 AM, December 17th, and this has been going on for nearly 24 hours. He has not yet sent me any citations, but if he does I will rush it all down to you, because I know you must be as worried about the devastating effect of Lambert and Green as I am."

From the following two letters, it appears that a frustrated and angry FF could not provide the citations and even denied making the remark.

December 16, 1957

Dear Felix:
Nobody in this office wants you to go through the ordeal by fire—especially at Christmas time.

But I never said that I thought the want of notice would "cut too deeply into the criminal law". I merely indicated at that time I was less sure of that ground than I was of the other on which I had done more work. But the more I got into the second ground, the clearer it became . . . .

I, too, would go to the stake for the accuracy of my quotation of what you said from the bench, i.e., that it would make a dissent much, much too long to list the statutes which would fall as a result of Lambert.

To be more specific, you stated from the bench the list would fill a volume.

So when we ask for just one, we are not asking for very much out of that long tabulation.

December 17, 1957

Dear Felix:

I guess my writing must be the opaque one. For all I wanted was a citation of one statute that would fall if the reasoning in *Lambert* were followed.

March 17, 1960

Dear Felix:

You may remember that when *Chicago* v. *Atchison T&S.F. RR Company*, 357 U.S. 77 [1958] was being argued, you and I had an exchange of notes about Phillip B. Kurland[1], one of the counsel in the case. He had been a law clerk to Jerome Frank before he was your law clerk. And in spite of all the things Jerry did to give him a boost up the professional ladder, he was spreading very derogatory things about Jerry since Jerry died. This was a matter you may remember disturbed me very much.

I have now just learned that Kurland is the man who was the architect of the report which the State Chief Justices filed against this Court about a year or so ago.[2] He farmed out various sections to various law professors. The reason I happen to know about it is because he approached one of Wiley Rutledge's old clerks who is now teaching somewhere in the middle west—at Indiana I believe, asking him to prepare a section for the State Chief Justices attack on this Court. Wiley's old clerk replied "I will not be a prostitute."

This came to me as a very interesting but disturbing piece of news.

---

1.   Kurland (1921–   ) has taught at the University of Chicago Law School since 1953; he is the author of numerous works, including three books on FF.

2.   The Conference of Chief Justices of the States had attacked the Court in 1958 for its alleged interference in policy-making as well as for intruding federal power into what had been traditionally considered state and local affairs, especially education. Kurland's involvement with the Conference may not have been publicly known, but he expressed views sharply critical of the Court in "The Supreme Court, the Due Process Clause and the *in personam* Jurisdiction of State Courts," 25 *U. Chicago L.R.* 569 (1958).

October 13, 1960

I have your memo asking for our votes on a conference to discuss the proposals made on Conference procedures in your memo of September 29, 1960.[1]

With all due respect, I vote against a meeting to discuss the proposals. The virtue of our present procedures is that they are very flexible. If anyone wants a *per curiam* held over, it is always held. If anyone wants to pass and not vote on a case until a later Conference, his wish is always respected. If anyone wants to circulate a memo stating his views on a case, the memo is always welcome.

If we unanimously adopted rules on such matters we would be plagued by them, bogged down, and interminably delayed. If we were not unanimous, the rules would be ineffective. I, for one, could not agree to give anyone more control over when I vote than over how I vote.

To repeat, if anyone wants delay on a particular case he always gets it. We need not put ourselves in the needless harness that is proposed.

---

1.   FF had proposed (and not for the first time) tightening up the procedures by which the Court processed its decisions, so that less time would elapse between hearing a case and handing down the opinion. In particular, he wanted the *per curiam* decisions, those which the Court decides without formal opinions, to be issued immediately; the current practice allowed any single justice to hold up announcement if he cared to think about it some more.

In two memoranda to the Conference on October 23, WOD expressed his opposition again. "We are not first-year law students who need to be put under strict restraints. . . . The blowing of whistles, the counting to three or ten, the suspension of all activity for a stated time may be desirable and necessary on playgrounds or in sports. But we are not children; we deal not with trivia; we are not engaged in contests. Our tasks involve deliberation, reflection, meditation. When opinions have jelled, the case is handed down. When jelling is not finished, the case is held."

FF had also suggested changing the manner in which dissenting and concurring opinions were filed, so as to make the entire opinion shorter. WOD opposed it. "I defend the right of any Justice to file anything he wants. I resist the effort to foist one system on all of us."

The friction between WOD and Frankfurter evidently reached a new high shortly after this latest conflict, in which the Court rejected FF's proposals. On November 21, 1960 WOD drafted a memorandum to the Conference which he evidently did not send after discussing the matter with the Chief Justice. In it he wrote:

> The continuous violent outbursts against me in Conference by my Brother Frankfurter give me great concern. They do not bother me. For I have been on the hustings too long.
>
> But he's an ill man; and these violent outbursts create a fear in my heart that one of them may be his end.
>
> I do not consciously do anything to annoy him. But twenty-odd years have shown that I am a disturbing symbol in his life. His outbursts against me are increasing in intensity. In the interest of his health and long life I have reluctantly concluded to participate in no more conferences while he is on the Court.
>
> For the cert lists I will leave my vote. On argued cases I will leave a short summary of my views.

It was, of course, impossible for any member of the Court to isolate himself from another member, no matter how tense their relationship, and the Douglas files include some short notes directly to FF over the next two years joining in opinions and occasionally making some brief suggestion. But the old camaraderie had gone.

Frankfurter's stuffiness and occasional "holier-than-thou" attitude never failed to annoy Douglas, and the latter took advantage of every occasion he could to point out FF's foibles. In a lengthy and somewhat condescending memo on March 27, 1961, FF lectured his Brethren on why the Court should not hastily overturn earlier decisions. WOD sent the following memorandum to the Conference the following day.

> Brother Frankfurter says . . . that he thinks "it is bad business for the Court to overrule a decision shortly following a change in the membership of the Court.
>
> Perhaps the most conspicuous precedent is *Helvering* v. *Hallock,* 309 U.S. 1—which was decided in 1940. It overruled a decision hardly nine years old and was done when a new Court came in.[1]

FF rose to the bait and justified the *Hallock* decision, which he had written, as really following precedent rather than overturning it. On March 29 , WOD followed up with another note to the effect that he "did not—and does not—disapprove of what [FF] did for the Court in *Helvering* v. *Hallock.*

> My disappointment was that he failed to follow his own precedent when *Girouard* v. *United States,* 328 U.S. 61 was decided—in which I wrote the opinion for the Court and explicitly followed the *Helvering* v. *Hallock* precedent. See 328 U.S. at 69–70.[2]

---

1.   In this case, FF wrote the Court's opinion overruling *Klein* v. *United States,* 283 U.S. 231 (1931) and adopting a new interpretation of section 302(c) of the Internal Revenue Code.

2.   WOD's opinion in this 1946 case, which said that in the absence of positive legislation, the Court could not assume that Congress had intended to impose a particular condition on naturalization, cited *Hallock:* "It would require very persuasive circumstances enveloping congressional silence to debar this Court from reexamining its own doctrines."

Douglas often dictated a "Memorandum to the Files" when he wanted to leave a record of his views or to justify his vote or position. After one bitter exchange between himself and FF, he dictated the following.

May 28, 1960

When Nos. 809 and 883[1] came up for our discussion on May 27, 1960, Frankfurter made a long speech telling what an awful record the judiciary had written in reorganization cases, referring particularly to *RFC* v. *Denver & RGW RR Company,* 328 U.S. 495 [1946], and to *Insurance Corporation* v. *Denver RGW RR Company,* 329 U.S. 607 [1947]. Those were cases where he dissented from the enforcement of the priority of the bondholders against the stockholders. We had quite a discussion about the problem, I defending the prior decisions both of which were written by Justice Reed.

Among other things, I stated that if the judiciary had not followed the standards of the Interstate Commerce Commission and approved drastic plans of reorganization that in substance turned over the Roads to the senior security holders, the Roads would be in much worse condition today than they are. This greatly inflamed Frankfurter who shouted that I had some ulterior motive in supporting those reorganization decisions.

I told him that I had never owned a bond or a single share of stock of any railroad company and so far as I knew, no member of my family ever had been such an owner nor had been identified in any way with any railroad system. I told him that those kind of accusations against me might raise in my mind the question of whether or not I should not tell the Conference the ignoble role he had performed in those two cases.

What happened is as follows: Frankfurter's close friend, Max Lowenthal[2] was heavily interested in railroad common stocks. He had a speculative position in the market. After the Denver & Rio Grande cases were argued, but before the opinion was written, Max Lowenthal used Frankfurter's office as his headquarters, bringing the Court closer to a scandal than anything in modern history. What Lowenthal did was to get into the offices of the Justices ostensibly to praise them or flatter them. And as Black told me, he suddenly realized that after a 30-minute conversation that Lowenthal had cleverly worked his conversation around so that Black was looking the issues of these reorganization cases squarely in the face. As a result, Black never again saw Lowenthal, but Lowenthal, with Frankfurter's connivance spent day after day in the building seeking conversations with the Brethren wherever possible. Happily he made no headway but it was the most glaring attempt I think I have ever seen made to use a speculator in the common stocks to try to get the

Court to give the common stocks the protection that Frankfurter thought they should have.

I do not think Frankfurter was financially involved in this Lowenthal maneuver, although of that I cannot be absolutely sure. The ties between the Lowenthal family and the Frankfurter family have been very close.

---

1. In the two cases, *Kern* v. *Columbia Gas System, Inc.* and *Vanston Bondholders Protective Committee* v. *Columbia Gas System, Inc.*, both 363 U.S. 813 (1960), the Court denied the petitions for certiorari.

2. Lowenthal (1888–1971), a New York lawyer and businessman, had been closely associated with FF in Zionist activities following the First World War.

Douglas often complained about what he considered Frankfurter's machinations off the bench. He recounted the disastrous effects of one such episode in a letter to his former law clerk John Frank.

November 18, 1958

Dear John:

. . .Wiley Rutledge was nominated as Associate Justice on November 11, 1943. A few days before his name went to the Senate, I had dinner with Roosevelt. During the course of the dinner he turned to me and said he supposed I was curious as to the person who was going to fill the vacancy. I said I was and asked him if he had made up his mind. He said he knew one he was not going to appoint, and I asked him what he meant. He said, "I am not going to appoint Learned Hand."[1] I said that Learned Hand had made quite a record on the District Court and the Court of Appeals and would make a fine Justice. Roosevelt's jaw was set as he replied. "Well, I am not going to appoint him." Then he relaxed and said, "This time Felix has overplayed his hand." I asked him what he meant by that and he replied, "You have never seen the kind of campaign that he has put on. Why, today I saw at least a dozen people with the same burning message—that I should appoint Hand. I saw so many that my Dutch is up, and I just ain't going to do it."

I said, "Have you made up your mind on someone else?" He said that he had. He said, "It is a man whose name is quite famous

in Supreme Court history." Then he added, "I mean Wiley Rutledge."[2]

---

1. (Billings) Learned Hand (1872–1961) served as a district court judge from
1909 to 1924 and then on the circuit court of appeals in New York until 1951. He
is generally conceded to be one of the finest of the lower federal court judges of
this century.

2. In a later note to Frank dated May 15, 1959, WOD wrote that he had learned
something else about this episode and claimed to have learned it from one of FF's
"former confidants." FF had merely been using Hand as a stalking horse to knock
off Rutledge and that his real candidate for the bench was Charles Fahy (1892–
1979), at this time solicitor general of the United States. Truman named Fahy to
the District of Columbia Circuit Court of Appeals in 1949; in 1967 he became chief
judge and served until his death.

Douglas suspected FF of working behind the scenes to deny Frank
and Vern Countryman, another former clerk, positions at Yale Law
School.

To John Frank

March 8, 1954

Dear John:

I hear that the Dean-elect of Yale Law[1] has advised you that your
services will no longer be needed. It does not surprise me. And I
suspect that it will not be the last move in the direction of making
Yale Law School safe, sound, and secure for the conservatives.

Harry Shulman is a fine person. I have known him a long time.
He is far to the right, however, and timid as well as conservative. He
is an agent of Justice Frankfurter who has long striven to make Yale
Law School a "farm" for his Harvard boys. He almost succeeded
before. His present victory gives him and his group a devastating
hold on Yale Law School . . . .

A great President of Yale once told me that he would know that
his law school and his economics department would be second-rate

unless they caused him constant trouble. Yale's President will never be troubled by Yale's Law School under Shulman.

---

1. Harry Shulman (1903–1955), a student of FF, had taught at Yale since 1930, with occasional absences for government service.

To Harry Shulman

January 11, 1955

Dear Harry:

Word has reached me through Law Clerk circles here at Court that Vern Countryman may not be kept on next year at Yale. I hope the rumors are not true. . . .

I do know, however, that these are crucial months of decision, that the great liberal tradition of Yale Law School is in the balance. There are many who look hopefully to you for vigorous sponsorship of Vern Countryman and men like him, so that none can ever say that the great liberal tradition at Yale was lost for failure of militant advocacy.[1]

---

1. WOD also wrote to A. Whitney Griswold, the president of Yale, on January 26, lecturing him that "A law school certainly should not be a 'conservative' school, a 'radical' school, a 'New Deal' school, or a school slanted to any one school of economic or political thought. That is the liberal tradition—the tradition that tolerates men of all schools because it knows that none has a monopoly on truth." Yale, despite WOD's efforts, let Countryman go, and he went out to teach at the University of New Mexico Law School. It was there that WOD wrote him the following.

To Vern Countryman

December 3, 1962

Dear Vern:

Scuttlebutt is that you are on your way to Harvard. It would be the best thing that ever happened to FF's old citadel.

Douglas also objected to what he saw as FF's involvement in the Oliver Wendell Holmes Devise, in which the jurist's bequest would be used to finance a history of the Supreme Court.

To L. Quincy Mumford[1]

January 7, 1959

Dear Mr. Mumford:

. . . My only regret is that the staff on the History of the Supreme Court is made up entirely of lawyers except for Julius Goebel, Jr.,[2] who is assigned pre-Constitution days. It always seemed to me that any appraisal of the work of the Court should be done by people other than lawyers—historians, political scientists, economists, sociologists, etc.[3]

---

1. Mumford was Librarian of Congress from 1954 to 1974 and a member of the Holmes Devise Committee.

2. Goebel (1892–1973) taught at the Columbia Law School from 1921 until his retirement. His volume of the project was not limited to the pre-Constitution era, although he spent many chapters on the Supreme Court's antecedents; he carried the story through the Court's first decade, until the appointment of John Marshall. Despite WOD's opinion of Goebel, critics have seen this volume as one of the weaker parts of the series.

3. In another letter to Mumford on January 20, WOD repeated his objections to lawyers writing the history. "But if lawyers are to do it, then a representative group should have been chosen, not one representing a single and rather narrow view of constitutional law."

To John Frank and Vern Countryman

May 18, 1959

A social gathering of ex-law clerks—drawn largely from FF's reserves—was recently discussing the History of the U.S. Supreme Court and the staff that was working on it.

The question came up as to why the authors selected were, with one exception, stooges of FF. The reply was an indignant one. There was a chorus of voices saying that only the roster of "scholars" was drawn on for the personnel, and that obviously men like you two could not qualify as "scholars."

I thought you would be interested in the new "party line" that has been established.

To James Ellison[1]

November 17, 1960

Dear Mr. Ellison:

. . . I think you should go ahead with your project for a book on the Supreme Court of the United States.

I do not think too highly of the so-called History of the Supreme Court to which my Brother Frankfurter referred in his letter to you. This is a history written almost entirely by lawyers, rather hand-picked for their orthodoxy. There is one non-lawyer in the group, but he is relegated to the pre-Constitution era. He is Julius Goebel of Columbia. . . .

I would not necessarily exclude a lawyer from the job you mention. But I think that one coming from outside the legal profession with high scholastic standards would be the best one for the task.[2]

---

1. Ellison was an editor at Holt, Rinehart and Winston.

2. WOD suggested several people whom he thought capable of writing an unbiased account, such as Irving Brant, Irving Dilliard, and Walter F. Murphy of Princeton.

In 1974, Douglas responded to an inquiry from Professor David Atkinson of the University of Missouri at Kansas City about a 1954 episode, in fact, the one WOD complains about in his letter to FF of May 29 of that year. Douglas said that he had "no recollection of the episode so it could not have been very critical or important." Then he went on to write the following:

"We were always twitting our Brother Frankfurter over his long and dramatic performances in Conference. He was an artist as well as an able advocate and his Conference presentations were dramatic and lengthy. Most of us thought the function of the Conference was to discover the consensus. His idea was different: he was there to proselytize and to gain converts. . . .

"One would err greatly to conclude that Frankfurter and I were at war. We clashed often at the ideological level but our personal relations were excellent and I always enjoyed being with him."

Chapter 5

. . . and the Brethren

THE SUPREME COURT is a unique institution in which nine strong-willed individuals wrestle with a broad range of topics, attempting to reach a consensus through which the lower courts, the other branches of government, and the American people will know what the Constitution commands. In some instances, the nine speak as one; more often, they agree to disagree, issuing a sometimes bewildering mixture of majority, concurring, and dissenting opinions.

Because the Court works behind closed doors, we have far less understanding of its internal dynamics than we do of the executive and legislative arms of government. Everyone who has sat on the high court has jealously guarded this privacy; some justices have gone so far as to destroy their papers so that historians will be unable to rummage, as it were, in the debris of the inner sanctum. But there are occasional bits of illumination—a letter here, an anecdote there—which shed light, and in recent years the papers of some justices have survived nearly intact.

The politics of the Court during Douglas's long tenure cannot be fully explicated here; he served, after all, with nearly a third of all the men ever to sit on that bench. But the Douglas Papers include letters to some of the Brethren dealing with Court business and personalities, as well as memoranda on many important cases, some of which are presented in the following chapter.

The inconsistencies in these letters, especially when compared to Douglas's later recollections, are striking. But they do cast light on the give-and-take of judicial politics, the way in which one justice with a particular viewpoint can "get a Court." They also show that, with the exception of Felix Frankfurter, Douglas enjoyed good to friendly relations with his colleagues even when, as so often happened, they agreed to disagree.

Harlan Fiske Stone

Harlan Fiske Stone (1872–1946) had originally been named to the Court by President Coolidge in 1925, and in 1941 Franklin Roosevelt elevated him to be Chief Justice. Although he had been a partner in a prestigious Wall Street firm, Stone had confounded those who expected him to vote with the conservative bloc. He joined Holmes and Brandeis, and in the 1930s he, Brandeis, and Cardozo formed the liberal core on the high bench.

WOD had known Stone since 1922, when he had been a student of his at Columbia Law School, and be used to visit with him frequently in Washington. In his memoirs, WOD says he knew three "active proselytizers" on the Court—Stone, Hugo Black, and Frankfurter. "These three were evangelists, each in his own right, each sincerely eloquent and unrelenting."

In a letter to Abdul Moneim Riad, a judge of the Egyptian High Court of Appeals, on April 5, 1947, WOD wrote:

> As I recall, I said that Chief Justice Stone did not believe in judicial supremacy. . . . [He] meant that in passing on the constitutionality of legislation, judges should not sit as a super-legislature and uphold or strike down a statute, depending upon whether it seemed to them to be wise or unsound. Stone stood firmly on the side of those who maintained that the legislatures were entitled to room for experimentation with new ideas, so that changing conditions of today could be adequately met.

For an affectionate portrait of Stone, see *Court Years*, 222–25.

August 21, 1940

My dear Justice Stone:
. . . I felt pretty relieved when the Convention[1] was over. For a while I feared that pressure might be put on me to go on the ticket. It was

not. Every one of my friends knew that I had no political ambitions and that I had but one desire viz. to stay where I am. But for extra protection I went with Jim Donald[2] on a fishing trip to spots where not even the Lone Ranger could find me.

I have always felt with you that one who has political ambitions should not go on the Court. To use the Court as a stepping stone would be most harmful in my opinion. . . .

---

1. The 1940 Democratic convention, at which WOD's name had been mentioned as a running mate to Roosevelt; the President chose Secretary of Agriculture Henry A. Wallace.

2. James T. Donald practiced law in Baker, Oregon; he had been a student of Stone's at Columbia.

April 24, 1941

Dear Justice Stone:

I have been reading your opinion in the above case.[1] So far, one question has arisen in my mind which I want to mention to you and which bothers me.

You state in several places and give emphasis to the fact that a primary choice in Louisiana, so far as a Democrat is concerned, is tantamount to final election. My difficulty is in seeing the relevancy of that fact to the problem in the case.

Suppose Congress passes a law regulating such primaries? I think it has the power to do so. But the validity of that law would hardly seem to me to be dependent on whether it was applied to a Democratic primary in the South, which for all practical purposes is a final election, or to a Democratic primary in Washington, which has no such practical effect.

In other words, a primary is or is not an integral part of the election process within the meaning of the Constitutional provision. To me it is not the less so because the successful Democratic primary candidate may lose, probably will lose, or so far has never won.

---

1. *United States* v. *Classic*, 313 U.S. 299 (1941), held the federal government could regulate a state primary where it constituted an integral part of the machinery for choosing candidates for federal office.

June 30, 1941

Dear Chief:

Let me congratulate you again, this time on the speedy & unanimous vote of confirmation.[1] I am delighted. And I can say this—that in our zig zag tour across the country during which we met literally hundreds of lawyers, your appointment was hailed enthusiastically without a single dissent.

The other purpose of this letter is to tell you of the fishing trip. I saw Jim Donald of Baker Ore. last night and here are our plans.

We want to leave Baker by car on July 14th. We hope to get into the Madison River country in Montana for a week or so. The first part of the fishing will be done on some lakes near Morida, Mont. I understand they have cabins there, nothing fancy but on the rough side. Yet I am told they are comfortable. We would fish from boats. After 4 to 6 days, we would push into the river country on horses and fish the streams. That part of the trip would be rough—camping on the ground and wading streams. I have never been in that country but they say it is fine scenery & good fishing.

In view of the new honor & responsibility which have been bestowed on you, you may have changed your summer plans. But if you are west & if you want to join us (even for a few days) let me know. We could pick you up at Shoshone Ida. or at some point in the Yellowstone Park.

If it does not work into your plans for this summer, we can do it another time. . . .

---

1. As Chief Justice of the United States; see, however, WOD's comment to Hugo Black, p. 107.

Re: Saboteur Cases[1]

October 17, 1942

. . . I would like to see the sentence which I have underlined on page 6 omitted. That sentence is susceptible of the interpretation that it would have been unlawful for the Executive to have disposed of the petitioners summarily without a trial by a tribunal. That may be true although if I had to vote today I would be inclined to vote the other way. The proposition, however, is not before us and I think we need not express any view on it one way or the other. . . .

---

1. *Ex parte Quirin,* 317 U.S. 1 (1942). The Germans had landed several saboteurs by submarine with orders to destroy American factories. All had been captured quickly and tried by a military commission. The Court confirmed the right of the President to have the men tried by military rather than civil courts, and Stone omitted the sentence WOD found objectionable.

May 31, 1943

Dear Chief:

Here are some suggestions on your first circulation.[1] They are aimed at the most part to eliminate any suggestion of racial discrimination. . . .

Is not the justification for dealing with Jap citizens as a group the fact that the exigencies of war and the necessities of quick action in defending the nation against invasion do not necessarily permit enough time to sort out the sheep from the goats? Is it not necessary to provide an opportunity at some stage (although not necessarily in lieu of obedience to the military order) for an individual member of the group to show that he has been improperly classified? Otherwise if the military commander knows there are only 10% of the group who are disloyal he can nevertheless hold the entire group in confinement for the duration without any opportunity on the part of the 90% to prove they are as loyal to the United States as the members of this Court.[2]

---

1. *Hirabayashi* v. *United States,* 320 U.S. 81 (1943), confirmed the Roosevelt administration's internment of Japanese Americans from the West Coast in concentration camps.

2. In a second note to the Chief Justice on June 7, WOD said: "I could not go along in an affirmance of the judgment below except on the assumptions (a) that the group treatment was temporary; (b) that the individual must have an opportunity to be reclassified as a loyal citizen. That may be too great a gap for us to bridge." In his memoirs, WOD admits that he had, like the others, been too easily swayed by the military but claims that he had written a concurring opinion objecting to the concentration camps. At the urging of Black and Frankfurter he did not publish it, a fact he later regretted. See *Court Years,* 279–80.

November 17, 1943

I was a member of the TNEC[1] from the date of its formation to the time of my appointment to the Court. I served on the TNEC as a representative of the Securities and Exchange Commission. . . .

While I was a member of the TNEC the Department of Justice presented to it at public hearings the Hartford-Empire story. I did not attend those hearings, my alternate, Jerome Frank, being present for the Securities and Exchange Commission. I had nothing to do with the making of the Hartford-Empire investigation. The decision to undertake it was made by the Department of Justice. And I had no recollection that the Hartford-Empire matter was presented to the TNEC while I was a member until after argument on the present case[2] had started. . . . I had nothing to do with that report as I was on this Court at that time.

I mention these matters to you for the reason that it now appears that there may be no quorum of the Court without me. I apologize for bringing it to your attention at this late date. But it was not until yesterday afternoon that I discovered to my surprise that the matter had been presented to the TNEC while I was still a member of that committee. I do not feel that I am disqualified to sit on the case. But I wanted you and the Brethren to have the facts so that I might withdraw in case there was the slightest feeling that I should not participate.[3]

---

1.   Congress created the Temporary National Economic Committee in 1938 at Roosevelt's request to examine problems of concentrated economic power in big business. The TNEC gathered a great deal of information, but the war cut short its operations and it never had much impact on governmental policy.

2.   *Hartford Empire Co.* v. *United States,* 323 u.s. 386 (1945), a complicated antitrust suit involving the nation's glass jar manufacturers, had originally been argued in 1944.

3.   WOD did not participate, and neither did Murphy and Jackson, both of whom had been involved with the case while attorneys general.

March 15, 1944

Dear Chief Justice:

I was talking at luncheon yesterday with some of the Brethren about the *Cramer* case[1] and your suggestion that it might be desirable to pass on the substantive question of treason instead of writing the opinion on evidence questions alone.

I rather thought that it would be desirable to follow the latter course and not reach the treason question. My reasons are as follows:

Counts 1 and 2 of the indictment clearly raise the troublesome question which we discussed at length in the Conference. But Count 10 is plainly valid whatever view may be taken of the meaning of treason. Hence, it may very well be that if there is a new trial, the Government, in view of the apparent difficulties on Counts 1 and 2, will try it on Count 10 alone. At least we do not have a situation where a new trial will inevitably raise the questions which we reserve. It seemed to me that that would be the more desirable course than to reach the substantive points at this time and inevitably get a close division of views on an important question in the middle of the war.[2]

---

1.   *Cramer* v. *United States*, 325 u.s. 1 (1945), involved charges of treason against an American citizen.

2. Of the original ten counts, seven had been withdrawn. Nos. 1 and 2 consisted of allegations that Cramer "did meet and confer for the purpose of giving aid and comfort," which even the Justice Department admitted were difficult to prove. The last count alleged that the defendant had given false information to the FBI in order to conceal the saboteurs. A bare majority of the Court found that even this did not meet the constitutional definition of treason and reversed. WOD, joined by the Chief Justice, Black, and Reed, dissented, on grounds that the last count did constitute the necessary treasonous activity.

November 28, 1944

I think an opinion in this case[1] should be announced on December 4, 1944, unless prior to that time Mitsuye Endo either has been released or has been promised her immediate and unqualified release.

The Court is unanimous in the view that she is unlawfully detained. An opinion in the case was distributed on November 8, 1944. A majority of the Court has agreed to it. But the matter is at a standstill because officers of the government have indicated that some change[s] in detention plans are under consideration. Their motives are beyond criticism and their request is doubtless based on important administrative considerations. Mitsuye Endo, however, has not asked that action of this Court be stayed. She is a citizen, insisting on her right to be released—a right which we all agree she has. I feel strongly that we should act promptly and not lend our aid in compounding the wrong by keeping her in unlawful confinement through our inaction any longer than necessary to reach a decision.[2]

---

1. *Ex parte Endo,* 323 U.S. 284 (1944), held that a native-born American citizen of Japanese ancestry, who had been able to prove her unquestioned loyalty, could not be detained. WOD wrote the majority opinion.

2. The decision in the case came down on December 18, 1944.

Hugo LaFayette Black

Hugo LaFayette Black (1886–1971), Douglas wrote, "was my closest friend on the Court, and my companion in many hard judicial battles." The two of them became identified as the Court's most liberal and activist members during the more than three decades they served together. C. Herman Pritchett, who did a statistical study of the Court's internal alignment, found the two men voted together about 80 percent of the time, and he described them as "generally more concerned for the protection of civil liberties and the rights of criminal defendants, more likely to support the government in its tax and regulatory activities, more desirous of limiting judicial review of administrative action, and more likely to vote for labor than their colleagues."

Black, however, proved the more profound thinker of the two, and scholars generally agree that he led the way in creating a new First Amendment jurisprudence, that greatly expanded constitutional protection of expression. Although a majority of the Court never completely accepted Black's argument that the Fourteenth Amendment wholly incorporated the guarantees of the Bill of Rights and applied them to the states, in practice he secured this goal. Black had the rare ability to abandon his earlier assumptions and think things through from the beginning.

Black reciprocated Douglas's affection and trust. In 1957 he and Mrs. Black sent the following birthday greetings:

A very happy birthday to
Our Judge with wanderlust—

Who likes to hit the auto trail
Or hike in foreign dust!

He likes to climb and ride and boat—
He's of the travelin' school—
He knows his way from Timbuctoo
To Turkey's Istanbuhl.

He takes his own mechanic, too,
So he can write a book,
While Mercedes, his faithful spouse
Crawls under and takes a look.

Since terms of court confine our judge
Who has this travel craze,
We thought at home he'd like to have
"Around the World in Eighty Days."

We hope he finds some exotic places,
Though some may not be bug-less;
So happy birthday to our friend,
Mar-co Po-lo Douglas!

The letters below marked with an asterisk are handwritten notes from Douglas to Black from the Hugo L. Black Papers in the Library of Congress.

June 22, 1941[*]

Dear Hugo:

. . . We were motoring across Arkansas on our way to New Mexico when we heard on the radio that Stone had been made c.j. I said to Mildred, "Felix has done it again." And there is no question in my mind that he was responsible.[1] You will recall that I expressed my fear that Felix would make that move. I am sorry that it did not go to you. I thought you deserved it. And I knew it would strengthen the Court greatly if you were the Chief. The bar—being a conservative outfit—hails the Stone appointment. But unless the old boy changes, it will not be a particularly happy or congenial atmosphere in which to work, at least as far as I am concerned.[2] I wired Stone, however, extending my congratulations. . . .[3]

It was an interesting conference of the Ninth Circuit here in San Francisco. I think I will try to attend each year. I think I can do some good behind the scenes once I get to know the judges personally. Some are very conservative; some are lightweights. But others are made of pretty good stuff. . . .[4]

---

1.   Frankfurter did advise the President to elevate Stone, a Republican, for the sake of national unity, but whether Frankfurter "engineered" Stone's appointment to the center chair is problematic.

2.   WOD's prediction proved accurate. Stone had been an outstanding associate justice, but he proved a disappointment as chief. Above all, he could not control the increasingly tense rift on the Court caused by such strong-willed colleagues as WOD, Black, Jackson, and above all, Frankfurter.

3.   See p. 102.

4.   Each member of the Supreme Court is assigned to oversee the work of one of the circuits and to provide liaison between the high court and the lower benches. WOD did attend the annual conferences of the Ninth Circuit (located on the West Coast) fairly frequently.

August 3, 1941[*]

Dear Hugo:

. . . I was delighted to learn that Alabama is giving you an LLD. It was much deserved & will mean much. I am also pleased to learn that you will address the Colorado Bar. I have felt that we do not do enough of that. I try to do two a year. I think I get quite a bit from it & I hope the Bar does. There are precious few of our kind in those associations. But there are some. And they appreciate the effort . . . .

September 8, 1941[*]

Dear Hugo:

The President has talked with me over the telephone. And decision has been deferred until I return to Wash. Sept. 19th. Here is the proposition.

He wants me to be the top guy in the defense work—to take it off his neck; to be his "alter ego." He apparently visualizes the present defense set-up continuing. Apparently I am to be the top holding company, so to speak.

I have not said yes; nor have I said no. He put it on a personal basis—that I was the only one who could swing it; that he needed me badly etc. etc.

I would have to resign from the Court.

I have no enthusiasm for the project. In fact there is no attraction in it for me whatsoever. I can think of nothing less attractive, except practicing law in New York City.

I cannot help thinking that the odds would be very much against me doing a real job—(1) because the present defense organization would continue; the fat cats would be entrenched; 561 guys would dedicate themselves to the task of ruining me; (2) because I would be a sort of C[ircuit]. C[ourt of]. A[ppeals]., no matter how carefully plans were laid; in other words the present crowd would be putting all sorts of pressure on the President to alter my policies; (3) much water has gone over the dam; I would be inheriting all the errors of the past; most of them could not be eradicated; there would be no such thing as a clean slate, at least so long as the present crowd remains in control of details.

Of course there comes a time when all bets are off & every man has to shoulder a musket or do some chore for his country. If things were utterly chaotic & we were in desperate straits, I would gladly make the sacrifice. But I do not see that such a crisis has developed. In absence of it I cannot see the desirability of taking a man off the Court, unless that man is unhappy there. As you know, I greatly enjoy the work of the Court. Furthermore, I think that as a member of the Court I can knock out a base hit once in a while. For the defense job I would go to the bat with 2 1/2 strikes on me.

Some of the President's inner circle whisper that there is a big chance that it will lead to the 1944 nomination. But that leaves me cold because I am not a bit interested in running for any office. Even if I were, I would doubt the wisdom of that observation of theirs.

I am quite sure that F.F. has inspired this offer, at least that he has been influential. It has come to me "straight" that he thinks I am the only man. If he could get me there & you back in the Senate I am sure he would be happier.

. . . We will be back the 19th. At that time (and before I see FDR) I want to talk this thing out with you. The President has put the real pressure on me. That's why it's hard to say no. But the wisdom of declining impresses me daily. It's hogwash to say that I am the "only one" for the job. Yet that is what he says & he is a hard one to get away from.[1]

---

1.   In his memoirs, WOD recalled that he asked Roosevelt "Is this a draft—a real draft, Mr. President?"

"A real draft," he replied.

"Then I'll do it," agreed WOD.

"Wonderful," he boomed back. "Call me the minute you get here."

WOD returned promptly to Washington and called the White House operator to let her know he was in town, then waited, but no call came from Roosevelt. A week later he opened the morning paper to learn that Donald Nelson had been given the job. "I soon learned," WOD said, "that Harry Hopkins, whose star was rising, had persuaded FDR to make the switch."

July 23, 1949

Dear Hugo:

I received a telephone call from the President. He wants to see me. I will be in Wash. D.C. Monday Aug. 4th. I do not know what he has in mind. He said over the telephone that he needed me in a "more active" job. I gave him no encouragement beyond my agreement to see him, which of course I could not refuse.

I am writing you this to make sure I can see you Aug. 4th after my talk with him.

I do not want to leave the Court. I desire to stay just where I am. I hate even to consider the prospect of leaving. I am very happy right there, and I want nothing but the opportunity to slug away alongside of you for the next 30 years.

Right now I cannot think of anything which would lead me to resign. If the country was in complete chaos or on the brink of a major disaster & I felt I could help, I would gladly do so. But it is not, so far as I know. And there are many able men who would do all that he possibly has in mind.

All this is very confidential. I will telephone you when I get into Wash. D.C. around 9 A.M. on Aug. 4th to see when I can see you. I would prefer to talk at your house.[1]

---

1.   WOD does not mention this episode in his memoirs. He had already turned Truman down twice, once in 1946 when the President had offered him the Interior

Department, and in 1948 when woD had been invited to run as the vice presidential candidate on the Democratic ticket. See p. 219.

November 3, 1949

Dear Hugo:

I am sitting up a few hours a day.[1] But the ribs get very painful after I have been up an hour. And getting in & out of bed is a most painful ordeal. I am stronger each day, my temperature has been normal for two weeks, and if all goes smoothly, the docs say I can leave by train for Tucson Nov. 10th. . . . I am lucky to be alive. I was in excellent physical condition or I would not be.

I have sent in my votes in the two 4–4 cases. But I've done no other Court work. And I will plan to do none except where my vote is crucial. . . .

1. woD had been badly injured in a riding accident. The horse had apparently been stung by a hornet and had thrown woD partly down the mountain, where he landed on a ledge unhurt. But then the horse came over the side and rolled over woD, crushing his chest, puncturing a lung, and breaking twenty-three of his twenty-four ribs. woD should have died of these injuries, but he made a remarkable recovery after convalescence in Arizona.

November 23, 1949*

Dear Hugo:

I am sorry you did not write in No. 20 Treichler v. Wisconsin.[1] You could have torn the opinion to pieces in a couple paragraphs. It's a very bad precedent & shows the clever handiwork of F.F.

1. 338 U.S. 251 (1949). For the Court, Justice Clark upheld a Wisconsin inheritance tax on property held by the decedent outside the state. Black entered a one-sentence dissent, opposing federal courts interfering with essentially local matters. woD did not participate.

September 12, 1953*

Dear Hugo:

. . . I wish Eisenhower would make you Chief Justice.[1] It would be the smartest thing he could do *politically* and the best possible appointment on the merits. But I do not think he's smart enough to do it. I shudder when I think of Dulles[2] or Vanderbilt[3] in the job. And the reactionary forces would want one of them (or a recent ABA president) over Dewey[4] or Warren.[5] Dewey would, I think, be much better (i.e. liberal) than is suspected. . . .

---

1. Chief Justice Fred Vinson had died unexpectedly on September 8.

2. John Foster Dulles (1888–1959), lawyer and diplomat, was then serving as Eisenhower's secretary of state.

3. Arthur T. Vanderbilt (1888–1957), the chief justice of the New Jersey Supreme Court, enjoyed high esteem in the legal community, even from those who thought him too conservative.

4. Thomas Edmund Dewey (1902–1971), an old friend of WOD, had been the Republican candidate for the presidency in 1944 and 1948; he was then in his third and last term as governor of New York.

5. Unknown to WOD, Eisenhower had promised former California governor Earl Warren the first vacancy that would arise on the Court, although Eisenhower had expected it would be a side judge rather than the center chair.

August 24, 1954*

Dear Hugo:

I have thought a lot about you this summer on my long and rather weary journey around the world.[1] On these lectures I get a lot of questions. A few—quite a few—concern Senator McCarthy.[2] I find myself in great difficulty explaining what is happening in America. For when I'm abroad, I do not like to criticize my country too much. I've met a lot of interesting people. My tour has only a few weeks left. It is one that you should have been on, instead of me.

---

1. WOD wrote from Hobart, Tasmania; he was in Australia lecturing on American law.

2. Senator Joseph Raymond McCarthy (1908–1957) of Wisconsin exploited the postwar fear of communism to inflict a second Red Scare on the United States during the early fifties.

August 24, 1956*

Dear Hugo:

I never had such an indolent & wasted summer. I had bursitis in my hip & in my two shoulders. Between treatments I got in two trips, one in Idaho & one in Alaska. It would have been better if I had skipped both of them for my bursitis got steadily worse. To make matters worse, I have an allergy to all the painkillers. So I had to ride out the pain raw, without any relief. For a few days I was not sure I could take it any longer.[1] But the crisis passed. Then the medication they were giving me produced a severe case of hives. It took me a week to recover from that. I am now about 100% better than I was last month. . . . But I haven't been able to hike nor to ride, both of which I greatly enjoy.

I was glad the Chief went to India. He'll make a lot of friends for us there.[2] Have you had any time to work on your dissent in the army-wife case? . . .[3]

There was very little to lift the heart in the conventions and hardly a reference to any basic issue, such as getting down to the business of living with the Soviets. I suppose the Democrats did the best they could, considering everything.[4]

---

1.   On August 14, Mercedes Douglas had written Black: "At best, bursitis is no fun—for an active person it is worse. . . . What worries me most is the depressions he gets in having to stay quiet. I thought a word from you might be cheering. You can say my letter to so/so brought you the word or he'd die if he thought I wrote you about him."

2.   Chief Justice Warren was on an official goodwill tour of the subcontinent.

3.   *Reid* v. *Covert*, 354 U.S. 1 (1957). Black's opinion evidently proved persuasive, for it emerged as the majority opinion. He ruled that a wife of an Air Force sergeant, herself not a member of the armed forces, could not be tried for his murder under military law but had to be prosecuted in civil court.

4.   The Democrats again nominated Adlai Stevenson of Illinois to run against Eisenhower; at the election, Eisenhower won easily, 35.6 million popular votes to 26 million for Stevenson.

[not dated 1958/59]*

Hugo—

I think if the Catholics get public money to finance their religious schools, we better insist on getting some good prayers in public schools or we Protestants are out of business.

July 14, 1960[*]

Dear Hugo:

That was quite a civil rights plank put into the platform.[1] I've been reading it; and its implications are so broad, it looks as if a constitutional amendment will be necessary.

Last night I heard the Governor of Alabama[2] say Kennedy, if nominated, would carry Alabama and the entire South.[3] That apparently means they do not think the platform pledge means much of anything.

---

1.   The 1960 Democratic platform included the strongest civil rights plank since Reconstruction.

2.   John Malcolm Patterson (1921-   ), after a term as attorney general, served as governor of Alabama from 1959 to 1963.

3.   Kennedy did not sweep the South; he took six of the former Confederate states, Nixon three, and Senator Harry Byrd of Virginia one. Byrd and Kennedy split Georgia.

December 26, 1963

Dear Hugo:

I received your note about No. 483—*Fook* v. *Esperdy,*[1] and called in one of your law clerks. We deleted the footnote in the text citation which mentioned the procedure used by our government in communicating these days with the Peking regime. This release was obtained for me by our Library, and it is of course official, and is in the public domain.

---

1.   375 U.S. 955 (1963). The case involved the complicated extradition of a person born on the Chinese mainland who had never lived in Formosa. Since the United States government did not recognize communist China, it tried to extradite Fook to Formosa, which would not take him. The opinion chastised the lower courts for trying to manipulate the law in order not to embarrass the government. WOD moved the material showing how the United States had maintained regular contact with the Chinese government since 1955 from the footnote to the text itself.

March 2, 1965

Dear Hugo:

I like your opinion very much.[1]

I have only one question and that concerns the new citizenship test described on pages eight and nine of your opinion. Your opinion does not explicitly approve it but does not disapprove it and I do not think I could approve it. Perhaps the way you treat it is to give it implied support or approval.

As you know, *Lassiter* from North Carolina was a close case for us.[2] That was bare literacy and I even had doubts about that in spite of the fact that I was the author of the opinion. But I do not think I could agree to expand *Lassiter* to include this new test in *Louisiana.* I would prefer that we say as much here and now rather than prolong the agony any longer.

I do not know how the Court feels about it, but I would hope you could get a Court for that. But if not, I may want to write separately on Part Two of your opinion.[3]

---

1.   In *Louisiana* v. *United States,* 380 U.S. 145 (1965), the Court struck down discriminatory use of voting tests.

2.   WOD had spoken for a unanimous Court in *Lassiter* v. *Northampton Election Board,* 360 U.S. 45 (1959), in rejecting a black petitioner's attack on the North Carolina literacy test. He had noted, however: "A literacy test, fair on its face, may be employed to perpetuate that discrimination which the Fifteenth Amendment was designed to uproot." When the Court found that to be the case, it voided the test.

3.   Black did "get a Court." Everyone joined his opinion except Harlan, who concurred but on different grounds.

August 1, 1965*

Dear Hugo,

. . . Abe Fortas's wife is very upset over Abe's appointment. It is apparently a very serious crisis. I thought maybe you & Elizabeth could think of something to do.[1]

---

1.   Many people in Washington believed that Carol Fortas opposed her husband's appointment to the Court, because he would take a huge salary cut from his share as a partner in one of Washington's most successful law firms. They had just bought an expensive house on R Street, which they planned to renovate extensively.

October 24, 1967

Dear Hugo:

I see that you assigned the *Marchetti-Grosso-Haynes* cases to John.[1]
I do not for the life of me see how John could possibly write an
opinion for the Court because John has quite a different feeling, as
you know, about the reach of the Fifth Amendment than most of
the rest of us.

---

1. The three cases, all of them handed down by Harlan on January 29,
1968, dealt with various infractions of the Fifth Amendment's right against self-
incrimination.

February 26, 1971

Dear Hugo:

The jurisdictional issue bothers me somewhat. I would like to defer
my vote in this matter until I have seen the opinion which Mr.
Justice Harlan is preparing. On the merits, I am in full agreement
with your conclusion.[1]

    . . . Sometime you might enlighten me as to the significance of
the word "competent" when the statute speaks of a "competent
licensed practitioner of medicine." I would have assumed that if a
physician is licensed, he is, at least presumably, competent, and,
therefore, that the word "competent" is redundant here. If he
proves to be incompetent, that, it seems to me, has no bearing on
the abortion problem. It would, of course, be more important where
malpractice is alleged.

---

1. *United States* v. *Vuitch*, 402 U.S. 62 (1971). In a 5–4 decision, the Court,
through Black, held that the Supreme Court did have jurisdiction over an appeal
from the District of Columbia court in an abortion case. In the second part of the
opinion, Black ruled that the abortion statute was not unconstitutionally vague.
WOD concurred in the jurisdictional matter but did not join in Part II. The four
dissenters wanted to deal with the merits of the issue, a matter the Court put off
for two years. An indication of the future problems the Court would have with this
issue is indicated by the fact that seven of the nine justices filed opinions.

Stanley Forman Reed

Stanley Forman Reed (1884–1980) had been Solicitor General in
the Roosevelt administration before his appointment to the Court

in 1938, and as such he had the burden of defending many New Deal measures before a hostile bench. An economic liberal in that he favored governmental regulation of the market, Reed also took the government's side in the growing number of civil liberties cases which came before the Court in the 1940s. Reed, according to Douglas, "was one of the most reactionary judges to occupy the Bench in my time."

But, he went on, "he was also the most gentle, the friendliest, the most warm-hearted individual one could meet. He never raised his voice; he never reflected anger or animus; he never said one unkind thing against another person. It was always a joy to be with him, though often he and I were poles apart."

December 2, 1941

Dear Stanley:

I like your opinion in No. 18 very much.[1] You have done an excellent job in a difficult field.

And I want to join in it. *But*—

(1) All of the first paragraph on page 8, beginning with the third line, forces me to kiss the big toes of more than one *bete noire*.

(2) The first full sentence on page 9 does likewise.

Are they necessary here? Sec. 6(b) says "The finding of the Commission as to the facts, if supported by substantial evidence, shall be conclusive."

You have shown that 6(b) was satisfied. Is not that sufficient? Can't we postpone to another day the evil thereof?[2]

---

1. In *Gray* v. *Powell*, 314 U.S. 402 (1941), the Court refused to overturn an administrative ruling, confirming that except where constitutional provisions apparently had been violated, the judiciary would not interfere with administrative procedure.

2. Evidently Reed removed the offending passages, since WOD joined his opinion.

February 1, 1949

Dear Stanley:

In No. 24, *Hynes* v. *Grimes Packing Co.*,[1] I am inclined to the view that the "equality" proviso in the White Act is not applicable to validly created Indian Reservations. From the beginning a Reservation has been a monopoly. This is ancestral land which the Indians are occupying. I have not found any indication that a purpose of the White Act was to make the Indians share their Reservation fishing rights with packing companies. Fishery reservations aimed at by the White Act were those covering 40 per cent of the fishing waters of Alaska granted by the Secretary of Commerce to a group of packing companies. Indian Reservations in Alaska had long had exclusive fishing rights. I have found nothing to indicate that the "equality" proviso of the White Act was designed to effect a reversal in Indian policy. The administrative construction has been to the contrary. . . .

The right to create Indian reservations should, I think, carry with it a right to grant to the Indians in question the exclusive right to fish therein.

The problem in Alaska has been to protect the Indians and the public against the packing houses, not to protect the packing houses against the Indians.[2]

1.   In *Hynes* v. *Grimes Packing Co.*, 337 U.S. 86 (1949), the Court upheld the government's claim that it could restrict Indian rights, even on reservations, in licensing companies to fish waters running through the reservation. Rutledge dissented and was joined by Black, Murphy, and WOD.

2.   Reed responded later this day, defending his opinion: "I think it is best for the Indians. If the Indians were given a monopoly of a three million dollar a year fishery . . . it would be too much to give the Indians." In later years, WOD teased Reed that the Indians remembered that he had gone against them. See letters of December 20, 1967, and June 17, 1968.

February 16, 1949

Dear Stanley:

One more word about *Penn Foundry*[1] and I'm through. . . .

One doesn't need to prove there was a war on, or that labor was in short supply, or that materials were being allocated.

We know these things and can make an informed judgment concerning them.

1.   In *United States* v. *Penn Foundry*, 337 U.S. 198 (1949), the Court dismissed an appeal to recover anticipated profits lost through cancellation of a government

contract. WOD voted with the majority; Reed and Jackson concurred with the result, but not with the order of implementation.

April 29, 1957

Dear Stanley:

(1) A friend of mine is director of General Motors. He is terribly worried about the size of the company in terms of

(a)   inefficiency

(b)   stifling competition

(c)   curbing individual initiative

(2) The men who know more about the problem than any other are O'Mahoney[1] and [Emanuel] Celler.

They can "curl your hair" on the awful fate of small business resulting from our decisions.

(3) A speech by you urging atomization of big business would certainly be welcome.

---

1.   Joseph Christopher O'Mahoney (1884–1962), a Democrat from Wyoming, sat in the Senate from 1934 until his death.

December 17, 1958

Dear Stanley:

I really think your treatment of the British practice is as unfair and distorting as your construction and interpretation of *Mallory*. [1]

I can imagine a judge of this Court resisting a decision like *Mallory* while he is a member of the Court, and doing everything he can to get it changed or altered. But for the life of me, I cannot understand how any judge in the lower court can conscientiously sabotage it.

Think of what would happen if the fine judges in the South allowed their own individual preferences to come through when they dealt with the integration cases.

---

1.   In *Mallory* v. *United States*, 354 U.S. 449 (1957), the Court unanimously reaffirmed the rule that confessions received during a period of illegal detention could not be admitted in federal cases.

December 20, 1967

Dear Stanley:

As I started reading Indian Warrior,[1] I realized I must have got it by mistake. For as you know, the Indians never had a better friend.

Who should have received it? Then it dawned on me—Stanley Reed, of course, who could doubtless use this lamp to light his way.

Merry Christmas.

---

1. Patrick E. Byrne, *The Indian Warrior* (1928), praised the Indian civilization which had existed before the white man.

June 17, 1968

Dear Stanley:

I'll see what I can do about your salmon. But what you did to the Indians since that time makes your cause difficult.

Robert Houghwout Jackson

Robert Houghwout Jackson (1892–1954) was undoubtedly one of the ablest men ever to serve as Solicitor General; someone once suggested that he be named to that post for life. A committed economic liberal, he disappointed some of his supporters by an inconsistent record on civil liberties. He also caused a major uproar in 1946 when he publicly washed the Court's dirty linen and exposed many of the feuds among the Brethren. Jackson had supposedly been promised the center chair by Roosevelt and felt betrayed when Truman named Fred Vinson. At the time, Jackson was out of the country, serving as the American prosecutor at the Nuremberg trials, a role some of his critics, including Douglas, believed inappropriate for a Supreme Court justice. Jackson's closeness to Frankfurter also did not endear him to Douglas, who wrote in his memoirs: "He was a lone wolf on the Court, having no close friend except Frankfurter. He loved to write essays and publish them as opinions, not necessarily to illuminate a problem, but to embarrass or harass a colleague. In that sense he was petty, but some of his opinions are enduring and contain ringing declarations of the democratic ideal. But his ambition to be Chief Justice truly poisoned his judicial career."

[not dated, circa 1942]

RHJ: I now remember that I never was admitted to practice before the Court. I wonder if you might sponsor me some Monday soon.[1]

---

1. WOD had passed this handwritten note down the bench; Jackson scribbled back on it: "Yes—the same way I make the best argument: *nunc pro tunc.*" The phrase means "now for then" and refers to a court's power to correct a record retroactively.

May 25, 1942

I have the copy of your proposed draft of order for reargument in the above case. While I did not have the benefit of the Conference discussion on the matter, I am of the view that we should decide the case now. The problem is a simple though plainly a very important one. All of the relevant material is before us. . . .[1]

---

1. The Court did hold the case for reargument in the fall. At that time, Jackson wrote for a unanimous bench in *Wickard* v. *Filburn*, 317 U.S. 111 (1942), upholding the 1938 Agricultural Adjustment Act. The case is significant for Jackson's broad interpretation of the federal government's commerce powers.

Frederic Moore Vinson

Douglas liked Frederic Moore Vinson (1890–1953), so much that he forbore from criticizing him in his memoirs the way he lambasted some of the other Brethren who took an equally conservative position. Scholars have not considered Vinson a particularly good Chief Justice, in part because of his inability to manage the Court effectively, and in part because he could not develop a jurisprudence equal to meet the great changes confronting the Court and the country in the postwar era. Although the Court began to grapple with civil rights and civil liberties issues, Vinson almost singlehandedly prevented the Court from coming to grips with the problem of school segregation. The cases were stalled in the Court when Vinson, an overweight chain-smoker, died of a heart attack; at his funeral, Felix Frankfurter commented that Vinson's death was the first proof he ever had of the existence of a deity.

June 15, 1949

If in my absence the Conference considers the question of getting reporters to transcribe the oral argument before the Court, would you kindly vote me in favor of the proposal? I think experience has shown that if we had transcriptions of the oral argument, it would be most helpful and would avoid the misunderstandings that have repeatedly arisen in the past.

November 20, 1949

Dear Fred:

I arrived here Thursday last and I must admit the sun feels good on my back.[1] My doctor is Roy Hewitt. . . . I am asking him to give you a report on me as soon as he finished his study. So far he has been quite optimistic—he not only thinks I'll live and raise hell for many a year; he thinks I am progressing better than a man has the right to expect.

I admit that for 15 minutes a day I'm hotter than a fox. I've a long way to go so far as restoration of energy is concerned. The right lung has cleared a great deal in the last two weeks, though there is still cloudiness in the lower portions. The total number of ribs broken will exceed 17. In fact they are sure of only one thing—that one rib is not broken. So I'll bring back a new championship, no doubt.

I'm chafing in all this idleness. Don't hesitate to shove things my way. I don't want to get too rusty.

---

1.   WOD had gone to Tucson, Arizona, to recuperate from his riding accident; see Simon, *Independent Journey*, pp. 281–283.

February 6, 1950

My dear Fred:

Your letter of February 1st has reached me and I cannot adequately express my gratitude for the sentiments which you expressed in it.[1]

. . . I am delighted that the business of the Court is so well in hand. I had a hunch when I gave you that gavel made of the Cedars of Lebanon that you would not have a need to use it down at the

Court House and I am glad to see that the Vinson efficiency has proven itself in other ways too.

I miss you all terribly and it will be a happy day when I can get back to work.[2] Time drags very heavily with me now.

---

1. The Chief Justice had written a warm and solicitous letter noting that woD would be welcomed back at the Court anytime but that he should not rush things; it was more important for him to recuperate fully than to rush back to work not fully healed.

2. woD thought he might be able to rejoin the Court on March 13.

Sherman Minton

Sherman Minton (1890–1965) was an unusual person, a man who wanted to be on the Supreme Court and yet resigned after only seven years. Douglas lumped Minton together with Fred Vinson in his rather cavalier disregard of defendant rights under the Fourth, Fifth, and Sixth Amendments, yet he also praised Minton. "When it came to the Equal Protection Clause," he wrote "no one was more adamant than Minton in insisting on equality in the treatment of blacks." Douglas restrained himself from telling stories about the internal affairs of the Court to strangers but felt that he could discuss Court matters freely with an ex-justice.

October 18, 1958

My dear Shay:

. . . I am glad you liked the Little Rock case.[1] We all hated to see Harold Burton leave. He is, as you said, a warm and loveable person—probably the best true Christian who sat on this Court for a long, long time. He is shaking pretty badly these days. His disease is diagnosed as Parkinson's disease. So far the tremors have affected only the left arm. . . .

---

1. *Cooper* v. *Aaron*, 358 U.S. 1 (1958), held the Little Rock, Arkansas schools, and by extension all school systems throughout the country, bound by the 1954 desegregation decision.

October 7, 1959

Dear Shay:

I am still with the White Sox if you give me good odds.[1]

---

1.   The Los Angeles Dodgers defeated the Chicago White Sox in the 1959
World Series in six games.

April 27, 1961

Dear Shay:

You know how enthusiastic we were when Earl Warren came to the
Court. But in retrospect it was a sad day. His attitude toward the
Court is the attitude of a prosecutor to his staff. We all know how
extravagant Felix often is in announcing his opinions. He often
embellishes them, as you know. Last Monday was the second time
Warren spoke up after Felix had finished, denouncing Felix for
"degrading" the Court. Warren had no opinion in the cases. He was
purporting to ride herd on Felix.

I've never been a Felix fan, as you know. But I never dreamed
I'd be here when a Chief Justice degraded the Court like Earl
Warren is doing. It's a nasty spectacle. Perhaps the old boy is off his
rocker.

May 8, 1961

Dear Shay:

The CJ fired that good colored barber we had because someone said
the police had picked him up drunk on weekends. He never drank
around here. I never thought it was my business what an employee
did on weekends.

The CJ thinks the Court is a bureau in Sacramento, and that he
runs it. He's headed for tragedy. We all got here on our own. I don't
know of a soul who respects him any more. I have defended him in
public and in private. But no more.

The Washington press is, I think, now laying in wait for the old
boy to pop off once more. The truth is, I think, that Earl Warren
is a cheap politico with a Christer complex. It's sad, but true.

Earl Warren

Shortly after Earl Warren (1891–1974) came to the Court, Douglas wrote Walter Jones, editor of the *Sacramento Bee*, that Warren "is a fine and a good man. And he is going to make an excellent Chief Justice." In a statement after the Chief Justice's death, Douglas wrote:

> I knew Earl Warren when he was Governor [of California] and instantly liked him for his honesty, and for his dedication to constitutional values. I was, therefore, more delighted than surprised when President Eisenhower named him to the office of Chief Justice. . . . He was an ideal Chief Justice. . . . He was one of the great men of the country; and I think when the history of the Court is written, Earl Warren will be rated with Marshall or Hughes as a great Chief Justice.

Yet in a letter to Irving Dilliard on March 27, 1961, Douglas wrote: "Earl Warren, in his personal relations, is a very petty man, but he has at the professional level stood up extremely well. I do not know how long this will continue. I often wonder how deep his roots really are." As his letters to Sherman Minton show, Douglas had a mixed mind about Warren. In his memoirs, however, he spoke glowingly of him, and well he might, for Warren helped swing the Court to the Black and Douglas position in favor of greater constitutional protection of civil rights and civil liberties. Warren did not have the erudition of a Marshall or Hughes, but, according to Douglas, "he had an understanding of the needs of the common man as opposed to those in corporate and other high hierarchies," and had "a passion for justice." In later years, Douglas often refered to Warren as "*the* Chief."

December 11, 1953

Dear Chief Justice:

I have learned since the argument in this case[1] and our discussion of it at the last Conference that my brother has either a financial interest or is undertaking financial transactions with one of the respondents. I do not know how important they may be—perhaps they are minor. But I think it is important to lean over backwards.

So I have concluded that I should withdraw from the case. . . . This unfortunately makes necessary a reassignment of the case. Perhaps you could find something else for me.[2]

---

1.   *Theatre Enterprises Inc.* v. *Paramount Film Distributing Corp.*, 346 u.s. 537 (1954).

2.   Warren reassigned the case to Justice Clark; woD recused.

April 25, 1955

Dear Chief Justice:
I agree with you in No. 8 . . . . I think your opinion in *Quinn* is magnificent, one of the very best in all the annals of the Court. I congratulate you for the wonderful job.

---

1.   In *Quinn* v. *United States*, 349 u.s. 155 (1955), the Chief Justice held that a defendant refusing to answer questions before a congressional subcommittee could invoke the Fifth Amendment right against self-incrimination.

October 18, 1958

Dear Chief:
I have received the revised Handbook for Jurors which you sent me. . . .

It has been my experience that jurors often get impatient coming down sometimes day after day and sitting there hour after hour waiting their turn to be called or waiting for the trial to start. They often have no idea of the necessity for the long drawn out examinations and the delays that sometimes take place at the start of the trial. It is very often in these early stages that settlements are in fact made.

I think a paragraph explaining why these preliminary delays take place would be helpful in many situations. Apart from this I have no suggestions to make. . . .

June 13, 1960

Dear Chief:
In No. 1—*Aquilino* v. *u.s.*, you will recall that I thought the Court of Appeals decision rested on state law and wrote an opinion to that effect.[1] But no one on the Court seems to agree with me.

Although I am still of the view that the Court of Appeals opinion does not need the clarification which your opinion suggests, I nevertheless withdraw my separate opinion and will acquiesce in your recirculation of June 10.

---

1.   363 U.S. 509 (1960). Warren, for a 7–2 Court, held that New York's highest court had failed to clarify state law over the priority of a mechanic's lien and remanded so the court could do so.

January 29, 1965

Dear Chief:

I guess I owe you an apology. At the Conference on No. 52— *Dombrowski* v. *Pfister et al*,[1] Hugo took no part, and I assumed it was a seven-man Court. If I had stopped to think about it, I would have remembered that you participated. But somehow or other, due to something which was said at the Conference, I thought it was down to seven.

That was why I wrote you the note saying I had assigned the case to Bill Brennan.

Assignment is none of my function and I apologize for interfering with your domain.

But I did this rather impulsively, because Bill Brennan's view seemed to come closer to the consensus of the meeting than some of the others.[2]

---

1.   380 U.S. 479 (1965). *Dombrowski* opened the door to prospective constitutional challenges to state criminal laws and provided relief against possible future state prosecutions. Specifically, it vacated Louisiana's subversive control act.

2.   Brennan did deliver the majority opinion.

May 24, 1965

Dear Chief:

Most memorial services are rather perfunctory, the speeches usually containing boilerplate which could be applicable to almost any judge.

I thought the one on Burton was delightfully different because of your humanistic treatment of the man. I thought it was indeed splendid.

---

1. Burton had died April 9, 1965; a report of the memorial service held at the Supreme Court can be found in the *New York Times*, May 25, 1965, 18:1.

Charles Evans Whittaker

Charles Evans Whittaker (1901–1973) had risen rapidly from district court judge to the circuit court to the Supreme Court in three years thanks to an affable personality and excellent political sponsorship. Ideologically, Douglas lumped him with "the Stone Age Man," the reactionary General Curtis LeMay. While Douglas liked Whittaker, he considered him a poor judge too easily influenced by others, especially Felix Frankfurter. "In Conference," Douglas wrote, "Whittaker would take one position when the Chief or Black spoke, change his mind when Frankfurter spoke, and change back again when some other Justice spoke. This eventually led to his 'nervous breakdown' and his retirement for being permanently disabled in 1962. No one can change his mind so often and not have a breakdown."

March 2, 1957

My dear Judge Whittaker:

It was a great pleasure meeting you this morning. As I told you, I was dictating a letter of congratulations to you when you came into my office. I repeat what I said, that it will be wonderful to have you here as a colleague. I look forward eagerly to many years of close association with you in the great work of the Court.

We have a wonderfully fine group under a great Chief Justice and you will make a great contribution to our work. I hope your confirmation is speedy and that you will be sitting with us in a few weeks. . . .

May 29, 1958

Dear Charlie:

Going back to our discussion[1]. . . the Internal Revenue Code, Section 311(a)(1) speaks of the liability "at law or in equity of a transferee of a taxpayer." . . .

You know this much better than any of us. I used to teach the subject and that is why I guess the words "liability at law or in equity" take me back to 13 Eliz. and the whole body of State law that developed after it.

Section 70 of the Bankruptcy Act shows that uniformity is not always the Federal policy and that these voidable transfers are tested by varying State laws. What is a good transfer in one jurisdiction might not be in another.

---

1. Of *Commissioner of Internal Revenue* v. *Stern,* 357 U.S. 39 (1958), and *United States* v. *Bess,* 357 U.S. 51; both dealt with tax code provisions for handling insurance proceeds for a decedent, and how they applied to a bankrupt's debts.

May 13, 1960

Dear Charlie:

. . . I agree with your fine opinion.[1] And I only add that I cannot imagine me changing my mind no matter who writes, no matter how long his dissenting opinion, no matter how many footnotes, etc. In other words, I think you are dead right and I think you have done a fine job.

---

1. *Hoffman* v. *Blaski* and *Sullivan* v. *Behimer,* argued and decided together at 363 U.S. 335 (1960); both dealt with a technical matter of civil procedure in transferring cases in federal district courts.

October 30, 1964

Dear Charlie:

The decision you are using as a cudgel to beat the Court is *Wickard* v. *Filburn,* 317 U.S. 111.[1] It was a unanimous decision, both Republican and Democratic appointees joining in it. So, unlike you, I do not see its relevancy to any political controversy.

It's too bad you left the Court, for up here you would at least have a chance at the proper time to convince a majority of the Court that *Wickard* v. *Filburn* was wrongly decided. To do so you would have to change your mind. For I note you joined in opinions that cited *Wickard* v. *Filburn* with approval. *Ivanhoe Irrigation Dist.* v. *McCracken,* 357 U.S. 275, 296 is one and *United States* v. *Haley,* 358 U.S. 644, is another.

The latter case involved indeed a reversal of a District Court for doing what you now say was constitutionally right. Yet you joined in the reversal!

---

1. See WOD to Robert Jackson, p. 121. Whittaker's attack on the doctrine may be found in "Confusion of Tongues," 27 *American Bar Association Journal* 597 (1964).

Potter Stewart

Douglas hardly mentions Potter Stewart (1915–1985) in his memoirs, and almost in passing characterizes him, together with Harlan, as "the nucleus of a new conservatism on the Court." The description is inaccurate, to say the least. Stewart is best seen as a moderate, and if he failed to join the Black-Douglas wing on the First Amendment, he nonetheless authored several of the Court's decisions expanding rights of the accused under the Fourth, Fifth, and Sixth Amendments.

January 9, 1962

Dear Potter:

I do not think that you have solved the difficulty in No. 68—*Hill* v. *United States* [1] on the recirculation.

I think it unwise to fall into the language of "jurisdiction." . . . I had hoped that you would put this on the same ground as Sunal, [2] namely, that where defendant has a lawyer, the error in question is one to be appropriately corrected by appeal rather than through collateral proceedings whether habeas corpus or otherwise.

I think the problem comes down to the common law approach, namely, case-by-case, weighing in each the magnitude of the error and the competence of the person to correct it on appeal. I would think, for example, that if the defendant had not been represented by counsel, his right of appeal would for all practical purposes be unavailable and that he should be allowed to raise the point under 2255.

---

1. *Hill* v. *United States*, 363 U.S. 424 (1962), involved the specific question of whether a defendant had to be allowed to make a statement and more generally referred to the Sixth Amendment right of counsel. Stewart ruled against the petitioner; Black, joined by WOD, Warren, and Brennan, dissented. At this time the

Court had not yet decided *Gideon* v. *Wainwright,* 372 U.S. 335 (1963), granting
a blanket right of counsel, but decided each challenge on a case-by-case basis.

2. *Sunal* v. *Large,* 332 U.S. 174 (1947), had held that one had to have
significant grounds to seek collateral relief after a conviction.

January 27, 1964

Dear Potter:

I have been back and forth in No. 83—*Costello* v. *Immigration
Service,* [1] voting first to affirm. Then, filled with considerable doubt
first from your opinion and then shaken up again by the dissent, I
have finally decided to go along with you.

---

1. 376 U.S. 120 (1964). The law allowed deportation of an alien convicted of
two offenses involving "moral turpitude." The Court ruled this provision could not
be applied to a person naturalized at the time of the offenses.

February 16, 1971

Dear Potter:

In Nos. 281, 349, and 436, I hope you turn this into an opinion—an
opinion designated as dissenting "in part."[1]

I also hope you can treat the District Court's use of the 79–21
ratio not as a fixed formula but merely as a guideline. You could say
that there is ambiguity in the language, but that we resolve the
ambiguity in favor of a purpose to use 79–21 merely as a guideline.
That would lead to an affirmance in No. 281.

With that modification I predict you'd have a court overnight—
JMH, WOD, WJB, and TM—and probably BW. . . .

We then could get the opinion down perhaps in April, giving
time for September opening of schools.

---

1. These cases were argued and decided together as *Swann* v. *Charlotte-
Mecklenburg Board of Education,* 402 U.S. 1 (1971). In a unanimous opinion
delivered by Chief Justice Burger on April 20, the Court ordered a North Carolina
city to adopt a plan for desegregating its schools which included suggested racial
mixtures and busing to achieve those ratios.

July 11, 1974

Dear Potter:

When *Marshall* v. *Ohio*[1] is presented to the Conference I'll be necessarily absent. Please note on the order that is entered that I would grant the stay since I believe the First Amendment as applied to the States by reason of the Fourteenth Amendment does not allow prosecutions for "obscenity."

---

1. 419 U.S. 1062 (1974). WOD dissented from the order dismissing an appeal of an obscenity conviction on grounds that it lacked a substantive federal question. Stewart, Brennan, and Marshall joined WOD, who believed the case raised an important question concerning the application of local community standards.

Byron R. White

Byron R. White (1917-   ), appointed by John Kennedy, disappointed those who had hoped he would join the liberal wing of the Court. He is perhaps best characterized as a moderate, although in recent years he has often voted with the conservative bloc. In his memoirs, Douglas included White as one of the seven ablest men with whom he served, one "who would have adorned any Court in our history." WOD had first met White when the latter had applied for a clerkship; for his initial characterization, see p. 48.

February 27, 1967

Dear Byron:

I have your memorandum dated February 27, together with a draft *per curiam* in No. 118—*Dombrowski* v. *Eastland,*[1] which I gather you did not write. I gather that you in this case are serving merely as a procurer. To you and your principal, may I say I could not join in this *per curiam.*

I think we owe it to the lower courts to state in a very responsible way what the contours of immunity are. There is no clear indication in this *per curiam* as to how Mr. Sourwine gets any immunity, if in fact he does. But there will be a stage in the proceedings below at which the lower court will have to make a ruling or determination or decision. The draft you sent is much too facile, inconclusive, and mercurial. Therefore I hope and pray that nothing like this will go down but that it will be spelled out as to what this immunity amounts to. After all, one of the purposes of the immunity, if it exists, is to keep a person from running the gauntlet.[2]

---

1.   387 U.S. 82 (1967). The decision held that Senator James Eastland, chairman of the Judiciary Committee, could not be held liable for the allegedly illegal conduct of one of the staff members.

2.   The opinion did not respond to WOD's concern and left the question of staff member (Sourwine) liability to rehearing.

April 8, 1969

Dear Byron:

. . . I join your opinion,[1] although for the life of me I don't see why you don't save three or four pages by giving Automatic Radio the decent burial it deserves.[2]

---

1.   *Zenith Radio Corp.* v. *Hazeltine Research, Inc.*, 395 U.S. 100 (1969), involved complicated questions of patent infringement and its effect on allegedly monopolistic activities.

2.   In fact, the case did overrule the holding in *Automatic Radio Mfg. Co.* v. *Hazeltine Research, Inc.*, 339 U.S. 827 (1950), that a holder of a patent could secure royalty payments for use of nonpatented items as a condition for licensing.

November 11, 1971

Dear Byron:

In Nos. 70–63 and 70–65, I voted to affirm as you know.[1] And I do not mind taking the "precarious leap" on which you frown at p. 12 of your memo of November 10, 1971. But since you have gone out of your way to cite my *Girouard* opinion at pp. 13–14 of your memo, my opposed views on the merits of these two cases have melted away and I'll acquiesce to your memo.[2]

In fact, with one or two more quotes from other decisions of mine, my joining of you might become truly enthusiastic.

---

1.   NLRB v. *Plasterers' Local No. 79* and *Texas State Tile and Terrazo Co.* v. *Plasterers' Local No. 79*, argued and decided together at 404 U.S. 116 (1971). The cases reversed NLRB rulings on the standing of employers in interunion jurisdictional disputes.

2.   White removed the "precarious leap" phrase but kept the quote from

wod's opinion in *Girouard* v. *United States*, 328 u.s. 61 (1946): "It is at best treacherous to find in Congressional silence alone the adoption of a controlling rule of law."

February 8, 1972

Dear Byron:

I got a big lift out of your "Dear Bill" letter when you said it was a pleasure reading my opinions.

Later I discovered it was for "Dear Bill Rehnquist", not "Dear Bill Douglas."

Can't we work out some code like Bill, Will and Willie?

June 21, 1973

Dear Byron:

I am glad you are keeping score on *Fausner*. It goes far to disprove the slanderous charge that with me on the Bench the taxpayer never loses.[1]

---

1. *Fausner* v. *Commissioner of Internal Revenue*, 413 u.s. 838 (1973), was a *per curiam* decision upholding an irs ruling. wod is referring to charges made against him by several scholars, including Bernard Wolfman of the University of Pennsylvania Law School, that he had been "reckless and irresponsible" in most of his tax case opinions, nearly always siding with the taxpayer against the irs regardless of the merits of the government case.

January 30, 1974

Dear Byron:

I was in Oxford, Mississippi at the Law School this week and all they talked about was you—your last visit, when you were coming next, could I help push you that way for a visit.

They are so damned enthusiastic I suspect they may want to run you for Governor or make you Chief Justice of the Mississippi Supreme Court. So if you go, accept no offices without talking with me first.

Abe Fortas

Probably "the best single legal argument" he ever heard during his tenure, Douglas asserted, had been made by Abe Fortas (1910–1982) in the *Gideon* case, when the powerful Washington lawyer had argued the indigent Clarence Earl Gideon's claim that he had been denied due process of law by not having a lawyer at his trial for theft.

Douglas had known Fortas ever since his days at Yale Law School, where Fortas had been his student. He had brought Fortas with him to the SEC and then had watched as his protégé, who had come to Washington like many other young New Dealers to do good, stayed on to do well. Fortas became a partner in an influential Washington law firm and an adviser to presidents. His close friendship with Lyndon Johnson led to his appointment to the Supreme Court and also played a part in his forced resignation four years later.

As Douglas wrote, "I was too close to Fortas . . . to be objective about him," and in his memoirs he defends his friend against charges of impropriety. Fortas's career as a justice is difficult to evaluate, although some scholars believe that in his brief tenure he proved himself a highly capable judicial craftsman.

March 18, 1966

Dear Abe:

. . . Would you kindly report to the Conference on the Escobedo[1] cases the following:

The other night at the Gridiron Dinner, I sat next to Stanley Reed and we were discussing various phases of the problem presented in this type of case. He seemed to think, and I certainly do, that the rule to adopt is substantially the rule in *California* v. *Stewart.* [2] I think this is not essentially a question of coerced confession. It pertains to the right to counsel and here as in other situations where preliminary stages in state procedure are critical, the right to counsel matures. I do not see any other answer than that.

---

1. *Escobedo* v. *Illinois*, 378 U.S. 478 (1964), held that when police move from general investigation to accusation, the subject has a right to counsel, and if denied that right, his statements cannot be used against him.

2.   *California* v. *Stewart* was one of the cases argued with *Miranda* v. *Arizona*, 384 U.S. 436 (1966), holding that statements obtained without informing defendants of their rights could not be used against them.

March 17, 1967

Dear Abe:

I have your typewritten draft in the bank merger cases[1] and tried to reach you after I finished reading it but you had left the building and I had to leave shortly.

From reading your draft opinion, which is certainly a competent and responsible job, I do not see any irreconcilable differences. It occurred to me that what you might like to do is take a draft of my opinion and mark the passages in it that seem to you to be objectionable because I am very free and easy in making changes to accommodate differences of views. And it may very well be that once I see your draft with the things that seem to you to raise difficulties in your mind, that a revision can be worked out that will be satisfactory with everybody.[2] I do not speak, of course, for Harlan. He said, among other things, that he was going to wait to see what you wrote and if you didn't write he would write on his own.

---

1.   *United States* v. *First City National Bank of Houston* and *United States* v. *Provident National Bank,* argued and decided together at 386 U.S. 361 (1967).

2.   In the end, WOD spoke for a unanimous Court, holding that despite the Bank Merger Act of 1966, the legality of any bank merger would ultimately be a matter for the courts to decide.

February 28, 1967

Dear Abe:

I have been hoping that you might write the dissent in the *National Bella Hess* case assigned to Potter Stewart.[1]

I have been writing in that area for so long (I wrote the dissent in *Miller* as you know) that I think perhaps a fresh point of view might be helpful.[2]

I suspect that you can pick up not only me, but Black and

Brennan and there is perhaps a fighting chance that you might get a majority of five.

---

1. *National Bella Hess, Inc.* v. *Dept. of Revenue of Illinois*, 386 U.S. 753 (1967), held that a state could collect taxes on mail order business conducted from offices wholly outside its territory.

2. Fortas did dissent, joined by Black and WOD, and his opinion relied heavily on WOD's dissent in *Miller Bros. Co.* v. *Maglin*, 347 U.S. 340 (1954).

Thurgood Marshall

Thurgood Marshall (1908-   ) had been the architect of the NAACP's legal attack on racial discrimination in the 1940s and 1950s and had successfully argued a number of cases before the Supreme Court, including the landmark *Brown* v. *Board of Education*. While Douglas liked Marshall, he thought little of him as a judge, and this comes through clearly in his memoirs.

Marshall, according to Douglas, "was named simply because he was black, and in the 1960s that was reason enough . . . . The public needed a competent black on the Court for symbolic reasons; none was needed to put the Court right on racial problems." Without naming Marshall personally, Douglas noted that "a black reaching the top was likely to be anxious to prove to society that he was safe and conservative and reliable. That at least had been the history of most black appointees to the judicial posts."

Marshall has not been so "conservative," but it is true that with the exception of civil rights and capital punishment cases, he has failed to carve out any distinct niche for himself on the Court.

October 17, 1961

My dear Judge Marshall:
My belated but hearty congratulations on the judicial honor which has been bestowed upon you.[1]

We will miss seeing you at the Bar. I hope you will not miss the hustings.

---

1. Kennedy had named Marshall as the first black circuit court judge.

March 6, 1972

Dear Thurgood:

I am still with you in No. 70–13, *Dunn* v. *Blumstein*, [1] and am particularly happy that you left in all of the material which I will use to demolish you very shortly in another case.

You said the reason I do not get any assignments is that I work too slowly. Would you put in a word for me, saying that with practice I might speed up?[2]

---

1.   405 U.S. 330 (1972). The decision invalidated Tennessee's durational residency requirements for voting.

2.   According to some sources, Chief Justice Burger, in an effort to dilute the allegedly liberal cast of the Court, had used his power to assign opinions to make sure that Douglas received as few civil-liberties-type cases as possible.

June 21, 1972

Dear Thurgood:

. . . My opinions were all supposed to be sent out on June 13, and most of them came except my dissent in No. 70–5106, *Graynel* v. *City of Rockford.* [1]

Then came your new circulation with a new Footnote 1 that says I was inaccurate in my dissent. It took three telephone calls for me to get my dissent out of my office to me at Goose Prairie. It arrived 15 minutes ago but nothing came with it—not the records—not the briefs—nothing I would need to revise my dissent.

I hate to hold you up, but I would like to have a chance to answer or at least to comment on what you say in Footnote 1. . . . I apologize. I am sorry. But that is all I can say.[2]

---

1.   408 U.S. 104 (1972). Marshall, for the majority, sustained an ordinance barring demonstrations near schools.

2.   WOD only dissented in part and claimed that the type of protest in question, blacks demanding more black history in the school curriculum, was the type protected by the First Amendment. Marshall's note said that issue had not been raised in the arguments. The decision came down a few days later on June 26.

Warren Earl Burger

In his memoirs, Douglas is quite harsh on Warren Earl Burger (1907-   ), whom he believed attempted to align the Court with the political views expounded by the Nixon administration. In their book *The Brethren*, Bob Woodward and Scott Armstrong portray a constant battle between Douglas and Burger over the latter's alleged efforts to exert greater authority over the Court, especially through control of assignments. Traditionally, when a preliminary vote at Conference is taken, the Chief Justice assigns the case if he is with the majority; if the Chief is in the minority, the senior justice in the majority chooses who will write. Hugo Black's retirement in 1971 left Douglas the senior justice, and since he and Burger often differed, it should have been his responsibility to make assignments. But Burger, as Douglas claimed, tried to manipulate this process by withholding his vote when he saw he would be in the minority.

It would be facile, however, to ascribe total conservatism to the Burger Court, as Douglas did. Scholars have noted how after 1975 the Court swung toward a more moderate position, and in some areas, such as abortion and women's rights, actually went much further than the Warren Court had ever done.

Moreover, Douglas pulls some of his punches, no doubt because Burger showed great kindness to Douglas during his illness. The Chief had a special ramp constructed in the court to accommodate Douglas's wheelchair. Douglas also greatly appreciated what Burger had done after Earl Warren's death, arranging for his predecessor to lie in state in the Great Hall foyer of the Supreme Court.

October 31, 1969

Dear Chief:

I was one of three to either grant or to note in the following cases:[1]

. . . At the time it seemed pretty much like a routine matter as I was sure we would get our ninth Justice soon. How long we will stay as a Court of eight, I do not know. But in view of the passing of time and the vast accumulation of these cases being held for Justice No. 9, I have decided to change my vote in each of the above cases to either dismiss or deny, depending of course on whether it is an appeal or a cert.

---

1. Nixon had been unable to secure Senate confirmation of his first two choices to replace Abe Fortas after the latter's resignation in early 1969. Because of the Court's rule that it will grant certiorari whenever four justices vote to accept a case, a pile of cert petitions had accumulated which had three votes, and it would be up to the new justice to determine which of these the Court would hear. WOD

believed the pile had grown too large and had therefore withdrawn his vote to grant cert on a dozen of the cases.

August 19, 1970

Dear Chief Justice:

I thank you for your effort to find the funds for my second law clerk. I meant no criticism of your retention of the three new ones, none at all. . . . My law clerk is moreover part of "a family" so to speak. A second one would not do IFP's[1] only. He & the other and myself would rotate on a weekly basis, sharing all types of work, except opinion writing.

My one law clerk and I are now handling all the IFP's and the regular certs. It means that I must do many of the IFP's. But the burden is not intolerable, and I rather enjoy it. But I must say it is a prodigious effort we are all making over such a few meritorious cases.

---

1. *In forma pauperis* petitions; the Court receives hundreds of these annually from indigent prisoners claiming they had been denied their rights. Each year the Court accepts a few, if they raise important questions. *Gideon* grew out of an IFP.

March 6, 1972

Dear Chief:

I think the assignment to Byron[1] (much as I love my friend) is not an appropriate one for the reason that he and two others including yourself voted to affirm on the statute, while there were five who voted to affirm on the Constitution. Those five were Brennan, Stewart, Marshall, myself and Powell.

You will recall that Lewis Powell said that to handle the government's problem of searching the country over for an appropriate magistrate to issue a warrant, an opinion should be written suggesting that the court here in the District of Columbia should handle all of the cases, which I thought was a splendid idea.

With all respect, I think Powell represents the consensus. I have not canvassed everybody, but I am sure that Byron, who goes on the statute, will not get a court.

To save time, may I suggest you have a huddle and see to it that

Powell gets the opinion to write? Or if you want me to suggest an assignment, that would be mine.

---

1. *United States* v. *United States District Court*, see letter to Lewis Powell, p. 144.

July 13, 1972

Dear Chief:

I have your memorandum concerning the pooling of law clerk talent to prepare cert memos on IFP cases. I do not desire to be included in the project for the following reasons.

1. I like to go over these petitions personally. They are interesting and absorbing, and for me much more meaningful than when they are reduced to a memorandum written by someone else.

2. With all respect to the strong differing views which you hold, I think the Court is overstaffed and underworked. The lecture I gave in March 1970 before the Bar of the City of New York contains all the statistics. We were much, much busier 25 or 30 years ago than we are today. I really think that today the job does not add up to more than about four days a week.

3. I think that the more Justices who look at these petitions, the better the end product will be. Different eyes see different things, and the merits of these petitions obviously cannot be routed through a computer.

The law clerks are fine. Most of them are sharp and able. But after all, they have never been confirmed by the Senate and the job here is so highly personal, depending upon the judgment, discretion, experience and point of view of each of the nine of us that in my view the fewer obstacles put in our way, the better. Pooling of the cert memos is, in my view, a rather major obstacle.

These are my own personal views. I of course have no objection if anyone else wants to use a different system. But since you asked for our reaction, I thought I would tell you frankly what my own is.

January 7, 1975

Dear Chief:

The purpose of this memorandum is to thank you for your kindness in arranging for Cathy to get back and forth from the hospital.[1] The parking conditions are terrible which makes it very difficult for an unchauffered person. In addition it is dangerous for an unescorted woman to be alone in this area due to the muggings and other crime. I am deeply grateful, Chief, for your kind arrangements.

My best to all of you.

---

1. WOD had been hospitalized following a stroke.

March 31, 1975

Dear Chief:

Many thanks for the bottle of French wine. It is delicious and has already become my favorite.

I am sorry I missed the session today. The reason was the Press. It ambushed me at the house at 7 A.M. to get more pictures of my wheelchair. If this keeps up, they'll make me wonder about the First Amendment—their big umbrella.

June 15, 1975

Dear Chief:

I was delighted to receive your warm little note; and that delicious bread will certainly give me something to look forward to at mealtime.

Again, I thank you for all your kindnesses and for thinking of me.[1]

---

1. On August 1 WOD dropped another line to the Chief Justice thanking him for a bottle of wine and inviting him out to visit at Goose Prairie. "Your acts of kindness and generosity," he wrote, "are greatly appreciated and I hope I can repay you in kind someday."

April 11, 1978

Dear Chief:

I know how concerned you are that unfounded claims against the Court not be filed. This note is sent to advise you that last Friday, April 7th, Datcher was temporarily absent from the office when I decided to move from my wheelchair to my big chair. Monty,[1] my law clerk, volunteered to do it. While moving me he fell and brought me down with him. . . . Later that evening, my physician . . . examined me and agreed that no damage had been done. I will, of course, file no claim against the Court.

---

1.   Monty James Podva, a graduate of the University of the Pacific, served as woD's last law clerk, from August 1977 until June 1980.

April 19, 1978

Dear Chief:

It was very thoughtful of you to remember that April 17th was a very important anniversary of mine,[1] and very generous of you to come by with a delicious bottle of wine for the occasion.

My best to you and Vera for a relaxing and happy summer. Please take it easy and slow down so you can be around for many years to come. The dinners one must attend during the winter months in Washington, D.C. exact a great toll—greater than one suspects at the time.

---

1.   woD had been sworn in as a justice on April 17, 1939.

Lewis F. Powell, Jr.

Few people who have come into contact with Lewis F. Powell (1907-   ) have failed to recognize the Virginian's innate gentility and decency. Douglas thought Powell too conservative, but in the years since Douglas left the bench, Powell has staked out an identifiable centrist position, and he has often been the swing vote in 5–4 cases.

December 7, 1971

Dear Mr. Justice:

Welcome! It will be grand having you here.

If the late Chief Justice Stone were present he would doubtless say "Welcome to the salt mines." There is, of course, drudgery but there is also much freedom and a relaxed pattern of life.

I am sure your good wife will be happy to learn that by coming here you are adding ten years to your life. Our congratulations to both of you.

March 8, 1972

Dear Lewis:

. . . The vote at Conference was to affirm but there were five of us who could not do it on the statute but went on the Constitution.[1] And according to my notes, you were one of the five. Byron, however, was explicit. He could not go on the Constitution but would have to go on the statute.

Traditionally an opinion would therefore be in the province of the senior Justice to assign. That was not done in this case and the matter is of no consequence to me as a matter of pride and privilege—but I think it makes a tremendous difference in the result.

I am writing you this note hoping you will put on paper the idea you expressed in Conference and I am sure you will get a majority. I gather from the Chief's memo that he is not at all averse to that being done.

---

1. In *United States* v. *United States District Court*, 407 U.S. 297 (1972), the Court ruled that the Omnibus Crime Control and Safe Streets Act of 1970 did not allow the President to initiate wiretaps without a warrant, even in cases of domestic security. Powell delivered the opinion of the Court; WOD, Burger, and White entered separate opinions concurring in the result but on differing grounds. Rehnquist, who had helped draft the law, recused.

May 4, 1972

Dear Lewis:

As you know, Bill Brennan is considerably disturbed by footnote 20 in your opinion.[1]

You state in the text: "We have not addressed, and express no opinion with respect to, the issues which may be involved with respect to activities of foreign powers or their agents."

I thought as I read that that it was a very proper reservation, and I still think it is.

Bill Brennan apparently thinks that footnote 20 squints toward a position that is in support of the American Bar position. It is a question which, as you know, is highly controversial, and Bill Brennan and I expressed our views on it in the *Katz* case.[2]

The Court has never spoken on it, and this certainly is not the time to do so.

But I was hoping that you could find some way to satisfy Bill Brennan so as to bring him into the opinion. It would be fine if this could be wholly unanimous.[3]

---

1. Powell did not change the note and in fact kept the reference to the ABA Project on Standards for Criminal Justice, Electronic Surveillance, which supported warrantless taps in cases involving foreign powers.

2. *Katz* v. *United States,* 389 U.S. 347 (1967), struck down wiretapping of a phone booth without a search warrant as a violation of the Fourth Amendment.

3. Brennan joined the opinion.

June 20, 1972

Dear Lewis:

You have convinced me I was in error in joining the Court's opinion.[1] I now believe you are right. So please join me in your dissent.

---

1. *Pennsylvania* v. *New York,* 407 U.S. 206 (1972), upheld a master's distribution of unclaimed assets between two states. Powell dissented, joined by Blackmun and Rehnquist, but WOD is not listed with them. Since the decree had in fact been handed down the preceding day, it is likely that WOD acted too late.

March 12, 1974

Dear Lewis:

I read your memo in 72–1598, *Labor Board* v. *Bell Aerospace.*[1] If this memo is turned into an opinion I will be happy to join it. I may want to file a separate opinion on the rule-making function and procedure. I realize that our decisions squint the other way and I do not plan to suggest they be overruled. The recent Ash Report to the President dated January 30, 1971 entitled A NEW REGULATORY FRAMEWORK touches on this as respects certain agencies and thinks that rule making is more efficient and expeditious than case-by-case adjudication. I doubt that very much, but my own experience at the S.E.C. was that public hearings on proposed rules brought in new, fresh points of view and considerations that busy bureaucrats, herded by a staff of eager beaver law clerks and other assistants, are apt to overlook, for at times they are so close to their knitting that they do not see the broader perspective. . . .

---

1.   416 u.s. 267 (1974). Powell wrote the opinion in this 5–4 decision (in which woD joined), holding that Congress had intended to exclude managerial employees from the reach of the National Labor Relations Act. woD did not file a separate opinion.

April 3, 1979

Dear Lewis:

My heart sank when I heard about ten days ago that you were scheduled for an operation.[1] My thoughts were with you and Jo often during those trying days.

I have been greatly cheered by the news since then, as I understand that you are coming along fine. I hope that you will take the time to regain your strength before your return to the bench, as I know how great the strains of the term can be. . . .

---

1.   Powell had a benign polyp removed from his colon on March 12.

William Hubbs Rehnquist

William Hubbs Rehnquist (1924-   ) is often considered the most conservative member of the Court, and one of the brightest. Some scholars have compared him to Hugo Black in that both of them are willing to rethink important issues from the beginning and not merely go on the accepted wisdom. Originally appointed to the bench by Nixon in 1971, President Reagan elevated Rehnquist to the center chair in 1986.

December 10, 1971

Dear Mr. Justice:

Welcome, and congratulations. Word reached us as we were about to close our Conference today. It will be nice having you here.

I realize that you were here before as a member of the so-called Junior Supreme Court. But I do not believe that we met while you were in Justice Jackson's service.[1]

It will be very nice, I assure you, to have you here on a permanent basis.

1. Rehnquist had been Jackson's law clerk in the 1953 Term.

Chapter 6

Rights

LIKE MOST government officials, Douglas received many letters from ordinary people, in his case concerned about what the Supreme Court meant by its decisions. Except for out-and-out crank mail, Douglas answered most of them. Sometimes his reply merely amplified a point already made by the Court; other times he tried to correct misconceptions. He especially took time to answer letters from schoolchildren.

Following are excerpts from such responses, all dealing in one way or another with individual rights. A few are to newspaper editors, but for the most part they are to ordinary citizens. Most show Douglas trying to educate, but a few also display his anger when he believed the writer ought to have known better.

To Robert W. Lucas

December 6, 1948

Dear Bob:

. . . The issues between totalitarianism and the parliamentary system strike deeper. They involve, as we all know, preservation of civil liberties in all their forms. The socialists of Europe are fighting for those liberties. They are our allies in that fight, irrespective of their different theories of economic organization. If the Commies can split them from us on the latter grounds, they will have made great gains.

To Harry Lincoln

April 3, 1954

Dear Mr. Lincoln:

As you know, I have an apartment and garage at 3701 Connecticut Avenue. Recently the police have been coming into the garage at night, tagging cars. Whether they also enter other places in the building, I do not know. . . . But I am sufficiently concerned to write you.

I have no quarrel with the police. . . . But I am alarmed to find the police patrolling inside a residence.

There is a way provided in the Constitution for a search of premises. Other searches are illegal and unwarranted. This is America, not Russia. If the police can invade the privacy of one part of my residence, they can invade another. I register this protest with all the vehemence I possess. I am registering it with you because you are the owner or manager from whom I lease the residence. I like the apartment building and the very nice Mrs. Young who supervises it for you. But I have decided I must terminate my lease if these unlawful searches by the police continue.[1]

---

1. Whether because of this incident or for other reasons, wod soon moved to another residence.

To C. Richard Leacy

June 6, 1955

Dear Mr. Leacy:

. . . Powerful political considerations led to the adoption of the Fourteenth Amendment. Powerful political considerations lay behind other provisions of the Constitution. But I never supposed that that made the construction of those provisions by courts on cases coming before them political decisions. I had supposed, and still believe, that construction of the Due Process Clause, of the Equal

Protection Clause, etc., as applied to individual cases and controversies is as much a legal as distinguished from a "political" question as is an interpretation of the *habeas corpus* statute.

To Robert W. Lucas

June 23, 1961

Dear Bob:

. . . People differ a great deal as to what kind of internal threat Communism offers to the continued existence of a free government (although everyone agrees that the danger here is less than it is anywhere else in the non-Communist world).

If one thinks the danger is small, then, of course, no legislation like the Internal Security Act[1] can be justified. But even if one thinks the danger is great, one cannot come up with an Internal Security Act unless he is willing to take all the bad effects which follow on denial of First Amendment rights. The tendency is, of course, to put on blinkers as to the bad effect of something, in this case the blinkers are labelled "Communist menace."

It's editorials like yours[2] that take off those blinkers and allow everyone to see how much it will cost—in terms of our own freedoms—to dispose of the "Communist menace" with a tool like the Internal Security Act.

---

1. The McCarran Internal Security Act of 1950 contained a variety of restraints intended to force the Communist Party to register with the government as a "subversive organization" and then to limit its activities.

2. Lucas had written approvingly of the Court's decisions in two companion cases, *Scales* v. *United States* and *Noto* v. *United States,* 367 U.S. 203 (1961) that undercut the registration requirements of the McCarran Act without actually ruling the law invalid.

To Edmond Nathaniel Cahn

January 10, 1962

Dear Edmond:

I have been thinking more about the Madison Lecture, and have decided to suggest as an alternative the title *A Bill of Rights Is Not Enough.* . . .

Our Bill of Rights is a series of "Thou shalt nots." They have served the useful purpose of hamstringing the group that is in control of the government. But they are negative and do not generate the forces of freedom. They are merely designed to see to it that opportunities for freedom are not destroyed by the government. But what may be needed for the development of freedom, and what the various opportunities may be depend on quite different circumstances. . . .

To Betty Whitesell

June 20, 1963

Dear Mrs. Whitesell:

. . . The First Amendment was added to the Constitution years ago—and one of its purposes was to prevent public institutions from serving sectarian ends. The reason was the history of religious conflicts that tore society apart.[1]

The Court, in adhering to the First Amendment, promotes rather than retards the full spiritual development of the people. To hold as you think, we would have to rewrite the First Amendment. The people can do that, not the Court.

---

1. WOD wrote numerous letters at this time explaining his view of the First Amendment religion clauses. The Court had recently handed down *Abington School District* v. *Schempp*, 374 U.S. 203 (1963), ruling that the First Amendment's Establishment Clause prohibited a required reading of Biblical passages at the opening of each school day.

To S.T. Leskosky

December 29, 1964

Dear Mr. Leskosky:

. . . The First and Fourteenth Amendments prevent either the federal government or the state government from "establishing" a religion.

I suppose you would be the first to object if the Moslims, having obtained control of your school board should introduce the Moslim prayer to the classroom. But the Moslim prayer is as precious to them as your Catholic prayer is to you and my Presbyterian prayer is to me. You see the aim of the First Amendment was to keep government from using public institutions for sectarian ends. I think you would be interested in reading the history of New York from 1840 to 1842 to see what terrible tensions were created when the Protestants, over the objections of the Catholics, used the Protestant Bible in New York's public schools. I think that if you were aware of the history of the First Amendment, you would be writing not to condemn me but to send a word of praise.[1]

---

1. For the *Schempp* case.

To John C. Love

January 25, 1965

Dear Mr. Love:

. . . I guess I did not make clear in my New York University School of Law lecture which school of thought I was in when it comes to Due Process.

I, along with Justice Black, have maintained in many opinions that the Due Process as used in the Constitution means those guarantees given in specific terms by provisions of the Constitution. That view has never prevailed, and that is why I took the liberty of calling the Clause "the wild card." . . .

To Rick Hawkins

April 13, 1965

Dear Rick:

. . . The Fourteenth Amendment, for example, provides that no state shall deny any person "equal protection" of the law. But to decide whether one person has been treated unequally as compared with others, the judge would have to know sociological, financial, business, agricultural and economic facts. The Constitution gives no guide except "equal protection."

To Charles T. Reeser

April 22, 1965

Dear Sgt. Reeser:

. . . The theory under which the First Amendment guarantees freedom of speech and of the press is that among all the conflicting views and charges and countercharges, the people will in time find what the true course is.

I think that has been the result in American history. What goes on today is probably not as venomous as what went on in the times of Thomas Jefferson.[1] Yet we survive!

---

1. During the early years of the Republic, a highly partisan press engaged in scurrilous attacks on leading political figures, using language which in England and even later in the United States would have been deemed libelous.

To Steve Smith[1]

October 6, 1965

Dear Steve:

I have your letter complaining about the regulations which your school has imposed on dress, wearing apparel, and haircuts.

Our Bill of Rights, as you indicate, is designed for the protection of a minority. But it does not cover all of man's idiosyncrasies. And you are talking about a field that is beyond the penumbra of any constitutional guarantees.

The price that all of us pay for living in a civilized society is a certain degree of regimentation, and the pressures of conformity are always great.

The part of wisdom is to find out when to bow and when to rebel.

Most people find it better in the long run to make their fights on basic issues.

---

1. A student in a St. Petersburg, Florida, high school.

To Harriet Jarzebski [1]

March 23, 1967

Dear Harriet:

... What we do is to apply the Constitution, not our own ideas, and the Constitution has in it some things that some people do not like. For example—the Constitution forbids the use of coerced confessions in criminal trials. The Constitution also requires that even a poor person be given a lawyer in criminal proceedings.

These are safeguards for everyone, innocent and guilty alike. And I always tell those people who are in favor of using confessions even though they are coerced, that they ought to go to Soviet Russia and see their system in operation. Then I think they would appreciate more than they do, our own system.

---

1. A student at Blessed Agnes School in Chicago.

To Charles E. Curran [1]

April 26, 1967

Dear Dr. Curran:

Congratulations on your stalwart stand for academic freedom. I know how lonely these situations can be and how rewarding as well.

The entire First Amendment community is grateful to you.

---

1. Catholic University had notified Curran, a popular teacher but one with decidedly liberal views, that his contract would not be renewed. Students and faculty in the Graduate Theological School protested by going on strike and were soon joined by most of the university. Pressure from leading Catholic laypersons and prelates forced the university's president to back down. He reinstated Curran and promoted him on April 24. In 1986 Curran became the focus of another uproar when Vatican officials suspended his right to teach theology because his views did not coincide with official dogma.

To Chester J. Niebler

May 8, 1967

Dear Mr. Niebler:

. . . You state "the validity of the propagation of ideas must be predicated in the validity of the ideas themselves."

By that I assume you mean that Jefferson, Madison, and the Declaration of Independence would all have been outlawed in the context of 1776, because they were at war with the views of the Establishment.

Does your system envisage a board of censors to determine what ideas are "valid?'

To the Editor, Christian Science Monitor

August 19, 1967

Dear Sir:

In your July 20, 1967 issue you carry an article by your distinguished Erwin D. Canham called "The right of dissent." In that article he says "There are laws against treason, in peacetime as well as in war. When does dissent become treason?'

The Constitution defines "treason" as follows:

Sec. 3. Treason against the United States, shall consist only in levying War against them, or in adhering to their Enemies, giving them Aid and Comfort.

This comes into play when there is "war" and "war" comes into being by a "declaration" by Congress, as provided in Article I, Sec. 8. The difference between "war" and a state of hostilities is tremendous—as constitutional students know.

So it is a form of illiteracy to talk about "treason" and "war" in the constitutional sense when speaking of those who voice their dissent against our Vietnam policies.

But the objection goes even deeper. Proof of "treason" requires proof of "overt" acts. Jefferson, who fought bitterly to exclude "constructive treason" in the old English sense from our Constitution, would turn in his grave at the suggestion that speech could be an "overt" act.[1]

Sedition, of course, is quite a different thing. Whether speech alone could ever qualify is a much mooted question. It was so condemned in one case where "war" had been declared and was in process.[2]

It was condemned in another case where there was a "conspiracy" to teach the noxious creed even though there was no "war" in existence.[3]

But there were qualifications originally stated by Mr. Justice Holmes in the "clear and present danger" test.

The terms "treason" and "war" as used in the Constitution are words of art. The truck drivers and field hands of the nation cannot be expected to understand subtle constitutional nuances.

But news editors who mold public opinion have a special trust, a special responsibility.

---

1. WOD's history was often less than precise. Jefferson had nothing to do with the drafting of the Constitution or of its treason clause, since he was then serving as ambassador to France. He did not learn of the contents of the document until James Madison sent him a draft at the end of the convention.

2. Probably *Abrams* v. *United States,* 250 U.S. 616 (1919), one of the World War One sedition cases in which the Court, over dissents by Holmes and Brandeis, upheld restrictions on free speech.

3. In *Dennis* v. *United States,* 341 U.S. 494 (1951), the Court, over dissent by WOD, sustained convictions of communist leaders for conspiring to teach a theory aimed at overthrowing the government.

To A.N. Jayaram[1]

January 9, 1968

Dear Mr. Secretary:

. . . The right to travel under the American Constitution is a basic "liberty" of which the citizen cannot be deprived without due process of law. The right of course is not absolute—a theatre of war may be too dangerous for travel; pestilences may rage in a given area, making it necessary to protect not only the traveler but those he might infect on his return, and the like. And while a passport is necessary for travel abroad, it is recognized by the courts that its issuance is a right which the law can deny only if some clear countervailing national interest stands in the way. . . .The right to travel within the United States and its territories is a privilege of national citizenship and is only one aspect of the free flow of people, articles, and commodities in the great Common Market constituted by our fifty states.[2]

---

1. Secretary of the International Conference of Jurists then meeting in Bangalore, India.
2. The Court had recently upheld the right of citizens with politically unpopular views to travel abroad in *Aptheker* v. *Secretary of State,* 378 U.S. 500 (1964), and *Zemel* v. *Rusk,* 381 U.S. 1 (1965).

To Ricky Tinsley[1]

October 10, 1968

Dear Ricky:

I think students should learn the constitutional principles governing the citizens and the police.

The Fourth and Fifth Amendments are central ones, and should be known.

In Russia a person can be held *incommunicado* for six months. There are no guarantees in that nation against police domination.

Police are very important to us; but our history indicates that the innocent as well as those who are guilty need protection against police short-cuts.

This is the area where I think students should start with the problem of law enforcement.

---

1. A student in Mrs. Harris's junior high school class in Columbia, Tennessee.

To Albert Castel[1]

November 4, 1968

Dear Professor Castel:

. . . You speak of "the brave, noble but unrealistic ideals" that I cherish. What are involved, Sir, are key provisions of the Bill of

Rights which no one now alive drafted, but which have come down to us with the commentaries of Jefferson and Madison and a long list of Justices starting with Marshall, all of whom construed the Bill of Rights against the repeated demands for a police state.

---

1. Professor of history at Western Michigan University.

To William R. Johnson[1]

April 24, 1969

Dear Mr. Johnson:

. . . I don't think many people really understand our Constitution.

It was designed by men who wanted to take government off the backs of the people. It is an eighteenth-century product, but it was written with the hope that it would be difficult for police, prosecutors, judges, legislatures, governors, and Presidents to do anything to the citizens.

It is the Constitution which the Court has followed quite faithfully, I think, over the decades—and not the views which uninformed people have concerning the Constitution.

---

1. Dean of students at Glenhard High School in Glen Ellyn, Illinois.

To Andrea Stone

November 19, 1969

Dear Andrea:

Socrates was condemned, as I recall, for impiety.

No one should ever be condemned on such a charge. It's part of our First Amendment traditions.

To Bart Crippa

February 18, 1970

Dear Bart:
All rioting is against the law. The problem of people everywhere is to settle their problems peacefully.

To Leon Quat[1]

December 11, 1970

Dear Leon:
I send you this note of greetings on the 179th anniversary of the Bill of Rights.

Our claim to greatness rests not on the technology but on the ideals of humanity that make possible a viable society made up of multi-racial, multi-religious, multi-ideological groups. They are among the values inscribed in the Bill of Rights. They mark indeed the differences between freedom and the great abyss.

---

1. Quat practiced law in New York with WOD's good friend, Sidney Davis.

To Evelyn R. Tiffin

December 4, 1972

Dear Ms. Tiffin:
. . . The problems of which you speak are real and varied as they relate to law enforcement at the local level.

The FBI, which has been our outstanding law enforcement agency, has always lived under the Constitution and they remain very efficient. So blaming the courts for what goes on is due to a misunderstanding of what role the courts play.

Law enforcement depends largely, as I see it, on the professional competence of the officers. When I grew up the police were chosen not for their brains but for their muscles. And the FBI has shown that brains are a more important issue.

To Michael Reagin

March 15, 1973

Dear Michael:
Under our Constitution there is no such being known as a "non-person."

To Robert C. Heling

March 5, 1974

Dear Mr. Heling:
. . . The questions you pose are in large part misconstructions of the Constitution.

The Constitution did not in all areas provide for majority control. In some areas it protects the smallest minority of all—one person.

Moreover the Constitution was designed to make it difficult for government to do things to people. It was drawn to keep government off their backs.

To Charles Burroughs Anderson [1]

September 23, 1974

Dear Mr. Anderson:
I rejoice with you and your associates on the 75th Anniversary of the American Booksellers Association, Inc. By reason of our First Amendment, books are supposed to be sacrosanct in this nation. Bookburning is anathema to us. Prior restraint is foreign to our Constitution, as is [sic] all forms of censorship. At least in the English speaking world, books have acquired a protective position never anticipated, I believe, when the bark of the beech was the first parchment used.

Books, however, are easy and tempting targets. Sedition—endangering national security—is the ready instrument of national leaders to suppress dissent, just as heresy was the tool used by ecclesiastical powers. Books seem dangerous to those in power, as they traffic in ideas. And there is nothing more dangerous than an idea which reaches fertile minds.

---

1. Anderson (1905-   ), the owner of a bookstore in Larchmont, New York, was then serving as head of the American Booksellers Association.

To Seth Amgott

November 25, 1974

Dear Seth:

. . . I have not thought much about the Equal Rights amendment, for the reason that under my view the Equal Protection clause of the Fourteenth Amendment has always made sex a suspect classification.

To H. Keith Thompson [1]

June 25, 1975

Dear Mr. Thompson:

. . . I thought at the time and still think that the Nuremberg trials were unprincipled.[2] Law was created *ex post facto* to suit the passion and clamour of the time. The concept of *ex post facto* law is not congenial to the Anglo-American viewpoint on law. Before criminal penalties can be imposed, there must be fair warning that the conduct which one undertook was criminal.

There has never been a code of International Law governing aggressive wars. So a punishment within the scope of domestic laws would have been impermissible and I think that a nation must practice abroad what it practices and preaches at home if it is to take its place among the nations of the world and still be true to its own ideals.

Scholars have searched frantically for little pieces of evidence of whether there was ever an International Law and have pieced together fragments that in their minds justify the conclusion that aggressive war is an international crime—but the reasoning in those cases is shaped to the urgent necessity to find an *ex post facto* justification for what was done.

---

1. An author at work on a study of the German Grand Admiral Karl Doenitz and his part in the war crimes trial at Nuremberg.

2. See *Court Years*, pp. 28–29.

To Young Lawyers Section of the Washington State
Bar Association [1]

September 10, 1976

Dear Friends:

. . . The Constitution and the Bill of Rights were designed to get Government off the backs of people—all the people. Those great documents did not give us the welfare state. Instead, they guarantee to us all the rights to personal and spiritual self-fulfillment.

But that guarantee is not self-executing. As nightfall does not come all at once, neither does oppression. In both instances, there is a twilight when everything remains seemingly unchanged. And it is in such twilight that we all must be most aware of change in the air—however slight—lest we become unwitting victims of the darkness.

Your award touches me deeply, and I thank you.

Keep the faith!

---

1. The Young Lawyers Section had voted its Distinguished Service Award to WOD, who was, however, too ill to attend the convention in person.

Chapter 7

Some Significant Issues

During his record tenure on the Court, Douglas took part in a number of momentous cases, ranging from validation of the New Deal's economic measures soon after he took his seat to abortion and restrictions on the death penalty shortly before his retirement.

In very few instances does a Supreme Court decision put an end to a controversy. The Court, as a matter of principle, always tries to decide the cases before it on as narrow grounds as possible, avoiding constitutional questions if technical or statutory reasons are sufficient. As a result, even the relatively few sweeping decisions are really only first steps; *Brown* v. *Board of Education* (1954) held segregation in public schools unconstitutional, but what did that mean in terms of implementation? How did this new interpretation of the Fourteenth Amendment's Equal Protection Clause affect segregation in other aspects of American life? What happened when protestors seeking to enjoy the rights the Court said belonged to them violated public-order regulations? Moreover, even though its members enjoy life tenure, the personnel of the Court changes, and with every new appointee there is the possibility that issues on which the Court has been closely divided may now go the other way.

As a result some issues, albeit in different form, come up before the Court time and again. Douglas's papers indicate how he tried to influence his colleagues on these issues, and in some instances, how he changed his own mind. The reader should know that often a letter to one of the brethren would be circulated to all of them;

memoranda to the Conference also went to all the justices and
served as a means of explaining his views in a somewhat more formal
manner. The memoranda to the files, however, did not circulate, and
despite Douglas's protest to Chief Justice Burger that he did not
write for posterity, he obviously did. According to one of his later
law clerks, Douglas wanted to make sure that historians would have
his views of what had happened, and, of course, in the most favorable light to him. Because the weekly conferences are private, it is
difficult to confirm the accuracy of these memoranda. One should
read them for what they are—one person's highly individualistic
interpretation of events.

Racial Segregation

No other issue before the Court in this century has been as important as racial segregation. In 1896 the Court ruled that the Civil
War amendments had not been intended to reach social or economic discrimination, and that so long as blacks had access to *equal*
facilities, they could be segregated. The NAACP, in a forty-year legal
campaign, chipped away at the "separate-but-equal" doctrine, and
when the school desegregation cases first came to the high court in
1952, the organization had made some significant gains. It had
gotten the Court to see that in certain circumstances separate could
never be equal, an argument eloquently stated by Chief Justice
Warren in *Brown* v. *Board of Education* (1954).

But southern white hostility, the growing anger of blacks, the
insipid political leadership of the Eisenhower administration all
combined to keep the Court busy in one racial discrimination case
after another. Some commentators saw the election of Richard
Nixon and his appointment of Warren Burger as a reaction to the
egalitarian decisions of the Warren Court. According to Douglas,
Burger did in fact try to subvert *Brown* in *Swann*, but the Chief
Justice eventually spoke for a unanimous Court in restating the
judicial power to enforce state compliance. How he came to that
position, however, is only partially explained in the documents, but
the story they tell runs counter to what the Chief Justice allegedly
told his clerks, as recounted in Woodward and Armstrong, *The
Brethren*, 180–81.

To Elon Gilbert

May 29, 1950

Dear Elon:

. . . The problem is an old one and comes back to us recurringly in different forms. Can a negro be given one-tenth of a vote and a white man a full vote? Can Jews, Catholics and others be deluded [*sic*] in voting power? How about farmers? These questions come up frequently and whenever the Court does not want to pass on them, they often call them "political" questions.[1] They deal with political issues in the broad sense but they are very vital personal problems which go to the purity and sanctity of elections as do any other election issues which the Court passes on continuously. At least that is my view. But I thought you would like to see what was written.[2]

---

1. A "political question" is one not subject to judicial determination because it has been committed to another branch of the government, or lacks manageable standards for judicial review. In practice, a "political question" is often an issue the Court chooses to avoid.

2. In *South* v. *Peters,* 339 U.S. 276 (1950), the Court upheld the Georgia county unit rule, which assigned a certain number of units to each county in the primary. WOD, joined by Black, dissented, because the units were not apportioned according to population but gave a disproportionate share of the units to sparsely settled rural areas.

Memorandum for the File

May 17, 1954

The above cases[1] which were decided today were twice argued— once in December 1952 and once in December 1953. At the original conference in December 1952 it was decided that there should be no recorded vote in the cases because of the likelihood that there might be some leaks.

In the original conference there were only four who voted that segregation in the public schools was unconstitutional. Those four were Black, Burton, Minton and myself. Vinson was of the opinion that the *Plessy* case[2] was right and that segregation was constitutional. Reed followed the view of Vinson and Clark was inclined that way. In the 1952 conference Frankfurter and Jackson viewed the problem with great alarm and thought that the Court should not decide the question if it was possible to avoid it. Both of them expressed the view that segregation in the public schools was probably constitutional. Frankfurter drew a distinction between segregation in the public schools in the States. He thought that segregation in the public schools of the District of Columbia violated due process but he thought that history was against the claim of unconstitutionality as applied to the public schools of the States.

So as a result of the informal vote at the 1952 conference, it seemed that if the case were to be then decided the vote would be five to four in favor of the constitutionality of segregation in the public schools in the States with Frankfurter indicating he would join the four of us when it came to the District of Columbia case.[3]

The matter dragged on during the 1952 Term until as a result of further discussions it was decided to put the case down for reargument. But it is apparent that if the cases had been decided during the 1952 Term there would probably have been many opinions and a wide divergence of views and a result that would have sustained, so far as the States were concerned, segregation of students.

By the time the cases were reached for reargument Vinson had died and Warren had taken his place. At the conference following that argument in December 1953 Black was absent but he sent in his vote indicating that he thought that segregation in the public schools was unconstitutional. His vote, together with Burton's, Minton's and my own made four. Chief Justice Warren was very clearly of the view that segregation in public schools was unconstitutional. That made a bare majority for the reversal of the judgments below. Reed voted the other way. He thought that segregation was constitutional. Clark was inclined that way although doubtful. So was Frankfurter and so was Jackson.[4] The latter two expressed the hope that the Court would not have to decide these cases but somehow avoid these decisions.

It was once more decided to treat the matter informally, not to take a vote and to have the Chief Justice prepare a memorandum.

The matter was brought back to conference for further discussion. During the Term I mentioned it to the Chief Justice and I think Harold Burton did also and each time he said he was working on the matter. He circulated proposed opinions in the two sets of cases on May 7th, bringing them around to our offices by hand. These were in typewritten form. After they were read and suggestions made, the opinions were typed up and they went through one revision between May 7th and May 15th, the date of our conference. Everyone thought that at least Justice Reed was going to write in dissent but he finally agreed to leave his doubts unsaid and to go along. Frankfurter, Jackson (who was in the hospital recovering from a mild heart attack) and Clark agreed to do the same. It was then decided to get the cases down either May 17th or May 24th. Someone suggested that they be delayed until May 24th because there were still some primaries in the South that the decision might adversely affect. But at the end of the Conference on Saturday, May 15th it was decided, if possible, to get them down on May 17th to prevent any leaks or advance information or tip-offs or rumors about the opinions.

It was decided by a few of us (Black, Burton and myself) who worked closely with Chief Justice Warren on the matter that these opinions should be short and concise and easily understood by everyone in the country, that they should be written for laymen and not for lawyers, that they should be brief, succinct and to the point.

---

1. The various state school segregation cases were argued and decided together in *Brown* v. *Board of Education of Topeka, Kan.*, 347 U.S. 483 (1954).

2. *Plessy* v. *Ferguson*, 163 U.S. 537 (1896), set out the original doctrine of "separate-but-equal."

3. *Bolling* v. *Sharpe*, 347 U.S. 497 (1954), held school segregation in the District of Columbia unconstitutional under the Due Process Clause of the Fifth Amendment.

4. A slightly different view of Frankfurter's position can be found in Richard Kluger, *Simple Justice* (New York: Knopf, 1976), chapter 25.

Memorandum for the Files

October 8, 1958

The opinion in this case[1] was assigned by the Chief Justice to Justice Brennan who worked long and hard on it. Several Conferences were had before the final draft was approved. It was first suggested by Justice Harlan and later enthusiastically endorsed by Justice Black that the format of the opinion be changed—that instead of it being an opinion of the Court delivered by Justice Brennan it be an opinion reciting the name of each Justice at the beginning. The reason for that proposal was that some newspaper articles had suggested that perhaps the three new members of the Court who had come on since 1954[2] had other views on the matter and the Court was being brow-beaten by Chief Justice Warren.

The new format seemed silly to some of us, particularly Brennan and myself as it seemed to add nothing in substance. It had a disadvantage because the Chief being named the lead-off man was the man to deliver the opinion written by Brennan. I thought, and Brennan thought, it would be much better if Brennan delivered the opinion.[3] As it turns out, the Chief continues to get the burden of the criticism for the segregation decisions.

The decision was to hand down the opinion on October 6 when Court convened for the 1958 Term. So I went away on a canoe trip to Minnesota and Canada. On September 27 a Forest Service plane put down on Elk Lake which Sigurd Olson and I were traversing by canoe, with the message that the opinion was coming down the next Monday, September 29. I sent out my approval by air. It appeared, however, that Justice Frankfurter who was writing in the case was not finished—or at least had not circulated. The Chief felt that the opinion should be announced because Burton's notice of retirement had been sent to the President and news of it would soon be out and he wanted Burton in on the opinion before news of his retirement reached the public. Burton's retirement is not to take effect until October 13. That did not seem to be a legitimate reason for rushing the opinion down, especially in view of the absence of Frankfurter's concurring opinion.

Frankfurter's concurring opinion was to several members of the Court pretty much of a bombshell. It left many suggestions and innuendoes which seemed to them to work against the effectiveness of the opinion handed down on September 29. A Conference of the Court was had about the matter. The Chief Justice and Justice Black spoke very strongly, their feeling being that his opinion would do damage. Harlan had spent several hours with Frankfurter trying to get him to alter some phraseology but Frankfurter was adamant. He blew up in Conference saying it was none of the Court's business what he wrote.[4] The suggestion of Brennan's and Black's that another short opinion of the Court be written addressed to Frankfurter's concurring opinion was voted down, they being the only two in favor of it.

---

1. *Cooper* v. *Aaron*, 358 U.S. 1 (1958), dealt with the refusal of Arkansas officials to permit school desegregation in Little Rock. The Court's opinion held the state bound by *Brown* and strongly reasserted judicial authority.

2. The three new members of the Court were John Marshall Harlan, appointed in 1955, William J. Brennan, Jr. (1956), and Charles E. Whittaker (1957).

3. The opinion carried no signature but indicated that it was the opinion of the Court; every justice was listed, first the Chief Justice, and then the others in order of seniority. There was no indication that Brennan had written it.

4. Frankfurter's concurrence consisted of a bitter and at times vitriolic attack on Arkansas officials for defying the law.

Memorandum

January 25, 1960

Today we had a Conference on the motion of the US in *US v. Thomas*[1] to vacate the stay granted by the Court of Appeals.

During the Conference discussion Frankfurter got very heated. He recalled how I, as far back as 1946, was urging the Court to meet the segregation issue and bring cases up. He said if the cases had been brought up then he would have voted that segregation in the schools was constitutional because "public opinion had not then crystallized against it." He said the arrival of the Eisenhower Court heralded a change in public opinion on this subject and therefore enabled him to vote against segregation.[2] Bill Brennan's response was "God Almighty!"

---

1. *United States* v. *Thomas*, 362 U.S. 58 (1960), invalidated discriminatory usage of voter challenges to disqualify blacks.

2. See Memorandum of May 17, 1954, p. 165.

Memorandum for the Files

June 18, 1963

This motion[1] was presented to Black and brought by Black to the Conference. He said the matter was of such grave importance he did not think that any single Justice should pass on it. He also stated he thought there would be a number of situations like this coming up during the summer and that since we were about to recess, he thought it desirable to have a discussion concerning the attitude of the Court toward the problem presented.

The case involved a rather broad, sweeping, temporary injunction issued by a State court in Mississippi. Black, in his presentation to the Conference said this was a case of demonstrations on the streets that tied up traffic, that caused fights, riots, etc.; and that these street parades should be stopped; and that the Court should not raise a hand to interfere in any way. He said that the situation between the races was getting to be more and more acute and that there would be many outbreaks this Summer and he thought the Court would probably have to have a Special Session to handle the crises that would arise. He reiterated what he has said before, that he thought it was time to clamp down on the Negroes. The Chief Justice seemed to agree with him. I pointed out that so far as we know there were no more than 2, 4, 6, or 8 Negroes picketing on the streets of Jackson. All the facts that we know were given on Page 4 of this Memorandum and it did not show the violent practices that Black was talking about. Therefore it seemed to me that the Court should not dip into conjectural, inflammatory facts for its decision, but stick closely to the law. Under the statute, we have no authority to review anything except a "final" judgment of the State court. Since this was an interlocutory order there was nothing here for review.[2] The discussion indicated that the Court was unanimous in its views that the stay should be denied, most of them thinking that we should act solely on the ground that this was a temporary injunction.

Goldberg and I, however, raised what seemed to us to be a rather serious question. If this were a final or permanent injunction, I told Black, I would think that certiorari should be granted because a substantial question would be presented and perhaps a stay should issue. He reacted rather violently to that suggestion. But Goldberg and I went on to point out that these papers were so broad as to prevent petitioners from doing any picketing, demonstrating, etc., that was "unlawful." The breadth of the decree makes the decree a trap because no one here any more than in the old labor injunction issues would be able to tell what was lawful and what was unlawful and would therefore risk contempt for anything he would protest against as unconstitutional segregation.

Black indicated that while that might theoretically be true, he would deny stays in any cases from State courts involving racial issues during the summer of 1963 merely because he thought that it was time to bear down on the Negroes and to make it appear at least that the Court was handing out justice even-handedly. But Goldberg and I pointed out that our problem was not to decide one case for the Negro and the next for the White, but decide each case strictly in accordance with the law and that we should decide this case solely on the grounds that it involved a temporary injunction and we should issue a stay and grant a petition for certiorari if this injunction is made permanent. But on that proposition Black seemed to have the Conference with him. Only Goldberg and I spoke strongly in favor of the proposition. Brennan somewhat lightly joined us.

---

1. *Salter* v. *City of Jackson*, 374 U.S. 818 (1963); in a memorandum opinion, the Court denied petition for review.

2. An interlocutory order is one determining an intermediate issue in the course of pending litigation; the Supreme Court does not usually review such orders, only the final outcomes.

Memorandum for the Files

June 18, 1963

This case[1] came up for discussion at the Conference June 7, 1963. Black said that it was high-time the Court handed down a decision against the Negroes. He said this was a flagrant case of Negroes invading a church and he made quite an impassioned plea to the effect that if the Negroes could go so far as to invade churches, nothing was sacrosanct. He thought a prompt denial of certiorari in this case would serve a healthy purpose.

I was the only one voting to grant. All the others voted to deny. The Chief Justice was prepared to pass on to the next case but I spoke up to ask that the case be held so that I could write in it. That led to a long discussion at the end of which Goldberg suggested that the case be held for the other sit-in cases which were being put down for argument for the October, 1963 Term. After the Conference I prepared the attached Memorandum to the Conference and circulated it among the Brethren, indicating why I thought a substantial question was presented.

---

1. *Ford* v. *Tennessee*, 377 U.S. 994 (1964), arose when black youths were arrested while trying to attend a religious revival billed as open to the public but in fact open only to whites. See next memorandum.

Memorandum to the Conference

June [14], 1963

. . . I believe any organization exercising associational rights within
the protection of the First Amendment—be they religious, political
or otherwise—can, within the limits imposed by *Terry* v. *Adams,*
345 U.S. 461 [1953], and *Marsh* v. *Alabama,* 326 U.S. 501 [1946],
elect or reject whomever they please as members. . . . But this case
does not present only the question of whether a religious group can
exclude Negroes from its membership or its services. It presents the
question of whether a State can lease public facilities to a religious
group, give them a permit to conduct a religious rally advertised as
being open to the public, and then convict Negroes of a crime for
doing no more than attending the rally, at which they learned for
the first time that they were unwelcome, merely because the presence of the Negroes upset the rest of the audience.

Since the Court has held many times that a State cannot enforce
racial segregation in public facilities . . . and has applied the same
rule when the property involved has been leased from the State
. . . and since it is clear that the only disturbance proved in this case
was a direct result of the audience's desire to remain segregated
while using public facilities . . . I do not find this case free from
doubt.

That is why I think certiorari should be granted.[1]

---

1.   The Court denied certiorari, with WOD dissenting.

To Arthur Goldberg

May 8, 1964

Dear Arthur:

As you know, I like your dissent in No. 12—*Bell* v. *Maryland*[1] very
much, and I would like to be able to stay with it right down to the
end. But Footnote 1 which you have added is one with which I
cannot agree.

Perhaps I am of the wrong school of constitutional philosophy.
But I have more or less consistently resisted efforts to avoid pressing
demanding constitutional adjudications for reasons technical, pica-

yune, or otherwise. Even Bill Brennan, you will recall, said the other day that if there were a majority of the Court to hold the sit-in convictions unconstitutional, he would not file the dissent he is now filing. That means that the principle he announces is a rather flimsy one in the sense that it is not durable for all occasions, but useable only as and when you want to use it. . . .

I hope you don't feel so strongly about the matter that you must leave Footnote 1 in.[2]

---

1.   378 U.S. 226 (1964) was one of the most important cases dealing with black sit-ins and other protests. The Court had avoided dealing with constitutional issues, despite WOD's urging, but in *Bell,* six members of the Court reached the merits and split. WOD, joined by Goldberg, saw restaurants as property affected with a public interest, and therefore the state could not impose or enforce segregation. Goldberg, joined by WOD and Earl Warren, argued that the Civil War amendments required all persons to be treated equally in public facilities. Brennan, who delivered what became the opinion of the Court, reversed and remanded on the narrow grounds that a new state public accommodations law might have superseded the old discriminatory statute, and this was a matter for the state court to decide. Black, joined by Harlan and White, dissented and claimed that the Fourteenth Amendment did not bar all forms of discrimination.

2.   WOD stayed with Goldberg, who evidently removed the offending note. The published Footnote 1 merely refers to two books on the Fourteenth Amendment.

Memorandum for the Files

June 20, 1964

Brennan's opinion[1] which will be filed on Monday, June 22, 1964, was the product of his plan to keep the Court from deciding the basic constitutional issue of the Fourteenth Amendment.

He wrote it only after the Court had voted, and the majority agreed to Black's opinion. He said at the time that he would not think of filing it if the Court had held that the sit-ins were constitutional. Later he changed his mind and decided to file it anyway, not as a matter of principle, but because he had been somewhat shamed into sticking to the position he had taken, which came about this way.

Clark for some reason finally left Black just before the opinions were to be announced, and joined Brennan's opinion that would vacate and remand. Goldberg also joined Brennan's opinion, even though he also filed an opinion on the merits. The Chief Justice joined my opinion, and he also joined Goldberg's opinion, so there were three to reverse outright. Then there were three for Brennan's opinion, which Brennan maintained was a reversal but which in fact was only a vacating and remanding for reconsideration. He dressed it up, however, with the word "reversing."

Black then amended his opinion, saying that there were only three who avoided the merits, the majority of the Court reached the merits, the three who avoided the merits did not really reverse but only vacated, and therefore if the vote had been taken of those who reached the merits the decision would be one of affirmance, since there were four to affirm and only three, myself, Goldberg, and the Chief Justice, voting to reverse.

This position greatly disturbed Clark, and at the noon Conference he said he wanted the cases to go over, as he might write something. It turned out that what he wrote was an opinion to reverse on the merits. This opinion was conceived in my office in a talk I had with Clark. After he finished it, he came back; I read it and approved it with a few minor changes. Then he went on and cleared it with the Chief, with Brennan and with Goldberg. At that point there was a majority of the Court to reach the basic constitutional issue and to reverse on the merits. At that point also, Stewart in Conference said something that apparently hit Brennan pretty deep, because he implied that Brennan's opinion merely to vacate was an opinion not of principle but of expediency; and if it was good principle to be applied on the judgments below which ought to be affirmed, it was good principle to apply on the judgments below which were about to be reversed. The exchange between them was brief, but Brennan said he would talk to Stewart. Several days passed and Potter Stewart got hold of Tom Clark and told Clark that if he would return to Brennan's opinion to vacate he, Potter Stewart, would join. That would leave Brennan with himself, Potter Stewart, and Clark, because in the meantime Goldberg had talked with me and decided he would not go along with Brennan's opinion to vacate.

The Chief had gone to Stanford to get an honorary degree and was out of the city that weekend. I saw him Monday, June 15. The issue on the sit-ins was still in doubt.

What had transpired between Brennan and Stewart, I do not

know, but Brennan at that point had Tom Clark and Potter Stewart only. At the same time Clark had not withdrawn his opinion to reverse on the merits, although he expressed a preference to go the way of Brennan's opinion rather than to reach the merits.

I saw the Chief and told him what the situation was. I suggested that if he indicated to Clark he would not join Brennan's opinion, Brennan then would still lack a majority for vacating and remanding and Clark's basic worry on that concern would still remain. The Chief said he did not think he should talk to Clark.

Between that conversation and the next day, which was June 16, Clark had talked with the Chief, and the Chief instead of staying put, not only joined Brennan, but got Goldberg also to join. That, together with Brennan, Clark, and Stewart, made up a majority of the Court to vacate and remand.

The Chief came in to see me about it after it was all over, and said he thought that was probably the best thing to do under the circumstances.

On thinking it over, he had decided not only to join Brennan, but also to join Goldberg and me on the merits.

Then I recirculated, adding Part I of my opinion, to be filed June 22, 1964, criticizing the Court for not meeting the issue on the merits.

The Chief decided to join only Goldberg and not me, although there was nothing in the other parts of my opinion with which he disagreed.

---

1. In *Bell* v. *Maryland*.

To Warren Earl Burger

August 25, 1970

Dear Chief Justice:

I have gone over the stay application in *Swann* v. *Charlotte-Mecklenburg Board of Education, et al.,* [1] and vote to deny the stay.

The hour is late; school is about to start. What adjustments may be needed in the future, no one knows. The decree will be under the continuing supervision of the Court of Appeals. Perhaps an appropriate addition should be made to our prior order in the case in order to make that clear. I believe Haynsworth[2] read it clear as vesting power of modification in us. I think we should return supervision of the decree to the Court of Appeals.

---

1.   402 U.S. 1 (1971) was the first major desegregation case decided after Warren Burger took the center chair. It involved a significant shift in the Court's position away from merely outlawing segregation toward requiring positive steps for integration.

2.   Clement Furman Haynsworth, Jr. (1912–   ) sat on the Fourth Circuit Court of Appeals; Nixon had failed in his effort to appoint Haynsworth to fill the seat vacated by Abe Fortas.

To Warren Earl Burger

December 10, 1970

Dear Chief:

First. You seem to intimate that racial balance is required by the District Court order [in *Swann*].

I read the District Court's opinions to mean that an all-white or all-black school is not *per se* improper. It may or may not be practical and feasible dependent on the facts. . . .

Second. You seemingly make irrelevant "imbalances resulting from residential patterns of the area," even when those patterns were created by state law. It is difficult to remove from *de jure* segregation any type of state action that was a cause of separate school systems. . . .

Third. United States v. *Montgomery County,* 395 U.S. 225 [1970], involved, as you say, faculty segregation. Judge Johnson[1] had ruled that in every school with less than 12 teachers at least one would have to be in the minority. The Court of Appeals struck this part of his order, calling it a quota. We reinstated the order. In so doing, we did not rule that "racial balance" was required, but held the order could only stand if the District Court had power, under the Constitution to "integrate" the faculties. The distinction between teachers and students would seem relevant on the issue of feasibility, but not on the issue of constitutional power to order integration.

Fourth. You state that a District Court can order optional transfers to deal with the problem of all-Black schools, but it does not have power to order the abolition of them "so long as the school assignment is not part of state-enforced school segregation."

As I read your opinion, transportation of students is limited to attaining the "distribution of students and those patterns of assignments that would have normally existed had the school authorities not previously practiced discrimination."

You state, I believe, that "discrimination" means the "discriminatory location of school sites or distortion of school sites in order to achieve or maintain an artificial racial separation." If this is the only "discrimination" that can be cured, the orders for integration would seem to be quite limited. Apparently the board could still build schools to serve the population of the area, but should place them on the basis of numbers and need, not on race. Presumably a school could be built in the ghetto, or in the white neighborhood, if numbers required, and need not be integrated. A District Court would seem to have the task of determining if the board built any schools for the purposes of racial segregation. If so, the District Court would determine where schools would have been built, absent such a motive, construct attendance lines around those areas, and bus students to the schools in those areas which they would have attended. This does not seem likely to result in Blacks attending suburban schools or Whites attending schools in the central city. It would only integrate the central city areas.

---

1. Frank Minis Johnson, Jr. (1918–) served as U.S. district judge in Alabama from 1955 to 1979, when President Carter named him to the Eleventh Circuit. Johnson is widely regarded as one of the most courageous of the southern federal court judges in his insistence on integration.

To Warren Earl Burger

March 16, 1971

Dear Chief:

I had hoped to be able to join you in *Swann*.

The case is rather a simple one, since it deals with a situation where there was a dual school system. Hence we need not get into other types of *de jure* segregation.

Your opinion decides that those other kinds are not relevant to any problem the federal court may have in working out a school integration program.

We have never heard argument on the issue. Many, if not most, of the lower federal courts have decided just the opposite. I think that the decision of that question in the *Swann* case is needless.

I regret it because I am now unable to join your opinion, and will write separately.

There will be no delay on my part, as I will be ready when you are—if necessary, next Monday, March 22.

To Warren Earl Burger

April 9, 1971

Dear Chief:

In No. 281—Swann v. Charlotte-Mecklenburg Board of Education, please join me.

I think it is a good job, and I hope it can come down real soon. Even next week would be better than the week after next.

Memorandum to the Files

April 20, 1971

The opinion handed down today[1] by Burger followed by six months or more our first conference on the case in October 1970. The vote in October was 6 for affirming the District Court. Burger was against that action. So was Blackmun. Black vigorously opposed any "busing" (Brennan said it was because the word "bus" is not found in the Constitution).[2] The case obviously was for me to assign, and I would have assigned it to Stewart.

To our surprise the Chief Justice assigned it to himself, using the artifice of not actually casting a vote.[3] But he took it to write Nixon's view of "freedom of choice" in the law. Weeks passed and when the opinion at last came around reversing the District Court, the six were astounded. I wrote a separate opinion. Brennan did; Marshall did; and finally Stewart did. Brennan and I saw Stewart and made several changes, indicating that if he made them he'd have a court opinion.[4] So he made the changes. Instead of circulating, he went to the Chief Justice saying he thought he had a court for the opposed view. That started the slow turn-around that eventually ended in the unanimous opinion of April 20, 1971. Changes were made haltingly and with great resistance. We circulated new opinions, setting forth our views. At long last—piece by piece—the suggestions were adopted. Black capitulated very, very reluctantly.

We were anxious to get the opinion down before Christmas 1970 so that all the school boards, waiting on us, would have criteria to guide them for the school year beginning September 1971.

The delay until April 20, 1971 partially defeated that purpose for many could not possibly have the hearings and/or adjudications between April and August 1971.

So the Nixon sabotage worked in part.

---

1. In *Swann.*

2. Despite Black's view of the total incorporation of the Bill of Rights through the Fourteenth Amendment, in many ways he was a strict constructionist. If in the Constitution, Black read a right as expansively as possible; but he insisted he would not read new rights into the document.

3. WOD had a continuing battle with Burger over this issue.

4. See WOD to Stewart, p. 131.

To William H. Alsup, Richard L. Jacobson, and Kenneth R. Reed[1]

April 28, 1971

This is a second memorandum concerning a summer project. . . . It relates to the problems of *de jure* segregation which occur when there has not been or is not present a dual school system. I refer of course to such matters as restrictive covenants, state or federally financed housing programs and the like. And beyond all forms of *de jure* segregation are the classical instances of *de facto* segregation.

I have treated phases of these problems in the fourth draft of No. 5210—*Deal* v. *Cincinnati Board of Education,*[2] and in a memorandum I wrote in the *Keyes* case (the Denver School case)[3] both of these being in the 1970 Term.

These memoranda of mine merely opened up the subject and I thought that apart from pursuing the analysis I proposed in those foregoing cases that [you] might look at the pattern of restrictive covenants in states where there has been no dual school system and the pattern of public housing projects.

The impingement of this problem will be primarily on the north, not on the south. Whether Senator Ribicoff's measure which was turned down by the Senate this spring of 1971 bears upon this problem, I do not know, but his proposed measure and the hearings behind it may be of some relevance.[4]

Whether the *Cincinnati* case or the *Keyes* case will get back here, I do not know. But we are almost certain to have some case involving the other types of *de jure* segregation which I mentioned above and also the simon-pure *de facto* segregation.

---

1. WOD addressed three separate memoranda to his new law clerks; for the other two assignments, see below pp. 193 and 201.

2. 402 U.S. 962 (1971). The Court denied certiorari in a case which might have dealt with *de facto* segregation; WOD entered a dissent, but it did not deal with the issue. Instead he detailed a terrible story of how the papers in this case had been lost several times, so that the petitioner could not meet the required deadline.

3. 402 U.S. 182 (1971). The Court vacated a stay of a lower court order and directed a rehearing on the basis of *Swann*. The case did come back to the high court, *Keyes* v. *School District No. 1, Denver*, 413 U.S. 189 (1973); although the Court ordered relief because it found evidence of purposeful discrimination, it did not deal directly with the problems of *de facto* segregation.

4. Abraham A. Ribicoff (1910–   ) had been governor of Connecticut, secretary of the Department of Health, Education and Welfare, and then Senator from 1963 to 1981. He had introduced a measure on March 16 to ensure racial integration by requiring suburban and urban school districts to merge; the Senate voted down the proposal, 51–35, on April 21.

Abortion

The 1954 desegregation decision came after a number of other racial discrimination cases had been heard, and even some southern newspapers conceded that *Brown* had been anticipated. But no such decisional history prepared the country for the Court's ruling in *Roe* v. *Wade* striking down every single state antiabortion law. Even legal commentators sympathetic to the ruling questioned whether the Court had not gone too far into an area where there was little scientific evidence, much less legal precedent, to back up their decision.

Douglas had long wanted the Court to deal with abortion, and he considered state laws on the subject an infringement on a woman's personal liberty to control her own body. He had little hope that a majority of the Brethren would agree, especially after the arrival of the four Nixon appointees. Yet a Court widely assumed to be antiactivist handed down one of the most controversial decisions of our time. Burger, according to the Douglas files, tried to kill the decision, and Douglas's angry responses no doubt helped forestall the new Chief.

To Warren Earl Burger

December 18, 1971

Dear Chief:

As respects your assignment in this case,[1] my notes show there were four votes to hold parts of the Georgia Act unconstitutional and to remand for further findings, e.g., on equal protection. Those four were Bill Brennan, Potter Stewart, Thurgood Marshall and me.

There were three to sustain the law as written—you, Byron White, and Harry Blackmun.[2]

I would think, therefore, that to save future time and trouble, one of the four, rather than one of the three, should write the opinion.[3]

---

1. *Doe* v. *Bolton*, 410 U.S. 179 (1973), challenged Georgia's "modern" anti-abortion statute, which had been patterned after the American Law Institute's Model Penal Code.

2. The two new appointees, Lewis Powell, Jr. and William Rehnquist, had not heard oral argument and did not participate in this stage of the deliberations.

2. Burger responded on December 20 that he had remarked to the Conference at the close of discussion "that there were, literally, not enough columns to mark up an accurate reflection of the voting. . . . I therefore marked down no votes and said this was a case that would have to stand or fall on the writing, when it was done."

To William Joseph Brennan, Jr.

December 22, 1971

Dear Bill:

I enclose herewith a rough draft of my memo in . . . the Georgia abortion case.[1]

Let me have any of your suggestions, criticisms, ideas, etc. and I will incorporate them, and then we can talk later as to strategy.[2]

---

1.   WOD rarely wasted time once he had made up his mind on a case, and he expected Blackmun's opinion to sustain the statutes or ignore the important questions. So he drafted a tentative dissent and sent it only to Brennan for comment.

2.   Brennan replied in a ten-page letter on December 30, urging WOD to show some restraint and wait for Blackmun's draft to be circulated. He then went on to lay out a strategy regarding how the constitutional issues should be addressed and emphasized that, in his mind, the abortion decision must belong to the woman alone.

To Harry Andrew Blackmun

May 19, 1972

Dear Harry:

In No. 70–18—*Roe* v. *Wade,* [1] my notes confirm what Bill Brennan wrote yesterday in his memo to you—that abortion statutes were invalid save as they required that an abortion be performed by a licensed physician within a limited time after conception.

That was the clear view of a majority of the seven who heard the argument.[2] My notes also indicate that the Chief had the opposed view, which made it puzzling as to why he made the assignment at all except that he indicated he might affirm on vagueness. My notes indicate that Byron was not firmly settled and that you might join the majority of four.

So I think we should meet what Bill Brennan calls the "core issue."[3]

I believe I gave you, some time back, my draft opinion in the *Georgia* case. I see no reason for reargument on that case.

It always seemed to me to be an easier case than *Texas.*

---

1.   410 U.S. 113 (1973) dealt with the older model Texas antiabortion statute.

2.   Blackmun realized, perhaps more than WOD, the public uproar that would greet this decision, and he worried that it had been decided by less than a full Court. Black and Harlan had both resigned due to illness in 1971, and the case had been argued and the initial vote taken before Powell and Rehnquist took their seats in early 1972. Both men properly refused to vote initially on the abortion cases since they had not heard the argument. Due to the close division within the Court, their votes, should they choose to cast them, could easily affect the outcome.

3. The "core issue," according to Brennan, involved the basic freedoms related to one's individual liberty and included "freedom from bodily restraint, freedom to do with one's body as one likes, and . . . freedom to care for one's health."

To Harry Andrew Blackmun

May 25, 1972

Dear Harry:

In No. 70–40, *Doe* v. *Bolton,* I think you have done a fine job. Please join me in your memo, which I hope will be the Court's opinion.

I may possibly file a separate opinion, indicating of course that I join you.[1]

---

1. This same day WOD informed Blackmun he would also join his opinion in *Roe* v. *Wade.*

To Harry Andrew Blackmun

May 31, 1972

Dear Harry:

I have your memorandum submitted to the Conference with the suggestion that these cases be reargued.

I feel quite strongly that they should not be reargued. My reasons are as follows.

In the first place, these cases which were argued last October have been as thoroughly worked over and considered as any cases ever before the Court in my time.

I know you have done yeoman service and have written two difficult cases, and you have opinions now for a majority, which is 5.

There are always minor differences in style, one writing differently than another. But those two opinions of yours in *Texas* and *Georgia* are creditable jobs of craftsmanship and will, I think, stand the test of time.

While we could sit around and make pages of suggestions, I really don't think that is important. The important thing is to get them down.

In the second place, I have a feeling that where the Court is split 4–4 or 4–2-1 or even in an important constitutional case 4–3, reargument may be desirable. But you have a firm 5 and the firm 5 will be behind you in these two opinions until they come down.[2] It is a difficult field and a difficult subject. But where there is that solid agreement of the majority I think it is important to announce the cases, and let the result be known so that the legislatures can go to work and draft their new laws.

Again, congratulations on a fine job. I hope the 5 can agree to get the cases down this Term, so that we can spend our energies next Term on other matters.

---

1. Reargument would allow Powell and Rehnquist to participate.
2. The five would have been Blackmun, WOD, Brennan, Marshall, and Stewart, and WOD counted Burger and White opposed.

To Warren Earl Burger

June 1, 1972

Dear Chief:

I have your memo to the Conference dated May 31, 1972 re *Abortion Cases.* [1]

If the vote of the Conference is to reargue, then I will file a statement telling what is happening to us and the tragedy it entails.[2]

---

1. Burger had complained that part of his problem with the abortion cases resulted from the poor quality of the oral argument. On reargument, he suggested, the Court could appoint amici for both sides, outside counsel who could make better presentations.
2. Brennan was as mad as WOD, and in a handwritten note he informed him not only of his anger at Burger's tactic, but also that Potter Stewart was equally outraged and prepared to make an issue of it.

Memorandum to the Conference

June 1972[1]

... THE CHIEF JUSTICE represented the minority view in the Conference and forcefully urged his viewpoint on the issues. It was a seven-man Court that heard the cases and voted on them. Out of that seven there were four who took the opposed view. Hence traditionally the senior Justice in the majority would make the assignment. The cases were, however, assigned by THE CHIEF JUSTICE, an action no Chief Justice in my time would ever have taken. For the tradition is a longstanding one that the senior Justice in the majority makes the assignment. . . .

The matter of assignment is not merely a matter of protocol. The main function of the Conference is to find what the consensus is. When that is known, it is only logical that the majority decide who their spokesman should be; and traditionally the selection has been made after a very informal discussion among the majority.

When that procedure is followed, the majority view is promptly written out and circulated, after which dissents or concurrences may be prepared.

When, however, the minority seeks to control the assignment, there is a destructive force at work in the Court. When a Chief Justice tries to bend the Court to his will by manipulating assignments, the integrity of the institution is imperilled. . . .

The *Abortion Cases* are symptomatic. This is an election year. Both parties have made abortion an issue. What the parties say or do is none of our business. We sit here not to make the path of any candidate easier or more difficult. We decide questions only on their constitutional merits. To prolong these *Abortion Cases* into the next election would in the eyes of many be a political gesture unworthy of the Court. . . .

Five members of the Court have agreed on a disposition of the Texas and Georgia *Abortion Cases*. One dissent has already been written. These opinions should go down forthwith. . . .

---

1. WOD worked this memo through six drafts and was ready to make good his threat. But Burger and Blackmun both backed off from their call for reargument, and on June 1, Lewis Powell informed his colleagues that he would participate, but did not require reargument.

To Warren Earl Burger

July 4, 1972

Dear Chief Justice:
Cathy. . . told me over the phone that the Washington Post today carried a nasty story about the *Abortion Cases,* my memo to the Conference, etc. etc.[1]

I am upset and appalled. I have never breathed a word concerning the cases, or my memo, to anyone outside the Court. I have no idea where the writer got the story.

We have our differences; but so far as I am concerned, they are wholly internal; and if revealed, they are mirrored in opinions filed, never in "leaks" to the press.

I am taking the liberty of sending a copy of this note to you to the other Brethren.

---

1. An unsigned page one story fairly accurately depicted the events on the Court in regard to the abortion cases, including Burger's assignment of the case to Blackmun, WOD's protest, and the Chief's efforts to delay for reargument; it also quoted extensively from WOD's memo.

To Warren Earl Burger

August 7, 1972

Dear Chief:

I have your memo relative to my earlier memo on the *Abortion Cases*. That chapter in the *Abortion Cases* is for me gone and forgotten.

I wrote the memo for internal consumption only. I showed it to no one not on our staff. I did not "leak" it to the press.

I believe in full candor on our internal procedures, for, as I said before, we are a group with fiercely opposed ideas but we have always been a friendly, harmonious group. That's the only way I want it.

I did not write the memo for posterity. It would be the least interesting of anything to those who follow. . . .

Thanks for your inquiry concerning Cathy. She is now in fine health, and we hope on August 11 to welcome the Rehnquists to Prairie House.

Can you and Vera be next?

To Harry Andrew Blackmun

November 24, 1972

Dear Harry:

Please join me in your *Abortion Cases* opinions—No. 70-18 and No. 70-40.

I will probably file a concurring opinion;[1] and a footnote in that opinion will state that I disagree with the dismissal of Dr. Hallford's complaint, as I still disagree with *Younger* v. *Harris*, 401 U.S. 37 and its progeny. But this is a mere fly speck in the total case.

You have done an excellent job.

---

1. WOD did file a concurrence, an exceptionally eloquent one explaining what he considered the liberty rights embodied in the Fourteenth Amendment and which ones he considered absolute and which subject to "some" government controls.

To Harry Andrew Blackmun

December 11, 1972

Dear Harry:

I favor the first trimester, rather than viability.[1]

---

1. Blackmun had balanced a woman's right to abortion with the state's police powers to care for the welfare of its citizens. During the first phase of pregnancy, a woman had a total right to an abortion; in the second stage, the state could regulate the conditions under which she secured the abortion but not deny it to her; in the third phase, the state's interest in the potential life of the fetus allowed it to prevent abortion. Blackmun and others went around on whether to mark the end of the first stage at viability, that is when a fetus could survive outside the womb, or at the end of the first twelve-week trimester. WOD and others suggested the trimester as a more precise point and also worried that medical advances would change the determination of viability.

To William Joseph Brennan, Jr. and Harry Andrew Blackmun

January 22, 1974

On this anniversary week of our decision on Abortion, I am getting about 50 letters a day. I'll be happy to share them with you if you feel neglected.

The Death Penalty

Interestingly enough, in neither volume of his autobiography does Douglas refer to one of the Court's major concerns during his last years on the bench, the constitutionality of the death penalty. As these documents show, Douglas initially had no qualms about capital punishment. He told his clerks that "the death penalty has been with us from the very beginning and would require considerable effort to read cruel and unusual punishment under the Eighth Amendment as outlawing it."

By 1963, although he had not changed his mind, Douglas began to rethink the question. Unlike nearly every other issue in which he quickly made up his mind, capital punishment left him somewhat bewildered. He never, it appeared, agreed with the Thurgood Marshall position (later joined by Brennan) that the death penalty in modern times constituted a cruel and unusual punishment. But the arbitrary and capricious manner in which judges and juries imposed the death penalty and its disproportionate application to poor and black defendants troubled him. He also began to ponder the relationship of the punishment to the crime. Shortly before he left the bench, as the Court prepared to deal with the various state statutes revised after *Furman*, Douglas penned a brief note confessing that he remained unsure on the issue.

Memorandum to the Conference

April 10, 1947

... I have now received a request for a stay of execution which takes place tomorrow morning. The stay is requested pending consideration by this Court of a petition for certiorari in a new habeas corpus case filed in the Supreme Court of California. According to [the lawyer's] letter of April 8th, which is attached, the writ raises the question whether the provision for punishment of death by the administration of lethal gas is too vague and indefinite, and whether it allows cruel and unusual punishment.

I would not myself grant the stay but in view of the shortness of time I thought the whole Court should consider it.[1]

---

1. The Court on this day denied the stay in *Peete* v. *People of California*, 331 U.S. 783.

Memorandum for the Files

October 17, 1963

Goldberg presented the matter of the death sentence to the Conference on October 11. As a result of the discussion, I suggested that the cases in question go over for another week. The Chief did not express himself. Black expressed the view that he was unalterably opposed to Goldberg's ideas on the death sentence. Brennan indicated interest in the matter and interest in having the point argued. I indicated my general sympathy toward Goldberg's view. Harlan thought that this was a very poor time to bring the matter up, especially since none of the questions has been raised in the cases covered by Goldberg's memorandum.

On the following Monday, October 14, Goldberg told me he had talked to the Chief and was persuaded, in view of the numerous attacks on the Court, that it would be best to let this matter sleep for a while as could be done because none of the cases raised the question specifically and the questions would have to be raised by us *sua sponte.* [1] In this group are some death cases quite unfit to raise the question; but in others the setting is more appropriate. I put to Goldberg the question: Would a state law imposing the death sentence for larceny of $25 or more (such as was once in effect in England) be constitutional? He did not think so, nor did I. In other words, the relation of the penalty to the crime needs careful scrutiny.

The consensus of the present Court would probably be against the Goldberg view six to three, Brennan and I being the only apparent supporters. [2]

---

1. Of its own accord.

2. Goldberg did not argue the unconstitutionality of the death penalty, but he wanted the Court to examine some basic issues in that regard. See next letter.

To George Virchick [1]

March 4, 1964

Dear Dr. Virchick:

. . . I am enclosing a recent dissenting opinion by Justice Goldberg, in which I joined. [2] You may also be interested in a survey of the problems of capital punishment which appears in a paperback recently out entitled THE DEATH PENALTY IN AMERICA.[3]

As I recall, fourteen American States have at one time or another abolished the death sentence but seven of those reinstated it, after experience without it, leaving seven States that are without it today. . . .

I also have the impression from studies I once made that the death sentence is not a deterrent. By following statistics from states that have abolished the death sentence, notably Minnesota and Michigan, one can see that they are not essentially different from those in New York and California. . . .

---

1. Pastor of the First Presbyterian Church in Mifflinburg, Pennsylvania.

2. *Rudolph* v. *Alabama*, 375 U.S. 889 (1963), in which the Court refused to take a case challenging the death penalty. Goldberg, joined by WOD and Brennan, dissented, saying he would have granted certiorari in order for the Court to consider several fundamental questions related to capital punishment.

3. Hugo Bedau, ed., *The Death Penalty in America: An Anthology* (1964), has been republished several times; it is considered one of the key documents in the death penalty debate.

To Jack S. Jordan

April 26, 1966

Dear Mr. Jordan:

I have your letter of April 18 inquiring about the stay of execution I ordered in the case of *Smith* v. *California*.[1]

The purpose of a stay is to prevent the execution from being carried out before the Court can give full and fair consideration to the case. Smith is applying for a writ of certiorari, and the schedule was such that he was to be executed before the Court could act on his application.

This is not a case, as you suggest, of "allowing convicted murderers to escape the just punishment they deserve." For, as you know, the stay terminates if certiorari should be denied or if the conviction should be affirmed. Its only purpose is to avoid the tragedy of an execution before the accused has had his full day in court.

---

1. There were at least four separate *Smith* v. *California* appeals that Term; the Court denied certiorari in all of them.

Memorandum to the Conference

April 4, 1969

I attach copy of a proposed opinion in this case.[1]

The case has bothered me considerably and I have tried to step up the preliminary work on it so as to put the problems presented in focus as I see them. . . .

As I recall, there never were more than four votes to hold that standards for the imposition of the death penalty were constitutionally necessary. There was finally, however, a majority vote holding that a bifurcated trial was constitutionally required. But those who made up the majority included perhaps one who felt that standards were not required.

As I got deeper into the two problems they became inseparable to me. . . .

---

1. *Maxwell* v. *Bishop*, 398 u.s. 262 (1970). The Court remanded the case, involving a death sentence imposed for rape, for reconsideration in light of *Witherspoon* v. *Illinois*, 391 u.s. 510 (1968), which struck down a state law permitting the screening out of potential jurors opposed to the death penalty. According to Woodward and Armstrong, a bare majority of the Court favored striking down the death penalty in *Bishop* when it had first been argued, but woo, who had been assigned the opinion, wrote such a sweeping decision that he lost the majority. Then Warren Burger came on the Court and the balance shifted in the opposite direction. *The Brethren*, 243–44.

Memorandum to the Conference

August 14, 1970

I denied a stay in a death case—*Tyler* v. *Washington*—execution set for August 25, 1970.

Not a shadow of a *Witherspoon* question was present. The questions of standards and bifurcation do not seem to be in the case. He presses hard the constitutionality of the death sentence—a question we did not even set for argument. The questions raised seemed to me to be state questions.

I denied without prejudice as I realize some may think that every death case should be held for *McGautha*.[1] But I am of the contrary view, though I respect the opposed position.

I am circulating this note so that you may be advised of what is coming your way.

---

1. *McGautha* v. *California*, 402 U.S. 183 (1971), held that the absence of standards to guide a jury's discretion in imposing the death penalty did not violate due process; WOD, Brennan, and Marshall dissented. Many thought that the Court would finally tackle the question of capital punishment in this case, but it deferred until the following Term.

Memorandum to the Conference

June 3, 1971

It occurs to me that the following guidelines might be helpful at our Conference on Monday, June seventh.

There are quite a few cases where the majority of the Court is granting and reversing on *Witherspoon* v. *Illinois*, 391 U.S. 510, *Maxwell* v. *Bishop*, 398 U.S. 262, and *Boulden* v. *Holman*, 394 U.S. 478.[1] I think these orders should go down forthwith. They, or at least many of them, will end up in penalties lesser than the death penalty presently imposed. So we did not reach the basic constitutional question that some are concerned about. . . .

There may be others of like tenure that will require a new trial. I know that I, personally, voted to grant and reverse for a new trial in light of confessions that seemed to me to be vulnerable.

And then there is the somewhat substantial group of cases involving rape without endangering life. The lead-off case there is the one just filed by Maryland in the Fourth Circuit. It can be noted and set down for argument the first argument week in October and all the other rape cases held for it.

That leaves the miscellaneous group of first degree murder cases. And for the life of me, [I don't see] how anyone would entertain the thought that as a matter of constitutional law the death penalty was prohibited in a straight, clear-cut first degree murder case. Any possible implication to the contrary would be wiped out in the consideration of the rape case from the Fourth Circuit, assuming that a majority of the Court in that case would hold that rape under those circumstances constitutes cruel and unusual punishment within the meaning of the Eighth Amendment. I am by no means sure that a majority of the Court would ever so hold, at least the

Court as presently constituted. But if it did not, it follows *a fortiori* that all other death cases on the present list have no infirmity on this score.

As I say, if the Court held in the Fourth Circuit case that in the special circumstances of that case it was cruel and unusual punishment, the exegesis of that point of view would leave unmistakably clear but for such special circumstances the death penalty is constitutional.

---

1. 1969. The Court remanded a case under *Witherspoon* where fifteen veniremen had been excused because of their doubts on the death sentence.

---

*To William H. Alsup, Richard L. Jacobson and
Kenneth R. Reed*

June 7, 1971

There is a third assignment that I would like to have one of you undertake. . . .

It relates to the death cases that the Court is handing down shortly and the designation of some of those cases for oral argument the first week of argument in October. When we took the *Maxwell* case a few terms back and the *McGautha* case and the *Crampton* case,[1] we limited the grant of certiorari so that the constitutionality of the death sentences would not be reached. There has been a drive on inside the Court to reach that issue so that, to use the words of Justice Black, "it may be disposed of once and for all," as if that were possible.

The death penalty has been with us from the very beginning and would require considerable effort to read cruel and unusual punishment in the Eighth Amendment as outlawing it. I suppose that if a State passed a law making it a capital offense for anyone to steal a loaf of bread or a set of food stamps, a court would hold that to be cruel and unusual. But the cases that we have involve either rape with or without injury in the physical sense; rape cases with or without beating; robbery without physical violence to the person, and then the run of the mill murder cases.

The Court decided on June seventh to name a committee composed of Brennan and White to go through the some 185 capital cases then before the Court and to pick cases from each of the three groups with the view of recommending that they be argued October 1971. Some of us opposed this procedure, arguing that the decision of appropriate penalty rested in the very broad discretion of the legislature and that therefore the choice of penalty lay in the legislative rather than in the judicial realm, absent a clear cut and extreme case which I have already mentioned—where the death penalty is exacted for stealing a food stamp.

Burger, Blackmun, Stewart, Brennan, Marshall and I were disposing of all the capital cases presently before us merely by denying . . . there was a majority of the Court willing to follow that course rather than to have these cases festering here for at least another Term.

The drive on the other side was very strong, Black demanding that we hear the cases next week and decide them the week after next. In other words, he wanted to make it clear to the nation that the death penalty and all of its aspects pass constitutional muster. But there were finally enough votes to let Brennan and White select cases from each of the three groups and put those cases down for argument in October.

Hence this memo and hence this summer research project. The question of the death penalty has been a hobby of mine for some years. I have always thought it was extremely unwise as a public policy to enforce it. That of course is a far cry from saying that it is cruel and unusual punishment under the meaning of the Eighth Amendment. We as a people have always had the death penalty. Why it should become suddenly unconstitutional is a puzzle because none of the rape cases, none of the murder cases, none of the burglary cases are anywhere near the loaf of bread case that I mentioned above.

We need a solid piece of work this summer on the sociological, penological, psychiatric, and legislative aspects of this whole problem. I do not think this Court is wise enough to make a decision on all these various facets of this problem. I think it is a decision that turns not on the meaning of a constitutional phrase but on the degree of maturity of the people. The question is not political in the sense of *Reynolds* v. *Sims*, [2] but in the framework of our Constitution it is non-legal as compared to legal. In other words it goes into the realm of what our public policy should be. I have long felt that where there is a mandate in the Constitution such as in the Fifth

Amendment or in the First Amendment we should enforce that freely and, if you please, expansively. But the words "cruel and unusual" allow no such manipulation if the historic frame of reference from which they are drawn is kept in mind. Great, great value judgments are involved. That is why sociological, penological, and other phases of the question which I have mentioned become germane. . . .

I am not interested in a collection of cases to show what judges have decided on the matter because judges by and large are pretty ignorant people. But I am interested in case workers, penologists, and others who are close to the phenomena with which capital punishment deals and their conclusions and observations.

I have not checked this, but I am quite sure that each of the colonies or States had the death penalty at the time they approved the Bill of Rights. I would like in a memo the crimes that were covered by those laws state-by-state and I would like some reference to the debates on the Bill of Rights that specifically refer to the death penalty.[3]

---

1. *Crampton* v. *Ohio* had been argued and decided with *McGautha,* and the Court had then approved a single proceeding which determined both guilt and punishment.

2. 377 U.S. 533 (1964) established the "one person, one vote" standard in state electoral apportionment.

3. The Court finally began to deal with the death penalty in *Furman* v. *Georgia,* 408 U.S. 238 (1972), and it struck down many state statutes because of the arbitrary and capricious manner in which the penalty was applied. The Court did not, however, declare capital punishment unconstitutional and, starting in 1976, began approving state statutes which met its new criteria. The Maryland case, along with dozens of other appeals to the Court on the death penalty, was remanded to the lower court for reconsideration in light of *Furman.*

Memorandum to Law Clerks

July 28, 1975

Tell Justice Brennan to pass on to the Conference that I am unsettled as to what disposition to recommend in the capital cases. On the new capital cases that have come this term I am undecided whether to affirm or deny. . . .

When the Chief Justice was here Friday he said he had put two people to work on these cases. . . . I'd like to see their memorandum before I cast my final vote.

The First Amendment

"The First Amendment," Douglas wrote, "sets us apart from most other nations. It marks the end of all censorship, it allows the ability of the mind to roam at will over the entire spectrum of ideas, and the sanctity of one's beliefs. . . . A symbol of our [national] health is the respect we show to First Amendment values."

Douglas, along with Hugo Black, came to be publicly identified as an ardent, even extreme advocate of an expansive interpretation of the First Amendment. They argued that it enjoyed a "preferred" position in the pantheon of constitutional values, because without freedom of expression, the core of all First Amendment rights, all other liberties meant nothing. The full Court never formally adopted this position, and even Black, who developed the preferred position doctrine, sometimes felt uncomfortable with Douglas's more extreme positions, especially on the question of obscenity.

But whether one agrees with this view or not, it has the virtue of consistency. The First Amendment says Congress (and through the Fourteenth Amendment, the states) shall make no law abridging freedom of speech, and this means *no* law whatsoever. The Court's tergiversations in trying to define what is and what is not obscenity, and how far the guarantees of free speech go, have amused Court watchers for nearly two decades. For Douglas, the danger of poronography never matched the danger of censoring free thought.

To Kotaro Tanaka[1]

April 9, 1957

My dear Chief Justice:

. . . We have quite a few cases this Term involving a related problem. As you indicated, the line between obscenity and art is sometimes a very difficult one to draw. We had this spring a case from Michigan known as the Butler case.[2] I am sending you a copy of that opinion under separate cover as I think you may enjoy reading it at your leisure. . . .

---

1.   The chief justice of Japan had sent wod clippings relating to a case involving *Lady Chatterley's Lover* before his Court.

2.   In *Butler* v. *Michigan*, 352 u.s. 380 (1957), the Court struck down a statute prohibiting making available to the general public material potentially deleterious to youth. Frankfurter said the statute would reduce the adult population to reading only what is fit for children.

To William Joseph Brennan, Jr.

May 9, 1957

I liked very much the major part of your opinion in No. 23, *Jencks v. United States,* [1] but I am greatly disturbed by the part on affiliation. . . .

A person might vote consistently over and over again with the Communists on slum clearance, minimum wages, desegregation of the races, and any other number of domestic issues without being affiliated with the Communists in any realistic sense. At least I think that the word "affiliation" as used has an invidious connotation. The fact that a person may take identical positions over and again on certain domestic issues does not mean that person should be condemned merely because those positions coincide with the Communist position. To condemn a man on that ground would, I think, raise serious questions under the First Amendment. . . .

---

1.   353 u.s. 657 (1957), reversed a prosecution for filing a false noncommunist affidavit with the nlrb; Brennan removed the passages on affiliation.

To John Marshall Harlan

April 22, 1958

Dear John:

I have your circulation in the above case,[1] and I must say you have unloaded a few very difficult problems onto me.

In the first place, I had always thought that if the Fourteenth

Amendment incorporated through the Due Process clause the right of free speech and assembly protected in the First Amendment that it came into the Fourteenth Amendment full-fledged, not watered down by some concept of due process. As I remember, you have written to the contrary. Perhaps I am thinking of the Obscenity cases last June.[2] I have never thought that would stand the test and I do not think that the Court has ever so held.

In other words, I think that the right of free speech is subject to no more and no less regulation by the states than it is by the Congress.

If I am wrong and if you in your Obscenity opinion were right, then I think we are all in even greater trouble. Because if the right of free speech is watered down by the Due Process clause of the Fourteenth Amendment and made subject to state regulation, then the police power of the state has a pretty broad area for application. If we are dealing here with something that can be regulated then I think we are in very deep water in this case, as for the life of me I do not see why a state could not have a rational judgment for believing that an organization like the NAACP was a source of a lot of trouble, friction and unrest. . . .

Once we admit the existence of that kind of test in these racial problems, then I think we are hopelessly lost. If that is the test, why were we right in the Segregation cases? Certainly there could be a "rational" basis for concluding that a mixture of the two races in public schools might give rise to social evils.[3]

I thought that when we dealt with these racial problems and with free speech and free assembly and religious problems we were dealing with something that is right close to the absolute. There undoubtedly are instances where the guaranteed right cannot prevail. But I cannot believe that the state can be denied the power to act here if "rationality" is the test. . . .

---

1. *NAACP* v. *Alabama*, 357 U.S. 449 (1958), held unconstitutional Alabama's demand that the NAACP reveal the names and addresses of all its Alabama members. WOD did not write separately, and Harlan's opinion certainly did not reflect any watered-down interpretation of the First Amendment's right of free association.

2. *Roth* v. *United States* and *Alberts* v. *California*, both decided at 354 U.S. 476 (1957), opened the Pandora's box of obscenity and its relation to free speech. The Court upheld a federal statute banning the mailing of obscene materials, as

well as a state law punishing the sale of obscene items. But while Justice Brennan reaffirmed the traditional rule that obscenity did not come within First Amendment protection, he indicated that if the material could be proved to have some redeeming social value, it might qualify, thus setting off over a decade's confusion over what constituted literary or social value and what standards should be applied.

wod, joined by Black, dissented on the grounds that the First Amendment prohibited any form of censorship. In concluding, he wrote: "I would give the broad sweep of the First Amendment full support. I have the same confidence in the ability of our people to reject noxious literature as I have in their capacity to sort out the true from the false in theology, economics, politics, or any other field."

3. The "rational basis" test is the minimal standard against which the Court will judge legislation, usually of an economic nature. The Court merely asks whether the legislature has the power, and if it has a rational basis for exercising it in this particular manner. For laws infringing on personal liberties, the Court applies a standard of strict scrutiny, in which the state has the burden of proving that there is a compelling interest justifying the restriction. All racial classifications are judged by strict scrutiny.

To Edmond Cahn

January 21, 1960

Dear Edmond:

. . . My views on obscenity are so far out of line with the majority view of the Court that it seems almost hopeless to keep pounding away for them.

Once in a while I see some minor step being taken which is a small, tiny advance, and hence I succumb to the feeling that perhaps I serve the cause of the First Amendment best by lending my weight to that meagre advance.

Yet in the long haul, I think that you are dead right and that these moments of acquiescence accomplish nothing.

To Robert Maynard Hutchins

February 27, 1961

Dear Bob:

I thank you kindly for your gracious letter about my dissenting opinion in the censorship case.[1] Your letter has a ring of optimism that I wish I could share. From this viewpoint the size of the bucket which a person can bail seems much too small for the volume of water coming into the leaky boat.

---

1.   *Times Film Corp.* v. *Chicago*, 365 U.S. 43 (1961), upheld a local ordinance controlling which films could be shown in the city; WOD, along with Black, Brennan, and the Chief Justice dissented.

To Hugo LaFayette Black

June 11, 1962

Dear Hugo:

As you know, I have had troubles with No. 408—*Engel* v. *Vitale*. [1]

I have put my troubles on paper—not with the view of filing a concurrence or a dissent but in order to define the narrow issue that seems to me involved. . . .

I am inclined to reverse if we are prepared to disallow public property and public funds to be used to finance a religious exercise.

If, however, we would strike down a New York requirement that public school teachers open each day with prayer, I think we could not consistently open each of our sessions with prayer. That's the kernel of my problem.

---

1.   In *Engel* v. *Vitale*, 370 U.S. 421 (1962), the Court invalidated a prayer which the New York Board of Regents had written to be recited at the start of each school day. Justice Black termed the mandated prayer a violation of the Establishment Clause of the First Amendment. WOD entered a brief concurrence in which he emphasized the danger of any financial involvement of the state in religious matters.

Memorandum to the Conference

March 31, 1965

Under our decisions involving issues of obscenity, the basic question is whether the literature has "even the slightest redeeming social importance." See *Roth* v. *United States*, 354 U.S. 476, 484 [1957]. Administration of that standard makes this Court the ultimate censor of every challenged book, paper, movie, and magazine in the

land. My view of the constitutional issue of obscenity is quite different from the Court's.[1] . . .

But my constitutional standards are not accepted by the Court.
Hence if these petitions for certiorari[2] are granted and the cases are
argued, the Court will sit as the supreme board of censorship applying to these challenged tracts the standard whether they have any
redeeming social value. Censorship is anathema to me and so dis-
tasteful, as well as unconstitutional, that I have decided not to make
the fourth vote to bring these cases here so that we can sit as censors
and apply our literary code to literature—a code which I have no
reason to believe to be better than that of the lower courts. If there
is to be censorship, I can see advantages in its being decentralized,
administered locally so as to reflect varying views. Should a case be
brought here without my help then I will have a different problem.[3]
But I do not want to be the one responsible for the performance of
what to me is an unseemly and unconstitutional role.

---

1. wod then quoted from his dissent in *Roth*, in which he stated his opposition to government censorship as a violation of the First Amendment.

2. *Ginzberg* v. *United States*, ultimately decided at 383 u.s. 463 (1965), and
Mishkin v. *New York*, 383 u.s. 502.

3. Even without wod's vote, the Court decided to hear the case and upheld
both convictions for sale of pornographic materials. wod entered a strong dissent,
in which he reaffirmed his belief that the Court has "no business acting as censors
or endowing any group with censorship powers."

---

*To William H. Alsup, Richard L. Jacobson and
Kenneth R. Reed*

April 22, 1971

As a summer project I would like one of you to do some research
for me on the construction and constitutionality of various Acts of
Congress and regulations of the Park Service dealing with (a) the
grounds of the Supreme Court; (b) the grounds of the Congress; and
(c) the Mall in general.

The use of these areas by dissident groups raises recurring
questions. There is one special Act that applies to the Court, and
as I recall, to the Court alone. I have always thought that that Act
was unconstitutional as applied to people who merely came in not

to pay their respects to the Court, but to express to the Court their dislike of opinions, provided of course they are not engaged in violence. . . .

I would like someone to take these regulations one by one, annotate them with decisions that have been made concerning them, and analyze them respecting their application in suppression or dilution of the exercise of First Amendment rights. As I said, the problem is a recurring one. It usually reaches the Court in an emergency situation where there is no time for any research or oral argument, but where action must be taken immediately. . . .

To George J. Stavros

January 4, 1972

Dear Mr. Stavros:

. . . I did not write the dissent.[1] But I joined it because I thought then and still think it was the correct view.

One of my great heroes was Holmes—another Black. Yet though I usually agreed with them I did not always agree.

But that is what the First Amendment is all about.

---

1.   Stavros, of Arlington, Virginia, had written about a friend distressed by WOD's position in *Powell* v. *Texas*, 392 U.S. 514 (1968). A 5–4 Court had upheld a conviction for public drunkenness of a person who was not an alcoholic; Fortas wrote the dissent in which WOD, Brennan, and Stewart joined.

To Alden Whitman[1]

January 24, 1972

Dear Mr. Whitman:

. . . In Dennis[2] I chose to make clear-and-present danger the target, showing it could not be satisfied. I did so because of the new dimensions given that concept by the Court in that case.

But I have never thought clear-and-present danger has a place in our constitutional scheme.[3]

---

1. A reporter with the *New York Times.*

2. *Dennis* v. *United States,* 341 U.S. 494 (1951), upheld the conviction of communists for allegedly conspiring to overthrow the government. Black and WOD entered vigorous dissents.

3. In *Brandenburg* v. *Ohio,* 395 U.S. 444 (1969), WOD came back to this idea: "Though I doubt if the 'clear and present danger' test is congenial to the First Amendment in time of a declared war, I am certain it is not reconcilable with the First Amendment in days of peace."

To Warren Earl Burger

June 14, 1973

Dear Chief:

I join your opinion in *Levitt*—72–269 and the companion cases.[1] I would prefer, however, to strike most of the paragraph starting on page 11. The question of what service a state may "mandate" a religious school to perform might include, for purposes of health, keeping room temperatures at 72 when outside temperatures are at a certain level.

But I doubt if the state constitutionally could take on the heating and sanitary services of a religious school. I'd prefer to let the problem rest, awaiting case by case solutions.

There are bound to be cases coming up—cases of all kinds.[2]

---

1. In *Levitt* v. *Committee for Public Education and Religious Liberty,* 413 U.S. 472 (1973), the Court struck down a New York provision providing reimbursement for the costs of state-mandated testing to religious schools with no means of auditing the funds to ensure they did not go for religious purposes.

2. The Chief Justice eventually omitted the paragraph after Brennan added his voice to WOD's objection. On June 19, WOD again wrote to Burger about reimbursement: "This is new ground in which I have serious doubts. We have never so held and I would prefer to keep our holdings as narrow as possible."

Rights of the Accused

Douglas, possibly because of his youthful experience riding the rails with drifters, always had a sympathy for the "little guy," even one accused of a crime. During the Warren years, he would be found on the majority side in practically every major decision expanding the rights of persons accused of crimes. The First Amendment plays an important role in making ours a free society, but the Fourth, Fifth, and Sixth Amendments help keep it a just one as well.

In fact, Douglas had anticipated the direction the Court would take. In 1942, for example, he, Black, and Murphy dissented in *Betts* v. *Brady*, in which a majority held that a state did not have to provide counsel to an indigent defendant on trial for a felony; twenty-one years later, a unanimous Court came around to his view in the famous *Gideon* decision. In a 1958 dissent in *Crooker* v. *California*, Douglas argued that criminal suspects should have access to counsel during interrogation, a view the Court later adopted; and Douglas fittingly wrote the majority opinion extending the right to counsel to misdemeanor cases in *Argersinger* v. *Hamlin* (1972).

Charges that the Court had gone "soft" on criminals struck him as absurd, and the first letter in this section, written at the beginning of the Court's expansion of rights for the accused, summed up his philosophy well. A society does not suffer, but benefits, when it treats those accused of criminal or civil deviancy with fairness.

To Irwin M. Jones

January 29, 1959

Dear Irwin:

... Whenever a person who carries a belief that is currently unpopular or even obnoxious to the prevailing point of view, or who is thought guilty of a repulsive criminal act, is shrouded with protections to which he is entitled under our scheme of things, a protest is usually sounded. That protest often comes from those who, standing under the banner of patriotism or public safety, fail to realize that the system which they seek to protect retains its vitality only as long as its basic principles are scrupulously honored. A person accused of a crime is entitled to all the safeguards given to defendants no matter how heinous the crime may be. . . .

These are the principles which recent decisions upheld. Rather than serving to destroy our country from within, I think they stand as landmarks in the fight to preserve the values upon which our society was originally conceived.

To Tom C. Clark

January 25, 1962

This last weekend at a social occasion I saw Attorney General Stanley Mosk[1] of California and his wife. He said out of the blue "Thank the good Lord for *Mapp* v. *Ohio.* "[2] I asked him what he meant and he went on to give an interesting account . . . which I thought I would pass on to you.

He said that the California Supreme Court decision in the Cahan case[3] was four to three and since it was decided, there had been two vacancies on the Court and two new appointments. He said that Phil Gibson[4] and the others who were for the Cahan opinion held their breath until the nominees took office and until they could find out where these nominees stood on Cahan. It so happened that one of the two nominees was for the Cahan decision and one was against it. So far as the Supreme Court of California went, Mosk said that it was barely holding its own.

The newspaper campaign, however, against the Cahan decision, continued unabated. Mosk said that with the system of elective judges they have in California, pressure on the trial courts was very, very great not to apply the Cahan case or to find there were more exceptions to it, or in other words, try to get around it. . . . He mentioned in addition to the newspaper pressure, the pressure of the head of the police in Los Angeles, a man named Parker who, I understand, is a lawyer and very vocal.

The result of *Mapp* v. *Ohio*, according to Mosk, is to take the pressure off the local judges to create exceptions and to follow the exclusionary rule and all its ramifications.

---

1. Mosk (1912–) himself became a justice of the California Supreme Court in 1964.

2. 367 U.S. 643 (1961) applied the Fourth Amendment to the states and held that the exclusionary rule (long in effect in federal cases) prohibited the introduction in state courts of evidence seized in violation of the Fourth Amendment.

3. In *People* v. *Cahan*, 44 Cal.2d 434 (1955), the California Supreme Court had adopted the exclusionary rule on the basis of the state constitution.

4. Phil Sheridan Gibson (19[?]–1984) was then chief justice of the California Supreme Court.

To William Joseph Brennan, Jr.

October 30, 1964

Dear Bill:

In No. 6—*Henry* v. *Mississippi*, [1] I am inclined to join your dissent, although I said at the Conference that I would go along with a dismissal.

Your last paragraph, however, bothers me . . . . Couldn't you indicate that if we dismiss, the case most assuredly will be back here in federal habeas corpus? You might refer to the fact that our Miscellaneous Docket has been increasing at a rapid rate and that one of the lessons it teaches is that we should, where possible, let the state courts resolve the issues.

It may be that Mississippi justice is so blind that this man could get no possible relief. But it is rather difficult to make that assumption. Certainly in this case he won a victory the first time around, and maybe he would win again if the case were remanded, as you suggest, for a hearing.

I guess what I am asking for is a little elaboration . . . and making more explicit what the nature of the problem is from the point of view of efficient judicial administration. [2]

---

1. 379 U.S. 443 (1965) involved a procedural question of when federal rights could be asserted.

2. Brennan evidently reworked the paragraph; the final version urged state courts to explore federal claims during the regular trial. He also added a footnote that federal habeas corpus claims had increased in federal courts 85.5 percent from 1963 to 1964.

To Thomas P. Murphy[1]

March 9, 1967

Dear Mr. Murphy:
I have your letter of February 28 about my *Miranda* article.[2] . . . I am sorry you think it's still too complex.

I am not only sorry; I am disturbed. I am upset not because it's my piece, but because the country needs to know about *Miranda.* Whether the reader agrees with it or not is not so important as understanding of its roots.

Think reaches a sophisticated audience. If they can't understand what you and I wrote, who can? If your clientele is beyond understanding, what hope is there in the entire Bill of Rights?

. . . Surely *Miranda* can be explained in terms of the stream of our history. Even so, many will not agree with it. But that's not important. The important thing is for people to take a look at the roots of the Fifth and Sixth Amendments. . . .

------

1. The editor of THINK, an in-house publication of IBM.

2. *Miranda* v. *Arizona,* 384 U.S. 436 (1966), was the highly controversial case in which the Court ruled that police had to inform suspects of their rights, or else statements taken in the absence of that knowledge would not be admissible in evidence. It was also highly unusual for a member of the Court to explain one of its decisions this way.

Memorandum for the Files

March 17, 1969

The above case,[1] which was announced Monday, March 10, resulted in a long series of conferences between the Department of Justice, the FBI and the CIA. On March 12 it was decided someone representing the Attorney General should come to see the Chief Justice, and then it was decided that perhaps that was not appropriate. So it was suggested that the public relations man from Justice, Mr. Jack Landau, who had a slight acquaintance with Justice Brennan, should come to see Justice Brennan.

Justice Brennan immediately took him in to talk with the Chief Justice, because it pertained to the Department of Justice's threat to the Court that something terrible would happen to the Court unless it changed its ruling in the *Alderman* case.

This is the first instance in the memory of anyone connected with the Court at the present time of the Executive Branch making threats to the Court.

It came out in the discussion of Mr. Landau with Justice Brennan and the Chief Justice that either the FBI or the CIA had been tapping all of the embassies in Washington—i.e., 109 of them. Later in a telephone call Mr. Landau reduced that figure from 109 to 46 active continuous taps, as distinguished from those made occasionally.

The embarrassment to the Executive Branch is the disclosure of the fact that they have been tapping embassies. But the disclosure was not made by the Court but by Graham in a NEW YORK TIMES article, an article which now appears to have been planted by Kleindienst,[2] the Deputy Attorney General.

None of the horrible fears and imaginary difficulties mentioned in Graham's article were adverted to even indirectly by the Solicitor General[3] when he argued the case. And the fact, of course, that the embassies are wiretapped has nothing to do with the legal nature of the problem.

Apart from national security cases (these are very few and far between in this Court), the wiretaps involve a miscellaneous run of crimes including the so-called draft evasion by Cassius Clay.[4] The fact that an embassy wire was the wire that was tapped has no bearing upon the Fourth Amendment problem of whether there should be disclosure or non-disclosure to the defendant.

On this the Court is eight to one, the one being Justice Black, who has felt all along that wiretapping and electronic surveillance are not covered by the Fourth Amendment at all. But the others, including Fortas and Harlan who made an exception only in cases of national security prosecutions, would require full disclosure to the defendant of the material obtained on the tap.

So the representations of Landau of this split court decision were wholly misinformed. Apparently the Department of Justice had not read the decision very carefully.

But in any event, Landau's specific threats made to the Chief Justice were that they would get laws passed by the Congress which would change the rule of admissibility of wiretaps and the processing of them during a trial, or they would get a law passed which would take away from the Court appellate jurisdiction of any case involving the constitutionality of wiretapping.[5]

It seems pretty apparent that Kleindienst, and perhaps Mitchell[6] himself, has a cause and the cause is to give the Court as much trouble as possible. So this is probably the opening salvo of a long and intense barrage.

The Chief Justice told Landau that the way to present the views of the Department of Justice was through a petition for rehearing, and that the Court would consider it, not on the argument advanced by the Attorney General and Kleindienst and Landau, but on the basis of the points of law that they may be willing to discuss in the petition for rehearing; and that the political considerations Landau was talking about were wholly irrelevant to any decision the Court would make.

Landau replied that the Solicitor General is hard at work on a petition for certiorari and that it would be filed soon.[7]

It is pretty clear that the Department of Justice has picked on a group who will not be panicked or frightened or pushed around and that it is headed for great trouble.

I asked the Chief Justice during this special conference held today whether he had asked Landau about the bug which I am sure exists in our conference room.

He said no, but he had asked whether his office (the Chief Justice's) was bugged, and Landau, expressing great surprise and astonishment, held up his hands and said certainly not.

------

1. *Alderman* v. *United States,* 394 U.S. 165 (1969), held that a homeowner whose house was subject to illegal electronic surveillance of conversations had standing to challenge any evidence obtained, whether or not he participated in the conversations.

2. Richard Gordon Kleindienst (1923–), then deputy, served as attorney general from 1972 to 1973 and was later indicted for perjury resulting from the Watergate scandals.

3. Erwin Nathan Griswold (1904–), longtime professor and sometime dean of the Harvard Law School, served as solicitor general from 1967 to 1973.

4. Newspaper stories indicated that the Justice Department had run wiretaps on Cassius Marcellus Clay, later known as Muhammad Ali, three-time world heavyweight boxing champion, who claimed draft exemption because of his newly adopted religion.

5. This "threat" makes very little sense. Congress always has power to limit

the Court's jurisdiction, but the Court has the power to review those statutes. Moreover, it is questionable whether the Court could be precluded from hearing challenges involving constitutionally protected rights.

6. John N. Mitchell served as Nixon's attorney general; he later went to jail for his part in the Watergate scandals.

7. The Court did not rehear the case.

Part III

A Very Public Justice

Chapter 8

Politics

THERE ARE, of course, politicians on the Supreme Court; one might say that only politicians ever get appointed to the bench. It should not surprise us that judges, despite their lip service to a strict separation of powers, continue to engage in political activities. Joseph Story drafted legislation which his good friend Daniel Webster then introduced into Congress; John McLean sought the Democratic presidential nomination in every election from 1832 to 1860; David Davis left the bench to become a senator, and Charles Evans Hughes to run for president. Even Louis D. Brandeis, whom many considered a model of judicial rectitude, advised both Woodrow Wilson and Franklin Roosevelt from the bench, and through surrogates played an active role in New Deal affairs. It would, in fact, be surprising if men and women who have been successful politicians suddenly abandoned this interest when they donned the black robe.

Douglas, who as SEC chairman had been an influential figure in Washington and a confidant of the President, had no intention of departing from the corridors of power. He knew he had to be more circumspect, but so long as he maintained his friendship with Roosevelt, Douglas could make his views known in the White House.

A far more difficult question is that of Douglas's personal ambitions. Within a single decade he had gained a national reputation as a scholar, become Sterling Professor of Law at Yale at age 32, joined the SEC and become its chairman at 38, and then had been named to the Supreme Court at 40. While for someone like Felix Frankfurter the nomination had come as the logical culmination of a career, Douglas might well have viewed his new position as a roadblock to a blossoming political future, a premature elevation out of the political arena. As he told some friends, "I'm too young to go on the Court."

From the time he joined the Court until the early fifties, Douglas's name figured prominently in the rumors surrounding every presidential election. Roosevelt seriously considered Douglas for the vice presidential nomination in 1944, but party leaders managed to steer the convention to Harry Truman. Privately Douglas would have welcomed this opportunity, although publicly he continued to insist that he had no ambitions other than to be a good justice, and he reaffirmed this view to the Brethren. In 1946, Truman offered Douglas the Interior Department, a position which appealed to him because of his conservationist ideas and which would have set him up for a serious run at political office in 1948. But Chief Justice Stone convinced Douglas that he owed it to the Brethren not to leave the Court at the time.

Then in 1948 Truman did offer the vice presidential slot, and Douglas declined for a number of reasons. Like most of the country, he did not believe Truman could win, so why leave the prestige and security of the Court to go onto a losing ticket? Moreover, Douglas had none of the affection and respect for Truman that he had for Roosevelt, and thought the man from Missouri to be second-rate. "Why be a number two man to a number two man?" was how Douglas's friend, Tommy Corcoran, described the Justice's views. Finally, on the personal side, his first marriage was falling apart, and at that time a divorced person had little hope of winning high elective office in the United States.

But because Douglas did not leave the bench does not mean that he remained apolitical. He spoke out, as no other justice of this century has done, in his speeches and writings on every important issue of his day. Privately, he pestered public officials to name his friends to office, efforts which for the most part failed.

To James P. Gifford[1]

May 29, 1939

My dear Jim:

I have your letter of May 12 relative to James A. Bough, who is seeking an appointment as Judge of the District Court of the Virgin Islands.

I personally adopted the policy when I took my seat on the Court of not recommending any one for any job in the government. That is a resolute policy to which I do not think I can start making exceptions. . . .

---

1. Assistant to the dean of Columbia Law School.

To Felix Frankfurter

July 2, 1940

Dear Felix:

There is considerable talk in Washington about putting me on the ticket [with Roosevelt in the fall presidential election]. I discount it very much. I do not really think it will come to anything. But it is sufficiently active to be disturbing. It is disturbing because I want none of it. I want to stay where I am. This line to you is to ask you, should the matter come your way, to scotch it. You need not be told any reasons. You know hosts of them—from the ones Brandeis would give, on down. I am *most* serious about this—probably more serious than the possibilities justify. But I write you just in case!

To Franklin Delano Roosevelt

January 3, 1941

Jerry Frank told me today that he would accept an appointment to the CCA in NY even subject to the condition that he would at any time step down if Patterson[1] wanted his old position back.

I did not tell him of my conversation with you. When he raised the question, I said that the position might not be unconditionally vacant. It was then that he expressed ready agreement.

I thought you should know this, as Jerry said he would try to see you soon to discuss his personal plans.

He would really be "tops" in CCA; and he would render grand service even if he were there only for a year or so.[2]

---

1. Robert Porter Patterson (1891–1952) had stepped down from the Second Circuit Court of Appeals to join the War Department, first as assistant secretary and then as secretary.

2. Frank enjoyed a long and distinguished tenure on the bench; Patterson stepped down as secretary of war in 1947 but did not return to the federal judiciary.

To Francis T. Maloney[1]

January 14, 1944

Dear Frank:

A few nights ago I attended a small dinner here in town which started as a purely social affair. It turned out, however, as an occasion to propose that I start a drive for either the Presidential or Vice-Presidential nomination. A person from New York whom I had met through a mutual friend wanted to raise funds for that purpose and to start an organization to get busy on it.

I said at once that I would not give my approval, that I had no political ambitions, that I wanted to stay on the Court for the rest of my life, that I would not authorize any such undertaking. I feel quite confident that that will be the end of the matter so far as the person in question is concerned.

But since in the years before I came on the Court you and I had been closely associated in various public projects, I thought it possible that the person who had approached me might also approach you. In case that came to pass I wanted you to have the facts and to know that I am not a candidate for any office, that my sole desire is to remain on the Court until I reach retirement, that any proposal to launch openly or silently any campaign for me is wholly without my authority and contrary to my desire, and that I do not think it would comport with judicial standards for one on the Court to nurture political ambitions.

---

1. Maloney (1894–1945), a friend of WOD's ever since he had moved to Connecticut, served as senator from that state from 1935 until his death.

To Harry S. Truman

February 23, 1946

My dear Mr. President:

Five days have passed since you offered me the post of Secretary of the Interior.[1] I hesitate to delay any longer a reply, not only because of the urgency of the matter to you but also because delay only generates rumors and speculation which bear not at all on the merits of the proposal.

During these five days I have given the matter my most earnest consideration. I have discussed the matter with the Chief Justice [Stone] and with some of my colleagues. The resignation of a member of the Court in the middle of a Term—when the Court already lacks a full bench[2]—would create serious difficulties. I have finally, though most reluctantly, concluded that in fairness to my colleagues and to the Court, I should not take that course.

Against this is the strong pull of the deep affection I have for you and the desire to help you with your present tremendous problems. I understand perfectly that the problems which confront a President after a war are even greater than those arising during a war. I appreciate more than I can adequately state the confidence you expressed in me that I could help you with them. . . .

My reluctance and regret at this conclusion are not because I desire to leave the Court, but because the call to a different service, coming from you, makes a strong appeal to me—an appeal that comes not only from my affection for you but from the gallant fight you are waging in a cynical post-war world to place human rights first and make our victory real.[3]

---

1. In *Court Years*, 288, WOD mistakenly says this offer came in 1947 and claims that he told Truman he would leave the Court for the cabinet, but only if the president named him as secretary of state.

2. Associate Justice Robert H. Jackson was absent from the bench from the summer of 1945 to the fall of 1946 while he served as the American prosecutor at the Nuremberg War Crimes trial.

3. Truman replied two days later that "although nothing in the world would have pleased me more than to have you as a member of the official family," he understood the necessity for WOD to remain on the bench. However, he added, "I hope you will remember that I expect to discuss a great many matters with you, which I believe will be a great asset to me."

To Fred Rodell[1]

April 9, 1948

Dear Fred:

Yesterday Miss Evelyn Brand of Friends of Democracy, Inc. came in to see me. She indicated that she had been working for her group in an effort to get a Democratic ticket of Eisenhower and Douglas. She said she was sure, on the basis of certain confidential information she had, that Truman would withdraw a few days before the convention. These plans that she spoke of are being perfected in order to draft Eisenhower as the Presidential nominee. She said it was indispensable that I run with Eisenhower because otherwise the so-called independent voters would not vote for him. She said that the voters did not know what Eisenhower stood for but that he was a sure winner, although he needed some liberal coloration. She was very anxious that I agree to run with him. She said she had confidential information that he would run if drafted.

I told her that I had no political aspirations or ambitions and that she should eliminate me completely from her political calculations.

---

1. Rodell (1907–1980) began his long tenure at the Yale Law School two years after WOD arrived there; he wrote widely on the Supreme Court and its business.

To Leland F. Hess [1]

July 3, 1948

Dear Leland:

I am writing you this letter at this time because I understand you will be leaving shortly for Philadelphia to attend the Democratic Convention. You asked me the other day in Portland what my reaction was to the current talk about nominating me in the first or second place on the Democratic ticket. I am putting my answer in writing, so that there may be no doubt where I stand.

I have not been and am not now a candidate for either office. I have done all in my power to stop individuals or groups from promoting me for either office. The rumors, however, persist that I am available and will allow my name to go before the convention, and that I will actively or passively seek one of the nominations.

These are not the facts. I am not available. No one is authorized to promote my candidacy. I have but one ambition and that is to stay on the Court and serve my country there to the best of my ability. And I am convinced that it would be a great disservice to the Court for one of its members to seek political office while he remains on it. It was that reason which caused me to keep my name from being presented to the Convention in 1944. It is the same reason why I am taking the same step through you at this time.

---

1. Hess was a Portland, Oregon, attorney; according to woo's memoirs, Lee and his brother Henry had tried to get woo to accept the vice presidential nomination in 1944.

To Harry S. Truman

July 31, 1948

Dear Mr. President:

You put me a most difficult question about two weeks ago.[1] My decision was not an easy one. Basic in my whole thinking was the thought that politics had never been my profession and that I could serve my country best where I am. I weighed the pros and cons many times before I called you back. I did want you to know that I greatly appreciated the confidence you expressed in me. I will always cherish our friendship. I assure you it would have been a pleasure to stand shoulder to shoulder with you in the fray.[2]

---

1. Truman had invited woo to be his running mate in the 1948 presidential election; see *Court Years*, 288–90.

2. On August 9, Truman acknowledged this note and affirmed his confidence that Senator Alben Barkley of Kentucky would make a fine running mate. Truman also indicated that he would wage a "give 'em hell" campaign, declaring that "Congress has certainly left a miserable record here and I don't believe they will be able to explain it to the people."

To James Paul Warburg[1]

January 21, 1952

Dear Mr. Warburg:

I have your letter of January 18th and find it difficult to put into words my deep and sincere appreciation for the sentiments which you expressed. I am greatly honored by the letter and by the confidence you have expressed in me.

These are perilous days in which no one is entitled to do a wholly selfish act. The question of where a particular individual functions

the best for the common good is a difficult one. There are many
things in the stream of events which I would like to change and some
which perhaps I could change. But the Court is a custodian of an
important tradition. If we can keep the tradition alive, perhaps that
is as great a contribution as one can expect to make.

The stupid things we are doing abroad are largely the result of
the fear and orthodoxy that have beset us at home. That is the reason
why I have concluded, after long reflection, that my place in public
life is on the Court.

---

1. Warburg (1896–1969), an author and member of the famous banking
family, had written WOD urging him to seek the Democratic presidential nomination; WOD received a number of letters to this same effect, and he answered all of
them in a similar manner.

To Students for Democratic Action [1]

February 11, 1952

Dear Friends:

The wonderful letter which you folks sent me, dated January 30th,
moved me deeply. I find it difficult to put in words the feeling that
I have for your expression of confidence and good will. I appreciate
more than I can tell you your kindness in writing me and your
forthright proposal that I enter the primaries in Ohio.

I have given this subject of my own personal career in public life
a lot of consideration. These are very difficult and dangerous times,
and the peril I think is much greater than the people in America
appreciate. At least that is my feeling after traveling Asia. I am
greatly alarmed that the political trend is going very strongly against
America in the world. The greatest thing for Americans to fear, in
my view, is the alignment of the political balance of the world
against us. And that would easily happen if Asia, which has the bulk
of the people of the world and the bulk of the wealth of the world,
is lost.

I know all these things and feel them deeply. Yet I also know
politics, and I know how perishable they have been and will continue
to be. The service to be rendered from the Court is a long and

continuous one, and I have concluded that it is the place where I can best serve my country. I state all this to you so that you may have an inkling of the considerations which have caused me to reach this decision. . . .

---

1.   At Antioch College in Ohio.

To John La Houd[1]

March 6, 1956

Dear Mr. La Houd:

I am honored that you should think of me as a candidate for the Presidency at your mock Democratic political convention to be held on your campus April 13th and 14th. An acceptance on my part would be wholly compatible in theory with my position on the Court, as your convention is only a mock one. But in view of the state of public opinion in the cases before us, I fear that if I sent you a statement of acceptance it might be misunderstood by a substantial number of people. Nevertheless I thank you for your kind thought of me.

---

1.   Secretary of the Omega Pi Alpha fraternity at Syracuse University.

To Lyndon Baines Johnson

May 21, 1959

Dear Lyndon:

As I told you over the phone, I saw Dugger[1] on Tuesday, May 19. He said he was writing articles for The Nation and Harper's promoting you for the Presidency.[2] He asked if it was true that I was for you. I said it was true; and I went on to tell him (1) how important it was to get you better known at the grass roots; (2) how you were able to hold the party together and get all-around progress in civil rights, etc. . . .

I told him to get the platform on which you ran for Congress in 1937 and feature it—that it is as fresh and challenging today as it was then. . . . If you think of anything I can do, please let me know.

---

1. Ronnie E. Dugger (1930–) edited the *Texas Observer;* he later wrote *The Politician: The Life and Times of Lyndon Johnson* (New York: Norton, 1982).

2. No articles by Dugger on Johnson appeared in these magazines.

To Edmund Gerald Brown [1]

November 3, 1959

Dear Pat:

This is a letter to you about one of my former outstanding law clerks, Stanley H. Sparrowe,[2] who I think would be an outstanding judge in one of your trial or appellate courts. Mr. Sparrowe was my law clerk for the 1947 Term. He served with distinction, being one of the ablest men I know that Boalt Hall[3] has turned out.

Since leaving Washington, Mr. Sparrowe has been practicing in Oakland. He is the man I have chosen to select for me each year a law clerk who is a graduate of the law schools in the Ninth Circuit. He has complete control. I take the man he selects, and he has rendered outstanding service in culling the law schools in the Ninth Circuit, and finding the most promising young man. This is a public service of high order.

Mr. Sparrowe is, I believe, a Republican. But I know you have been appointing men and women from both parties, and I did want you to know that this is a man in whom you could have the utmost confidence. He is a person of fine character who would serve his State with great distinction. His politics have never been highly partisan. He has been more interested in the men who have been running than in party labels.

He has such a fine record of achievement that I thought I should bring his name to your attention in case there was a vacancy in his part of the State for which you needed a man of distinction and ability.

---

1. Brown (1905–), the highly popular attorney general of California from 1951 to 1958, was then elected to two terms as governor of the state.

2. Sparrowe had contacted WOD about this matter on October 20, and WOD immediately told him that he would be glad to write to Brown, provided that Sparrowe sound out the situation first. He wanted to make sure that the vacancy had not already been promised, or that Brown would only appoint a Democrat. Sparrowe did not receive an appointment.

3. The law school of the University of California, Berkeley.

To John Fitzgerald Kennedy

November 10, 1960

Dear Jack:

It was a wonderful victory[1] and I send you my heartfelt congratulations.

About a week before the election, the Soviet Ambassador[2] asked to see me. I had a long talk with him, a talk that lasted an hour or an hour and a half and when I finished and returned to my office, I reported the substance of it to Chip Bohlen[3] in the State Department who said he would pass it on to Herter.[4]

The Soviet Ambassador was obviously under instructions from his government to find out how the election was going and who was going to win. I told him you would win by at least 400 electoral votes. (I wasn't very far wrong.[5])

He then said that his government had decided not to endeavor to conduct any more conversations with the Eisenhower Administration because their relationships had worsened and there did not seem to be any prospect under Eisenhower of making an advance toward a solution of any of the difficulties between the two nations. He said that when the election was over, he and his government thought it very important to start informal exploratory talks at once. As he put it, these talks would be confidential and unofficial. But he thought it was important for his government and our government to try to reach some common ground for the solution of at least some of the irritating and pressing problems between now and the time the new President was inaugurated.

He repeated over and over again that he thought it would be too bad if the two countries let the two months between election and the inauguration pass without these exploratory talks.

He did not state what items he thought should be on the agenda.

He left the impression that the agenda could include what either government thought proper to bring up.

He repeated his government's great concern lest the cold war break out into some kind of hostility. He expressed real dread at the thought of any nuclear conflict.

When I reported this conversation to Chip Bohlen, he said that the Soviet Ambassador had talked to several other people along the same line. Who these other people are, I do not know. But I had the distinct impression that I was perhaps the third one he had approached.

He did not ask me to carry any message but he spoke with such apparent sincerity and concern that I thought I should relate the conversation to you for what it may be worth.

Needless to say, I am always at your service.

---

1. Kennedy had just won the 1960 presidential election.

2. Mikhail Alexeyevich Menshikov.

3. Charles Eustis Bohlen (1904–1974), a career foreign service officer, was then special assistant for Soviet affairs to the secretary of state.

4. Christian Archibald Herter (1895–1967), a former governor of Massachusetts, served as secretary of state from 1959 to the end of the Eisenhower administration.

5. Kennedy won the presidential election by only 118,574 popular votes out of 68 million cast, but he had a comfortable margin in the Electoral College of 303 to 219.

To Robert Francis Kennedy

December 16, 1960

Dear Bobby:

Wonderful congratulations on the news of your appointment as Attorney General.

That must be a great relief—having the decision made. You will do a fine job and be a great credit to the Administration. It is great to know that you and Ethel will be in town at least for a while longer.

I hope you don't forget what we talked about and the other prospects for your own personal plans, come another year or so.

Meanwhile, my warm and affectionate regards.

To Robert Francis Kennedy

December 27, 1960

Dear Bobby:

I am very much concerned about the Under-Secretary of the Interior.

Stu Udall[1] is a wonderful choice as Secretary. But some really bad actors are manipulating to get in the Under-Secretary's spot.

It seemed to me from this vantage point that all of the problems would be over and Stu would have a wonderful working partner if Dewey Anderson were named as Under-Secretary.[2]

---

1. Stewart Lee Udall (1920–   ), a Tucson lawyer, served as secretary of the interior under both Kennedy and Johnson.

2. Kennedy named former senator Frank Briggs and James K. Carr to the two undersecretary positions in the Interior Department.

To Robert Francis Kennedy

December 30, 1960

Dear Bobby:

I think I have a real find for you for Assistant Attorney General in charge of the Criminal Division. He is Professor Abraham S. Goldstein[1] who is a full professor at Yale Law School. . . . He is in his middle or late thirties. He once was a clerk for Judge David L. Bazelon.[2] He is one of the most enlightened young men I know, very personable, very able, and a Kennedy fan.[3]

---

1. Goldstein (1925–   ) joined the Yale faculty in 1956 after practicing law in Washington; he served as dean from 1970 to 1975 and wrote several books on criminal law. He did not join the administration.

2. David Lionel Bazelon (1909–   ) joined the Circuit Court of Appeals for the District of Columbia in 1949 and was chief judge from 1962 until he took senior status in 1979. He was one of the most liberal of all federal judges during this time.

3. WOD evidently thought that his longtime friendship with the Kennedy family entitled his recommendations to special consideration. He peppered Robert Kennedy with many similar letters, but it appears that the administration ignored all of them.

To Lyndon Baines Johnson

August 26, 1961

My dear Lyndon:

To use a phrase of the late Fred Vinson, I was not "bitter" when I wrote you last nor am I now "bitter." I am for my friends—right or wrong. My only effort is to put them right.[1]

The Pakistan conversation to which you would not listen was in 1951. It was at Lister Hill's home.[2] I was fresh out of Pakistan and full of news. You let me talk about two minutes when you jumped up and said "That's just like Texas." You held the floor for the rest of the evening, obviously not interested in Pakistan. I never was able to get back to you; and I know you never read my books. . . .

My test of an overseas regime is highly personal. I ask "If Lyndon Johnson were a citizen of that country, where would he be?'

In the old Pakistan I knew, you would be pulling the various political parties together and making a viable society. Under Ayub you would be in prison; and you would be in prison if you were a Taiwanese under Chiang Kai-Shek. . . .

Only the Lyndon Johnsons of Pakistan can turn back the tides of communism. The Ayubs command armies; the Lyndon Johnsons command the hearts and minds of men. . . . When the Lyndon Johnsons of Pakistan are back in control, the sun will rise in Pakistan again.

---

1. WOD had written Johnson on August 2, warning that America should not rely on Field Marshall Mohammed Ayub Khan (1907–1974), who had seized control of Pakistan in a bloodless coup in 1958. He retained power until ousted in 1969.

2. Lister Hill (1894–1984) represented Alabama in the Senate from 1938 to 1969.

To Stephen A. Mitchell[1]

May 19, 1962

Dear Steve:

I have been greatly puzzled and somewhat distressed as to the lack of consideration you have received for judicial appointment. The many times I have talked about this I have always had a very warm reception and very cordial response. But the long drawn-out silence has become rather ominous. So I took the liberty of pigeon-holing the man close to Bobby [Kennedy] who has been processing some of these vacancies. He did not want his name to be used but this is the information that I discovered. It is very disheartening information but something I thought you should know.

I am told that in view of the credentials you have and your high qualifications that your case was very carefully considered and proc-essed but that both Senators have expressed themselves to the De-partment of Justice in the negative. In other words they have said thumbs-down on Steve Mitchell. . . .

I hesitated for some days to write you. But I decided I should do so—not only to get it off my chest—but to let you know the facts. The judgment of this man at Justice was there was no chance at all of your being appointed either to the District Court or to the Court of Appeals. This has nothing to do with the merits. It is merely a political blockade.

You will know better whether anything can be done than I. But in view of this report, I think . . . this the time for your friends in New Mexico who are important to . . . start becoming indignant and doing some pounding of the table and screaming.

You should not of course bring in the source of this information because that might have some repercussions in Justice and I do want to protect my informant. . . .

---

1. A lawyer in Taos, New Mexico, and a friend of woD.

To Edmund Gerald Brown

November 13, 1962

Dear Pat:

May I make a suggestion concerning the forthcoming appointment to the California Supreme Court?

I am bold enough to ask the question because several times you have asked me about the qualifications of certain men for judicial work.

My suggestion for this vacancy is Warren Christopher,[1] who was my law clerk during the 1949 Term.

I think if all the law clerks of all the Justices during my 23 years on the Court were sorted and classified, Christopher would be in the first ten. He is unusually able, and is young and industrious. He is also a person of the highest character. But equally important, he has a liberal, progressive outlook on law; he is not wedded to the cliches of bygone days. He views the Constitution as a living force that embodies our democratic ideals. And in his construction of law he has a high regard for human rights.

---

1.   Warren Minor Christopher (1925–   ), a successful Los Angeles attorney, was well-known to Brown, since he served as special counsel to the governor for a number of years. He did not get the judicial appointment. Christopher did serve as deputy attorney general under Lyndon Johnson and as secretary of state in the Carter administration.

To Nelson Aldrich Rockefeller [1]

March 22, 1968

Dear Nelson:
I read with a feeling of sadness your announcement that you would not run in the 1968 campaign. I think you would have brought a brand new dimension to the thinking of our people.

This has not even the slightest note of criticism, because these decisions are highly personal and no one can make them but the person involved.

---

1.   Rockefeller (1917–1979) had been governor of New York from 1959 to 1973 and vice president under Gerald Ford. He had made several unsuccessful bids for the Republican nomination but realized early on in 1968 that he would be unable to defeat Richard Nixon.

To Lewis B. Merrifield [1]

April 16, 1968

Dear Lew:
There had been a few minor indications that LBJ would not run, so his announcement did not come as a total surprise to me.[2]

But who knows—maybe the decision not to run is the best possible way to run. If things between now and August are handled in a masterful way which tends to make the others look like amateurs, it might not be beyond possibility to have a real draft. In other words, I don't know what the announcement meant!

1. A professor at the UCLA Law Center.
2. On March 31, Johnson had announced on nationwide television that he would not accept renomination for the presidency. He wanted to devote his efforts to ending the war in Vietnam and did not want partisan politics to intrude in that process. By then, of course, Johnson's popularity had sunk to an all-time low, and a number of polls indicated that not only would he lose the general election, but might not even receive the Democratic nomination.

To Isabelle Lynn[1]

November 7, 1968
Dear Isabelle:
I know a lady in my office who has spent years hoping that something terrible would happen to a man we can call Tricky Dick.[2] She now realizes that if anything terrible happens to him we will have one, Spiro [Agnew], on our hands.
   Let this be a lesson to you also!

1. A longtime friend and summer neighbor of WOD and co-owner of the Double K Ranch in Goose Prairie, Washington.
2. Richard Milhous Nixon, whom WOD had long detested, had just been elected President of the United States.

To Patricia Hanzook[1]

January 9, 1970
Dear Patricia:
I have your letter asking whether an elected official should vote on issues as the majority of his constituents believe or according to his own belief.
   I had assumed that it was part of the American tradition that an elected official be independent, using his best judgment in the exercise of the responsibilities of his office.

1. A high school student in nearby Maryland.

To Edward Moore Kennedy

February 4, 1976

Dear Senator:

I will try to keep in touch with you during the next few months as the big problems of the day appear. Both Mrs. Douglas and I hope you go for the White House.[1] I know it is a hard decision but there is such a thing as a stream of history and that stream is now at your doorstep.

Mrs. Douglas, as you know, is a practicing attorney here in the District. Do not hesitate to draft her anytime. We're all Kennedy people in this corner.

---

1. Kennedy was then a semiactive candidate for the Democratic nomination, but he later withdrew when it became apparent that Governor Carter of Georgia would capture the prize.

To Jimmy Carter

November 15, 1976

Dear Mr. President:

I get many letters and calls from people who think that I'm closely associated with you and they think I can influence you to put them in your new cabinet or give them an important job in your new administration.

You have no reason to remember me but I was told years ago that you were the new leader of the south and that you were a person of great ability worthy of holding any office in the government.

Some of the men who have contacted me are ex-law clerks of mine and they are all people I know intimately. You may have great need for all of them or no need for any of them. The purpose of this letter is to inquire as to what I should tell them. Whom should I ask them to see or write?

Chapter 9

Environmentalist

IF WILLIAM DOUGLAS had any lifelong passion, it had to be the outdoors. He wrote several books on mountains and wilderness, and there is a lyric strain that runs through nearly all of them. As a boy partially crippled by polio, he regained his health through long and arduous hikes in the Cascade Mountains near his home. The mountains came to mean not only physical renewal, but mental well-being also. He later wrote in his memoirs what being on the mountains meant to him:

> As I walked the ridge that evening, I could hear the chinook on distant ridges before it reached me. Then it touched the sage at my feet and made it sing. It brushed my cheek, warm and soft. It ran its fingers through my hair and rippled away in the darkness. It was a friendly wind, friendly to man throughout time. It was beneficent. . . .
>
> It became for me that night a measure of the kindliness of the universe to man, a token of the hospitality that awaits man when he puts foot on this earth. It became for me a promise of the fullness of life to him who, instead of shaking his fist at the sky, looks to it for health and strength and courage.
>
> That night I felt at peace. I felt that I was part of the universe, a companion to the friendly chinook that brought the promise of life and adventure. That night, I think, there first came to me the germ of a philosophy of life: that man's best measure of the universe is in his hopes and his dreams, not his fears, that man is

a part of a plan, only a fraction of which he, perhaps, can ever comprehend.

For the rest of his life, Douglas proselytized the joys and benefits of nature. At a moment's notice he would leave for a hike, a hunt, or best of all, a fishing trip. A purist, according to one of his many fishing companions, Douglas fished primarily with dry fly and light tackle and rod. "I would rather hook a one pound rainbow with a dry fly on a 3 1/2 ounce rod," he declared, "than a four pounder with bait or hardware."

Early on Douglas realized the conflict between man's desire to dominate the earth, to expand cities and mine minerals, and the need to preserve the environment. He had no doubt on which side he stood, and in his travel and nature books he lashed out at government agencies, utility companies, large ranchers, and anyone else who despoiled the land for profit. He encouraged others to join in the fight, and he provided a highly visible and a highly vocal symbol of the struggle.

His best-known campaign, and victory, came in thwarting efforts to build a modern highway along the old Chesapeake & Ohio Canal, which runs northwest from Washington next to the Potomac River. His well-publicized hikes and annual reunions drew attention to the recreational potential for the canal, and Douglas succeeded in having the area turned into a national park in 1971. Six years later the government dedicated the area in his name.

There is, however, a certain irony about much of Douglas's crusading. The C & O is unique in that it is easily accessible to large numbers of people; on a nice day one will encounter literally hundreds of hikers, campers, joggers, bicyclists, and canoers, just the type of crowd that Douglas tried to avoid. He wanted his wilderness raw and untouched, so that it would be a challenge that only a few people could attempt. He disdained national parks that tried to make nature easy or interpreted wilderness as a "natural" amusement area. Nonetheless, his fight to preserve the less than 2 percent of the nation which remains in its pristine state captured the imagination of many people, and it may well have been his finest battle.

To Fred A. Stackpole[1]

April 29, 1937

Dear Mr. Stackpole:

. . . You can appreciate the point of view of our Association[2] that jurisdiction of the now proposed commission over low water is as important, if not more so, than its jurisdiction over high water.

There is a growing sentiment on the part of some of our members that the only effective way in which the Association can get its program of control over low water started is for the summer people on Lake Wentworth to make a boycott against the merchants of Wolfboro. I do not know whether this idea will develop or not, but the letters which I have been receiving from various summer residents are rather vehement and indicate clearly that such course is the only one for the summer residents to follow. I would like to get your thoughts and reactions on this. I do not think it would be raised as an official matter before the Association. But I would not be surprised if it gathered considerable momentum in view of the rather rough treatment and lack of interest and support which many of them feel they have received at the hands of the town.

1. An officer of the Wolfboro National Bank in Wolfboro, New Hampshire.

2. wod had purchased a summer place on Lake Wentworth near Wolfboro; the association of property owners, as happens in many places, found itself in friction with the year-round residents on a number of issues.

To Ted Powell[1]

November 29, 1946

Dear Mr. Powell:

. . . I had two interesting visits to Silver Creek this last summer. As you probably know, it runs south of Hailey, Idaho. It is a slow, meandering stream, with water from six to eighteen feet deep. It runs for miles through the valley which has very few trees except willows in it. The elevation of the stream is about 6,000 feet. There is no white water. There are three or four feet of grass, moss, etc., on the bottom. It is the most ideal stream for trout which I have seen. And while I have not seen all of the good trout spots in the

United States, this Silver Creek is by all odds the best dry-fly trout stream I have seen. The average catch will run around two pounds. You will not hook anything under one pound. There are rainbow trout in there up to fourteen pounds. You can see them and you will hook them, but you will very seldom be able to land a trout of that size in that water in view of the brush and the grass. It is very delicate fishing. We usually use a No. 14 or 16 fly. We cast upstream, quartering the creek and feed out the line with a flick of the tip of the rod. It is not at all unusual to be able to get a float with 40 or 50 yards. The best time for dry-fly fishing is at the opening of the season around July 1st or near its end in September or even early October. During the dog days of August, it is very slow for fly fishing. But at the other times, you will have during a fishing day a dozen or more fish on. The size of the fish and the light tackle necessarily mean that you lose a lot of fish. But they are there in great abundance and you will have at the end of the day as many as you possibly want. . . .

While you are in that neighborhood, you would probably want to fish Wood River, which is a fast-running stream and connects up with Silver Creek. You will catch small fish in Wood River but there are some big lunkers in there also.[2]

---

1. Fish and game editor of the *San Francisco Chronicle.*

2. WOD once told Fred Rodell that Silver Creek is "the best fly stream I have seen. . . . It's a honey. Any day you wish me to meet you at Silver Creek, I'll be there."

To Roy Rudolph [1]

June 24, 1947

My dear Roy:
. . . The Game Commission of Oregon has woefully neglected the lakes and streams of Eastern Oregon. Perhaps it was due largely to your influence that I concluded some years ago that what the lakes needed was some scientific planning. I went through them with a fish expert about six years ago and I found that many of the lakes were woefully deficient in food. The Oregon Commission has never made a study of the lakes. They have dropped fish in, indiscrimi-

nately mixing brook trout and rainbow trout. They have done no planting of food worth mentioning in Eastern Oregon. Now they contend that the lakes of Eastern Oregon are overstocked and as a result they have increased the limit. The limit on eastern brook in the Wallowa Mountains is unlimited now. That may be the answer on a few lakes but from my experience it would be the answer for only a very few. As a result of lack of planning they are not able to take care of the demands of the new tourist season. Lakes which six or seven years ago were wonderful lakes are completely fished out. One of the best streams in Eastern Oregon for trout is Minam River but they have never stocked it. You can still get some rainbow but it is way below what it should be.

So the sum of my answer to your question is that fishing in Eastern Oregon is not what it used to be. . . .

---

1. A fishing friend from Los Angeles.

To Wilbur LaRoe, Jr. [1]

September 24, 1951

Dear Mr. LaRoe:
The report of your Chicago friend about the art of rubbing muskies on the belly and quieting them is so plainly a truthful account that I cannot understand your lingering doubt. Those fish, however, were on a hook at boatside. The fish I speak of are wild, untamed, and free. It's an art to approach them under water, touch them gently, and then with the help of a sleepy under-belly massage, lift them with bare hands from the stream.[2]

I met a negro in Oklahoma City who swore he'd done it. The judge he worked for cast a disbelieving look at both of us. All of which proves, *first* that your friend from Chicago is on the road to real fishing, and *second* that not all judges know the truth when it knocks.

Come some day with a judge who does; we'll go to the mossy banked stream flowing into Long Lake in the high Wallowas. A rainbow—perhaps 16 inches long—will be waiting for us in water

two feet deep. You'll catch him with your bare hands and everyone
will start calling you a liar.

---

1.   LaRoe (1888–1957), a Washington lawyer, was active in a number of civic
affairs.
2.   wod recounts how he learned this art in *Go East*, 233.

To the Editor, the Washington Post

January 15, 1954
Dear Sir:
The discussion concerning the construction of a Parkway along the
Chesapeake & Ohio Canal[1] arouses many people. Fishermen, hunt-
ers, hikers, campers, ornithologists, and others who like to get acquainted with nature first-hand and on their own are opposed to
making a highway out of this Sanctuary.

The stretch of 185 miles of country from Washington, D.C. to
Cumberland, Maryland is one of the most fascinating and pictur-
esque in the nation. The river and its islands are part of the charm.
The cliffs, the streams, the draws, the benches and beaches, the
swamps are another part. The birds and game, the blaze of color in
the Spring and Fall, the cattails in the swamp, the blush of buds in
late Winter—these are also some of the glory of the place.

In the early twenties Mr. Justice Brandeis travelled the canal and
river by canoe to Cumberland. It was for him exciting adventure and
recreation. Hundreds of us still use this Sanctuary for hiking and
camping. It is a refuge, a place of retreat, a long stretch of quiet and
peace at the Capitol's back door—a wilderness area where man can
be alone with his thoughts, a sanctuary where he can commune with
God and with nature, a place not yet marred by the roar of wheels
and the sound of horns.

It is a place for boys and girls, men and women. One can hike
15 or 20 miles on a Sunday afternoon, or sleep on high dry ground
in the quiet of a forest, or just go and sit with no sound except water
lapping at one's feet. It is a Sanctuary for everyone who loves
woods—a Sanctuary that would be utterly destroyed by a fine two-
lane highway.

I wish the man who wrote your editorial of January 3, 1954

approving the Parkway would take time off and come with me. We would go with packs on our backs and walk the 185 miles to Cumberland. I feel that if your editor did, he would return a new man and use the power of your great editorial page to help keep this Sanctuary untouched.

One who walked the Canal its full length could plead that cause with the eloquence of a John Muir.[2] He would get to know muskrats, badgers, and fox; he would hear the roar of wind in thickets; he would see strange islands and promontories through the fantasy of fog; he would discover the glory there is in the first flower of spring, the glory there is even in a blade of grass; the whistling wings of ducks would make silence have new values for him. Certain it is that he could never acquire that understanding going 60, or even 25, miles an hour.

---

1.   wod recounted the background of his crusade to save the C & O Canal in a letter to Frederick W. Luehring on June 9, 1966:

My 189-mile hike took place in March, 1954. The C & O Canal property had come under federal ownership as a result of the B & O Railroad transferring it at an agreed upon evaluation for credit on an account to the Reconstruction Finance Corporation. This was back in the days of Franklin D. Roosevelt. It lay idle and largely untouched and unsupervised. The Park Service was not interested in it at that time. Under Eisenhower the Park Service decided it would get rid of it and fell in with the plans of the highway builders (the Bureau of Public Roads and the Maryland Highway Commission) to put a highway down the Canal which would give a water level connection between Cumberland and Washington, D.C. There was great propaganda for that kind of highway because the existing highway went up and down, up and down, between many small ridges that became slippery in wintertime.

The thing that triggered my hike was an editorial in the Washington Post which said in effect that the Post was delighted that at last some good use was to be made of the C & O Canal property. The editorial got under my skin and I wrote a letter to the Editor in which I said that I would like to challenge the man who wrote the editorial to hike the 189 miles with me because I was sure that after he had hiked its entirety he would not want to have it destroyed. Bob Estabrook of the Post said that two of them worked on it—he, and Merlo Pusey—and could the two of them accept my challenge. I said that would be fine. So the three of us planned a backpacking trip but when they wrote a news item about it, we had about 600 applications come in from people who wanted to go along. So Bob Estabrook and I got together and we sorted out those letters. First, we eliminated all women; second, we eliminated all publicists; third, we tried to select only those who had some real, legitimate interest in the outdoors. We ended up with a group of 37. That presented a problem of logistics because finding a campground for 37 people and finding wood and water for 37 people would present quite a problem. So we decided instead of backpacking we would rent a truck and have a cook and send the truck with the cook out to find a place each night to camp and haul in the water and wood necessary.

We started in Cumberland, going up by train, and walked back. Nine of us walked the whole distance. Of those nine, seven are still alive. There was tremendous news coverage—the news apparently lying in the fact that people still walk! ABC, CBS and NBC covered us every day. We had local radio interviews, etc. We got in on the eighth day and there were an estimated 50,000 people who greeted us in Georgetown.

The public interest was so great that the Director of the Park Service, Conrad Wirth, directed that restudy be made and nobody in the Park Service talked or commented on the C & O Canal until the restudy had been completed. That took a year and the Park Service came out for a park. Within two months after the hike, the Washington Post reversed itself with a ringing editorial saying the park must be preserved. Those are the highlights of the hike that I took in 1954.

2.   WOD admired Muir (1838–1914), the great naturalist who helped preserve much of the California wilds, and wrote a book for children about him, *Muir of the Mountains* (Boston: Houghton Mifflin, 1961).

To Douglas McKay[1]

April 22, 1954

My dear Mr. Secretary:

As I told you, the group that made the trek down the C & O Canal last month selected a committee to make recommendations to you, concerning the preservation and development of this national property. We call this Committee *The C & O Canal Committee;* and I am Chairman of it.

The members of the Committee have put their ideas in writing. At this time, I am not going to burden you with those individual reports, but rather, as Chairman, give you a brief Report on the preliminary recommendations of the Committee. A more detailed Report containing the views of the various members will be prepared in the near future and sent to you. The views of Mr. Robert Estabrook[2] of the Washington Post, who is a member of the Committee, have been separately stated in the Post's editorial, dated March 31, 1954.

The Committee proposes four major points:

1. The Canal property should be preserved as a recreational and historical entity.

2. The Canal property should remain a unit of the National Park System, bearing some historic name, with a budget adequate for its maintenance and supervision.

3. The Canal property should be developed as a recreational area.

4. A parkway system should be developed from Cumberland, Maryland to Washington, D.C. following existing state, county, and federal-aid roads where practicable, perhaps at places parallel to, but not on the Canal proper. This should be located wherever possible on high ground, safe from damaging flood waters, and follow routes from which spectacular views of the river can be obtained.

The ideas for the development of the Canal as a recreational area are numerous and will be elaborated upon in our detailed Report. They are in the main as follows:

1. Preservation (and repair) of the tow path for use by hikers and by cyclists, and the possible development of supplementary bridle paths.

2. Cleaning out parts of the Canal, restoration of some of the locks, and filling some additional sections with water. This is for the purpose of establishing canoe-ways with portages around the locks, and for the planting and propagation of fish.

3. Maintaining some features of the Canal as ruins of an interesting historical era, and the development of some of the sites, such as the famous Paw Paw Tunnel, as an attraction for tourists.

4. The establishment at frequent intervals (at least every ten miles) of camp sites, having shelters, pure water, fireplaces, toilet facilities, etc.

5. Acquisition by the Federal Government of additional lands, both for camp sites and for effective management and control of the entire property.

6. Preservation and expansion of some tracts, such as that which lies next to the Green Ridge State Forest downstream from Paw Paw, as an area of wild land. This would entail a cooperative project with the State of Maryland.

7. The development of access roads, which would make it possible for people to reach the Canal at many points throughout its length. There are existing access roads, some of which need improvement. Some new ones may need to be built. These access roads should be tied into the parkway system.

8. The cleaning up of the Potomac River, a program which would deal first with the sewage and industrial waste problem. The fish and wildlife potential of the Canal has hardly been tapped. This can be greatly developed, once the river is free of pollution.

The area is rich in history. It has great charm and beauty. In some of its western-most reaches it is as pretty as any country one will find east of the Rocky Mountains. It can be made an attractive tourist area, where people can come by car with their families and spend a week-end, or for a few dollars have a real vacation.

---

1. McKay (1893–1959) had been governor of Oregon before becoming secretary of the interior in the Eisenhower administration.

2. Robert Harley Estabrook (1918–) had joined the *Washington Post* in 1946 and was the editor from 1953 to 1961; he later served as chief foreign correspondent before buying a small newspaper in Lakeville, Connecticut.

To Sharon Fairley [1]

November 6, 1954

Dear Sharon:

A person's experience on a mountainside turns so much on his own personality. For myself it is a testing ground of my strength and endurance, a pitting of finite man against one of the great rigors of the universe. It is an interesting testing ground. A man—or girl— can get to know himself—or herself—on the mountain. He gets to know his inner strength—the power of the soul to add to the power of the legs and lungs.

In the solitude of the mountains—especially on the highest peaks—he is close to the heavens, close to the outer limits of the earthly zone. It is for me easy, therefore, to have communion with God and to come on understanding terms with my own being.

Other people may have different experiences. These are the essence of mine. [2]

---

1. A schoolgirl in Seattle, Washington.

2. WOD wrote of his love of mountains in his first book, which in many ways is also the first of his three autobiographical volumes, *Of Men and Mountains* (New York: Harpers, 1950).

To Merlo John Pusey[1]

April 4, 1956

Dear Merlo:

A short while ago Secretary of the Interior McKay wrote me that he and National Park Service officials had decided not to build a highway on the old canal, and would seek legislation to make the canal property a National Historic Park.

This was very good news. I think we should celebrate by getting together again.

We discussed plans for the reunion at a recent meeting of the C & O Canal Committee, and have settled on an overnight camp at Fort Frederick State Park and a dinner at the Hilltop Hotel at Harper's Ferry, to which we will invite our Hagerstown hosts of last year.[2]. . .

---

1. Pusey (1902–   ), then with the *Post,* also wrote a biography of Charles Evans Hughes.

2. The reunion became an annual event.

To Conrad L. Wirth[1]

March 9, 1957

Dear Dr. Wirth:

As you know, the Olympic National Park has a strip along the Pacific Ocean that is the last primitive beach in the United States. At least I think it is the last primitive beach. I know of no other quite comparable. I have hiked this primitive beach in the State of Washington. I did so in 1953 with pack. As a result of that hike I fell in love with that primitive beach and its great charm and beauty, and its abundant wildlife.

When I was West this summer I learned of the many local pressures that work to get a road built along that beach or above it on the bluffs. Many of the local people are anxious to get a better highway connection with Neah Bay.

I hope that no final decision has been made by the National Park Service to put a highway along that beach. A highway would destroy many of the unique values that the primitive beach now has. If there is a highway I think it should be set back four or five miles. There should be trails running to the beach from the highway. But the highway, if close to the beach, would drive out the game and we'd end up with just another ordinary beach.

I'd like to talk to you some time about this. There are not many people who have hiked that beach. I believe a couple members of your Park Service at Port Angeles did so but I don't believe that there have ever been more than a couple dozen do it. As one of that small number I would like to discuss the matter with you to see if the highway couldn't be put back a sufficiently long distance so as not to disturb the wildlife in that secluded area. Putting the highway even close to the cliffs would present considerable problems because those cliffs are constantly crumbling. This is a part of the sea coast that is still very much in the process of erosion.[2]

---

1. Wirth (1899–   ) had become director of the National Park Service in 1951, after twenty years with the agency.

2. U.S. Route 101 runs along the southernmost ten miles of Olympic National Park; the other forty-five miles is accessible only by foot. Two dirt roads do connect to the beach near the two Indian reservations which are part of the park.

To Warren Grant Magnuson[1]

April 6, 1960

Dear Maggie:

I understand that you have introduced a bill proposing that the Secretary of the Interior make a study of the Northern Cascades area, to see if that region would fit into the National Parks system.[2]

As you know, I have traveled that country on foot and on horseback, and I have included in my new book *My Wilderness*, which is to be published in September, a chapter on the area.

This is a wonderful region, which presents unique problems concerning its preservation, as I know I do not have to tell you.

I just wanted to tell you that I think this bill is probably just what

we need—not the least of the reasons being that it would allow a
sort of cooling-off period.

---

1. Magnuson (1905–) served as senator from the State of Washington from
1944 to 1981.
2. Magnuson's bill died in committee. However, in January 1967 President
Johnson recommended the creation of a national park in the Cascades. Magnuson
cosponsored the enabling legislation, which passed Congress later in the year, and
was signed into law by the President on October 2, 1968.

To Jean-Paul Harroy[1]

May 5, 1960

Dear Governor Harroy:
I have recently heard of your plans to preserve the mountain gorilla
in Albert Park. I congratulate you on your fine conservation program. We Americans sometimes get the reputation of people who
want animals around merely to hunt and shoot. But there are millions of us who also love the life of the forests and plains for what
it is and who try to keep civilization from crowding it out of existence.

I often think how awful it would be if as a result of our practice
of extermination we ended up with nothing but people on this earth.

---

1. Vice-governor general of Uranda, now Burundi.

To David Ross Brower[1]

August 25, 1960

Dear Dave:
There was a United States Forest Service official in Oregon who—
ten years or so ago—vetoed putting a chair lift to the top of Mt.
Hood.

What would you say to us getting a plaque and next summer commemorating the man for this veto against invading the peaks?

---

1. Brower (1912–) served as executive director of the Sierra Club from 1952 to 1969 and was involved in numerous conservation programs.

To Percival Proctor Baxter [1]

November 8, 1960

Dear Governor:

May I write you confidentially for your advice and help?

This last September I ran the Allagash. I finished the trip with a feeling of great concern that that fine wilderness river would soon be lost due to the encroachments of civilization. The roads are penetrating closer and closer, and in view of the nature of modern lumbering operations the roads that are built are easy invitation to all the jeeps and other cars that can travel dirt roads.

There is some concern in the minds of the people in northern Maine at the idea of the National Parks Service taking over the Allagash. The Park Service to them means roads and hotels. What the Allagash needs is not roads and hotels as I see it, but a corridor from one to three or four miles on each side of the river and lakes that make up the Allagash water, and the restoration of the natural flow of the Allagash. This means eliminating relics of the old dams there, sealing up the Telos cut, taking out the dam at Chamberlain Lake and giving America once more a great unrestricted river run which is, I think, incomparable in this country.

It seemed to me, just between us, that the ideal solution would be to make some arrangements to put the Allagash under the Baxter State Authority. I wonder if there are men in Maine of your proportions that have your vision and dimension of thought who would take steps to make that a reality?

I don't know all the landowners. I do know the pulp company and the paper company and the hydro-electric company are involved. There may be for the most part only three. Those three could do it in large part. If it could be done under conditions similar to those that cover your Baxter State Park, we would be assured of an enduring recreational area for those who love canoes and the feel of fast water under them.

It may be that some slight concessions would have to be made to allow motors to be used on canoes. It may be that in some stretches hunting for deer at least could be allowed.

But by and large I think that the framework of the Baxter State Park fits the Allagash perfectly.[2]

---

1.   Baxter (1876–1969) had been governor of Maine in the 1920s and then became the state's leading conservationist; an extremely wealthy man, whose family had vast holdings in the state, he donated 201,018 acres to the state for a park.

2.   A number of other people felt the same way about the Allagash, and the state eventually set aside the entire length of the river as a state park.

To Wayne Morse

August 2, 1961

Dear Wayne:

A start of an investigation of the forces of monopoly and corruption at work on the Minam River would be a demand on every major lumber company in the United States to give the names of ex-Forest Service men in its employ, the position held, the salary and expense account, and the period they have been employed.

Then a check could be made to see if these ex-Forest Service men are also draining government retirement pay.

How can a public servant represent we the people fairly if his reward eventually will be a high post in the company he regulates?

To Conrad L. Wirth

December 4, 1961

Dear Connie:

Many thanks for your letter of November 20. I may not be the best friend of the Park Service in this country but it would be difficult to prepare a list of the top ten best friends and exclude me.[1]

One of the prerogatives of friends is criticism—not malicious criticism, not destructive criticism, but criticism in the sense of helping improve conditions and policies. You say my book EAST TO KATAHDIN contains disparaging remarks on the Park Service. That would, however, require some extra-special editing. What I was trying to do was merely to be a faithful reporter. People like Connie Wirth and Bill Douglas who are canoeists on the Allagash had those things to say that I reported in the book. I did not quote them. But it was an attempt to give a faithful reporting account of the forces that are making up part of the opposition to having the Park Service proposal carried through. They can easily be made your allies.

I hope and pray that the Allagash is made a National Park and I think that all the misgivings of the local people can be cleared up by some official announcement as to what Park Service policy in that area will be. I would like to see a big public hearing of the Park Service put on somewhere in northern Maine. Wintertime would not be the best, but come early Summer or late Spring, it could be arranged. Fort Kent would be one possible place. They have a college there and hearing facilities might be available. Fort Kent is on the St. John into which the Allagash River runs. It is the largest city anywhere near the waters of the Allagash, but any hearing in the State, say at Bangor, would enlist a lot of interest and get a lot of people mobilized.

---

1.   In *Go East, Young Man* 215, WOD included the Park Service in his list of the top ten public enemies of conservation.

To Paul B. Sullivan

January 8, 1962

Dear Mr. Sullivan:

I have your letter of January 5 and I thank you for your gracious comments.

Most American writings on wildernesses as of now relate to

adventurous conflicts and struggles—near-encounters or actual encounters with wild animals, etc., some relating how the biggest fish was caught or the biggest bear killed, etc. There is another level of interest in the wilderness which I hope to get at least some people interested in. That is the nature of the botanical and biological life which is present for those who are interested in knowing something about the earth out of which they came.

I am by no means an expert, but it adds greatly to the enjoyment of trips if one has a pocketbook of flowers or birds when he takes his hike.

To Richard T. Sterling[1]

April 2, 1962

Dear Mr. Sterling:

... What you say about nature healing the scars caused by lumbering at one time was true. One has only to go to the northern Minnesota area or to New England to see how the old tote roads were built, camps established, and lumber floated out on the spring freshets. But these days with the permanent roads and bulldozers there is no such thing as healing, at least not in the lifetime of one man or even of one man and his sons and his grandsons. I can show you places in Washington and Oregon where the caterpillars have taken everything off the slopes that it took perhaps 10,000 years or more to put there.

Generalizations are of course difficult. But the more I see of modern logging methods the more frightened I become.

I think you perhaps would best appreciate what I mean if you could get into a small plane and fly around for several days in the State of Maine.

---

1. Sterling owned a tree farm in the state of Washington and had written objecting to some comments wod had made about the bad practices of lumber companies in *My Wilderness—The Pacific West* (Garden City: Doubleday, 1960).

A VERY PUBLIC JUSTICE

To Editor, Yakima Daily Republic

July 28, 1965

Dear Sir:

Your issue of July 21 contains editorial comment which contains a misconception both of multiple use and of wilderness values.

A piece of land paved for highway use is dedicated to one single use, not multiple uses. An impoundment of water may serve irrigation needs, hydroelectric power, flood control, and boating and fishing. It preempts all other uses. An area set aside as wilderness does not "bar" trails as your editorial states, although it does bar roads. Wilderness use covers a variety of multiple uses—refuges for elk and goats, hiking and horseback travel, fishing, watershed protection, and the maintenance of the biotic community in complete ecological balance. These values cannot be preserved if logging, highways, hot dog stands, and motels take over.

Wilderness has the special values I have mentioned; and it also has spiritual values as well. Wherever cars can go crowds now go. Campgrounds for those who travel by cars and trailers are needed in increasing quantities. Wooded areas can be logged and campgrounds for autoists can be built on those sites, those tracts serving these two multiple uses. But the wilderness advocates do not want those two uses to preempt every section of land. We want some of the original America left in primitive condition so that one hundred years from now a lad can walk the North Cascades in the manner of Daniel Boone and see what God has wrought.

Your editorial assumes that the values of our mountains are dollar values. There are those values to be exploited. But a tree is measurable not only by its board feet or its cellulose content, but by its beauty, the wildlife it shelters, the biotic community it nourishes, and the watershed protection it gives.

There are spiritual values in the mountains that highway engineers, real estate promoters, chambers of commerce, and editorial writers often overlook. The Psalmist said, "I will lift up mine eyes unto the hills from whence cometh my help. My help cometh from the Lord who made heaven and earth."

Those values disappear once Blankenship Meadows are converted into a Swiss alpine resort area, when the roar of traffic fills the ridges, when man's last refuge (except the ocean) is converted to commercial uses.

Your editorial to the contrary notwithstanding, multiple use means more than logging trucks and highways and the exploitation of dollar values.

To Robert Strange McNamara[1]

July 3, 1967

Dear Mr. Secretary:

Mrs. Douglas and I have our home (official residence) at Goose Prairie, Washington, which is near the Bumping River and three miles below Bumping Lake. Mt. Aix is to the south; American Ridge to the north.

At 20,000 feet or 30,000 feet the area would seem wild and largely unused. But from June 1 to late October it is filled with people, many of whom use horses to travel the steep trails. We have our own horses; and nearby is a dude ranch, Double K, which uses them extensively.

The sonic boom is having disastrous consequences in the valley. We are now accustomed to having pictures knocked off our walls. Our neighbor lost many rocks from his chimney.

One day last week a horse wrangler riding on American Ridge was nearly killed, being thrown violently into a tree.

The next day Mrs. Douglas and I were up Thunder Creek, and happily not in a part of the trail that has a precipitous drop-off. A sonic boom sent our horses about two feet into the air, and three feet sideways.

No one has yet been killed. But someone will be shortly, if the practice continues.

There is no precaution a rider can take. The sonic boom may catch him in a safe place or in a dangerous one.

Air research must go on. But these wild sanctuaries should be left alone. The nearby Pacific Ocean should offer plenty of space for maneuvering.

I write you because local objections go unnoticed. Your Air Force people out this way are very callous.

---

1. McNamara (1916–) headed the Defense Department from 1961 to 1968 and then the World Bank from 1968 to 1981.

To Robert Strange McNamara

July 28, 1967

Dear Mr. Secretary:
Your letter of July 15 relative to disastrous effects of your sonic boom in the wilderness areas of the Pacific Northwest has been received.

The victims of this callous federal program for which you claim responsibility are so helpless that I am arranging to put your letter in a public file so that their attorneys will have the benefit of your confession of responsibility.

I assure you, Mr. Secretary, that your "villagers" here are not as voiceless and impotent as your "villagers" in VietNam.

To Lyndon Baines Johnson

August 12, 1967

Dear Mr. President:
The sonic boom is doing us in at Goose Prairie. . . . We have had very close squeaks riding horseback in those mountains. Some people have been badly injured; none as yet has been killed. But someone will be soon. . . .

Why can't McNamara set practice times for the sonic boom— say 2:00 P.M. to 6:00 P.M. Tuesdays and Thursdays or any other time convenient?

Then we could keep the horses in the corral during those times. McNamara writes polite letters that tell us to go to hell. . . .

People here are up in arms; and many lawsuits will follow.

To Lyndon Baines Johnson

September 7, 1967

Dear Mr. President:
I thank you for your good letter of August twenty-eighth.

Out here there are U.S. Army artillery ranges that reach 20,000 feet in the air. The Army is thoughtful enough to list at airports the hours and days when planes should stay away. All we want is like treatment respecting the sonic boom. Could we have, say, two hours a week during daylight to ride horses in June, July, August, and September?

Would that be "impractical" or "perilous" in the sense in which you use those words?

To Henry Martin Jackson [1]

February 1, 1968

Dear Scoop:

I see by the press that Frank Church[2] has convinced the Pentagon it should keep the sonic boom away from Sun Valley in the wintertime, in view of the risk of snow avalanches.

By the same token I wonder why we can't get the Pentagon to keep the sonic boom away from the eastern slopes of the Cascades in the State of Washington from July 1st to October 1st, when those slopes are so heavily occupied by people on horseback.

Cathy and I have personally experienced the panic which horses experience when that noise hits without warning.

It makes it extremely difficult and dangerous.

---

1. Jackson (1912–1983) represented Washington in the Senate from 1953 until his death.

2. Church (1924–1984) was United States senator from Idaho from 1957 to 1981.

To Frank Harden and Jackson Weaver [1]

April 30, 1968

Dear Sirs:

There were 843 people on the hike, my private secret service telling me that it was the biggest yet because word had spread that you two were hiking the 15 miles with us.[2]

Typical of the answers to the poll that was conducted are the following:

"Those two jokers coming? *That* will be the day."

"Movies of them hiking? That would be worth a fortune."

The Welcoming Committee figured you would show up Friday night. So they kept the bartender awake until midnight. He said if you really "loved Nature" you would have come even as late as midnight, because you could have gotten back by 6:00 AM for your radio program.

---

1. The hosts on a popular morning radio show in Washington.

2. WOD kept up an annual ribbing of the two for failing to join him on the hike to support the saving of the C & O Canal.

To David Brower

October 25, 1968

Dear Dave:

I have your letter of October 24. If there is anything in particular you would like to have me do apropos of the Sierra Club salute to the First Lady,[1] I would be happy to do it. I think it would be very nice.

But I take with a grain of salt the so-called conservation achievements of LBJ. If we had had a fighting conservationist in the White House, we would certainly have more than 58,000 acres in the Redwood National Park. If we had had such a person in the White House we would not have lost the Little Tennessee River to the TVA.

I don't think any credit is coming to him for the Red River Gorge or Allerton Park in Illinois, both of which I had something to do with. Everything that was done was in spite of LBJ's attitudes.

I can go through the whole list that way.

Anyway it doesn't detract from the salute to the First Lady.

But I hope any publicity which is released will play down the achievements of LBJ as a conservationist, because the guy, in my view, is a complete phoney on that score. He is the one who has given the Corps of Engineers more promotion, more backing, more encouragement, than any other person in our history.

---

1. Lady Bird Johnson.

To Nancy Weber[1]

February 26, 1969

Dear Miss Weber:

I met a lady at a reception recently who told me about her visit last summer to one of our great national parks in the Pacific West. She told me how she came to love the bears. "I trained one," she said, "so that he would take a piece of toast right out of my mouth."

I told her she should be committed to Saint Elizabeth's.[2] For the most dangerous animal on this continent is a bear who has lost his fear of man.

So I guess my only fear is of people like this lady who do not know what to fear!

---

1. A New York schoolgirl who had written asking WOD if he had any fears.
2. A hospital in Washington, D.C. for the mentally ill.

To Edgar Tompkins[1]

May 6, 1972

Dear Mr. Tompkins:

A stroll can be very tiring. A hike, in contrast, is exhilarating. One who hikes a distance comes back with a different perspective. His worries and concerns have faded away and he is once more in tune with the world. His subconscious may have solved knotty problems for him as he hiked.

Beyond all that is the function that hiking performs in forcing man to relate himself once more to the earth from which he came and to which he soon returns. The pileated woodpecker, the bared owl, the red fox, and muskrat reintroduce themselves, reminding man that they and he are only one community that prospers together or that perishes together.

---

1. Director of the Albany (New York) Public Library.

To Scott Deindorfer

November 16, 1977

My dear Scott:

I have your letter of November 4th asking about my favorite quotation.

I suppose if one could obtain a movie of spaceship earth passing through the stratosphere one hundred years ago, it would look very much like it does today. But there is a vast difference because this century man has discovered how to destroy life on this planet as well as others. The nuclear bomb and the means of delivering it to its targets have made this possible.

This arrival of the nuclear age has made me think that the most important statement we can make, and keep on making until the message is understood by every person in the universe, is this:

"The most dangerous thing a person
can do these days is to be alive."

Good luck and best wishes on your publishing adventure.

To the Editor, The New York Times

April 23, 1979

To the Editor:

In 1972 I devoted a chapter to radiation in *The Three Hundred Year War,* a chronicle of ecological disaster. I did so only after studying the facts about radiation and nuclear energy.

Then and now, most scientists agree that the safest exposure to radiation is none at all. Our government regulators have recently given further support to this basic fact. They are considering a 50 percent reduction in the amount of annual radiation to which a nuclear power plant employee may be exposed.

The Three-Mile Island cooling system breakdown[1] has made us all aware of the real potential for a peacetime nuclear holocaust. But even if the reactor cooling systems were "foolproof" there is still the greater problem of nuclear waste disposal. At present most spent reactor fuel is simply transferred to the "temporary" storage tanks adjacent to the reactor. It is held there indefinitely in hopes that a solution will arise as to what should ultimately be done with these deadly wastes.

This problem of disposal has plagued scientists since the peaceful use of the atom was sought to justify its development after the bombings of Hiroshima and Nagasaki. Until this problem is resolved there can be no truly safe use of nuclear power. It is time once again to consider the wisdom of Senator Gravel's[2] assertion in 1971:

> If this country ever grows dependent on nuclear energy for more than a few percent of its electricity, the entire economy could be rippled by one bad nuclear accident which required the shutdown of all nuclear plants.

The message is clear. The benefits of nuclear power are far outweighed by the greater risks imposed upon an unsuspecting public. If we should treat the energy crisis as the "moral equivalent of war" then we should view the continued use of nuclear power plants as the "moral equivalent of suicide".

---

1. The country's worst nuclear energy accident had occurred on March 28, with a meltdown in one of the reactors at Metropolitan Edison's Three Mile Island facility near Middletown, Pennsylvania.

2. Maurice Robert "Mike" Gravel (1930–) served two terms as senator from Alaska.

Chapter 10

Travel and Foreign Affairs

Hugo Black once called him "Marco Polo," and indeed few men of his generation saw as much of the world as did William Douglas. Next to tramping around the mountains of the Pacific Northwest, Douglas loved nothing as much as exploring new countries, especially their rural and wilderness areas. He had little use for Europe as a place to visit; it had already been tamed and examined and cataloged. He wanted to go where few Americans had been and then tell the country about it through magazine articles or books.

The books, however, went far beyond simple travelogs. They provided a running commentary—and a liberal one—on the ills besetting the world. Wherever he went, Douglas tried to seek out the nonestablishment groups, to find out how the common people lived and what problems they faced. And as even his critics conceded, Douglas had a magic touch with the peasants and hill people he met, and he learned a great deal about the countries he visited and their customs in a way unavailable to him had he taken the usual VIP tour.

A visit, even a hurried one, nonetheless led Douglas to believe he knew a great deal about a place; two or more trips and he considered himself an expert. And since he *was* a justice of the United States Supreme Court, he also made the acquaintance of influential local leaders on his trips, and he utilized these relationships to bolster his claims of expertise. Sometimes his judgments proved wrong, and there is more than just a hint of naïveté about some of these letters. Yet Douglas did have an uncanny ability to spot the weaknesses in American foreign policy, and his predictions regarding its failure often came true.

He did try to share his insights with those responsible for directing American foreign affairs; he told Harry Truman, John Kennedy, and Lyndon Johnson what he had learned, but for the most part they paid him very little heed. When people he had met abroad came to the United States, Douglas did his best to introduce them to congressional leaders, although there is little evidence that any of his efforts bore much fruit.

At least until the mid-sixties, Douglas also had no qualms about serving the military or intelligence branches of the government on his trips overseas. He willingly field-tested army camping equipment and clothing, and the Central Intelligence Agency alerted him to watch for certain things in which they had an interest and then debriefed him on his return home.

Douglas's writings, discussed in the next chapter, played a key role in his foreign travels. Although not poor, he had little money to spend on such trips and financed them through writing contracts with magazines such as *Look* or *National Geographic* or with advances against the books he would write. The magazine articles turned out to be fairly popular, and his first travel book, *Strange Lands and Friendly People* (1951) became a Book-of-the-Month Club selection.

Africa

To Abdel Khalek Hassouna [1]

December 11, 1954

Dear Mr. Hassouna:

. . . The Moroccans have a just cause but not many voices to plead for them in the Western world. I hope the West understands the conditions that are brewing there before it is too late. If the existing conditions continue, only communism will be the beneficiary.

If France is smart she will move soon and introduce real reforms, including the return of the Sultan and the restoration of the dynasty. I do not know many Moors who are anxious to have France leave Morocco completely. The French have done much for the country but the Moors deserve their independence and must have it if the democratic way is to survive in Africa.[2]

---

1. Secretary general of the League of Arab States.

2. Morocco was still a French colony, and there were frequent street demonstrations calling for independence, which France finally granted in 1956.

To Emanuel Celler

March 1, 1955

Dear Mannie:

. . . I was all through Morocco last summer. The jails are filled with political prisoners. The only people who are making political capital are the Communists. In my opinion independence should be a thing that comes in stages. But it should start now and contain sure guarantees for the Jewish minority. One of the most exploited minorities I saw in Morocco were the Jews themselves, exploited by the French.

To Kenneth Pendar[1]

November 20, 1958

Dear Ken:

. . . In spite of everything that we hear, I gathered that DeGaulle has failed. Does it look to you to be a hopeless situation? The American press has been ominously silent in recent days about the situation but it seemed to me, reading between the lines, that the Algerian problems are far from a solution.[2]

I hope all is well with you and that you will be visiting us soon.

---

1. An American friend of WOD then living in Morocco.

2. Algeria had been racked all year by violence. DeGaulle finally agreed to independence, which aroused extremely strong right-wing resentment from army officers who asserted that Algeria could never be cut off from France.

To Stuart Guthrie[1]

December 6, 1960

Dear Stu:

Don't write off Africa so quickly. It's the richest of all the continents. Even the Sahara—long a windblown dry desert—has turned out to be richer than the Saar Valley. Mr. K[hrushchev]. would love to have all those in his arsenal.

---

1. A San Francisco businessman and friend of WOD.

To Stuart Guthrie

December 23, 1960

Dear Stu:

I cannot help but wonder who taught you African geography. You seem to think that Africa is the land of jungles. You can find them there, but by far the greatest percentage of African land is high, rolling plateau-land.

The dangers to man have not been the heat and humidity but the flies and bugs which are now pretty well under control. So if you get into a poker game with Mr. K over Africa don't discard so fast—treat Africa as your wild card. White men thrive there much better than they do in Cuba, Mississippi, Louisiana, Guatemala, or any of the other more familiar places.

Asia

To Selig S. Harrison[1]

October 16, 1951

Dear Zig:

Your letter of September 2nd was a most gracious expression of confidence and admiration. I hope I am worthy. It warmed my heart to read what you had to say.

This is the City of Fear. Officialdom is mostly against what I said on Asia.[2] The letters I received—there were hundreds of them from all walks of life—were 4 in favor, 1 against. The grass roots here are worried, concerned, and unsympathetic to all we are doing in Asia.

My new book—*Strange Lands and Friendly People*—will be out in a couple of weeks and will stir the waters more. It touches lightly on India and gives a bow both to Nehru[3] and to j.p.[4]

---

1. A reporter with the Associated Press then stationed in New Delhi.

2. See p. 266.

3. Jawaharlal Nehru (1889–1964), Gandhi's closest disciple, served as prime minister of India from its independence in 1947 until his death.

4. Vallabhbhai Jhaverbhai Patel (1875–1951) was deputy prime minister of India.

To Remsen Du Bois Bird[1]

February 6, 1952

Dear Dr. Bird:

I have enjoyed greatly your letters. I have been thinking much about the recent ones. The trend of education in Asia has been away from the villages. All the brains were seeking to escape into an ivory tower where they could sit in comfort reflecting upon eternal truths while the needs and wants of the villages went unheeded. That is why China capitulated to the Communists. It was not a military conquest. It was not so much a military default as it was an educational default.

The big problem is to get education in Asia back to the villages. We can't do it by flying squadrons of Point IV experts.[2] The important thing is what happens after the experts leave the villages. It is not enough to hand out DDT, kill flies, clean up the water supplies and reduce the death rate. Those are all good things and ease the conscience a bit. But in many respects they are ultimately cruel things because without more they merely increase the people among whom the poverty must be rationed. It means that those who go out there among these people must be revolutionaries as well as technical experts. If they are not revolutionaries they will end up on the side of the landlords and misery may be only compounded. It would be easy to conduct this revolution even though our State Department would be shocked, horrified and amazed.

---

1. Bird (1888–1971) was president of Occidental College in California from 1921 to 1946 and had a longtime interest in Asia.

2. Truman had outlined a four-point plan to provide American aid to developing nations; the fourth point, which became a fairly successful program, involved making technical assistance available to increase agricultural and industrial production.

To Ramon R. Magsaysay [1]

March 7, 1953

My dear Monching:

. . . There is a tide in the affairs of all men some of which can be shaped and some of which cannot be. I think that destiny has marked you for a very brilliant chapter in Philippine history. That chapter has already started. And when it will be renewed no one knows. But my prayers and thoughts are always with you.

---

1. Magsaysay (1907–1957), then head of the Philippines Defense Department, would soon be elected president of the country.

To William Love [1]

April 3, 1953

Dear Mr. Love:

You probably have received by now a copy of the letter, dated February 2, 1953, from the Malayan Chinese Association of Kuala Lumpur, Malaya, together with the Resolution in which they condemn as a "scurrilous libel" my article in Look Magazine on the Malayan situation. [2]

This Resolution does not state in what way my article was misleading or what statements contained in it were false. There are, of course, many high-minded Chinese in Malaya, men and women with a sense of civic righteousness. But the following facts are uncontestable.

1.   It is a fact that over 90 per cent of the Communist guerrillas in Malaya are Chinese.

2.   It is a fact that the Communist Politburo in Malaya is composed of Chinese.

3.   It is a fact that the great bulk of the Chinese in Malaya are "fence sitters", waiting to see whether Red China or Formosa emerges victorious.

4.   It is a fact that the Chinese Communist guerrillas have a secret society called Min Yuen composed of 100,000 members who furnish the guerrillas with food, ammunition, medicine, and intelligence.

5.   It was a fact at the time the Look article was published that Malaya's Chinese sent to Red China $3,000,000 (Malay) per month, a figure that since then has dropped to $2,000,000 (Malay) a month.

It was the figure of $3,000,000 a month that the Chinese said was false. But it is an official figure which cannot be disproved. It was apparently that figure that aroused the greatest resentment in Chinese circles to the Look article.

---

1.   An editor with *Look* magazine.

2.   wod published five articles on Asia in *Look* in November and December of 1952; the one on Malaya appeared in the November 18 issue, 34. wod attributed a great deal of influence—both good and bad—to the Chinese living in Malaya.

To Ramon R. Magsaysay

December 31, 1953

My dear Monching:

You will be much, much too busy to answer mail, so please do not bother to reply to this. I just wanted you to know that I deeply appreciated the letter which you wrote me on December 15th. I drank a toast to your Inauguration at the Philippine Embassy and rejoiced with a lot of your friends that it was the beginning of a new era for the Philippines. I hope 1954 brings you great joy and happiness.

As you start your new job I have two suggestions to make.

First. You are at this point in history in the strongest political position that you will be in. At least that is what history teaches. So this is the time to strike hard and fast at the basic things that you want to get done. And I would think that the basic thing would be the land reform program. Much of the ammunition to carry it through is in the Hardie Report, as you know.

Second. After you get your land reform program through, which I would hope would be in the spring of 1954, I wish that you would take a swing through Southeast Asia, going as far west as Karachi. I hope you go through all of those countries, making several speeches in each place and telling them what independence means, what the Philippines under your leadership have already done with their independence and what your plans for the future are. I think that Asia needs leadership and I think that once you get your land reform program behind you that you will be in a very important, strategic position to supply that leadership.

Good luck and God bless you.

To Amos A. Jordan[1]

June 17, 1956

Dear Colonel Jordan:

. . . Nehru, U Nu[2] and Sukarno[3] are all very controversial figures. Many feel the same as you do about Sukarno and you probably could write a strong brief to support that point of view. There is no doubt but what the last government was a government in which Communists were powerfully represented. It had elements of real crises in it. However, the storm was weathered and the new government seems more firmly anchored against Communist blasts. Sukarno has represented to me that he feels that most of the Indonesian Communists are merely another species of disgruntled people not tied strongly to ideological lines. That may be true of many. It cannot be true of all of them. But I do not think he has ever taken the Communist threat in Indonesia as seriously as some of the rest of us. I do think he is a great democratic leader. He is basically and fundamentally opposed to Communism. He is a person that we must include in our allies. . . .

_____

1. Jordan taught social sciences at West Point.

2. U Nu (1907–) served as Burma's first prime minister after independence, from 1948 to 1958 and again from 1960 to 1962.

3. Sukarno (1901–1970) was president of Indonesia from 1945 to 1967.

_____

To Mrs. Stanley Young [1]

February 18, 1963

Dear Nancy:

. . . I visited Sikkim in 1955 and was entertained by the Maharajah. I also met the young Maharajkumar—the one who is about to be married. His wife was a Tibetan woman and was among the very loveliest people I had ever seen anywhere. She died shortly thereafter of some mysterious disease.

When I was having tea with the Maharajah one afternoon about dusk I asked him about the Abominable Snowman. He got up and took me to the window. He drew the curtains and pointed across the lawn and showed me where, a few days earlier, he had seen the Abominable Snowman. I asked him what he was doing, and he said he was running. He described the Abominable Snowman in such vivid terms that I began to think that there probably was such an animal (or that the Maharajah and I were more than slightly fey).

One day I went to the Buddhist monastery near the residence of the Maharajah. I say monastery—I guess it was only a temple. It is a small beautiful thing which you will see. The secretary of the Maharajah asked me if I would like to see the costumes of the devil dancers. . . . As we were leaving the storeroom where the masks and gowns are kept, the secretary asked me if there were any I would like to have. I said yes, and pointed to one. He ordered a man to go up and get it for me. Down it came. It now hangs in my office. It is the mask of the god of the Kangchenjunga, the second highest mountain in the Himalayas, and one that dominates the Sikkim scene. I am sorry you did not see the mask. It has a very ferocious face, but a kind heart. The ferocious face scares away the evil people, but he is a protector of the good, which of course includes you and Stan and me. . . .

---

1. A friend from Florida, about to travel to Asia, who had written asking for any advice he might give.

To M. M. Shafik Kanawi [1]

October 24, 1964

My dear Shafik:

I have thought of you many, many times and especially when I get copies of the Afghanistan News which I find to be very interesting. When the October, 1964 issue arrived, I was compelled to write you because in it, as you know, is the draft constitution of Afghanistan.

I thought this was a splendid, modern document and I felt as I read on from paragraph to paragraph that I found your hand and philosophy in many of the provisions. I hope that it turns out to be a workable one and practical in all of its aspects, as I am sure it will be. It is, as all constitutions should be, indigenous and yet ties Afghanistan into the grand mosaic of law running through all civilized regimes. I congratulate you and send you my warm and affectionate regards. . . .

---

1. Minister of justice in Afghanistan.

To David Frost [1]

December 4, 1971

Dear Mr. Frost:

I have been very concerned over your interview a week or so ago with the King and Queen of Sikkim.

You obviously have never been to Gangtok; and though British you apparently have the crude qualities that Britishers usually associate with Americans.

These were very special people on your program. I know the King and I knew his father. I knew the King's first wife, a lovely Tibetan lady. With all respect to the present Queen, reporting in depth would have led you to inquire why Lhasa was no longer the source of brides, even before the Chinese took over. Many wondered why you failed to inquire whether Sikkim was in the United Nations and if not, why. I wondered why you did not inquire whether the altitude of the site where the house of the Indian Commissioner stands is higher or lower than the site of the royal palace.

The mask of Kangchenjunga hangs in my office, the gift of the late father of the present King. It was amazing that you did not try to bring out many interesting facets of the famous mountain.

Instead, you struggled to produce a laugh.

It's depressing that you never see the potential for adult education in serious problems—with or without a laugh.

The King and Queen of Sikkim deserve an apology for their crude western reception on your program.

---

1. At this time Frost, a popular British television personality, ran a weekly American interview program as well.

China

To Harry S. Truman

September 25, 1951

Dear Mr. President:

. . . I regret that a public statement of mine embarrassed and offended you.[1] Never have I said or done anything in public or private with the purpose of injuring you or with the thought that it might. . . . I write what follows merely to make sure no misunderstanding grows up between us. I respect your judgment; and I only want you to know the basis of mine.

I know how you feel about Asia and China. I remember our talk in the fall of 1950, after I had returned from an earlier trip to Asia, including Hong Kong. I reported to you my conversations with various non-Communist men and women of the colored races of the Far East.

They urged that America make a political settlement with Red China.

They said that if United Nations forces crossed the 38th parallel, China would enter the war.

They did not want Russia to succeed in doing what Teddy Roosevelt most feared—getting the Mongol races to fighting her battles for her.

They wanted China to have an alternative to a Russian alliance.

They especially pleaded that Mao Tse-tung not be publicly called another Tito, as that would make his breaking with Russia more and more difficult.

At the time I expressed the hope that war with China would be avoided, that we would not cross the 38th parallel, and that a political settlement with China would be worked out. I felt the same as my Far East friends—that by diplomatic and political means we should promote in China the kind of counter revolution against Russia that we have been promoting in Yugoslavia. You emphatically espoused the other view—the view expressed in your letter of September 13th.

Your view is an understandable one. It is today perhaps the popular one. But my travels in Asia during the last three summers have convinced me that there is only tragedy to our country if it is maintained. History shows, Mr. President, that as China goes so goes Southeast Asia. The key group in each country in Southeast Asia is the Chinese population. Those Chinese are today shifting their support—moral and financial—to Red China. . . .

I hate Communism. I have been in Communist lands; I have traveled Communist borders; I have talked with Communist refugees; I have seen with my eyes the impact of its venal, godless system, of its regime of terror. But I have also seen at close range, Mr. President, the Achilles heel of Soviet imperialism. It lies in the intense nationalism of these separate countries and their resistance to Soviet regimentation. Yugoslavia, where I visited last July is a notable example. We of the West are doing a brilliant job in giving Tito and the other members of the Politburo an alternative to Russian serfdom. What we are doing on a small scale in Yugoslavia we can do on a grand scale in Asia.

To do it we must pry China loose from Russia.

This is the way we can give affirmative meaning to war in Korea. For certainly it will not profit us to gain Korea if in so doing we lose China.

Clearly the great victory we can win in Korea is to split China away from Russia. To do that we would have to make a political settlement with China. . . .

I am sorry you thought my statement was politically motivated. But the questions I touched on were not matters of politics; they are matters of citizenship and humanity—matters on which many during these anxious days are even afraid to speak. That is the reason, Mr. President, why I felt I should not hold back.

---

1.   On returning from the Far East on August 31, WOD had called for American recognition of the People's Republic of China in order to help undermine Peking's ties to Moscow. Such a policy, he declared, would be "a real political victory," but it would "require straightforward and courageous thinking." A few days later in a speech in Seattle, WOD had warned that the balance of power in the world would shift against the West unless China could be split away from Russian influence.

To Anna Eleanor Roosevelt[1]

September 28, 1951

Dear Mrs. Roosevelt:

I thank you for your interesting letter of September 26th.

I suppose there is no doubt that the Communists control the vast expanse of China, except Formosa. I had not thought that Formosa should make the difference between recognition and non-recognition. And I had felt strongly that if we recognized Nationalist China because of its hold on Formosa, we should recognize Red China for its hold on the mainland. Certainly Formosa in the economy of all of China is hardly more important than Long Island is in our own. Formosa is or would be the sticking point in any political settlement with China. I have thought that perhaps the best course would be to make it a United Nations trusteeship. At least that is an alternative worth exploring. Under our present policy all of Asia will explode in our faces and the Soviet scheme will have on its side
      —the bulk of the peoples of the world
      —the bulk of the wealth of the world.

There is in my mind a serious question whether we then could ever win a war.

Of course, Franklin D. Roosevelt would never have let it drift so far into dangerous waters.

---

1. Mrs. Roosevelt (1884–1962) had, after her husband's death, assumed an ever more prominent role in American political life. She then served as one of the American representatives to the United Nations and had become the doyenne of the liberal wing of the Democratic Party.

To Marvin S. Kincheloe[1]

March 5, 1952

Dear Dr. Kincheloe:

. . . In China our primary goal, I think, is to extricate that nation from the Soviet orbit. I am convinced that this cannot be accomplished by diplomatic isolation, which indeed will almost surely serve to accomplish the exact opposite of this objective. Astute diplomatic management is necessary if China is to be won over. And such a program presupposes recognition.

---

1. Pastor of the First Methodist Church in Johnson City, Tennessee.

To Clovis McSoud[1]

December 9, 1952

My dear Clovis:

. . . I never did say or think that the Chiang Kai-shek government should be recognized. All I said was that internally the government was doing a good job on Formosa in terms of land reform, education, medical care, etc. If they had done that same job on the mainland, then the mainland would not, in my view, have gone Communist. Chiang Kai-shek and his Nationalist Party represent an out-worn, out-moded symbol in Asian politics. Chiang Kai-shek is a symbol of something that has failed, not something that holds promise for the future. I think it is of the utmost importance to try to work out an over-all political settlement with Red China. I think there are many indications that Red China does not want to become dependent upon Russia. At the same time, I do not think that she would rush into the arms of the United States. But I do think there is a real opportunity under the leadership of India and Burma to work out a regional alliance in the Asian community, an alliance among Asians or South Asian people, that can be a real Third Force. It can be as powerful a force as the Middle East would be if it were allied in a common cause of reform and return of the country to the people. . . .

---

1.   McSoud, an American lawyer, was then in Beirut about to leave for the Far East.

To Robert Daniel Murphy[1]

June 19, 1959

Dear Mr. Secretary:

Upon returning to the city after a brief absence, I found in my mail a copy of a letter dated June 27, written to the National Geographic Magazine by a Mr. Kretzman, stating the Department of State was unwilling to validate a passport for me for travel this summer to Red China to represent the National Geographic.

This letter comes as a great shock and as a surprise. I had hoped to have a chance to sit down and talk to you about it. I cannot believe that it represents your view and the view of the Secretary and that of President Eisenhower.

The National Geographic is of course well known. I have done other travel pieces for them. I am sending with this letter two issues of the National Geographic showing the kind of work that I have done for them in the past.

My trip would not be in any sense a junket or publicity stunt. It would be a serious news-gathering project. I would be giving my full time to it for the two months I would be there. It would be my sole endeavor for that time. . . .

I urge with great earnestness that you give this matter your personal consideration. I think I can be of real service to my country in going to Red China for the National Geographic. What they want is four picture stories. I have traveled enough in Communist lands not to be taken in by propaganda. My writings on my travels through Russia speak for themselves. . . . I am writing you this note with the hope that you can find the time to give it your own personal consideration and if necessary to discuss it with Secretary [of State Christian] Herter and President Eisenhower.

---

1. Murphy (1894–1978), a career foreign service officer, was then serving as deputy undersecretary of state.

To Gabriel Reiner[1]

April 23, 1962

Dear Mr. Reiner:

. . . We sounded out through a European neutral nation the prospect of getting into Red China in the Summer of 1961. That particular Ambassador contacted Peking and the word came back that they did not want me. The main reason was they did not want any American, but they also said they were not sure what my position was on Formosa.

I am sending you under separate cover a copy of my book Democracy's Manifesto, which is something that no communist will like because it is definitely pro-Democratic. But that is a review of the Asian situation which you may want to keep in mind when you discuss this with your Chinese Ambassador friend again.

You should also know that one of the things which would probably militate against my getting into Red China is the fact that I was one of three who formed the American Emergency Committee for Tibetan Refugees, Inc. We have collected several hundreds of thousands of dollars to take care of those people who fled the Chinese army and are now in India.

I mention these facts not for you to pass on, but just to let you know that your efforts are appreciated and that I would greatly like to go to Red China should you be able to arrange it.

---

1. Reiner headed the Cosmos Travel Bureau in New York and had undertaken to package tours to Third World and communist countries.

To Sidney Reiner[1]

January 15, 1972

Dear Mr. Reiner:

. . . You ask whether we are still interested in a visit to Mainland China. I have been trying to get in since 1950. My interest has lagged considerably, however, in view of the fact that I could not get there in 1971.

You might say as a preliminary matter that I have no objection to your raising the question with some of the Chinese delegates to the U.N. I think, however, from information I have received, that it would be extremely difficult to get me into Mainland China on a basis where I would have any freedom. The reason why I think that is true is the following:

For your own information, quite confidentially, Edgar Snow[2] wrote me last fall as a result of his canvassing the situation in Peking, and he indicated there were considerable difficulties. Unfortunately you sent Peking a copy of my book INTERNATIONAL DISSENT. That book explains the anti-Chinese attitude in Southeast Asia. My writings and speeches have pretty well covered the perimeter of China. I have not only discussed at length the anti-Chinese attitude in Southeast Asia but the anti-Chinese attitude in Outer Mongolia. Peking thinks Outer Mongolia is a part of China, and I have indicated why it is not. Peking thinks that Tibet is a part of China and has gone so far as to invade Tibet and take it over. I have made speeches indicating that what they did was wrong and that, moreover, they filled up Tibet with about six million Chinese, drowning out the ancient Tibetan civilization.

These and other things too numerous to mention indicate, as I understand it, that Peking does not relish any visit from me. That is not important to me one way or the other except it means that if I did go I would be carefully confined and not allowed to travel as I would like.

---

1. Reiner had taken over his father's travel agency.

2. Snow (1905–1972) had been a correspondent in China from 1929 to 1941 and had accompanied Mao Tse-tung on the Long March. He therefore had access to China and to Chinese officials unavailable to most western journalists.

To Yao Quang[1]

March 29, 1973

Dear Mr. Ambassador:

Secretary [of State William] Rogers has advised me of the invitation from the Chinese Peoples Institute to Mrs. Douglas and me, and to my doctor, N. Thomas Connally, and Mrs. Connally, to visit China for two weeks beginning August 15th next.

The four of us are happy to accept.

We will plan to arrive in Hong Kong no later than August 14, and go by train to Canton.

Or we could go to Japan and fly to Peking on August 14, if there is plane service available.

Should we send our passports to you for visas or arrange for them through your Ambassador at the United Nations?

---

1. Ambassador of the People's Republic of China to Canada.
2. WOD finally realized his wish and did travel to China the following summer.

India

To Paul Gray Hoffman[1]

May 14, 1951

Dear Mr. Hoffman:

Since talking with you last week, I have had some further thoughts about the proposed Asiatic Commission or the Commission on Asia. It would perhaps be undesirable to include in the scope of the Commission, at least to begin with, all of Asia. Asia is wide and diverse and complex. Each situation may require different and diverse treatment. Perhaps the best thing to do would be to set up the Asiatic Commission and have it address itself immediately to the problems of India. When I say the problems of India, I mean the problems of the relations between India and the United States. . . .

Why not have this Commission sit down with Nehru and his cabinet and representatives of the Congress Party (and perhaps the Socialist Party which recently has split away from the Congress

Party) and work out a simple, concrete program for submission to America? It might be a one-year, five-year, or ten-year plan.

In other words, I think it might be better to take up the one critically important area right at the start and build from that later on into the other areas. I really believe that if India is held firm, given encouragement and support, that India can and will stabilize the rest of Asia and develop a strong democratic front. There is such a powerful spiritual force in India [so] as never really to succumb to the Communist ideology.

---

1.   Hoffman (1891–1974) had started as an auto salesman and ultimately became chairman of the board of Studebaker-Packard. He won international attention as administrator of the Marshall Plan and had just become president of the Ford Foundation. WOD wrote because of the foundation's interest in bettering American relations with Asia.

To Loy Wesley Henderson[1]

May 24, 1951

Dear Mr. Ambassador:

I am completing my arrangements to make a return visit to India this summer for the purpose of going on a long trek into the Himalayas. I am stopping first in Kabul and in Karachi and should arrive in New Delhi somewhere between the 15th and 20th of July. Then I will go direct to the hill station where I will start the trek. The trek will last about thirty days, or perhaps even longer.

I have had several talks with Army officials while I have been making plans for the trip. They have asked me to collect certain information for them relative to the movement of men and animals at those high altitudes. They have also asked me to try out for them a good deal of equipment, some new and experimental and other material untried in that particular region.

My arrangements with the Army have finally been completed and they are shipping a half dozen or more packages, some in duffle bags and some in cartons, to me in care of the American Embassy at New Delhi or in care of the Military Attache there. I am not quite sure what the final billing will be. MATS is handling it.

The purpose of this note is two-fold. The first is to advise you of the shipment of material and equipment and the second is to tell you how happy I am that I will have a chance of seeing you again soon. I will stop in New Delhi very briefly—just long enough to get the necessary permits and make a few supplementary purchases. I will push on immediately to the jumping off point, which will probably be Manali.

After this long trek I will return to New Delhi. I have received from the Living Buddha, who is at present in Baltimore, credentials to the Dalai Lama, who is now in a monastery near the southern border of Tibet. If he is still there the first part of September, I plan to fly to Darjeeling and then go in from the roadhead on a three or four day trek to see him. I would then come back to New Delhi and fly on across the Pacific, stopping in Indo-China and Indonesia. . . .

---

1. Henderson (1892–ᅠ), a career diplomat, was then serving as American ambassador to India.

To Craig Smyser[1]

December 21, 1951

Dear Colonel Smyser:

. . . I think you are quite right that India has not known the color problem as we know the problem in this country. There are strong vestiges of it, however, running throughout Indian public life. As one prominent Indian told me last summer, "I am sure I do not have any color prejudices whatsoever because ever since I was a small child we always had white servants."

The role of Britain in Asia will become more clarified with the passing of time. It has been, as you suggest, an empire builder and used India as a raw commodity warehouse. England did leave some fine things behind. It left the Indian Civil Service and a fine governmental tradition. It is the Indian Civil Service that has staffed all the embassies and legations in the world, the various offices in the UN, and the various offices in the state and federal governments in India. The great demands on the Indian Civil Service stretched that service to its capacity and there may recently have been a deterioration in it. But the good in it is owed to the British. I think the Indians themselves are the first to recognize it.

When one sees the empire building done by the Soviets, it makes one realize that Rome, France and the British, in spite of all their cruelties, were in large measure on the side of the angels compared with the Communists.

---

1. Colonel Smyser was with the Office of the Chief of Engineers of the U.S. Army.

To Jawaharlal Nehru

January 21, 1953

Dear Mr. Prime Minister:

Last December I was granted the Sidney Hillman Award, an award given each year by the Sidney Hillman Foundation for Meritorious Public Service . . . .

At the dinner tendered me on the occasion of the presentation of the award, I spoke of some of the problems of trade unionism in Asia. After the dinner I expressed my desire that this award, which amounts to $1,000, be devoted to the cause of Indian trade unionism. I have had discussions with Madame Pandit and Ambassador Mehta, who have been most cooperative and helpful. The idea has emerged that this $1,000 be used so as to enable one or more Indians to obtain education in trade unionism. it is my desire that the money be spent under your supervision, and that it be used for educational purposes in India, not to bring an Indian to the United States. In this way I thought the money would do the most good. . . .

To Geoffrey E. Myers [1]

June 15, 1953

Dear Mr. Myers:

. . . I did not intend to condemn British achievements in India. Perhaps the impression remains that I did so do. I was not attempting so much to write about the past as to get some projection of the future. I felt then and still feel that England left a very fine heritage in India: first, in its tolerance for minorities and minority views which is in line with the great British tradition of civil liberties; and second, the development of the civil service, without which the great work of India could not have been carried on so successfully.

---

1. Myers, a New Zealander, had written to WOD complaining about what he thought was an anti-British attitude in *Strange Lands and Friendly People.*

To Walter White[1]

June 5, 1954

Dear Mr. White:

. . . I also think it very important that the people out there hear your voice. Your voice out there will be a much more powerful one than most others, in view of the long struggle you have made on the side of human rights.

There are many, many things you can tell the people of India and Asia that will help them in their thinking and attitude toward us. Among other things, you can speak with authority on the tremendous progress which has been made in the last 80 years or so in the treatment of races and minorities in this country.

The people of Asia need to know that America has a warm heart and a tolerant attitude and that the great bulk of us are not like those that are depicted in the headlines.

You will be a wonderful emissary of America. By all means go. When you do go, the East will get into your blood and you will go again and again. And that is the way it should be, because I feel you have a great and important mission to perform out there.

---

1. White (1893–1955), the longtime secretary of the NAACP, had been invited to visit Singapore and India and wrote WOD seeking his advice on whether he should go.

To Edward R. Murrow

February 2, 1955

Dear Ed:

I'm delighted you are seeing Nehru. Start off with two questions—
(1) Is Red China on an expansionist move?

(2) Are the overseas Chinese in Asia (12–1/2 million) advance agents for the Red Chinese Communists?

I talked with him about these two matters last July for two hours; and he was most eloquent.

To Dag Hammarskjöld [1]

October 9, 1958

Dear Mr. Secretary-General:

There is an outstanding Indian by the name of R. N. Rahul.[2] He has wonderful qualifications for work in the United Nations and I want personally to bring him to your attention.

He is probably the foremost Indian authority on Central Asia. He speaks English, Hindustani and Tibetan. He is a great Tibetan scholar, and is a Buddhist by religious faith.

I crossed the Himalayas with him in 1951. Following that he came to America for a year of graduate work at Harvard and another year at Columbia.

He has such wonderful qualifications it seemed to me that you might find a place for him in the Secretariat.

---

1.   Hammarskjöld (1905–1961), a Swedish economist and statesman, served as the second secretary-general of the United Nations from 1953 until his death in a plane crash in the Congo.

2.   This letter is typical of many WOD wrote over the years. He would assume a mentor or patron role toward a young native he had met on a trip and then try (sometimes successfully) to arrange for a period of study in the United States or to place that person in a government job. WOD had previously written, without success, to Nehru seeking to place Rahul in the Indian government.

To Jawaharlal Nehru

August 1, 1961

Dear Mr. Prime Minister:

I was rather shocked at the arrogance of Ayub who, as you know, recently visited us. He was head of state, and entitled to every courtesy. But his authoritarian attitude toward us and our policies was disturbing to many of us.

After all, he tore up a Constitution and instituted instead a "basic democracy." But certainly Pakistanis are as intelligent as Indians; and the Pakistan Bar and Bench were as deeply imbued with Due Process as their Indian counterparts. Yet in Pakistan today even civil suits are commonly tried to military tribunals; and so are criminal cases with no right to counsel, no right to appeal.

Ayub stands for what we Americans long ago rejected. He is authoritarian; we are democratic. Here as in India if there is corruption in government we arrest the malefactors or drive them from government. It is strange indeed that we should honor a man whose remedy for dishonesty is destruction of the Constitution.[1]

---

1. See p. 226.

To Indira Priyadarshini Gandhi[1]

January 19, 1966

My dear Indira:

I am writing you this informal note today, the 19th of January by Washington, D.C. calendar, because it will be one of the last times I can address you so informally.

The robes of an exalted office are about to be put around your shoulders.

Your friends throughout the world are very happy and excited about it, and have renewed confidence in the great and glorious destiny of India.

---

1. Mrs. Gandhi (1917–1984), Nehru's daughter, became prime minister of India in 1966 and she served until 1977; she then served again from 1980 until her assassination.

Iran

To Gerald F. P. Dooher[1]

June 14, 1950

Dear Gerry:

As you can tell from my series of letters in the last month or so, there has been an element of uncertainty in my plans for the proposed trip.

I have been torn between Iran and India and had just about decided to take some time in each, cutting short the Iran trip by ten days or two weeks. But the reports from India as to weather conditions in the Himalayas during the month of September are not very encouraging. So I have about decided to spend practically all of my time in Iran and shoot the works on that pack trip which would take thirty days or so.

That decision has been partly influenced by a visit I received this morning from several gentlemen from our Central Intelligence Agency. They are very anxious that I go and are preparing a list of things that they would like to have me look into. This, of course, is in the utmost confidence. I told them that I would tell it to you but no one else. . . .

Central Intelligence is very anxious for me to go up to Tabriz and at least visit Amar Khan. They are also anxious to have me visit the other Kurds north of Amar Khan and south of him. These are probably names that I do not have readily at hand but you will know which ones they mean.

---

1. A member of the American embassy staff in Iran.

To Harry S. Truman

October 6, 1950

Dear Mr. President:

When I left on my trip to the Middle East and India, you asked me to pass on to you any ideas bearing on the Communist programs in those areas. I have several suggestions to make and will start with one relating to Iran.

Contrary to the common impression, the situation in Iran from the standpoint of our policy of containment of the USSR is critical. Henry Grady[1] went to Iran with a program of economic aid. The economic aid, however, has not developed, and Henry, like John Wiley[2] before him, is now forced to play in a game for enormous stakes without any chips. Both Wiley and Grady have done almost impossible tasks with little support from back home, beyond vague and unfulfilled promises.

In Iran today the Soviets are waging an important and effective campaign to win public opinion to their side. . . . Were it not that the Razmara Government[3] in Iran is pro-American—thanks to the efforts of Wiley and Grady—we might already have lost the game in that vital area.

If Iran is to be kept this side of the Iron Curtain, I am convinced that Grady needs substantial and immediate economic aid to be utilized at his discretion—just as Wiley recommended last year. He should have a $100 million line of credit that he can draw from quickly and with ease. He has not even been given the inadequate 25 million dollar Export-Import Bank loan promised him last June. That is still being processed here in Washington, D.C., after weeks of delay.[4] If something is not done in the immediate future, the Razmara Government may fall. . . .

Henry Grady does not know I am sending you this message. I do so on my own, out of my feeling of urgency of the situation in the Middle East. I hope you will excuse any intemperate note that may have crept into this letter. It is not written in an attitude of criticism but solely in a desire to help salvage a critical situation. . . .

---

1. Henry Francis Grady (1882–1957), a career foreign service officer, served as ambassador to Iran in 1950.

2. John Cooper Wiley (1893–1967), another career diplomat, represented the United States in Tehran from 1948 to 1950.

3. Lt. Gen. Ali Razmara (1901–1951), chief of the General Staff, had become premier of Iran the preceding June; he was assassinated the following year by Muslim fundamentalists who opposed modernization and economic ties to the West.

4. Truman did speed up aid to Iran, although the combined economic and military aid fell far short of the figure WOD suggested.

To Mohammed Mossadegh[1]

November 15, 1951

Dear Mr. Prime Minister:

I want to add one word before you leave the country and return to Iran. I am sure that your visit has been a very worthwhile one and productive of good will between America and Iran. You may today feel discouraged by reason of the kind of editorial which appeared this morning in the Washington Post.[2] That editorial expresses the British point of view on Iran. I do not think it represents the American point of view. I am sure that the American people, as well as the American officials, are coming to see as a result of your visit the great issues at stake in your country.

There may be disappointment in your heart as you leave. But much good has been done. I think the great body of American sentiment will grow and grow in favor of you and your wonderful people, as the ugly and greedy British policy under [Winston] Churchill's management becomes as plain to everyone as it is to you and to me.

---

1. Mossadegh (1880–1967) served as prime minister of Iran from 1951 to 1953 and during that time nationalized most of the British oil holdings in that country. He almost managed to depose the Shah, but failed, according to some sources, because of covert American and British interference.

2. The editorial, entitled "Dismal Swan-Song," attacked Mossadegh for a speech he had given at the National Press Club. Newsmen, according to the editorial, had come wanting to hear about plans for modernizing Iran; instead they heard "another dreary recital of the alleged misdeeds of the Anglo-Iranian Oil Company."

To Kurish Shahbaz[1]

February 2, 1952

My dear Shahbaz:

. . . I have been trying to promote in every way I can the cause of Iran and its very wonderful leader, Mossadegh. I saw a lot of him when he was in Washington, D.C., and was very much impressed. Right now I am in the process of making a movie about Iran which will be shown on our television stations. Some of these are the movies I took on my two trips to Iran. They have been supplemented by other movies. This is a movie which sustains pretty much the theme of my book, *Strange Lands and Friendly People*. . . .

You can tell His Majesty[2] that I will be very happy to cooperate in every way in the dissemination of the information about his land distribution program. Perhaps the thing to do would be for him to write the article. If he prefers, I would be very happy to undertake it myself, if he would send me, with the appropriate English translations, the documents involved, together with photographs.

Or, if His Majesty prefers, it might be possible for me to make a flying trip out to Iran for a few weeks in June, have the conversations with the necessary people, get perhaps additional pictures, and then do the article.

In this connection you might mention to His Majesty that this movie on Persia which I am presently preparing will have great educational and propaganda value in the cause of Iran and its national interests and that perhaps if I flew out to Iran we could prepare another documentary, one for distribution in this country on his very challenging and inspiring land project.

---

1. WOD had met Shahbaz on one of his earlier trips to Iran and had taken him on as a protégé, arranging for him to work in the American embassy.

2. Mohammad Reza Shah Pahlavi (1919–1980) ruled Iran from 1941 until overthrown by Muslim fundamentalists in 1979. His reign was marked by efforts to modernize Iran and also by the brutal use of SAVAK, the secret police, against his opponents.

To Mohammad Reza Shah Pahlavi

November 18, 1955

Your Majesty:

On hearing that our mutual friend His Excellency John C. Wiley was going to revisit Iran during the course of his present journey abroad, I took the liberty of asking him if he would hand you this note. It concerns the Baha'is and their condition in Iran.

I have many Baha'i friends in America. They are uniformly people of high standing and they command a great deal of respect in this country.

The Baha'i problem in Iran is very much in the American press these days. This next year is an election year in America in which all sorts of issues are likely to be stirred. I venture to invite Your Majesty's attention to this matter only because of my own feelings of deep friendship for Your Majesty and your country and my concern over possible future developments. I wanted you personally to know that the Baha'i problem has now reached the point where it can, in my judgment, seriously affect Iran's great prestige with the American people and with the American Government.

To Selden Chapin[1]

January 3, 1957

Dear Mr. Ambassador:

I have been hearing some very disconcerting things concerning my old friends the Ghashgais.[2] Malek Mansour Ghashgai has been here for a visit and I have also received reports from Abdollah, the son of Nasser Khan, who is now a medical student in New York. I hear that legislation has been introduced, or is about to be introduced, that would appropriate the lands of the four Khans under the pretext of paying fair value. This distresses me very much, not only because of the high regard that I have for the Ghashgais, but because of my belief that they are a very important mainstay in the fragile Iranian society.

You know, of course, that there has not been a good relationship between the Shah and the Ghashgais for some time and that the relationship was further strained under the regime of Mossadegh. But the Ghashgais are willing to pledge their honor, which to them is sacred, that they will keep hands off the government and not interfere in any way in politics, and support the Shah and his regime in every way. They have been most anxious to make this pledge to someone high in our government who can bear witness to their fidelity and earnestness. . . .

Perhaps I am intruding where I should not intrude, but I felt that you would understand my deep concern. I hope that the opportunity may come your way to turn the tide. I would write the Shah myself in a personal vein if I thought the letter would reach him. I know him and admire and respect him very much. . . .

---

1. Chapin (1899–1963), a career diplomat, served as ambassador to Iran from 1955 to 1958.

2. The Ghashgai, or Qashqai, tribal confederation consisted of a number of related nomadic groups led by a patriarchal clan. The Qashqai resisted the Shah's

plans for modernization, since these would have substantially affected their traditional ways. Because of their prominence in Iran, they became a special target for
the Shah, who believed he had to triumph over their opposition in order to advance
his program.

To Thomas Edmund Dewey [1]

March 11, 1957

Dear Tom:

I have been in correspondence with Ambassador Chapin our envoy
to Iran. . . . From all reports things are going from bad to worse in
Iran. It is a very fragile situation and I think almost anything can
happen.

The thing that distresses me most is the massive inertia at this
end. It seems impossible to move anybody to action. I think some
hard-headed, positive, sensible person should be sent out to talk
turkey to the Shah, and I still think you are the one that should go.

If there is civil war in Iran no one would gain but the Russians.
If Iran collapses, as I think she well may under the tremendous
internal pressures, then there will be profound repercussions
throughout the whole Middle East. I hate to sound like an alarmist
but I am truly alarmed from the reports I get. The sad thing is that
the Ghashghais are the true friends of the West and are strong and
irrevocably on the democratic side.

---

1. WOD had first met Dewey (1902–1971) when the latter had been a crusading U.S. attorney in New York. Dewey went on to be governor of New York for three
terms and twice ran unsuccessfully as the Republican candidate for president. At
this time he had returned to private practice in New York.

To Irving Dilliard

April 18, 1957

Dear Irving:

I wish you could get under the surface in Iran. Dreadful things are
happening there. At the level of non-commissioned officers, the
army is filled with Communists. There are bills before the Parlia-

ment to do three things: first, to give the government power to arrest anyone who criticizes the government; second, the dissolution of all political parties except one which is a national socialist party that has a program reminiscent of Mr. Hitler and Mr. Mussolini; and third, the confiscation of the properties of the Ghashgais. The Ghashgais are old friends of mine and are the one truly democratic, powerful force in the country. There is not a word of this in the American press because it does not cover Iran. I do hope you can ferret some of this out.

To Christian Archibald Herter[1]

June 8, 1957

Dear Mr. Secretary:

This is in answer to your letter of May 29, 1957.

I appreciate all of the consideration which you have given to the problems of the United States in its joint interests with Iran, particularly with respect to the moves which are being taken against the Ghashgais to deprive them of their organization, their position, and their power. Perhaps I did not make clear the reasons why I think it is not in the best interests of the United States to fail to take the necessary steps to stop these undemocratic and discriminatory moves. In brief summary it seems to me that we should try

(1) to assist Iran in becoming as independent and as democratic and strong as possible, politically, economically and otherwise.

Obviously the United States, which fought a revolution to establish its independence, is not in the tradition of trying to deprive other countries of their independence or to dominate them. We also know from our own experience and from what has happened elsewhere in the world that in war and crisis, as well as in peacetime, the strength of free democratic peoples is our surest safeguard of survival in struggles with dictators and police states.

(2) jointly with Iran to prevent communism from taking over Iran from without or within and to take the steps which are reasonably adapted to accomplish this joint objective.

We have a joint objective with Iran to fight communism. We are indeed supplying armaments and economic aid in substantial amounts to Iran to combat communism and to strengthen Iran economically as well as militarily.

When we help a country such as Iran in such a joint program we reasonably expect it will not be taking steps which will weaken the ongoing program or go in the opposite direction. . . . It does not seem to be in the best interests of the United States or the joint interests of the United States and Iran politically or morally to stand silently by and fail to act when our friends, who have demonstrated their actions against communism and who have saved the lives of Americans in this struggle, are being exiled, having their property confiscated, and deprived of their position, their power and above all, their capacity to continue with us in the struggle against communism.

---

1. Herter (1895–1967) had been governor of Massachusetts, then undersecretary of state, and then secretary after John Foster Dulles died.

To Malek Mansour Ghashgai

February 27, 1962

Dear Malek:

I will see Bobby Kennedy soon and write you again.

The stumbling block used to be Allen Dulles.[1]

The office has changed hands, but the stumbling block remains the same.

---

1. Allen Welsh Dulles (1893–1969) headed the Central Intelligence Agency during the Eisenhower administration.

Memorandum [1]

February 24, 1972

It is authoritatively reported to me through my Iranian friends that there are at least 20,000 dissidents in jail in Iran. These people have protested various actions of their government either while abroad or at home and have been apprehended.

Many of them, although I do not have the exact number, have been tried and executed. The trials are uniformly before military courts, not civilian courts. The executions take place immediately, without any appeal, and they are done secretly.

Even the closest relative of the condemned man is not allowed to see his remains nor is the family ever apprised as to the place of burial or other disposal of the body. This *in terrorem* method has been going on for sometime. It was indeed rampant at the time Robert F. Kennedy was Attorney General. But it seems to be getting worse and worse and it occurs to me that someone with authority and prestige should speak out against it saying that civilized nations do not follow the pattern of West Pakistan and bring the wrath of their military regimes down on the heads of dissenters.

What is happening to civil rights in Iran shocks the conscience of the free world.

The *Manchester Guardian* recently suggested "that torture is routine in Iranian prisons, that accused persons frequently die before they can be brought to trial, and that the authorities are taking advantage of the situation to send opponents to gaol, even those who have nothing to do with violence."

It went on to say that the world Federation of the Rights of Man have described Iran as "instituting a reign of terror."

That paper concluded:

"Strikes, unrest in the universities, and the growth of urban guerrilla movements demonstrate that Iran has not solved its most pressing social and political problems. The outlawing of all Opposition parties, complemented by a pitiless repression and the absence of even the most fundamental liberties, deprive the Iranian people of an indispensable safety valve—and serve to accentuate grievances that a more liberal policy would no doubt have tackled far more effectively." [2] . . .

Those who prize liberty and the right to dissent should let their voices be heard. Freedom never flourishes unless her defenders are vigilant and outspoken.

---

1. It is uncertain for whom this memorandum was intended; it is labeled "Oppressive Conditions in Iran—November 1971" and is signed and dated by WOD in February 1972.

2. At this point in the memorandum the bulk of the second and third paragraphs are repeated practically verbatim.

Israel

To Stephen B. L. Penrose, Jr. [1]

March 2, 1949

Dear Binx:

I have been toying with the idea of flying to Tel Aviv in June with my son, going up to Beirut to see you, and then buying a jeep and driving through Lebanon, Iraq, Iran and perhaps Afghanistan.

Do you think the idea is practical?

My idea is to see that part of the world and to stay off the beaten path.

If you think it practical, would there be serious health problems to guard against?. . .

---

1. Penrose (1908–1954), a childhood friend of woD, had recently become president of the American University in Beirut.

To James Hugh Keeley [1]

June 12, 1954

My dear Mr. Keeley:

. . . I understand and fully appreciate your attitude towards Israel. Many people have that point of view. I have heard many denounce it in even stronger words as a neo-fascist project. I have always looked at it differently. I have seen it from top to bottom, traveled from Dan far below Beersheba, stopping in the cooperatives and seeing all phases of the life there. Within its borders it is far advanced as a political, economic, and social democracy. But these are points of argument and differences which many people share. All I can say is that I respect your frankness, your independence, your integrity. My present-day concern is over the settlement of this controversy which should be done, and which I think can be done. I would hope that the constructive forces would move in that direction.

---

1. Keeley, the American consul general in Palermo, Italy, had written to object to woD's favorable comments about Israel and his public support of the Jewish state.

To Miriam Kottler Freund[1]

January 20, 1958

Dear Mrs. Freund:

I have your kind letter of January 7th inviting me to come to Israel to present the 1958 Hadassah award to Prime Minister David Ben-Gurion. I assure you nothing would give me greater pleasure, and I have tried hard to see if I could work it into my schedule for the week in which June 12th falls.

I have reluctantly concluded that I cannot with certainty make a commitment to be in Israel that day. The reason is that in all probability the Court will still be in session. . . . Another consideration is that I have such an emotional investment in Israel that I would hate very much to stay overnight and fly back at once. I have friends in the Negev, friends near Dan, and all over that fine little country. I have not been back for several years, and I would hate to go on a strictly flying visit. I would need at least three days, and preferably a week, to re-visit the scenes of my earlier trip.

This combination of considerations has led me to conclude it would be improvident for me to try to accept, for there might be some development in the work of the Court which would make it imperative that I cancel things out and stay here. . . .

---

1. Mrs. Freund (1906–) served as president of Hadassah, the American women's Zionist organization, from 1956 to 1960.

To Moshe Landau[1]

April 13, 1962

Dear Justice Landau:

I hesitate to intrude on you, but perhaps your secretary or law clerk could do this favor for me.

I have in my notes that the Supreme Court of Israel in its very first judgment in criminal appeal said "It is better that ten guilty persons be acquitted than one innocent person be convicted."[2]

We are at a disadvantage here because we have no reports of your Court in the English language. While your reports are available in Hebrew, the ones in charge of that particular department in the

Library of Congress are not trained in the law. So they do not go through the material with very great facility. If you could send me the name of the case verifying the accuracy of the quotation, I would be most grateful. . . .

1. Landau (1912–), a member of the Israeli Supreme Court, had presided over the trial of Adolf Eichmann the preceding year.

2. The sentiment is an ancient one, and the Court probably quoted a variant of it from the Talmud, the repository of traditional Jewish law.

To Mrs. and Mrs. Paul S. Berger[1]

January 25, 1973

Dear Paul and Debbie:
It was a lovely dinner and I am sorry if I upset anyone. Tell your friend the Ambassador that when the crunch comes and it's Rabin or oil, oil will win.[2]

1. Friends of WOD in Chevy Chase, Maryland.

2. Written before the Arab oil embargo of 1973, WOD's prediction failed to materialize. The heavy-handedness of the OPEC embargo did not create, as many had feared, an anti-Israel sentiment in the United States. Yitzhak Rabin (1922–), later prime minister of Israel, was then ambassador to the United States. As chief of staff, he had been responsible for the stunning Israeli victory in the Six Day War of 1967.

Latin America

To John Cooper Wiley[1]

April 24, 1953

Dear John:
. . . I have been pretty much under the weather and came down to Panama against my doctor's advice. But I think the trip probably did me good by getting away from the office routine for a while and basking in the wonderful hospitality which the Wileys always tender. But I felt pretty miserable most of the time. And therefore if my performances were not up to expectation, I tender this alibi.

I am very happy that you induced me to go down to Central America. I began to understand at first hand what you said last winter that there was no nexus between the intellectuals in this country and the intellectuals in that part of the world. That is a tremendous long-term advantage which the Communists have. I think some well worked-out program should be designed to take care of the situation, not only in Central and South America but in Asia as well. I will be writing you further ideas as they develop. . . .

---

1.   Wiley was then serving a stint as American ambassador to Panama.

To Yang-Chu James Yen [1]

December 12, 1962

Dear Jimmie:

. . . I think it is obvious by now that while Mr. Moscoso[2] is for village reform programs the staff (that he inherited) like old old I[nternational] C[ooperation] A[gency] is against it and will do all in their power to prevent it.

If they were for village reforms they would not be casting obstacle after obstacle in the path of those who promote it, but would be seeking out people like you who have created the techniques for doing this vitally important work.

Those who defeat village reform programs are honest and sincere citizens; but they will in time deliver Latin America to the communists. For the main root of the evils that beset Latin America is the *hacienda.* [3]

---

1.   Yen (1893–   ), an old friend of woD, had fled China after the communist takeover and continued his educational work through the International Mass Education Movement, an agency devoted to improving political and economic conditions in developing countries through education.

2.   José Teodoro Moscoso Mora Rodríguez (1910–   ), a Puerto Rican official, had been chosen to head the Alliance for Progress, the Kennedy administration's aid program for Latin America.

3.   The semi-feudal land system, in which peons worked on the large estates (*haciendas*) owned by a few wealthy people.

To William B. Sowash[1] *(Memorandum)*

March 18, 1963

I have just returned from a trip to the Dominican Republic, which I visited at the request of the Constituent Assembly, the group which is in charge of drafting their new constitution.

I was there from March 14–17. On the evening of March 14 the President, Juan Bosch,[2] gave me a very urgent message to pass on to the Secretary of State and the President. I thought the matter could await my return to Washington today.

But on March 16 the American Ambassador[3] in Santo Domingo received notice concerning the matter which President Bosch was most anxious about.

President Bosch was most earnest in his request that Ambassador Martin be kept in his present post. When Juan Bosch was here in January he apparently had a different point of view on the matter.

Either he or people speaking for him made representations both to the White House and the Secretary of State that it would be helpful to have someone else other than Ambassador Martin. Juan Bosch now realizes that he made a serious mistake in taking that position. He pleads with great earnestness for the retention of Ambassador Martin in his present position. He says that without Ambassador Martin he will not be able to do the many difficult things which need to be done. He has come to have great confidence in Ambassador Martin, and the two of them work together very closely.

Ambassador Martin is of course very independent, yet the relationship between them is warm and I think very productive.

Juan Bosch is going through such a critical time that I felt that I was derelict in not transmitting this message by the overseas telephone on the evening of March 14.

But I hope it is not too late.

---

1. An official on the State Department's Latin America desk.

2. Joan Bosch (1909–) had been elected in December 1962 in the Dominican Republic's first free elections in years. Bosch had been one of the leaders against the Trujillos, and he headed a leftist but non-communist government which tried to implement moderate reforms. This aroused the opposition of the rightists, especially in the military, and they toppled the Bosch regime in September 1963. Bosch fled into exile.

3. John Bartlow Martin (1915–), an author of numerous books on political

subjects, served as American ambassador to the Dominican Republic from 1962 to 1964. As wod noted, Martin's relationship with Bosch often proved stormy.

To Juan Bosch

April 28, 1965

Dear Mr. President:

We have been sitting very anxiously with our ears glued to the radio for news from the Dominican Republic. As of this writing things look very bleak. But do not give up, because events will certainly turn your way.[1]

I miss you greatly and hope there will be a chance of visiting with you.

---

1. The year 1965 saw one coup after another in the Dominican Republic; as conditions deteriorated, the United States decided to intervene. On this day, President Johnson sent in American troops to restore order and to prevent a suspected communist revolution.

To Sol Myron Linowitz[1]

February 26, 1968

Dear Mr. Ambassador:

. . . As a result of my studies and my observations I have found that in Latin America [Guatemala] is the one fascist anti-democratic program which we are actively promoting as a government, and I hate to see people that I like and friends of mine associated with it. I have read everything you have said and I know the great pressures you are under. But I still get nauseated at your misleading public utterances and the half-lies distributed to the public.

You see, I went down to Latin America twenty years ago. No one paid my way, I bought my own tickets, and I paid my own expenses. I spent my time at the universities trying to persuade these young Latinos not to join the communist party. That was the awakening of my interest. I have not seen every Latin American country, but I have seen most of them. A group in which I am interested and am guiding and promoting has a village program both in Colombia and Guatemala. A Foundation with which I am associated is financing the education of Latinos. We make a point not of taking the top English-speaking group who represent the vested interests, the fat cats, but of searching for men and women of talent who do not speak English and who come from more deprived areas. We bring them to Los Angeles to UCLA. We have been very proud of what we are trying to do in inculcating in them the traditions of the Free Society.

I know you are not personally responsible for the liquidation in the last eighteen months of 1500 Guatemalans. But it is your program and that of the Pentagon which made it possible.

These people were not communists—they were fine outstanding people who were trying to improve the lot of the Indians by introducing simple non-communist ideas, such as co-operatives, trade unionism, etc.

I should have mentioned that I swore in Ted Moscoso when President Kennedy appointed him. And I stood beside Ted Moscoso in those long anguished days when he was trying to turn the Alliance for Progress into a constructive democratic force. And I saw the whole thing end in bitterness, and his eventual disappearance from the scene.

Perhaps he was not the best for the job. But one thing you can say for Ted Moscoso was that he tried. He was on the side of the villagers and on the side of the democratic forces. He was not endlessly and enthusiastically promoting a fascist or anti-democratic regime in any country.

I know all about the great and wondrous things which military regimes sometimes do. I have made a study in my travels of the anatomy of Turkey, and it was Ataturk, the dictator, who took his country by the neck and started it down the path of modernity. Those things are sometimes done, and it may be some things of that kind are possible under the present regimes you are promoting and fostering in Latin America. But they are not discernible, and the liquidation of the democratic forces continues. . . .

1. Linowitz (1913–) a lawyer and then head of the Xerox Corporation, had become American ambassador to the Organization of American States in 1966.

The Soviet Union

To Alexander Semyenovich Panyushkin[1]

February 10, 1951

Dear Mr. Ambassador:

I am writing this letter to see if it would be possible for me to get a visa to go to Soviet Russia the summer of 1951. The period available to me would be from about July 15th to September 15th, as that is the time when the Court is in recess.

My interest in going to your country is as follows:

1.   I would like very much to see something of the judicial system in operation in your country. Comparative jurisprudence has been a matter of some interest to me.

2.   I would like to see some of your collective farms, as I made something of a study of the kibbitzim in Israel and I was much interested in seeing how the collective farms operated in Russia as compared to those in Israel.

3.   I would like to see parts of the Ural Mountains. The fauna and flora of those mountains have been of interest to me, especially the flora.

4.   I would like to visit Central Asia. I have heard of the irrigation projects and hydro-electric projects that have brought vast sections of Central Asia under cultivation. I have also heard that those projects have greatly altered the nomadic life of the tribes and settled people on very fertile land. Those types of agricultural projects are of interest to me because of the fact that Bonneville and Grand Coulee here in my own home country have always excited me. Moreover, I have spent the last two summers in the Middle East and have seen what these vast irrigation and hydro-electric projects can accomplish in a semi-arid country.

I would like to spend about two-thirds of the time available to me on projects 3 and 4, namely the Ural Mountains and Central Asia.

I would be traveling alone.[2]

---

1.   Panyushkin (1905–   ) had become Soviet ambassador to the United States in 1947.

2.   WOD's application for a visa was not approved until 1955.

To Anna Eleanor Roosevelt

June 12, 1954

Dear Mrs. Roosevelt:

. . . I have been much, much interested in seeing what the Russians did to these various nationalities in Central Asia. There are very few Russians down there. They are the Turco-Mongol group of people. Tashkent is one of their towns, Samarkand is another. You could probably get to both. It has been my dream to do so. But my visa application, while in for five consecutive years, has never been favorably acted upon. I am delighted you are going. I wish you every success on the journey. I am very, very jealous and needless to say, very, very proud that you can go and that you have the energy, courage, and imagination which will make this trip a very unique and successful one.

The Russians, I am told, use Tashkent pretty much as a show place. We are prone to think that Russia does only vile things because she uses Communist techniques. We know the Communist techniques are vile and that perhaps the Russian industrial achievements are the blood and bones of many people. We know that she uses slave labor to build her cities just like ancient emperors used slaves to build pyramids. But I understand that the Russians have produced some cities which in Asian eyes, at least, are splendid cities. Tashkent has been sketched to me in very glowing terms. It might still be a second-rate city according to our standards, yet seem to Asians something very fascinating. Anyway, I hope you can take a look and find out for yourself. I trust you are taking a good camera along.

To Ernest H. Kirachien[1]

March 31, 1955

Dear Ernest:

. . . I am just getting up steam for the Russian trip. The visa has been promised but a lot of details have to be worked out. Some of the details may present hurdles. I do not want to go if I cannot have my own interpreter chosen by me in this country. He will have to be cleared by the Russians.[2] I submitted a detailed itinerary for approval. I have not heard on that. The cost is a considerable factor because the rate of exchange is 4 rubles to one dollar. Each ruble therefore costs 25 cents but according to the best information, you can only purchase a nickel's worth of things with one ruble. So for practical effect you are getting 20 cents on the dollar. That makes it pretty expensive but I am trying to get Intourist to quote a flat rate or per diem rate. I have not heard from them on that but it is quite conceivable that they may exact too high a price in dollars so that it will not be possible to go.

Since it will be a pretty remote country, I will take a camping outfit along which also adds to the expense of the preparations. But I hope it all goes well. If so, we should have an interesting time. . . .

---

1. A reporter with the *St. Louis Post-Dispatch*.

2. The State Department arranged for Robert Curran to go along as WOD's interpreter, but the Russians denied him a visa.

To Walter John Stoessel, Jr. [1]

May 23, 1955

Dear Mr. Stoessel:

Colonel Moreau of the CIA and some of the men from his office were in today going over with Mr. Kennedy[2] and me some of the details of our proposed trip to Soviet Central Asia. The conversation with them proved to be very interesting and helpful. I hope we can turn up some information of value to them on our return from Soviet Central Asia.

One of the men made a suggestion with which I think Colonel Moreau was quite sympathetic; and that is that we arrange through the American Embassy in Moscow for some air attache or other person designated by the American Ambassador to meet us at Baku and to travel with us over to Alma Ata and back to Moscow. . . .

I talked with Mr. Kennedy about this and while we did not want to jeopardize the trip or drastically curtail it by having such a person assigned to us, we thought it was sufficiently interesting to pass along to you to get your reaction to it. Perhaps we can discuss it some time within the next few days.

---

1. Stoessel (1920–) served as the chief desk officer in the State Department for Russian affairs from 1952 to 1956; he later put in stints as ambassador to Poland, Russia, and West Germany.

2. Robert Kennedy accompanied woo on this trip; see *The Court Years*, 305–7.

To William D. Jackson [1]

October 18, 1955

Dear Colonel Jackson:

This letter is an accounting of the army equipment which the War Department forwarded to Teheran for my use in connection with my Russian journey this last summer. . . .

I learned when I got to Teheran more about the travel conditions in Russia and decided that we had picked out much too many materials, that we were heavily overloaded with baggage and that we could not afford to carry much of the equipment on the Russian airplanes which have a very high excess baggage rate.

Accordingly I picked out of the Army material which you sent me the light-weight trousers and jacket to match, an air mattress, two duffle bags, two of the DDT bombs, three cans of the lice powder and two or three small bottles of the Halezone tablets, plus a large jar of powdered milk.

I gave the balance of the Army materials . . . to the military attache at the American Embassy in Teheran. His office seemed happy to get them as they thought the items would be useful in their work in Iran.

I took the small selection that I had made with me to Baku. When I got to Baku I discovered that I was still very much over-weighted in baggage and that I was going to travel practically the entire distance in Russia by air. Air travel was very expensive and I did not have much money. So I thinned down my baggage and sent my sleeping bag and two duffle bags and the large can of powdered milk to the American Embassy in Moscow. When I reached Moscow later on I turned them over to the military attache in Moscow for his use.

I found the light-weight trousers and the jacket extremely well suited to travel in Russia during the summer months. It was extremely hot through the Central Asian stretch, temperatures averaging around 120° and one day reaching 145° . These two items of clothing were very tough and fairly cool and I thought ideally suited for that kind of travel. I found the Halezone tablets very necessary because until I reached Moscow it was not safe to drink out of any tap. In Central Asia the water is very badly polluted.

I found the DDT bombs to be most effective on all insects and while I did not have as much occasion to use the lice powder I have reason to believe that it too is most effective in that region.

I expect Mr. Robert F. Kennedy will give his own account of the army material which he took. His selection was somewhat different from mine.

---

1. Colonel Jackson was a member of the army's Research and Development Division in the Office of the Quartermaster General.

To Walter Newbold Walmsley, Jr. [1]

December 23, 1955

Dear Mr. Walmsley:
. . . The Soviets apparently do not like objective reporting, judging from their reaction to my piece in *Look*.

---

1. Walmsley (1904–1973) was then minister in the Moscow embassy.

To William R. Robbins [1]

December 29, 1956

Dear Mr. Robbins:
. . . I think that education is the only answer to the provincial attitude many Americans still have regarding world affairs. I do not know if you saw my book entitled *Russian Journey* giving my impres-

sions of Russia during a six or seven weeks' tour in which I covered about 8,000 miles in 1955. The Russians have made some very serious political mistakes and have alienated large areas of the world in their policy toward Hungary. But that is Russian colonialism. Insofar as internal conditions in Russia are concerned, the system seems to work far beyond our expectations or wishes. I certainly would not want to live under it myself but it is a way of life that has considerably raised the standard of living of the Russians over what the standard once was. . . .

---

1. A Florida businessman who had written to WOD about Russian affairs.

To Robert Francis Kennedy

January 29, 1962

Dear Bobby:
I thought you would say when invited to Russia:
    "I can't go without Bill Douglas."[1]

---

1. Robert and Ethel Kennedy were about to embark on a world tour; they had received an informal invitation to visit the Soviet Union but declined because of schedule conflicts.

To Foy D. Kohler [1]

June 17, 1963

Dear Mr. Ambassador:
You will be interested in the final outcome of the plans to have me cross Siberia this summer with a team of National Geographic photographers. I am writing you because you were so kind as to round up some American women who might be willing to go along. You might want to pass along to them and their families the reason why the whole project fell through.

The original application was made in February, 1962, and in May, 1962, the Russian Ambassador sent his First Secretary over to visit me and to advice [sic] that permission could not be granted. The National Geographic at that time retained Mr. Gabriel Reiner of the Cosmos Travel Agency who in late August or early September, 1962, obtained permission. The Soviets seemed to be very enthusiastic about me and the National Geographic team coming, but the trouble was Court was about to convene and I did not have the necessary six weeks to make the journey. So we put the matter off until this year.

This year Mr. Reiner went so far as to see Khrushchev whom he knows personally and everything seemed to be in order for us to leave on June 20. But once again the First Secretary came over and at the direction of the Foreign Office in Moscow, told me that permission would not be granted. This trip, as you know, is offbeat so to speak, not being on the regular tourist run. He said they were seriously considering giving me permission to make the trip and then concluded it would be "harmful" to the Soviet Union if I went. In explanation he stated he was instructed to advise me that my statements concerning the Soviet Union had been deemed to be "harmful" to the relations between the United States and Russia and therefore this privilege was being withheld.

This may or may not have been the reason. I am inclined to think it was not. I think the real reason lies deeper. I have a feeling that the Russians are full of spy scares and a little on edge and are clamping down on sensitive areas which includes of course parts at least of Siberia.

---

1. Kohler (1908–   ), a career diplomat, served as ambassador to the USSR from 1962 to 1966.

To Gabriel Reiner

October 7, 1965

Dear Mr. Reiner:

. . . The Russian trip was for me a great success. I was very cordially received in Moscow, thanks largely to you and your efforts. Mme. Mamadov of the Soviet American Institute was wonderfully helpful, and your friends at Intourist worked things out which helped me enormously. They opened doors which otherwise would have been closed, and although I was unable to get into many towns in Siberia, I greatly enjoyed my visit to those which were open.

I was everywhere very cordially received. At Bratsk I arranged to spend an evening in a Soviet home. While these Russians drink more than I am accustomed to, and while I can in no way compete with them, I greatly enjoyed their conviviality and friendship.

I wanted you to know this so that you could pass the word back to your Soviet friends that the trip they arranged was from my point of view eminently successful.

In due course I may write you about another trip, and that concerns Lake Baikal. . . .

What I was wondering is whether or not it would be possible to get permission to travel the east coast of Lake Baikal come another year, provided I took along my own tent, sleeping bag, cookstove, and food?

I would need my Russian counterpart to go with me, a man who personally knows the area and is somewhat acquainted with the outdoor world. We would travel by the river ports, putting down in the various places which are there for several days at a time.

I thought I would just mention this to you at this time so that when you do get to Moscow on a visit you could explore this possibility. It is entirely off the beat for Intourist, of course, but with advance planning and with the cooperation of a suitable outdoor man furnished by Intourist it might be arranged. If so, it would be a unique and interesting journey. . . .

To Anatolii Fedorovich Dobrynin [1]

October 7, 1965

Dear Mr. Ambassador:

I have just returned to Washington after an absence of some four months, during which time I spent a month in Siberia.

I want to thank you kindly for the part you played in getting the visa for me.

I spent five days in Moscow. I was very kindly and graciously received, and as I went throughout Siberia I met the warm hand of friendship. I greatly enjoyed the trip—every minute of it, and made my way entirely across Siberia, although the stops were of course not more than about six in number.

I did not want the occasion to pass without thanking you for the generous role you played in making the trip possible.

---

1. Dobrynin (1919–) served as Russian ambassador to the United States from 1962 to 1986.

Vietnam

To Ngo Dinh Diem [1]

October 11, 1952

Dear Sir:

I was in Indo-China for two weeks this summer and on numerous occasions heard people speak of you. I am very anxious to meet you. I am writing to find out if you ever get to Washington, D.C., or New York City and, if so, whether you have any plans to visit either of those places soon. I would like very much to visit with you.

---

1. Diem (1901–1963), an opponent to French rule in Vietnam, was then in the United States at the Maryknoll seminary in New Jersey. He returned to his country and became prime minister in 1954 and president in an orderly election in 1955. Reelected in 1961, he was unable to bring the war to a conclusion and lost favor in American eyes. A member of the Roman Catholic minority, he also aroused Buddhist opposition. A coup in November 1963, supposedly ordered by the American government, led to Diem's execution, although apparently that was not part of the original plan.

To Ngo Dinh Diem

January 2, 1953

Dear Mr. Diem:

Your letter of December 31st arrived on New Year's Day, together with your suggestions and recommendations for Part III of my new book[1] entitled "Indo-China—A Nation in Disintegration". Your suggestions have entailed many long hours of work and I do not know how to express to you my deep appreciation. Indo-China is a new country to me and, as you know, most of the material published in English has a corrupting French influence about it. So it is very easy to be misled.

What you have done is to help me put the whole part in accurate historical perspective and to give me insight which I did not have into the various characters on the stage, their motivations and background, etc. Your suggestions are of inestimable help to me. I do not know how to put into words my deep feeling of gratitude. I hope some day I may be able to repay you for your great kindness.

---

1. *North from Malaya* (Garden City: Doubleday, 1953).

To Clark McAdams Clifford[1]

February 7, 1953

Dear Clark:

I keep forgetting to give you a present which I brought back from Southeast Asia and which was finally put together in the form I wanted some weeks back. I deliver it herewith.

As you know, there is in Indo-China an armed revolt under the leadership of a Communist by the name of Ho Chi Minh. He commands a big army in the northern part of that country. I was pretty close to the front lines north of Hanoi in August 1952. As a matter of fact, I unwittingly got into a battle up there between the French forces and the forces of Ho Chi Minh. I also went in with the French into the village of Dong Khe right after it was captured by the Communists. One of the first things that the French army did was to collect all the money from the people. This money was mostly in the form of coins. The French army disposed of these coins in a half-bushel basket. As I was going through one of the streets of the village, I saw this basket of coins and grabbed up a few. It is one of them that I am sending you and with it come my affectionate regards.

---

1. Clifford (1906–   ), a highly successful Washington attorney, served as secretary of defense in the last year of the Johnson administration and strongly urged an American pullout from Vietnam.

To Jan Hartman [1]

June 5, 1953
Dear Mr. Hartman:
. . . My position on the French in Viet Nam is fully expressed in
my book, out this last week, entitled North From Malaya. I do not
condemn the French people nor the French government in Paris.
But the colonial administrators and the army in Viet Nam have been
cruel and ruthless not only recently but through the years. And what
Hitler did at Lidice was done over and again by them. The whole
problem is presented in my new book which I hope your library has
by now. . . .

1. A professor at the Fletcher School of Law and Diplomacy.

To Ngo Dinh Diem

October 8, 1954
Dear Mr. President:
. . . I think of you often. And I know from all the press accounts
that you are beset with enormous problems. You have already come
through many dark days. And there may be many more ahead of you.
Colonialism in Viet-Nam produced a host of complex problems, as
you know better than anyone else. But what you may not know is
the great and abiding faith that millions of us in the free world have
in you and your associates. . . .
    The winning of independence is, of course, only the first step
toward freedom. Maintenance and management of that independence are sometimes almost as difficult, perhaps more so. Today the
problems facing you and your colleagues are legion. They are complex and troublesome. They would be difficult even if Viet-Nam
were not divided. They are tremendously intensified by reason of the
division between the democratic south and the communist north.
    The communists in the north have had years to work together
as a political team. You and your associates have had only a few
months in which to learn and practice the art of collaboration.
    Moreover the communists operating as a totalitarian group use
the Fascist technique of tolerating no opposition. Any minority

voice is stilled wither by the censor or by bullets. You, on the other hand, represent the parliamentary tradition where free speech and free press are permitted, where opposing views are tolerated and even encouraged, where differences of opinion shape the course of events, where there is no dictator, where men debate and air their differences and then settle on a compromise course.

You represent, in addition, a regime dedicated to the principle that all men are created equal, are endowed by their Creator with unalienable rights. You believe in the dignity and worth of the individual, his right to equal justice under law, his right to worship as he pleases, his divine right to follow the dictates of his own conscience. These values which you and your colleagues represent in Viet-Nam align you with the forces of freedom the world around, with America and Britain, with India, Pakistan and Burma, with Australia and the Philippines.

I mentioned these things to let you know why the prayers of millions of free people are with you in the difficult days through which you are passing. You and your colleagues are men of good will; you believe in God and in the brotherhood of man. That is the source of your great spiritual strength. Whatever differences there may be between you and your colleagues—and from time to time there are certain to be many—those differences are nothing as compared to the great things you have in common. You are one in spirit, one in ideals, one in purpose. Your dream is to unite your people in a government of the people, by the people and for the people. Your dream was Abraham Lincoln's dream. His dream was realized on this continent. Your dream can be realized on your continent.[1] . . .

---

1. Reports of Diem's treatment of his opponents do not quite coincide with WOD's fulsome praise.

To Gene Gregory[1]

December 4, 1965

Dear Gene:

. . . I have thought of you often during these recurring UN crises, and I wondered where you were and how you were surviving. I am comforted by the thought that you were out of Saigon in a more stable environs. I hope your enterprise in Saigon survives, and that in time you can go back and participate in more placid community life than has been possible for some years.

Your intimation that Diem might possibly be alive is intriguing.[2] If you get any further clues you might pass them along, because I had a great admiration for him and he always called me "my good luck piece."

When things were piling up on him and the tension between this country and his regime was thickening, I almost went to Jack Kennedy to suggest that he send me out to spend some time with Diem. I don't know whether I could have bridged the gap between the two or not. Then when the crisis came and Diem was assassinated, I felt terrible, because I thought perhaps that might not have happened if I had followed my original impulse. . . .

---

1. Gregory had published *Vietnamese Times,* an English-language newspaper in Saigon; he had been released from the Eisenhower administration as a "poor security risk" because, according to WOD, he had argued against supporting the French in Vietnam.

2. Diem had been assassinated on the night of November 2–3 1963, allegedly through a CIA operation.

To Jorge Gonzalez [1]

March 15, 1969

Dear Jorge, et al.:

. . . I am not sure I know what you mean by the Vietnam lobby. I was never a member of any lobby concerned with Vietnam. I did help form a committee called Friends of Vietnam for the purpose of supplying the University of Hue with a modern, up-to-date library and this committee over a period of a few years sent thousands of books to that library.

Later on I learned that the Friends of Vietnam had been infiltrated by the CIA so I resigned from the committee. . . .

---

1. Gonzalez, a high school student in Mission Hills, California, had written on behalf of several students to ask if WOD had ever worked for Vietnam.

Chapter 11

Writer and Speaker

WHEN DOUGLAS went onto the Court in 1939, he decided to emulate his predecessor's example in regard to outside appearances. Louis Brandeis, during nearly twenty-three years on the bench, had never granted interviews, had given only one speech (at a closed Zionist meeting), and restricted his writings to letters and judicial opinions. Douglas responded to an early speaking invitation by firmly declaring: "I have adopted a policy, since coming on the Court, of not making any public addresses." (See p. 43.) During the war years, he stuck to this decision, since he had enough to do learning the business of the Court and quietly satisfying Roosevelt's demands for advice and other assignments.

After the war, several things led Douglas first to take up writing and then lecturing. To secure a divorce from his first wife, he agreed to very stiff alimony payments, and he needed to supplement his rather modest salary as a Supreme Court justice. (At the House hearings on his proposed impeachment, it turned out that from 1960 to 1969, Douglas received $389,749.26 in judicial salary; in the same period, he earned $377,260.19 in writing and lecturing fees and accepted nearly $100,000 more from the Parvin Foundation.) Wanderlust also bit him, and he financed his traveling, whether in the American wilderness or in Asia, by selling articles and books about these adventures.

Above all, Douglas could not contain his energy or his views within the confines of the Court. Even in those first years, he never found Court business taking up more than three or four days a week. He wrote his first book (other than his earlier legal texts), the autobiographical *Of Men and Mountains*, in his spare time, and he claimed that his writing never interfered with his judicial obligations. In fact, there are no letters in the voluminous Douglas Papers even hinting that Douglas ever felt overburdened by the combination of judicial and extrajudicial activities.

Douglas, finally, could not shut off his drive to reform. Important issues confronted the world and the nation, and so long as these matters did not come up in litigation before the Court, he saw no reason why he could not speak his mind. He was a taxpayer; he had to breathe the atmosphere and drink the water, he had to face the possibility of nuclear holocaust, the same as everybody else, and the fact that he wore judicial robes—in his eyes—made no difference. He had things to say, and he would say them.

To Cass Canfield[1]

December 24, 1947

Dear Mr. Canfield:

John Gunther[2] is right in saying that I have been working on a book. I do not know whether it will ever see the light of day. I have made no arrangements for its publication although I have talked with Mr. McCormick[3] of Doubleday several times about it. The book has at least one unique characteristic and that is that it is not about my recollections of Roosevelt or the workings of the New Deal of which I was a part.

---

1.   Canfield (1897–   ) was the longtime president of Harper & Row.

2.   Gunther (1901–1970), a newspaper correspondent before the war, had embarked on a highly successful career as a writer of current affairs books.

3.   Kenneth Dale McCormick (1906–   ) rose from book clerk to editor in chief and then vice president of Doubleday.

To Kenneth Dale McCormick

June 1, 1948

Dear Mr. McCormick:

I received the galleys of The Lincoln Papers[1] to be published by Doubleday just about the time the Doubleday suit[2] was brought to this Court. I meant to write you at the time but have delayed doing so in view of the fact that the case will not be argued until Fall.

One of the important responsibilities of the office here is to avoid activities which will disqualify one from participating in the business which comes to the Court. A disqualification to sit in any case should be avoided if at all possible. Therefore, it seemed clear to me that I should not send you any statement on The Lincoln Papers but should return it to you. Furthermore, I believe for the same reason that I should not contemplate submitting the manuscript of Men and Mountains to you. In fact, if I signed a contract for the publication of a book, I would feel disqualified to participate in any case which the publisher had here.

As you can readily understand, the work of the Court comes first and it is of paramount importance to keep free of business arrangements that interfere with the performance of one's function here. . . .

---

1. David C. Mearns, *The Lincoln Papers* (2 vols., New York: Doubleday, 1948).

2. *Doubleday & Co., Inc.* v. *People of the State of New York,* 335 u.s. 848 (1948). By a split vote (with wod participating), the Court in a memorandum opinion validated the ruling of the New York Court of Appeals against Doubleday.

To Bradley Emery [1]

October 29, 1948

Dear Brad:

I will be sending you before very long some rough drafts of parts of the book I have been working on, which involve you and some early experiences you and I had together. I would certainly appreciate it if you could find time to go over them and write me your views. Memories are pretty faulty and I would like to be as accurate as possible, though too much detail is perhaps a bore and relatively unimportant.

Meanwhile I wonder if you could send me the recipe for the pancake bread which you and I used to fry in the frying-pan. And I also wonder if you have any recipes from your own personal experience or that of your boys in cooking trout on sticks or on rocks before an open fire. I am having a chapter on cooking in the book. It is not a collection of outdoor recipes in the broad sense. Rather it is designed to show how to cook when you haven't very much to cook with or when you have no utensils at all. Anything along that line which you could contribute would be deeply appreciated and it would go in the book under your byline.

---

1. A boyhood friend of WOD and a reporter on the *Yakima Daily Republic*.

To Phil Parrish [1]

December 11, 1948

Dear Phil:

I decided long ago that so long as I was on the Court I would try never to do or say anything which would disqualify me from sitting on cases coming before the Court or otherwise interfere with my duties here. But I also decided that the fact that I was on the Court would not deter me from speaking on large issues involving the fate of the nation, provided they did not involve the Court's work. This is unorthodox and not in the tradition of the Court. But these are fateful days for the world. I am a taxpayer like everyone else. I claim the rights and responsibilities of citizenship. And I cannot stand mute on important questions that transcend political or judicial considerations.[2] . . .

---

1. A reporter on the *Portland Oregonian*.
2. Compare this sentiment to the one expressed on p. 215.

To John Fisher [1]

March 29, 1949

Dear Mr. Fisher:

I am sending you herewith a copy of the manuscript of the book which I have just finished. It comes to you under the title Men and Mountains, although that is not the title I had in mind for it. I have another which I will tell you about later.

I am sending you this manuscript at this time because I would like to get your reactions and suggestions. Several other publishing houses have shown some interest in it although none has as yet seen it. But in the next few days I am going to send copies to two other publishers. I am not sure whether any of them will be interested in the book. But I am asking each one who is interested to send me its ideas concerning it. The royalties that would be paid, the program for advertising the book, etc. I will decide on the basis of those proposals which publisher to go ahead with.[2]

I am doing this on my own, without benefit of any intermediary.

In case you are interested in the book, I would be very happy to discuss some other ideas I have concerning it. I might say at this time that I thought a few photographs, though not many, and some etchings should go into the book. I also thought that perhaps a map of the two regions involved should be printed, one inside the front cover and the other inside the back one. There is a glossary that goes with the manuscript, containing definitions of terms and some folklore concerning geographic, Indian, and botanical names.[3] . . .

---

1. Fisher (1910–1978) was then a senior editor with Harper & Brothers; he later edited *Harper's* magazine for a number of years.

2. WOD sent similar letters and copies of the manuscript to Simon & Schuster and to Farrar, Straus & Co.

3. In the end, Harper & Row published the book in 1950.

To Selden Smyser[1]

May 8, 1950

Dear Dr. Smyser:

When my former English professor tells me that I have done a fine job of writing and interpretation, I glow all over. Your words of praise are deeply appreciated. I am very happy that you are enjoying the book.

---

1. Formerly at Whitman College, Smyser was then with the Central Washington College of Education.

To Helen Strauss[1]

October 1, 1951

Dear Helen:

I am beginning to wonder if the William Morris Agency has the standard of fair dealing which I had assumed. I am beginning to wonder if I should continue my relations with it.

When it became apparent that Doubleday's advance would not finance my Asian trip[2] and that I would have to draw on my own funds, I asked that the agent's commission on the last $1000 be deferred for a later accounting. That was agreed upon I thought. But when the checks came through, William Morris (as was its legal right) took its $100 out. It's a small matter but highly disruptive of confidence.

---

1. Helen Strauss of the William Morris Agency served for a number of years as WOD's literary agent.

2. Recounted in *North from Malaya*.

To Kenneth Dale McCormick

March 24, 1952

Dear Ken:

I finished the new section or chapter to lead off Three Worlds.[1] I prepared it along the lines of our discussion in your office last week. But I am not sending it to you because after seeing it and realizing what it will do to the book, I am very much opposed to adding it or anything like it to the book. I tried to phone you today but could not reach you. Hence I am writing you this letter instead.

There are several reasons why I cannot add the lead-off material which we discussed.

(1) It makes the book too patently a political book rather than a book of adventures and experiences, partly but not predominantly political.

(2) It detracts from the force of the book. As written, the book turns up in unexpected places a number of political stories. To announce those at the start is to make them too obvious and to detract from the casual atmosphere of their telling.

(3) No matter how written, the introductory material sounds too

much like a book review. I am not the one to write it. If any summary by the author were to be added, it should be placed at the end, as I did in Strange Lands and Friendly People. But I do not think it should be added even at the end.

(4) Those who worked with me on the book are strongly opposed to any addition of the political theme of the book. They feel it will give a new and different emphasis to the book—that as written it has a wider range and broader appeal than the political theme. Its appeal is in the music, the personalities, the hardships of the trail, the experiences at high altitudes, the problems of the mule train, the flowers, the family institutions, etc., etc.

As a result of these various considerations, I have decided not to send to you the lead-off material which we discussed. I think no such additions should be made.

I also think that any effort to put the political theme into each chapter should be abandoned.

I do not desire to change the character of the book. I do not desire to place the weight of it on the political theme alone. If that is to be done, some one must write a new and a different book.

Nor do I desire to rewrite the book into a travelogue as was suggested.

---

1. The book was published under the title *North from Malaya*.

To Simon Michael Bessie [1]

January 18, 1956

Dear Mr. Bessie:
I have your letter of January 17th and I thank you for writing me. I deeply appreciate the sentiments you express.

I had a four-book contract with Doubleday and I have just submitted the last manuscript due under that contract.[2] I have no idea whether or not I will ever write another book. I took a vow New Year's that I would let my literary contributions rest. I have no immediate plans for writing . . . nor do I have any plans for any more trips.

---

1. Bessie (1916–   ), a general editor at Harper & Row during these years, left to cofound Atheneum Press in 1959.

2. The four books were *Beyond the High Himalayas* (1952), *North from Malaya* (1953), *An Almanac of Liberty* (1954), and *Russian Journey* (1956).

To Fred Rodell

April 19, 1956

Dear Fred:

I took *Woe Unto Ye Lawyers*[1] home last night to refresh my recollection and to try my hand at a draft foreword. But Mercedes vetoed the project and I think probably she is right. She is decidedly of the view that it would do what Laski and his small coterie used to do.[2]

Perhaps it is just as well that I don't try it at this busy time. I easily agreed to do a foreword on Hugo Black for the anniversary issue of the Yale Law Journal.[3] When I came down to writing it, it was the hardest thing I had ever undertaken. I actually spent eight days on it, with at least thirty-two drafts. I was just too close to undertake it and you are in the same small circle as he is so far as my respect and affections are concerned. . . .

---

1. Rodell had first published *Woe Unto You, Lawyers!*, a volume of humor and criticism of the legal profession, in 1939; he had asked WOD to write an introduction to a new edition to be published in 1957.
2. The implication is that Harold Joseph Laski (1893–1950), the noted British political scientist, and his friends—including Felix Frankfurter—used to write laudatory introductions to each other's books.
3. "Mr. Justice Black—A Symposium," 65 *Yale L.J.* 449 (1956).

To Phil Tippin[1]

March 8, 1957

Dear Mr. Tippin:

Perhaps I have neglected to tell you in my earlier letters that I would be very happy to have you represent me in getting lectures without my films. And your suggestion in your letter of December 20, of a fee of $1,000 and commission of 30% is quite agreeable with me.

I thought I had made explicit in our conversation when you visited me in my office that I would be talking on matters of foreign policy, not on matters that pertain to the work of the Court. I have given some lectures on the Court, but they are more formal ones. I am, for example, giving three lectures at Franklin and Marshall College next May on Civil Liberties.[2] But these lectures are very painfully worked out and written in detail. It is the kind of lecture I cannot give very often because of the tremendous amount of preparatory work necessary. When I am lecturing on work of the Court I have to talk with extreme care and great precision. And I must avoid the really controversial matters that stir the country.

When it comes to foreign policy I mention matters that do not concern the Court so I can speak readily as a citizen. My expertise in the foreign field concerns the Middle East, Asia, and Russia. The talk I make with considerable variations deals with the issue of Democracy v. Communism in Asia, and discusses the rising democratic institutions out there notably in Israel, India, and Burma. It discusses the impact of Marxism on that part of the world, communistic tactics in that part of the world and the manner of repelling them. It also covers Red China and the race between it and India for the hearts and minds of the people. It ends with a summary of the Western relations with Soviet Russia and an appraisal of the ultimate outcome. It is in this field and this field only that I feel I could make lectures except on very special occasions such as presented by the Franklin and Marshall lectures this May where I take time out to write what is in effect a scholarly treatise.

---

1. An agent with National Artists Corporation who would book lecture engagements for woo for several years.

2. Published as *The Right of the People* (Garden City: Doubleday, 1958).

To Helen Strauss

March 21, 1959

Dear Helen:

I hear that Bennett Cerf[1] has started a new children's series entitled *Myths* or something like that.

The next time you are by there, see if they have any ideas in it for me.[2]

---

1. Bennett Alfred Cerf (1898–1971), the founder and head of Random House, also wrote a number of humorous books.

2. WOD did not do a children's book for that series.

To Sterling North [1]

January 4, 1960

Dear Mr. North:

I enclose the manuscript for the book MUIR OF THE MOUNTAINS. I submitted it to a jury of two youngsters and adopted all of their criticisms. These were ten and twelve-year old girls who are rather precocious.

I hope you like the book. Do you plan to have illustrations or drawings for it? The young people who read the manuscript are very anxious to know about when it will come out. So when you work out your publishing schedule, I would appreciate it if you will let me know.[2]

---

1. North (1906–1974) did a number of things during his life, including editing, writing, lecturing, and publishing.

2. Houghton Mifflin published *Muir of the Mountains,* a children's biography of the great naturalist, with illustrations by Harve Stein in 1961.

To Kenneth Dale McCormick

August 7, 1960

Dear Ken:

Your letter arrived asking what you can do to correct the errors in *My Wilderness.* [1]

There is nothing you can do. When your letter arrived last Spring saying the number of lines per page would be reduced as I suggested and an open effect given the pages, Mrs. Douglas made a bet. She bet your promise would get lost in the maze of red tape at Doubleday. I bet your promise would be kept. I lost the bet and with it all confidence in Doubleday's bureaucracy.

---

1. *My Wilderness: The Pacific West* (1960).

To Helen Strauss

December 17, 1960

Dear Helen:

You have been hearing for years about the straw that broke the camel's back. I thought I better pass on to you the latest in that series.

Some friends wanted Christmas copies of *MY WILDERNESS*. They lived in small towns in the west where they had no book-stores and wrote me asking if I could send them copies. We had none in stock and we wrote Doubleday, only to find out that Doubleday did not have any copies. I did not take that too seriously until I went across town to try to find some for my western friends. I find that other bookstores have run out and are unable to get a supply for the Christmas trade. This is a matter that I simply do not understand and it comes as a shock and surprise that MY WILDERNESS apparently misses the Christmas market.

Matters of this kind were in my mind when Ken McCormick called me last summer wanting to put off the publication date from the first week in October to the first week in November. I asked him if it would interfere with the Christmas sale and he assured me it would not. But it certainly has because you can go all over Washington, D.C. today and you can find very, very few copies of MY WILDER-NESS and no more supplies will come in until after the Christmas period is past.[1]

I think this is a matter that you can take up with Mr. McCormick on a day when you feel mean and ugly, if you ever do feel that way.

A Merry Christmas and a Happy New Year to you.

---

1. According to a former Doubleday editor, WOD had probably turned in his manuscript too late for the firm to get it out in time for the normal Christmas ordering by bookstores. "As a general rule, only major best sellers are ordered by bookstores after the first week in November. Ken knew that and so did Helen Strauss."

To Robert Alan Gutwillig[1]

November 13, 1964

Dear Mr. Gutwillig:

The more I have thought about the mountain series the more I think it could be given broader contemporary interest by putting it on a different axis.

I enclose an outline for 12 volumes which pretty well covers the country. The heading is THE AMERICAN OUTDOORS. The format is broad enough to cover boating and canoeing as well as hiking and mountain climbing. It includes the coastlines, the beaches, and the bays. It is not as encyclopedic as the mountain series would be. It would pick out the most scenic recreational places that are left and describe them in historical, botanical, geological, and recreational terms.

The emphasis in each chapter would be more on the 1960s and 1970s than on history. *The Mountains of the Southwest,* which I have already started on, would have of course historical material, but it would be primarily in terms of the present-day recreational potentials of that area.

Each of the chapters should, I think, have a strong conservation overtone. The volumes would not be road guides or trail guides to recreational areas, although they would be very useful to families who wanted to explore any area. For example, Volume 11—New England Appalachia—should, I think, have in it a description of the hut system of the Appalachian Mountain Club in the White Mountains of New Hampshire.

I would like your thinking on this matter in the near future. I will be leaving the city in a month—about the 14th of December to be precise to do some field work. The kind of field work I will do will depend on the nature of the book. If you like this new and somewhat different approach, *The Mountains of the Southwest* would be be less history, less geology, and contain more modern current events relating to hunting, fishing, camping, and hiking prospects.

---

1. Gutwillig (1931–   ) was then a senior editor with McGraw-Hill. The company did not take up wod's idea, although he did start what was supposed to be a series on various wilderness areas in the United States.

To Phil Tippin

February 21, 1966

Dear Mr. Tippin:

I found the Richmond Forum a rather pleasant experience in spite of my fears previously expressed to you. It was the largest Forum they ever had—some 3500 being in attendance and they kept me there for 2–1/2 hours which means that I really sang for my supper. But I enjoyed it.

There were all sorts of groups in the audience but it was not, by any means, predominately John Birch[1] influence that pervaded the auditorium.

I forgot to mention to you that when I was in Miami a member of the student committee tendered me a check which I refused, saying it should be sent to you. But I noticed that it was a check for precisely half the correct amount for the engagement.

---

1. A right-wing organization which, among other things, attacked the Supreme Court for being too liberal.

To Helen Strauss

March 29, 1967

Dear Helen:

I have completely reworked that autobiographical manuscript which I sent you a year or so ago. I have entitled it GO EAST YOUNG MAN and I am sending it to you herewith.

I am frankly very much up in the air as to what to do with it and that is the threshold of the problem that I tender you. It is 98 per cent final, I think—perhaps more so than that. One alternative is to leave it in your hands with instructions to arrange with my executors for publication of it when I die.

Another is to publish it in the next few years. I am frankly torn between the two and very uncertain as to what would be the best. There are still living people involved. It is a very intimate account of my life.

If you think it should be published while I am alive, then some other problems are presented. Of course the initial problem is the publisher and I cannot think of any publisher that I have had that I would like to give this book to. I liked Harpers very much indeed except for Jack Fisher who developed a tremendous animosity toward me. I have never done business with Bennett Cerf but I have always thought perhaps I should. Anyway, these are questions on which you have much better judgment than I.

But the other questions relate to a different matter. Would it be possible to sell the copyright on this book, payment to be in installments over say the next 10, 12, or 15 years? Or would a better deal be to sell it on a royalty basis, limiting the amount of royalties payable in any one year? As you will recall, we tried that one time with Doubleday and got very badly loused up with their Accounting Department which meant that one year a large accumulation was dumped on me at a time when it went into the high brackets and I lost most of it in very high income taxes.

There is no rush at all about these matters—take your own time. Perhaps sometime between now and summer we can talk about it. I think for the time being, however, I do not want you to show it to anyone.[1]

---

1. WOD went back and forth on what to do about the book. He needed and wanted the money for it, yet a sense of propriety as a sitting justice held him back; see

pp. 324, 328. He finally decided not to withhold publication until after his death, and Random House issued *Go East, Young Man* in 1974.

To Irving Dilliard

January 8, 1969

Dear Irving:

This is an unusual request and if there is any feeling of impropriety in it please forget it.

It concerns some lectures which I gave at New York University last March and which were published by the New York University Press under the title *Towards a Global Federalism.*

The publication date was originally August; then it was moved to September, then to October, and finally to December 4. It apparently was not distributed to book review channels, as it was not even mentioned in the lists that were published.

Since a month has passed since publication date it is unlikely that the book review sections would undertake to review it at this time.

It occurred to me that if you looked over the book you might find it sufficiently provocative to write an article.[1] The article would not pertain to the publisher's neglect of the book, but to the basic theme which deals with the need for a breakthrough in law as an alternative to the nuclear contest, the ABM race, etc., and also to the problems of the underdeveloped nations, politically, economically, and from the point of view of managerial abilities. . . .

But the ideas need circulating and discussion, and it occurred to me that you might like to take it on for some magazine. . . .

---

1.   There is no record of whether Dilliard ever took up WOD's suggestion.

To Phil Tippin

March 24, 1969

Dear Mr. Tippin:

This letter is for you alone and should by no means ever be passed on to the Boston group I was with last night, or its contents revealed to them for they are very fine people and well intentioned.

But I should not undertake assignments of that character. In the first place, I stood in a receiving line for two hours, which of course is wholly needless. I stepped into an adjoining room and performed on two television shows, which again is wholly needless. The dinner was nice but it was a half-hour late starting and as it turned out, I was speaker or performer No. 11. I was introduced a little before 10:00 which is no time of the night to be speaking, especially on a Sunday when I had to get up at 6:00 the next morning. It was an extremely arduous thing. I was happy to do it and they seemed pleased with the talk I made—but there again I had problems.

Just as I was going into the dinner, the Rabbi who was in charge of the Hebrew Academy insisted that my talk be directed to the value of religious training to the youth of this country. I told him I had been asked originally to speak about the value of the day school but that I was not an educator and that I had told you they should therefore get someone else to speak. When they wanted me anyway, we worked out an agreement for a substitute subject which was EDUCATION, ISRAEL, AND THE WORLD ORDER, and that is what I talked on. But the Rabbi was very unhappy when I left him prior to the dinner. I did not talk to him at a later point of time, but my position was an extremely unhappy one. I handled it as best I could, and as I say, I think it was a very successful occasion. Nevertheless, I write this for your own information alone as you screen future arrangements for my public appearances.

To Robert Lantz [1]

September 5, 1972

Dear Mr. Lantz:

. . . The point of this letter is that I am withdrawing GO EAST YOUNG MAN from publication.

I crossed the bridges that you and Mr. Silberman [2] raised some years back with Helen Strauss of the William Morris Agency who, as she was leaving that agency for the movie field, urged me to write my autobiography. I replied that OF MEN AND MOUNTAINS was a partial autobiography. She replied that it made no difference, that it was prologue and would explain much in subsequent chapters. She was prophetic at least in part, for the Bernhard Lown syndrome which led to my pacemaker was presumably occasioned by the polio. So the polio chapter becomes a new echoing prophetic incident that was not possible until 1969—20 years after OF MEN AND MOUNTAINS was published.

The truth is the whole bloody business, my dismal encounters with life, and the grief-laden episodes I often relate humorously have wrung me dry.

Volume II trenches very closely on modern life; and I have concluded I want none of it. A year ago, I told Dagmar Hamilton[3] who worked on the manuscript, that I should burn the whole thing. She broke into tears; but I should have followed my instinct.

Volume II relates how I easily could have become Public Enemy No. 1 by showing the malefactors how to do things they never should do. So I turned my back. But the turning was not merely a philosophical turning, but the show of a strength which I got from my own ghettoes which I loved in a curious way, and in which I found more humanity than one finds on Broadway or Park Avenue.

But the whole thing becomes a make-believe Madison Avenue creation unless the whole bloody mess is exposed. I have written and spoken about how it seems to be a migrant worker, hunted down by cops in dirty railroad yards. So that comes out because it was once mentioned. . . .[4]

1. A New York literary agent who took Ms. Strauss's place.
2. An editor at Random House.
3. Ms. Hamilton, then an instructor in government at the University of Texas, had been a research assistant for WOD on several books. She was married to Professor Robert Hamilton, the son of WOD's old friend from Yale.
4. In the final version WOD kept in what he wanted.

To Ed Hinshaw[1]

January 31, 1974

Dear Mr. Hinshaw:

. . . When I have a prepared speech I have no objections at all to a television or tape recording of it. When I speak extemporaneously I have as a matter of bitter experience asked not to be taped.

The reason is that the unethical segment of the press has in the past edited the topic changing my "noes" to "yeses". Another reason is that when I am talking to students I answer questions. Very often a statement I make is not accurate because I have misunderstood the question; and I find that the unethical press will use an isolated comment out of context even though I have corrected it a few moments later. I do not allow any interviews in private to be taped for the same reason.

---

1. A newsman with wtmj-tv in Milwaukee, Wisconsin.

To Phil Tippin

March 7, 1974

Dear Phil:

My premonition against going to the University of Texas turned out prophetic. When I got off the plane I was served with a Court order directing that my speech be recorded on tape and on t.v.

After a long talk with the Committee it was agreed

1. I would not give my speech at all.
2. In lieu thereof, I would stand to questions.

I did just that, answering questions for 1 1/2 hours. At the end of the hour the audience rose to its feet and started screaming at the tv men and news men shouting "Go home—get out of here—you're ruining our evening."

The press stayed. In answer to some questions I said, "In view of the unethical element of the press who work hard to distort what I say, I'll pass that question by."

There was no court order in Lubbock, but the press was there in mass

1. Denouncing me at the airport for violating the First Amendment (I replied that my copy of the Bill of Rights does not even mention tape recorders);

2. And at the question and answer period they were once more screaming at me. I explained how tapes could not only be "erased" (at which the audience howled[1]) but edited—moving "noes" where "yeses" had been the answer.

All in all I think I'll never go back to Texas. If you get future inquiries you can tell them exactly why.

---

1. A reference to the eighteen minutes "accidentally" erased on the Nixon Watergate tapes.

To Leonard Lyons[1]

March 29, 1974

Dear Lennie:

I never thought of writing my autobiography until Helen Strauss (then with the William Morris Agency) about 15 years ago suggested it. That was after a decade or so of travelling the far reaches of the world and my thoughts then centered on an autobiography that mirrored the world overseas. By then I had dozens of notebooks, covering these travels; and I started to go through them in my spare time—the visit with the aboriginals on Melville Island off Australia's north coast—my running of the MacKenzie River in Canada from Fort Smith to the Arctic; my sojourn with the Canadian Eskimoes, not to mention Morocco and the French occupation, Vietnam and the French occupation, our obsession with Chiang Kai-shek and my efforts to get into Peking, American involvement in the assassination of Ngo Dinh Diem, my many notebooks on Nehru of India, Sukarno of Indonesia, Magsaysay of the Philippines, U Nu of Burma, Korea, Borneo, the Fizii Islands—not to mention Israel, the Arab World, Mossadegh of Persia and the machinations of the CIA in the Middle East, Asia, and the Caribbean.

That was the start in putting an autobiography together, and that is the part I did first. Yet it obviously is only the middle part. First, what I did before I was 40 and second, life on the Court.

So I did the middle part first and hopefully it will be Volume II. Then I did Volume I, GO EAST YOUNG MAN, and finally I did the Court through Hughes, Stone, Vinson, Warren, and now Burger.[2]

I never thought much of biographies, for those written about men or women I knew were distorted versions. The autobiography is a challenge. It takes courage to tell the truth as one sees it and there is always the gnawing doubt that one's own life has so many subjective aspects that objectivity is hard to achieve.

Yet what is "objectivity" after all?

The essence of life is the zest with which it is lived.

The jury is usually out a long long time before it renders a verdict.

---

1. Lyons (1906–1976), an old friend of WOD, wrote a syndicated Broadway gossip column for many years.

2.   Published posthumously in 1980 as *The Court Years, 1939–1975* by Random House.

To Dagmar Hamilton

April 23, 1974

Dear Dagmar:

. . . Random House called up to say the sales of the book[1] are booming along, which from their point of view is good. In retrospect I regret I didn't put the whole manuscript through the shredder about a year ago because those who hate make up the big majority and are the ones with the great endurance and I will never live it down. This was all made very clear last month when I visited the University of Texas. It may be interesting to you to know the only person in the entire University that dropped me a note of apology was a man I hardly know but that you know is Professor Wright[2] of the Law School faculty.

---

1.   *Go East, Young Man.*
2.   Charles Alan Wright (1927–   ), a distinguished professor of law at the University of Texas Law School, had served as President Nixon's lawyer the preceding year.

To Robert Lantz

January 31, 1978

Dear Mr. Lantz:

I have written you before about the manuscript that would be used if one of my books produces a movie. I have thought all along that I should not consent to a movie unless it was based on my books, and not what an outsider thinks of me and my work. That idea was recently reinforced when I went to see the play "First Monday in October" at the Kennedy Center in which Henry Fonda has a leading part.[1] The men who wrote the manuscript obviously did not have an adequate understanding of the First Amendment debate that was going on and that they tried to build the play around. One who did not know what those Constitutional principles were would get no clear idea as to what my contributions to the Court work in that field were. For me to explain all my objections in this letter would result in a rather long treatise, but we can talk about it when I see you again—which I hope will be soon.

---

1. Jerome Lawrence and Robert E. Lee, *First Monday in October,* had opened at the Kennedy Center in late 1977 with Henry Fonda and Jane Alexander. It dealt with the appointment of the first woman to the Supreme Court, a very conservative woman, and the relationship between her and the Court's senior member, a liberal who believes in an absolutist interpretation of the First Amendment. Although many people believed WOD had been the model for Justice Daniel Snow, others commented that the stage character was a much nicer person.

Part IV

Husband, Father, and Friend

Chapter 12

Wives

IN HIS admirable biography of Douglas, James F. Simon points out the many contradictions inherent in the Justice's personality. Outwardly strong and independent, he had a fragile ego which needed constant reassurances. A "man's man" in the wilderness, he never got over his closeness to and dependence upon his mother, against whom he measured all other women—and found them lacking. He wrote eloquently of the sanctity of the marital chamber, yet the evidence points to frequent womanizing.

Douglas had four wives. While teaching school in Yakima before going off to study law, he fell in love with a colleague, Mildred Riddle; he married her in 1924, and she bore him two children, a son and a daughter. Millie accompanied him on his climb up the academic ladder at Columbia and Yale, on to the SEC, and finally to the Supreme Court. Originally she no doubt felt proud of her husband's success, but she did not like the Washington social scene. At New Haven she had known her place and been a person in her own right; she loved the academic environment and did her best to make a home in which her husband and family would be happy.

In the mid-thirties and early forties, people stopped describing Millie Douglas as bright and cheerful, and Douglas's friends intimated that she lacked ambition, that she could not keep up with her husband intellectually. She seemed to fit Fannie Holmes's description of Washington as a place full of famous men and the women they had married when young. It is true that Millie dreaded and disliked life in the capital, but according to her children she remained the bright and responsive person they had always known and loved.

William Douglas, they claimed, had been the one who changed. He began to bark orders, demand attention, and when Millie failed to live up to his expectations, he either glared at her, or worse yet, ignored her. (In his memoirs, he devoted less than a page to his wife of twenty-nine years.) The marriage had ended in all but name before the divorce in 1953, but Douglas had to pay a stiff price to gain his freedom.

He paid willingly, however, for by then, as one of Douglas's friends said, the Justice had taken up "openly and notoriously" with Mercedes Hester Davidson (1917–   ), the wife of former Assistant Secretary of the Interior D. Girard Davidson. The two couples had been, according to one gossip columnist, "a popular and happy foursome in Washington until Cupid intervened." Mercedes, whom Douglas married in December 1954, had all of the attributes Millie supposedly lacked. Spirited, a fine conversationalist as well as a good listener, at home at political dinners and cocktail parties, aware of and interested in world events, she could also, as Douglas loved to boast, change a tire in the middle of the desert.

But Mercedes also had a mind of her own, and while she tried to cater to her husband's whims, she refused to be bullied by him. Perhaps because of his own philandering, Douglas suspected his wife of infidelity. The marriage lasted until 1961, when Douglas went out to lecture at Allegheny College in Pennslyvania and met Joan Martin (1940–   ). He wooed her over the next two years, sending her presents and calling her from all over the world, until she finally agreed to marry him.

Mercedes tried to salvage the marriage, but as she wrote Douglas's daughter, the Justice seemed "mesmerized" and under the spell of "a twenty-year-old problem child." In the end they agreed to a divorce, and soon after Mercedes herself remarried, to an old friend she had known for more than twenty years.

Douglas married Joan in her parents' home in the summer of 1963. The pressures on the young woman proved unbearable. She felt herself inadequate in the heady Washington society where her husband moved so easily, so she turned inward. "I had been raised to be a wife," she declared, and so she tried to make the Douglas home perfect, with the cocktails chilled and the Justice's slippers ready when he came home. But nothing she did seemed to please him. Like Mercedes, Joan found out that Douglas demanded everything and gave little in return. In the spring of 1964, after less than a year of marriage, a suffocating Joan Douglas ran off to Europe to find some breathing space and to regain a sense of personal identity. After a brief reconciliation upon her return, the marriage faded away.

Douglas met his match at last. Cathleen Heffernan (1943–), a student at the Catholic Marylhurst College in Oregon, was twenty-two when she met the sixty-six year old jurist. A strong-willed woman who had learned to make her own way, she was "the only one of Dad's wives," according to his daughter Millie, "who categorically refused to wait on him." Moreover, she refused to be intimidated either. For whatever reason—her youth, her high spirits, her willing-ness to try new adventures, her independence—Cathy acted as a tonic on Douglas.

He willingly took her to places that interested her, such as the ballet; she in turn learned to hike and ride and to enjoy the outdoors with a zest all her own. She finished college and went through law school, and rather than resent her independence, Douglas took great pride in her accomplishments. When he grew sick, she tended him lovingly through the very difficult months and years leading up to his death. The two Douglas children, who never forgave him for walking out on their mother, came to appreciate all that Cathy did and what she meant to their father, although as Millie put it, "He made Cathy into what he wanted all of us to be. . . . She is his product." No doubt Douglas contributed to her success, but in a very candid note (see p. 346), he acknowledged her own special abilities. It was the type of praise he had been unable to give to his other wives.

To Mercedes Hester Davidson

October 26, 1954

Dear Mercedes:
You worked on *An Almanac of Liberty* for six months this year—January to June inclusive—without being paid the $350.00 a month I had promised. The delay has been due to lack of funds to pay you. Now that I am in funds I enclose herewith a check for $2100.00 covering the salary for those six months.

The salary is not high. It is not enough. I wish I could have paid more. For your services were excellent and deserve more than that amount.

To Joan Martin

April 10, 1962

Dear Joanie:

It was nice to get your letter, and I have done the following things.

First, I have asked Miss Burgess[1] to get a reservation for you at the Statler for the night of your arrival, June 4, as you may be getting in late and it would be nice to have a place to go to right from the airport. The rooms there are air-conditioned. This reservation will be in your name, of course, and you may want to keep it more than one night. But at least you will have it for one night.

Second, I have asked Miss Burgess to call the YWCA to see if they take permanent residents and if so, if they would have something for you beginning the 5th or 6th of June. She will also get information as to the rates, by the week and by the month. I have also asked her to find out from the YWCA if their rooms are air-conditioned, or if they have any which are air-conditioned.

Third, your idea of getting an apartment with two or three other young ladies who are also working for the government is probably a good one. But I am asking Miss Burgess to write you about what ideas she may have on that. She may have some ideas as to apartments where you could eventually look. I don't know that much could be done about it until you arrive. If, however, there is an efficiency apartment not too far from where you will be working, which is air-conditioned, it might be taken and held so that before a month was out you could find suitable roommates.

Fourth, the book *A Short Speech by Mr. Lincoln* is being typed and will be all ready when you arrive the first part of June.

I would like very much to hire you to check this manuscript. You can use room 210 upstairs, and put all the *Lincoln* books in there. The problem would be to find the exact quotations in Basler's edition of *Lincoln,* and then to check the dates and other things in the manuscript from books like Sandberg's *Lincoln.*

This is a job which need not be done quickly, as the manuscript need not be turned in until the first of September, I believe. So there will be no great pressure on it. But if you could do it, I would be more than grateful.[2]

If there are any things that we can do in preparation of your arrival, please let me or Miss Burgess know. . . .

Give my very best to your dear mother when you see her.

---

1. Nan Burgess had been WOD's secretary for years.

2. Joan Martin was coming to Washington to work for the Agency for International Development that summer, and WOD offered her an additional job as his research aide. The manuscript was ultimately published as *Mr. Lincoln and the Negroes: The Long Road to Equality* (New York: Atheneum, 1963).

To Mercedes Hester Douglas

February 22, 1963

Dear Merci:

When we were married, I had zero assets—except for two insurance policies (one payable to Millie and one to Bill)—and I was $80,000 in debt.

The debts are paid, and during our marriage we accumulated:

    1.   Hutchins Place.

    2.   Glenwood.

As to Glenwood: The deed was a gift to you. But after that we put $10,000 to $15,000 into the property. So that we now have a very nice place worth say, $20,000, not to mention the horses worth $2,000, and the jeep worth $500.

As to Hutchins Place: We bought it for $35,000 and put $5,000 more into it, or perhaps $7,000. It is paid for except for the balance of the mortgage - $18,000. We have say, $40,000 in it. But it is worth, I would say, $60,000.

On that assumption we have (apart from household goods) two properties:

Glenwood	$20,000
Hutchins Place	60,000
Total	$80,000

Under Washington law what we acquired is divisible 50–50, apart from gifts. But most of Glenwood—the stove, washer, TV, refrigerator, water pump, water system, irrigation district, fences, the two buildings, the pastures—was the product of our joint efforts.

In equity, it seems to me we should try to divide things 50–50. We can do it the easiest way as follows.

1.   If you want Glenwood, you get $20,000 and need $20,000 more, to get half of the $80,000.

2.   That would mean that I would get Hutchins Place, and pay you $20,000. I could do that by putting a mortgage on Hutchins Place for $20,000 and paying it over to you.

This would result in a 50–50 division of property accumulated during our marriage. If you got the horses (which I am willing to grant you), you would be getting more than 50 percent, assuming Hutchins Place is not worth more than $60,000. (I doubt very much if it's worth more. . . .)

I cannot in good faith take the insurance away from Millie and Bill, for it is all I can for certain leave them. But I am trying to effectuate a $20,000 policy for you; and I believe I can work it out.

It might be best for you to keep Hutchins Place. It is practically free and clear and, as I said, it is probably worth $60,000. The upkeep will be small and it would mean you would have no rent to pay. If you want it, I'll be glad to take Glenwood, though that would give me only $20,000 out of the $80,000—apart from personal property.[1]

---

1.   Mercedes decided to keep Glenwood, and wod paid out the amount he owed her in yearly installments.

To Clark McAdams Clifford

November 5, 1965

Dear Clark:

Joanie called from Buffalo today. She is returning to Washington tomorrow and will be at the house from about 10:00 AM until Noon on Sunday. I mention this not because I think you should talk with her, but if anything is on your mind you could reach her by telephone at that time.

She says she does not want to see me and wants me to evacuate the house over the weekend, which I will try to do. But where I will go, I am not sure.

For November 25 she has engaged the movers to come out to the house to take out the furniture. She is not taking all of it, but a substantial part of it, as perhaps you know by now. I asked her to reconsider that because it would entail the cost of sorting it, and she certainly will not need it for four, five or six months until she gets settled. At that time I could ship it on to her. She said in reply that she is fearful of two things. First, that I might change my mind and refuse to release the things I promised to release, which of course is not true. Second, she fears I might drop dead and then she would have a problem proving to someone else these things belong to her. I told her that worry could be taken care of by a detailed list which both of us could initial, and which should present no problem whatsoever.

You might want to explore these with her attorney. If she insists upon taking the furniture on November 15 that is all right with me. But I would much prefer to have the house undisturbed for selfish reasons. I would then have four or five more months to replenish my treasury and refurnish the house.

The truth of the matter is that I have been pretty much in a financial bind and I am completely depleted, at the present time, with only enough to pay the next installment of income tax.

However, I don't want to make this any point. I pass it on to you for reflection and discussion with her attorney. . . .

To Clark McAdams Clifford

November 8, 1965

Dear Clark:

Several other things have occurred to me which I don't think I have mentioned and which will be relevant to your conversation with Mr. Kohn.[1]

In the first place, Joanie has a horse called WILLOW. I bought it as a present for her, paying something around $300. It is now out on pasture on an open range with my other horse. There should be some division of property settlement for the disposition of WILLOW.

I would suggest the following, if it is agreeable. That next Summer I sell the horse, if I can get $ 300.00 or more, and remit the sum to Joanie. Or if I cannot sell it readily that I buy it, paying $300.

The man who will represent me in the State of Washington is Charles Horowitz, Northern Life Tower, Seattle. He is an old, old friend. I gather from him that Joanie, being a resident of the State of Washington, will have no problem. The state law requires a year's residence and she has been a registered voter for longer than that, her residence being Yakima County.

She said that she wanted to avoid Yakima County and file in Seattle, where she is not a resident. According to Charlie that would mean that she would have to take a trip out there and establish some kind of a residence in Seattle for a few days or a few weeks. Moreover, my Seattle friends tell me that the publicity out of Seattle would be much greater than the publicity out of Yakima, which is a relatively small place. Moreover, if Joanie should file in Yakima, she would not have to go out there in order to file. All she would have to do would be to get her Washington State lawyer to file. Then she would appear ninety days later. That would save one trip with the attendant expenses and problems and would, I think, be a desirable course. Anyway, you will want to discuss this with Kohn.

Joanie was in town this weekend and I had a long talk with her. I think she will now agree to leave most of the big items of furniture in the house until she knows where she wants them shipped. As I wrote you earlier, if she took them out now there would be storage as a further item of expense. And it may be some months, perhaps even a year, before she will actually have a place where she can use much of the furniture.

She is rightfully concerned with my dropping dead and some relative stepping in and saying that these things do not belong to her.

So there should be attached to the property settlement an inventory of the things which are hers. That inventory should be sufficiently detailed as to avoid any embarrassment if I am not still alive when she comes to claim the property. She and I have been over the property that she wants, and there is no disagreement between us. So I think there will be no problem there.

---

1. The lawyer representing Joan Douglas in Oregon.

To Clark McAdams Clifford

February 17, 1966

Dear Clark:

. . . When you see Mercedes, you may find she has changed. The chances are that she has not. But if she has mellowed, then here are the facts for the alternate proposal.

First as to the note of $2,500 due June 1966. She has the

following property of mine that she can keep, crediting its value on the note.

1. The Himalayan tent cost $150 and is brand new.

2. The painting of the water buffalo which Cleomie Wadsworth gave me is worth at least $150, probably more.

3. The horse Lady was worth $2,500 or more, and even now is worth every bit of $1,500. . . .

4. The gazelle horns are priceless. I shot the animal myself in Iran. They are the only ones I have. I miss them greatly. I understand that comparable items have sold for $500 up at New York auctions.

5. The cougar skin cost me $250 to mount and $500 to get (that being the fee to Marvin Glenn of Douglas, Arizona, who took me on the hunt).

These items total more than $2,500.

Second as to the note due June 1967. Her medical expenses, as shown in the breakdown Mr. Novin has, which will be covered in any settlement, are in excess of $2,500. I paid all of them. On that basis, the second note should be considered paid.

To Sidney Davis

June 6, 1966

Dear Sid:

When you get around to the matter of the escalator clause and the talk with Ernest Cuneo[1] there will be a question as a practical matter as to what can be done for me.

What I need is cancellation of the escalator clause, but to do that I would probably have to pay something.

What I am paying now [to Mildred Douglas] is $910 a month, plus $145 on the house. What I could agree to do would be to just increase the $910 by $145 when the house is paid for, as it will be in the next year or so.

There does not seem to be any other possibility under the property settlement. She gets under my will 50% of my estate over $100,000, so I don't have very much to offer, as I have already assigned to her all my insurance policies totalling $75,000 except for two that I have for the children. And I have already transferred to her my summer property in Oregon, which was worth at least $10,000 and probably more.

So this may be too sticky a situation to do anything about as a practical matter, and Ernie may not be in a position to get his partner to move at all.

Any suggestions after you have had a chance to review the situation would be deeply appreciated.

---

1.   Ernest L. Cuneo (1905–   ), who evidently represented Mildred Douglas, had been an aide to Fiorello La Guardia and remained active in Democratic Party politics.

To Joan Martin Douglas

June 9, 1966

Dear Joanie:

Keep this letter so you will have it when I die.

You, by agreement, have a life estate in Prairie House, Goose Prairie, Washington, after which it goes to Nature Conservancy. The monthly mortgage payments at present are $191.00. Whether my estate will have enough in it to pay the mortgage, I do not know. But I rather doubt it.

So when I die, if I were you, I would sit down at once with Nature Conservancy, 1522 K Street, N.W., Washington, D.C. whose present head is Mr. Herbert Hiller, and work out with them a plan whereby they, if possible, take over the mortgage payments or pay off the mortgage in a lump sum or work out with my executors a plan whereby the debt is somehow shared.

I suggest this course as you may not be able to assume the financial burden. On the other hand, you may by then be affluent in which case you and Nature Conservancy can work it out equitably.

To Cathleen Heffernan

June 11, 1966

Dearest Cathy:

In view of your work with disturbed persons, I thought you might be interested in the enclosed article from a recent magazine entitled PSYCHIATRY.

I am enclosing copies of letters to some of the colleges in this area in case you desire to finish up here, sending your credits back to Marylhurst College.

To Mercedes Hester Eichholz

June 15, 1966

Dear Mercedes:

I enclose herewith $2,500 check in payment of the note which falls due June 15.

Before the last and final payment is made in June 1967, we must come to some understanding and reach an agreement respecting my personal property still in your possession.

As you remember, we had an oral agreement that each of us was to take from Glenwood his own personal property.

But I have been unable, except for my mother's rocking chair which you returned to me, to get any of mine.[1] Clark Clifford has the complete inventory.

---

1. On June 21 Mercedes replied: "As you well know in the summer of 1963 I packed up all your personal possessions at Glenwood including clothing, your share of the camping equipment, books, pictures, Persian carpet and had them delivered to you care of Bekins Storage in Yakima. I also had your quarter horse, King, delivered to you at Goose Prairie. I never found your little axe but I purchased a new one from Abercrombie and Fitch and had it sent to you. I take great exception to your saying the only thing I turned over to you was your mother's rocking chair. . . . As far as I am concerned there is nothing left of the Glenwood property that is not mine."

To Mercedes Hester Eichholz

June 28, 1966

Dear Mercedes:

I have your letter of June 21.

Clark Clifford has a copy of the inventory of my personal effects at Glenwood which you have never released to me. These items must be settled before the last installment of the note falls due next year.

You know in your heart that they belong to me—either because they were gifts to me personally or trophies personally acquired.

We will be very happy to submit the inventory to court for adjudication.

To Samuel David McIlwain [1]

February 22, 1967

Dear Mac:

. . . I enclose xerox copies of the two opinions you wrote me on the duty to pay alimony [to Joan] after her remarriage, and if you don't mind dropping them in the mail to her, I would appreciate it.

I sent Charlie Horowitz in Seattle a copy of the letter I gave you when you came in for lunch. He called yesterday, saying he agreed with your opinion that in spite of the peculiar wording of the Yakima decree there was no obligation to pay alimony after she had remarried. The only function of the twelve-months clause was to make sure she would get twelve monthly payments in case she did not remarry, in case I died. He also said that he talked to her Seattle lawyer, Dan Reagh, who agreed with him.

There is apparently some difficulty in amending the Yakima decree absent contested litigation. I am not quite clear on that from his telephone talk, but will send you a copy of his letter when it arrives.

After you have given Joan this oral message, I think perhaps we should just wait and see what happens. I think she is very desperate, although having been raised in a family which never made more than $50 a month, I can't quite figure out why she is.

If you think I am going about this whole thing the wrong way, please let me know. I suppose if she made some more concessions— for example, releasing the coffee table, I would probably bow and go along. But when I got to adding all these things up last night, I began to think perhaps I was soft in the head!

---

1. McIlwain (1912–   ), an associate in Clark Clifford's law firm, handled WOD's postmarital obligations.

To Edward Kiatta [1]

March 16, 1967

Dear Mr. Kiatta:

As I told you on the telephone, Mrs. Douglas was in Larimer's shopping the other day at the meat counter buying a leg of lamb. The exact day was March 10. There were two butchers behind the counter and the one that this complaint is filed about is the short one. I have never seen him. I do not know his name. But I am going on Mrs. Douglas' account of what happened, which upset her very much.

This man in your employ insinuated that she was a slut who was in the store soliciting as a prostitute.

Mrs. Douglas is young and very pretty and one of the most wholesome ladies who has ever come to Washington.

This has upset her greatly and upset me even more. So I am sending this on to you as a written protest in the hope that you will give me a full report.

---

1. The manager of Larimer's Market in northwest Washington.

To Charles Horowitz

April 4, 1969

Dear Charlie:

I thought I would never have to touch the will again, but now it appears that a codicil is necessary. I am dictating this from the hospital, where I have just had my appendix removed, and I don't have a copy of the will in front of me.

In the section which sets up the trust with the National Bank of Commerce of Seattle is a provision that Cathy may draw down a certain amount of capital per year or per some other stated period of time. I think that draw-down provision is applicable only to Trust #1. But I think the codicil should eliminate it completely.

The reason is that the other night Cathy came in from a shopping trip and was very impressed with a lady clerk she had met in one of the stores who seemed to her to be very reliable, honest, and trustworthy. She had never met her before, but she was very much impressed with the lady's character. This lady told her a story about her proposed trip abroad and how the money was somehow or other not forthcoming, and the lady was just sick at the thought of losing out completely. She apparently asked Cathy for a loan, and when Cathy got home she wanted to advance her the money. Whether it was $1,000 or $5,000 is immaterial. But I felt in view of Cathy's insistence that if she were operating under the trust with a draw-down provision in it she would have taken the money to advance to this complete stranger, that provision should therefore be changed.

The reason for the trust was to give Cathy some security. I have always told her she is a "soft touch," so I think to increase that security the draw-down provision should be eliminated. You will know precisely how to do it, and I think a codicil would be enough.

We should be West a little after mid-June, going through Seattle, and we will try to see you while there. . . .

To Richard Joyce Smith

March 27, 1973

Dear Dick:

Cathy thanks you for your nice compliments.

She told me she was going to support me. Later she said she was going into poverty work. I replied that poverty law would not support me in the style to which I am accustomed! . . .

To Cathleen Heffernan Douglas

February 9, 1978

Dear Cathy:

You said that someone told you today that someone had called me your "Kingpin." A kingpin is a metal shaft that holds two or more parts of an engine together. You have no need for a kingpin. You have gotten along famously all your life without one. If you go back in your memory and think of all the hard decisions you have had to make, you will realize that you made most of them correctly. You are wholly self-contained and the only enemy you have is your own fear that you are not. I am not suggesting that you try to do the impossible because no one can, but in the physical, emotional and intellectual areas you are self-sustaining. So, your only problem is to keep your emotional side from getting hold of the steering wheel and the gas pedal.

Everyone is dependent upon someone else to a greater or lesser degree. Everyone knows how dependent I am on you and if you are dependent on me that does not decrease your worth because you have already gone through the worst part of the school of hard knocks and have survived in a resounding way.

Chapter 13

Children

IN HIS MEMOIRS, Douglas talks lovingly and proudly of his two children, Mildred (1929–   ) and William Jr. (1932–   ), called "Bumble." But he also admits candidly "I doubt if I rated high as a father although I did receive a Father of the Year award once." He proved most successful at implanting in them his love of the outdoors, and he boasted at the end of the seven-page chapter he devoted to them in *Go East, Young Man* that "either of my children can be dropped by parachute anywhere in our temperate zone and survive, though there are no matches, knives, or food in their pockets."

It seems that Douglas's relations with his children, like that with his wife, changed significantly after they moved from New Haven to Washington. Douglas had less and less time to spend with them in the free and easy frolicking they had earlier enjoyed. What galled the children most, however, was their father's public posturing. Photographers would come out to the house to see Douglas, and he would have the children line up to catch a ball or do something else with him to make it look as if he played with them all the time. They both came to resent his lack of attention, his posturing, and above all his estrangement from their mother. Their rebellion took different forms; Bill Jr. turned inward, became sullen, and refused to communicate with his father; Millie rebelled openly, defying her father and daring him to do anything about it. She even managed, with considerable difficulty, to fail every course at school one year. The following term, to make her point even sharper, she brought home straight "A"s.

James Simon interviewed both Bill Jr. and Millie for *Indepen-*

dent Journey, and their comments are harrowing. "Dad was scary," Bill Jr. recalled. "I felt from an early age I needed help in talking to that man. He would turn those blue eyes on me and make me squirm and feel self-conscious." "He didn't get angry," Millie agreed. "He just gave you that cold stare—and that cut you off immediately."

The letters to his children show a man unable to determine how he should deal with them. He would try to be supportive but always wanted to dictate what they should do. He claimed pride in their independence and then tried to interfere with their lives. Both children lived far from him. Millie married twice, both times to Englishmen, and settled in Great Britain. Bill Jr. lived in France for a while, then in California, and at times did not even want his father to know where he could be found.

The justice had relatively little contact with his grandchildren, although he seems to have gotten on with them fairly well. He had no responsibility for them, and instead of trying to run their lives he just enjoyed their company. Bill Jr. and his wife Joan had three children—Seana, Pierre, and Eva Marie, while Millie and her first husband had two children, Tyrone and Leslie Lee.

To Deanna Durbin [1]

February 1, 1941

My dear Miss Durbin:
I was under strict instructions from my eleven year old daughter, Mildred, to ask you for your autograph when I met you at the President's Birthday Dinner at the Hotel Willard the other evening. But it completely slipped my mind at that time.

To square myself with my little girl I am writing you now to ask if you would be so kind as to forward her one in the enclosed envelope. You can readily understand why she would deeply cherish it. . . .

---

1. Durbin (1922–   ) was a popular singer and actress in the late thirties and early forties.

To Mildred Douglas

October 13, 1947

Dear Milly:

I paid your bills and my nose is just barely out of water, so go easy on this charge account which I have authorized the Book Nook to open for you.[1]

---

1. At Whitman College.

To Mildred Douglas (Telegram)

December 5, 1947

Your mother is worried not hearing from you. Wire me collect whether you are sick, too busy to write, etc.

To Lawrenceville School

January 6, 1951

Dear Sirs:

This letter is written with great reluctance. But after considerable deliberation and discussion, my son Bill and I have decided that he should leave Lawrenceville at the end of the present semester. Both of us had counted heavily on him being there through the spring semester so that he might finish his regular course next June.

But the development in the world situation and the fact that he becomes nineteen on April 23rd have caused us to change our plans. No one can look forward with any great certainty to the future but our best opinion is that he will be drafted this summer. He prefers not to be drafted because he has a desire to go into the Marine Corps. He can go into the Marine Corps Reserves if he transfers to an accredited college at this time. He has passed his physical examination for the Marine Corps Reserves. I took up with the Marine Corps his desire to become a Marine Reserve and to stay at Lawrenceville until June and then go to Quantico for his training. The Marine Corps turned down that request saying that on the basis of past experience they found it undesirable to have men in the Marine Reserves who were in preparatory school.

The sum of the matter is that we have decided that Bill should withdraw from Lawrenceville and enter Whitman College next month.

As I stated above, both of us have reached this decision with reluctance. Lawrenceville has been very good to Bill—he has grown immensely, he has great admiration for the place and a strong attachment to it. I want to take this opportunity to express to the faculty of the School my great appreciation for the fine training they have given him.

To Allan Vanderhoef Heely[1]

April 28, 1951

Dear Dr. Heely:

. . . Bill seems to be thriving at Whitman. I think he appreciates that he would not have been able to do so but for the excellence of the training and instruction he received at Lawrenceville. He has a very high regard and deep affection for you and your colleagues and the boys of Lawrenceville. I think Lawrenceville did great service for him and I know he will always be grateful, as will I.

I was planning to write you since Mrs. Douglas and I talked the other night about a matter pertaining to Lawrenceville. Bill would have graduated from Lawrenceville with flying colors this June but for the intervention of the United States government and its military program. We were wondering whether some kind of diploma could be granted him. I do not want any special considerations or exceptions, but if on the basis of the work he actually did at Lawrenceville, he could receive some kind of certificate, I know it would be greatly appreciated and deeply cherished.

He is in the Marine Corps Reserves and will spend the summer at Quantico.

---

1. Heely (1897–1959) was the longtime headmaster of the Lawrenceville School in New Jersey.

To Chester Maxey

January 26, 1955

Dear Chet:

I understand Bill has finished Whitman and is on his way to the Army for a tour of duty. Whitman meant a lot to him and contributed greatly to his growth at a critical period of his life. At Whitman he found himself and took a good measure of life. This was not accidental. It was due to you and Rod and others. And I want you to know I am eternally grateful. For Bill means more to me than anything else in life.

To William O. Douglas, Jr.

January 26, 1955

Dear Bill:

This is an assignment to you of [one of my savings accounts]. There is about $2500 in it. The book itself is in the safe in my office in Washington, D.C.

I want you to have the money for graduate work when you finish your tour of duty in the Army. This amount is not much. But it will pay for the main part of two years, one of which I hope is abroad. So, no matter what happens, you have this assurance, that you can pursue graduate work. And if I'm alive, I will of course put in enough more so that you can do it the right way.

To William O. Douglas, Jr.

March 17, 1955

Dear Bill:

Last night Mercedes and I saw the preview of Kirk Douglas' new Western movie entitled "Man Without A Star".[1] It was quite a show and I enjoyed it very much. It is packed with action.

We met Kirk Douglas afterwards and had a nice visit with him. I told him that you may be headed for the theatre after your tour of duty in the Army. He spoke up expressing a great interest in meeting you. . . . He said that while you are stationed in California[2] you doubtless will have a free weekend. If you drop him a note in advance or send him a wire, he would like to have you come down and stay with him and spend some time with him. I think you will like the guy. He is around 40 I imagine. He has come up the hard way. He seemed like a very decent, wholesome person.

I hope all is well with you. Please do write. It is nice to get just a postal card. How about money? Do you need any?

---

1. Douglas (1918–   ) starred in the humorous movie, directed by King Vidor, and costarring Jeanne Crain and Claire Trevor, about a drifter and the strong-willed woman he confronts.

2. WOD, Jr. was then stationed with the Sixth Infantry Division at Fort Ord, California.

To William O. Douglas, Jr.

December 7, 1955

Dear Bill:

I'll respect your desire to be on your own in graduate school. I understand it and though I'm not too sure you are right, I defer to your decision.

But don't leave me out completely. Let me backstop. I'll hold the $2500 savings account in trust for you. You'll need a ticket. Perhaps you'll have extra expense. Perhaps you'll want to come home for Christmas. Perhaps you'll get married (I hope you do soon). A lot of contingencies will arise that will require money. Be on your own so far as you can. But don't leave me out completely. You mean everything to me and I want to be in a little at least on the great future that will be coming up for you.

To Mildred Douglas Wells

January 3, 1956

Dear Millie:

Bill cabled you about the wedding.[1] He was sorry that you and Frank could not have been there, but of course that was impossible. He called me on the 29th and I flew out on the 31st and flew back on the night of the 1st after the wedding.

It was a very nice affair. Joan, whom I believe you know, is a very lovely girl. I am sure that she and Bill are going to be very happy. She still has a semester to finish at Whitman. But she is going to take the credits needed for a Whitman diploma at the University of Washington this spring. A year from now Bill will be out of the army and she will go back to Whitman for a semester to get her degree in teaching. To do that she has some field work in the Walla Walla public schools to complete. Bill will also return to Whitman for a semester in February 1957, polishing up on his French before the two of them go to the Sorbonne for graduate work in the summer of 1957.

I thought you might like to have these details of the event. It was a very nice occasion; although, as I said, it would have been nice if you and Frank could have been there.

---

1. To Joan Fredrickson.

To William O. Douglas, Jr.

March 3, 1958

Dear Bill:

This is a letter you may want to discuss with Joan and your mother.

You will recall that some years ago Saul Haas had a general talk with you about the possibility of your coming with him to KIRO. The talk was vague, I gather. But it did evince a great interest by him in you and your future.

Since then Saul has a TV license and will open this week. In due course his radio and TV should be a most valuable property.

I have seen him twice this winter and each time he speaks of you and asks if you have any interest in TV. Moreover, he is recasting his will as he has some premonition of early decease. He has had skin cancer, as you know; and it is dangerously close to his eyes. I am, I believe, one of his executors. He hopes to keep KIRO running after his death under an uninterrupted arrangement.

That's where you fit into the picture. If you came with him in June as assistant TV producer, you'd grow up with this business and be in a position to take over in five or ten years.

He has not authorized me to make you an offer. I am merely putting together pieces of conversations and giving you a drift of his thinking. He's extremely fond of you. You might want to consider opening up the whole subject with him and planning, if it works out, to join KIRO in June or September.

That would entail a possibility of continuing on the side some work at the University of Washington.

Anyway—think it over. This may be an important crossroads.[1]

---

1. The younger Douglas was then studying in France.

To William O. Douglas, Jr.

January 7, 1959

Dear Bill:

Since writing you about jobs for this next fall, I have been talking around a bit among various friends. As a result, it is my recommendation to you to latch on to that Exeter job. All these teaching jobs are pretty well gone by the first of March. They sign up their faculties about Christmas time and January of each year so by spring it is too late to look.

You are at a great disadvantage since you are in France and cannot take a weekend off and visit campuses here, although if you thought it was imperative to do so, I would arrange for you to get a ticket just for that purpose.

I do think that Exeter is the choice place. It has a terrific reputation. It puts you right in the middle of New England within easy reach of a lot of different colleges including Middlebury, Vermont which you once mentioned. Secondly, it puts you down on a campus where there is an active theatre group. At Exeter you can put on your own theatrical productions; you could put on a French play; you could experiment with all sorts of things connected with drama and the stage.

I have no idea whether it would be a good place to stay more than a year or so—only you could tell that after being there. But it offers wonderful credentials and I would snap it up and make it the base of operations for at least a year. It would be a wonderful place for you, Joan and the kiddies. It is one of the prettiest spots you ever saw and I imagine they pay a pretty good salary. . . .

To Mildred Douglas Wells

February 25, 1959

Dear Millie:

I for one am wonderfully happy that I am going to have another grandchild. The more the merrier! And I hope that you have selected the right birthday. I hope all goes well. Please keep in touch with us.

This is just a hurried note.

There is a possibility of an opening at the University of Alaska for Bill either in French or in Dramatics. I think he believes it is too much on the off-beat—too far removed from the center of things.

But I have been urging him to apply and if he gets accepted, to take it. I believe it is a wonderful opportunity. After all, Fairbanks these days is only a few hours by air from Seattle, closer than Harvard or Yale would be.

Love to all of you.

To Joan Douglas

March 2, 1959

Dear Joan:

I was mighty sorry to have to write you the other day that Saul Haas won't take Bill on his TV staff. I rather suspect that Bill had his heart set on it. When I spoke to Saul last summer he indicated that it was a bright prospect and I think he must have had some words of encouragement for Bill because Bill had that pretty close to his heart. At least that is my impression.

I have known Saul a long time and I have never asked him any favor but this one. So it came somewhat of a great shock to me to realize that the Douglases were not welcome there. This would perhaps have been an understandable decision if he had been deep in his cups, but I think it was a decision that was long coming. I suspect it is the reason he lost Bill's letter of two or three months ago.

This matter I think is somewhat on his conscience. So that may mean he will be of great help to Bill. I wrote Bill, as you know, that he should follow up on Saul's suggestion because I think Saul is in his own way anxious to help. But I am quite certain now for some reason or other that we cannot count on Saul in a pinch and must work out other solutions. That is why I think that it is perhaps more important than ever to latch on to the University of Alaska job. The reason I think so is that these openings that Saul has in mind involve the TV world in New York and Bill cannot possibly have the chance to explore those until he gets back in June and then nothing may turn up. So the best anchor to windward is the job in dramatics at the University of Alaska. At least that seems to me to be the best thing yet. The fact that Bill accepts this Alaska thing does not mean necessarily that he would have to go if he found something better in the next month or so. It probably does mean, however, that he could not accept and then wait until June or July and back out because that would leave them high and dry.

To William O. Douglas, Jr.

April 11, 1959

Dear Bill:

I have your interesting letter concerning your global plans.[1]

First, let me say that we will look into the transportation problem in the next few days and try to get space for you on the LIBERTE that leaves France on July 11.

Second, I would above everything else latch on to a job at CBS if it offers one to you. I think the chances are they will offer you a job as an Assistant Producer. This is only surmised but it was an estimate that Saul passed on to me. He was here again the other day and while he had no definite assurance CBS would employ you, he had high hopes that if you and they hit it off they would make you a proposition.

I understand an Assistant Producer, who of course starts at the bottom, receives an initial salary of $85 per week and moves up from that to several times more—$10,000 a year if he makes good.

If you have a definite job with CBS or if you have a definite job teaching drama at some college like the University of Alaska, then you can do almost anything afterwards that you may want, but it will take time.

I would strongly urge you to follow that course rather than trying to get into the cabaret and night club work right off the bat. That is really tough competition stuff. You have to have a booking agent and the only way you can get that is to make contacts in New York.

If you latch on to the CBS job you can in due course develop your mime acts. You can do them perhaps in the TV theatre.

I would like to see you stamped as a TV producer or as a teacher of drama because I think that will be the best for you professionally in the long run. The cabaret business can be done successfully only over a long term. For example, the bookings for next year are almost pretty well completed. I tried to get an agency in New York City— the National Artists Corporation—to take on a Burmese friend of mine for bookings next spring. They told me just this last week it was too late to start. I do not think you could possibly do that in the winter of 1959–60 unless you had had your auditions started and lined up your bookings. So I would strongly urge you to head for New York and CBS and see if you can latch on to a good job. With that as a base then the world would be your oyster. But I really think you need a base of operations. After you have been in that job for a half year or a year you will know all about these things we are talking about in a rather expert way. And as I say, you probably could work out your own mime productions in TV, making that one of your distinct professional contributions.

You mention in your letter about going west after you have been in New York for a few days. I would strongly urge you not to do that but to latch on to the CBS job right away and get as much behind you as you can in terms of professional training. CBS, if it is interested at all, would be interested in you right away and they certainly would not be interested in you if they thought you would be going into cabaret work.

To repeat, what I think you really need is a base of operations and a good professional connection like CBS and then you can make your plans. Without such a base of operations I am afraid you are going to waste a lot of time and end up doing nothing really interesting for some time after you get back. You certainly can arrange for the Belgium artist to come on at a later date. Meanwhile you need a platform, a connection of prestige value which only a university job or a network job in TV can give you immediately.

I think it would be best if I arranged for a ticket for Joan to meet you in New York when you arrive so then you can make your plans together. If CBS offers you a job right away you could not afford to say no and take a chance they might offer you another one in three, six, or nine months. What I am trying to say is, if you arrive on July

18, you may be at work on July 20. Therefore the family should be on hand.

---

1. WOD, Jr. had returned to France to study pantomime.

To William O. Douglas, Jr.

April 27, 1959

Dear Bill:

A letter from Martha[1] says that the $10,000 life insurance policy on your life has been delivered to her and everything is now paid up until March 3, 1960. She says that there is a policy issued by the State Mutual Life Insurance Co. of Worcester, Massachusetts, which can insure you for $50,000 at a premium of $394 a year. That would require a physical examination. You might think this over and if the policy is still available when you get back, perhaps something could be worked out.

We have space on the Liberte for you. I will send the steamship company a check and have them deliver the ticket direct to you. I think that will be the best way of handling it. You should be hearing from them in the next week or so. If you don't, let me know and if your plans change and you want to come on a different ship, also let me know so we can get in a new application. From all indications on this side of the Atlantic, travel is going to be very heavy this summer.

Your letter of April 23 written on your birthday just arrived. I am sorry that we have not had a chance to talk all these things over face to face. It is difficult to put all this conversation into writing because the written words may have the wrong implication.

I was merely trying to let you know everything that came up in conversations on this side of the water.

I think you have always known all your life that anything you want to do is all right with me. I have never had any blueprint I thought you should follow. I realize every man has to work out his own path to maturity and happiness and realization.

I do not think any pointed swords hang over your head or any risk of disaster or insecurity surrounds you. I have never for a moment thought that.

I think that the one important problem, whether it is law or medicine, or the theatre or teaching or athletics, or anything else, is to have friends and allies and points of reference. Because one needs that support in order to get ahead and realize his ambitions.

I am delighted you ran across some William Morris Agency people. I do not know that field at all in which you are working, but I do know their reputation is about the best. . . .

---

1.   Martha Bost, WOD's sister.

To Mildred Douglas Wells

December 18, 1959

Dear Millie:

I am enclosing a stamp you may want to have for your album.

I hope the Christmas presents have gotten there and were not broken or did not cost you a lot of customs duty.

There is one thing I would like to have you do for me. As you know, your old horse Lightning was always very choice in my mind. He was a fine horse. We heard from Bill and Joan last summer that Lightning was somewhere in the Grande Ronde Valley at pasture and was very fat and happy.

For sentimental reasons I would like to buy Lightning, now that I have a corral at Glenwood. If anyone knew I was the one who wanted to buy him, the price would probably go skyhigh. I have hesitated to write Katherine[1] about it for that reason. She undoubtedly knows where the horse is located, who owns it, and so on.

I wonder if you would get off a note to Katherine and casually inquire about Lightning, who owns him, how he is these days, etc. She can send you the information in due course and you can send it on to me. Then this Spring I will send somebody to La Grande and have him buy the horse and take him over to Glenwood. We have a nice pasture now of about 6 acres, which is being fenced, and a nice corral. I probably would not actually have very much use for him, but I would like to see that he has real social security and old age pensions. I think the best thing to do is not to mention to Katherine I have any interest in the matter.

Maybe you should send us new measurements for the children. I imagine they have both shot up pretty fast, and perhaps what we sent will not fit them.

Merry, Merry Christmas and a Happy New Year to all of you. We shall be thinking of you through the holidays.

---

1. Possibly Kay Kershaw, WOD's friend and co-owner of the Double-K ranch in Washington.

To William O. Douglas, Jr.

January 17, 1961

Dear Bill:

I will be very happy to see Marcel Marceau[1] when he gets back to Washington, D.C.

I hardly know what to recommend to you. I have a feeling that now is the time for you to fly your own kite and not be the tail to somebody else's kite. I have the feeling that if you go now to Europe for a year or so you will get out of the main current of the American theatre where you have already made an impression. I don't think they pay much attention over here to understudies in European companies.

But this is a matter in which I cannot have very good judgment. The field is not known to me. I do hope, however, that offers that are challenging will open up from the American scene this Spring which will lead you and Joan to think that this is the place to stay for a while.

I guess it comes down to the fact that I would like to see your return to Europe based on the return of someone who has reached the peak here in his own right and is being acclaimed abroad for the things he achieved here.

---

1. WOD, Jr. had met and studied with Marceau (1923–   ), the famed French mime, while living in France.

To Mildred Douglas Wells

December 16, 1961

Dear Millie:

I am glad that Ty[1] is turning out to be a rebel. Any boy who is any good has that spark in him when he is about Ty's age. The problem is to see that it does not die out, and that he retains the capacity to tell his old lady or his old man where to get off.

The only dangerous people in the world are those who are rebels without a cause, and the problem is as the years go by to find a good cause to which Ty can tie his rebellion. On that you and he can get together and come up with something pretty special and I am sure it will all work out to the best of the order.

Merry Christmas to you all.

---

1. Tyrone Wells, Millie's son.

To Leonard Lyons

February 1, 1962

Dear Lennie:

My son's . . . screen name is William Douglas. . . .

I thank you from my heart for anything that you can do. But it would be, as I told you, extremely unwise for Bill to know that you or I had any part to play because he insists on being completely on his own.

To Max Gordon [1]

March 21, 1962

Dear Max:

My son, Bill, whom you met, should I think be screened for Warners new picture which is going to be built around Kennedy's exploits in the Pacific as a young officer. It will be called *PT Boat 109*.

There is a resemblance between Bill and Kennedy and he is about the same height. I do not know anybody at Warners. Perhaps you know someone there who would at least give Bill a chance to be screened. His resemblance to Kennedy, at least from his mouth upward should put him in a good position for the role if he turns out well on the screening as I am sure he would.[2]

---

1.   Gordon (1892–1978), the legendary theatrical producer, had a career spanning vaudeville through movies to television.

2.   Cliff Robertson played the Kennedy role in PT-109, but WOD, Jr. landed a supporting role as a member of Kennedy's crew. In reviewing the film, *Variety* (March 20, 1963) wrote: "Others who merit more than passing attention are William Douglas. . . ."

To Mildred Douglas Wells

May 9, 1964

Dear Millie:

I have your letter. I am sending you herewith a check for $250 just to prime the pump and to keep things going. Sometime [before] the first of June I will send you some more and then before I leave for the Summer I will arrange to send the balance you need. Meanwhile I am writing you a long letter, as I am dictating this pretty much on the run.

I have been sending Ty a series of corny jokes, and I will try to continue to do so if I can run across some more.[1]

Give my love to all.

---

1.   The jokes were indeed corny, one might even say terrible. Examples include:

Q.   What has 18 legs and catches flies?
A.   A baseball team.

Q.   Did you hear about the rich flea?
A.   He bought a dog.

Q.   What has 4 heads, 17 legs, and a bushel of feathers?
A.   No one has been able to figure it out. But it is worth wondering about!

To William O. Douglas, Jr.

March 25, 1965

Dear Bill:

Joannie[1] saw Jack Benny here the other day and he said he had called you twice but got no response. He cannot do anything for you except give you a chance. But that's all you want. You can count on him as a real friend, interested in your career.

Al Parvin called saying he has some ideas for you and Danny Thomas. Why not give Parvin a ring? He's anxious to get you and Danny Thomas together. . . .

---

1. WOD, Jr's wife.

To Mildred Douglas Wells

April 22, 1965

Dear Millie:

Ask Ty if he knows how to catch a squirrel. The answer is, climb a tree and act like a nut.

Why don't you forget the so-called "loan" I made you and figure that you already repaid it with love, affection, and everything.

To Mildred Douglas Wells (Telegram)

October 7, 1966

Am with you in spirit. Good luck.[1] God bless you.

---

1. Millie, after separation and divorce from Frank Wells, married Norman Read; she continued to live in England.

To Mildred Douglas Reed

January 9, 1967

Dear Millie:

I wonder if it would work a great hardship on you if I did not send the usual $50 monthly check for a while?

I hate to ask this, as I know you may have been counting on it.

But the truth of the matter is that things have been piling up on me for several months and times are getting to be pretty tight in the financial department. There have been extraordinary dental bills amounting to around $8,000. And also a number of really necessary expenditures in connection with furnishing the house, inasmuch I was left with considerably less than adequate supplies this past Summer.

Please be perfectly frank in letting me know exactly what this would do to your own situation, as I certainly would not want you to lack for anything essential, as I am sure you realize.

Give my love to all the children. And my regards to your husband.

To William Albert Norris [1]

October 23, 1967

Dear Bill:

I hear that my son Bill and his wife have separated for good. That leaves me without a mail or telephone contact with him. He will of course let me know in time what they are.

But meanwhile, if you could give them to me, I can forward some things that need to get along.

---

1. Norris (1927–   ), a successful Los Angeles attorney and active in state Democratic politics, would be appointed to the Ninth Circuit Court of Appeals in 1980.

To William O. Douglas, Jr.

February 25, 1969

Dear Bill:

I was terribly sorry to hear that your mother died.[1] I wish you-all had called me and told me at the time.

Here is a matter that may be of interest to you and Millie. As a part of our property settlement, I signed to her, irrevocably, $75,000 worth of insurance on my life. She had it for some 14 or

15 years to do with as she liked and what she did with it, I do not know.

She may have turned it in and got a cash surrender value, or she could have converted it into a paid-up policy on my life, or she could have kept it as it was and paid the annual premium.

I am writing you not to find out what she did with it, but to alert you to the fact that if she kept it as it was, someone having an interest in the estate should make a very early decision as to what to do with it. You will know where to inquire and how to go about it.

---

1.   WOD's first wife had died on February 20 of cancer in La Grande, California. The end had come painlessly, and both her children were with her at the time.

To William O. Douglas, Jr.

March 20, 1969

Dear Bill:

I have your letter of March 18 written from Newport News, and I thank you for it.

I agree with what you say, and I am happy that you wrote me fully and frankly.

As you know from my letter, I wrote Joan but did not promise her anything. I merely asked her questions. I have not as yet heard from her, although I doubtless will.

I have talked this over with Cathy and I think the best thing for us to do is to send you $150 a month. We can afford it, and there will be no strings attached, and you can disburse it as you see fit.

Moreover, while I am happy that you and Millie got Lapover,[1] I am disturbed there isn't money enough to even buy an insurance policy. Please let me know what the insurance requirement is, and I will send you at once a check for that also.

I am surprised that your mother did not make you and Millie her beneficiaries. Under my will that was made last year when I did not think I was long for this earth, I set up a trust which will include my main assets, and the trust is to be divided into three equal parts, one for you, one for Millie, and one for Cathy.

I have finished an autobiography under the title GO EAST YOUNG

MAN, and that will be published after I die. All the proceeds from it, which should be very, very substantial, will go into that trust.

---

1. Property in Washington which went to the first Mrs. Douglas as part of the divorce settlement.

To Mildred Douglas Read

April 18, 1972

Dear Millie:

. . . I went west to Spokane to deliver a lecture at Gonzaga University and missed Leslie[1] because at the time she was visiting in Los Angeles with Joan. Then I went to Los Angeles last week to give a lecture and Leslie had returned to Whitman. I did, however, talk to Joan and I wrote Leslie at some length. I have not heard from her. But I will tell you of my conversation with Joan.[2]

According to Joan, Leslie is having real academic problems at Whitman. I cannot imagine that they are problems relating to her ability to do assignments or to understand what is going on because I think she is very bright. I think it must express another kind of conflict—presumably her effort to pick up some money on the side through baby sitting, etc. and her inability to do the college work at the same time.

Joan said that Leslie wanted to come to Los Angeles and get a job and to either save enough money to go back to college or to go to college while she worked. Joan said there was room in her home for Leslie but then of course Leslie would have to contribute to the kitchen fund as they are living on a narrow margin. According to Joan, Leslie seems wholly agreeable to that and plans to go down to Los Angeles in June.

I asked Joan if Leslie's father had come through with the financing for Whitman and she said she did not know. She did try to find out from Leslie but could not quite make out what the full story was. She told Leslie—and when I wrote Leslie, I told her the same thing—that if she got her father on the phone or wrote him that he *must* do the financing, he would somehow or other come through.

The cost of a college education here is now astronomical. It probably costs between three and four thousand dollars a year to go to Whitman. It costs four thousand dollars or more to go to Yale. Jobs are scarce and Leslie would have great difficulty making enough money on which to live; and certainly could not come anywhere near saving the funds needed to send her back to Whitman.

Perhaps I will know more when I hear from Leslie—although she is not a good correspondent, having not answered any of my other earlier letters. She may have the feeling that I am anxious for her to stay on at Whitman, which is true. I have the feeling that if she leaves and gets into the swim of a job in Los Angeles, which would certainly be no higher than that of a waitress, she will be swimming against a very strong tide and be swept away—probably never going back to school and never getting a chance to obtain the credentials for a higher paying job.

If I don't hear from Leslie by the end of this week, I will write her again or try to get her on the phone. Whitman closes fairly early, as you know. I think she has just about five more weeks left of school so it is important that she be making her plans right soon.

I mention all these things because you may want to talk to her father and put a hot iron right on his back where it belongs. Leslie can get through the next three years at Whitman for less than ten thousand dollars and with that as a background she can go on to almost anything she wants—whether it be teaching, music, business, or what not.

My love to you all.

---

1. Leslie Wells, Millie's daughter.
2. WOD, Jr.'s wife.

To William O. Douglas, Jr.

November 28, 1972

Dear Bill:

. . . I do not know what you should do in the years ahead. You have great talent in writing and speaking. I hope you cultivate both.

I think you mastered the short story years ago. You can write them—and novels—and plays. While you are marking time, take my play THE DEVIL AND THE LORD and rewrite it. It should be produced, and you'll know how to do it.

Your speaking should be more than playing roles. You should run for public office, perhaps. Or get a series of Lectures and go on the Lecture tour. Your Lectures could cover the modern world—the needs of a pluralistic society—the danger of keeping government on the backs of people, etc.

Once you start down a road of writing and speaking, unknown avenues will open up to you.

Keep on display and keep punching.

It's a hard, hard life. But it is worth it.

They want my seat so badly they will try again in 1973 to unseat me.[1] I hope you do not have to suffer for my unpopularity with the powers-that-be.

---

1. WOD had just survived an effort to impeach him; see chapter 15.

To Joan Douglas

May 16, 1973

Dear Joan:

Thanks for your note. I have no address for Bill. Mail sent to him at Sonoma is returned. I called his former associate at the Berkeley Little Theatre and he has no idea where Bill is. I called Lostine and learned that he has not been there. I am very anxious to talk with him.

To Mildred Douglas Read

November 15, 1974

Dear Millie:

Yes, we keep in touch with Joan.

Yes, we write Pierre and discover he's not as sick as you said.

Yes, we write Seana and Eva Marie.

Yes, we write Martha [Bost] and talk with her on the phone.

Yes, I write Bill—many times.

No, Bill never answers.

No, his sister is superb in writing nasty letters.

To Mildred Douglas Read

January 15, 1975

Dear Millie:

A lot of changes have taken place since the last letter I wrote you. . . . Leslie came on schedule, stayed with us, and we enjoyed her visit very much.

She has matured greatly and I think that the American College that she has attended has helped her considerably. She is composed and self-reliant and getting along very well. She left here on schedule on January 4th going back to Spokane by air and then by bus to Pullman.

I hope your plans to come here next summer go through. Please let me know and I'll try to send some funds to assist you. We'd like very much to see you.

When I was in the hospital in Portland a man who was a stranger to me came in with a letter from Ty. The letter Ty wrote was very gracious and tell Ty I greatly appreciated it.

Bill was here until yesterday and has now gone West.

To William O. Douglas, Jr.

January 15, 1975

Dear Bill:

. . . It was great having you with us. We may have had a few cross words but they don't mean anything. My respect for you is unbounded as is my admiration and love. I respect you greatly. You are welcome anytime.

To William O. Douglas, Jr.

October 12, 1975

Dear Bill,

Since by your account everything I do is "evil", I began to wonder why helping you financially was not also "evil". Joan always has blamed me for your irresponsibility.

You have a Nikon camera and light meter which cost about $600. You want a lens which will cost $500. Is this not evil coming from me if I finance this? If I do would you insure the articles against loss or theft making the policy payable to me?

Or is that another evidence of my "evil nature"?

To Mildred Douglas Read

May 4, 1976

Dear Millie:

Cathy is quite upset about my going to Goose Prairie for the summer. She says that it is too remote from doctors, which is one of its advantages from my point of view. I don't want to spend the summer in a hospital or medical institute taking therapy. I really need a place where I can relax, sleep, and do some work.

The only other possibility I can think of is Lapover. I've asked her to ask you if we can work out an arrangement whereby we might rent the place for the month of July or something along those lines. . . .

I'm [anxious to see you] so hurry and write to me at Goose Prairie. I'd like to send you some money to help pay for your air fare. . . .

I'm hoping to get to the Prairie in time to attend the Joseph Rodeo. It is held the last weekend in July. We might be able to fly from Yakima as we did once before or perhaps we could drive over if we are at Lapover.

Chapter 14

The Powell C Club

Douglas had, it seemed, thousands of acquaintances, many of whom he referred to as "good" or "close" friends. But there was a smaller group of really close friends, men and a few women he had known from his early years, and with whom he kept contact over the years. Dipping at random into those various files does not provide the true flavor of these friendships, so it seemed more appropriate to take one file and reprint it in full. The correspondence with Thomas Reed Powell (1880–1955) shows Douglas at his wittiest, and how much he enjoyed intellectual give and take, especially when it dealt with matters of the law.

Powell provided a model for Douglas and other young Realists in that he not only had a law degree (Harvard, 1904), but a doctorate in political science (Columbia, 1913) as well. He taught administrative law at Columbia in the early twenties, and then moved to Harvard in 1925. Douglas described him as "an iconoclast. He was the offbeat intellectual who could cut the Supreme Court into ribbons in any field of constitutional law."

Douglas took his course in the third year and turned in a paper he felt sure would receive an A; instead, Powell gave him a C, the lowest grade Douglas received at Columbia. Shortly afterwards, Douglas and some others who had fared similarly joined to form the Powell C Club, which met irregularly afterwards. In a letter to a law school friend, Phil Graham, on October 2, 1939, Douglas wrote:

> . . . You have been elected President of the Powell C Club. Your tenure is in nowise dependent on your good behavior. To make

it such would be out of harmony with the Club's spirit and not consonant with those qualities which our preceptor has and which we seek to perpetuate.

Perhaps you do not know of the Powell C Club. It was formed at Columbia in 1925 as a reprisal against a professor who taught:

'Law's not imperishably writ in ink
It turns upon what judges think
And by and large you'll find they ———.'[1]

The creed was not new to him in 1925. He had followed it ever since it started giving him a living years before. But it was new and startling to the unsophisticated lads who sat at his feet. Those who reserved decision or substituted "occasionally" for "by and large" did not make out so well. Yet he was by nature a kindly man and tolerant. And instead of flunking those students he adopted the policy of giving them all C's—perhaps as a concession to the role of dissenting opinions. As a result, by the time I got my Powell C in May 1925 the ranks of that group had so swollen that we feared the mere weight of numbers would leave the false impression that mediocrity was our outstanding distinction. So we formed the Powell C Club. It was exclusive—one must have a C to join. It was fraternal—we were bound together for the purpose of keeping alive the memories of the mistaken judgment of our former master.

The years rolled by and in 1930 at the end of a long and convivial evening in New Haven, I was made President of the Club. At that time our preceptor was taken in as an Honorary Member. He was so touched by that that he endeavored to get the Columbia authorities to raise the grade of myself and other Powell C Club members from a C to a B. He was thwarted in that endeavor, however, by the condition precedent which was attached—viz., that a new examination need be taken and all parties would have to abide by the results. That prospect was so terrifying that the matter was dropped. Hence we gave up all hope of escaping from our lowly rating and decided to capitalize on it. If, as a result, humiliation was heaped upon our preceptor, it did not exceed what, in view of all the circumstances, was proper.

But recently time and tide have wrought great changes. I can no longer with comfort remain as President of the Powell C Club. Back in 1925 I thought I had written my last examination paper in Constitutional Law. As it now turns out that was merely a warming up exercise. I will now be writing them all my life. But that isn't half of it. The same guy reads the papers. More than that he grades them. I am not intimating that I want to escape the Powell C Club because I think I can now get an A or even a B. From what has transpired so far, I think I will be lucky to have that particular score-keeper give me another C.

Despite the grade, Douglas remained friends with Powell, and the latter did in fact "grade" his Supreme Court opinions with an irregular "Report Card." The two men drifted apart in the mid-forties. In his memoirs, Douglas derided Powell for becoming "a spokesman for the Establishment when he reached Harvard." More likely Powell's intellectual support for Felix Frankfurter's doctrine of judicial restraint irked Douglas, who by then had joined with Hugo Black in advocating a more activist role for the Court, especially in civil liberties.

---

1. WOD had added, as a footnote, "My class notes are blurred at this point."

November 18, 1930

Dear T.R.:

I never realized before I received your letter of the 14th what the functional approach was. Now that I have found out I have climbed on the band wagon. Evidently I have been a functionalist for years and did not know it.

I thank you for your statement of the law. I consider it authoritative without the customary footnote material. However, I have a hunch that the Supreme Court will have to reverse another district court.[1]

In the future I will do all that is in my power to equalize the equation between the amount received for concocting nonsense and the amount expended to offend.

---

1. WOD had written a few days earlier to ask Powell if he had any ideas about how the Eighteenth Amendment might be declared unconstitutional, since Judge Clark was about to decide a prohibition case; see p. 14.

February 9, 1931

Dear T. R.:

That you of all persons should think that I would go to Chicago for $18,000 is most distressing, especially in view of the fact that I thought I had passed through that stage when I did not recognize applied functionalism when I saw it.[1]

I never took the Supreme Court seriously because you taught me not to. For a monastic life I think both you and they are vastly underpaid. Salaries should be adjusted upwards on the basis of what you may not do rather than in accordance with what you may do and do do. (By reading the last sentence hurriedly, a better effect can be secured.) On this theory you can see why the Supreme Court should receive more than you—since you always have the last word—and why I should receive more than the paltry sum you so lightly mention—since I will have not even the security of a monastery. . . .

If I could predict all decisions as well as I did Clark's, I might stand a chance of getting to Harvard. Applying my formula again I think the price you mention would be close enough.

At four o'clock the other morning Al McCormack and I had a toast to you, affirmed you twice and were about to reverse you once—all on the same case—when someone got a little incoherent and the discussion got off on Judge Lindsey's new book.[2] Which proves that the Powell approach has endless possibilities.

---

1. Powell had heard rumors that WOD had accepted an offer at Chicago for $18,000 (see p. 13), and said that if WOD got that much, then he would want at least $24,000. "But why not go on the Supreme Court?" he asked. "They pay well there too, and you don't have to be intellectual."

2. Benjamin Barr Lindsey (1869–1943) of Denver was probably best known for his pioneering work in juvenile justice. He had just published his autobiography, *The Dangerous Life*.

July 14, 1931

My dear T.R.:

Now that your dean and curator has gone functional how are you going to handle the problem of the dynasty?[1] In sporting circles here the odds are 9 to 1 against it. (We know that the boys of Harvard Square always rated him higher.)

Strange to say we had taken it as a personal accomplishment until some Princeton wag (or perhaps it was a Columbia realist) suggested that the Commission[2] had considerable to do about it. There is also some opinion that hereafter Jurisprudence will have a little more realism in it.

I hope you made your party of the 18th as great a success as you did our bankruptcy dinner.

---

1. Pound, then sixty-one and a widower, had just remarried; he and Mrs. Lucy Miller would be married for twenty-eight years before she died. According to Powell, "The lady has reached the mature age of forty or thereabouts. Our earlier reports were that she had been chasing him ever since he went to Washington, but that he was inclined to flee. I trust the consummation will make him happier."

2. The President's Commission on Law Enforcement, of which Pound was a member.

January 24, 1934

My dearest Reed:

Having just recovered from the shock received in reading your letter of April 6, 1933, I hasten to reply to it. The various animadversions which you cast from time to time to my little note in 25 Columbia Law Review 470[1] had me so completely baffled that I did not have the nerve to read it until I received your letter of April 6, 1933. At that time I did read it. I cannot say that my chest swelled out so far that I lost any buttons, but nevertheless I did not hide my face in shame. I do not think the note is anything more nor less than an interesting exercise and it probably did me no great damage to get my exercise that way instead of playing handball with Eachenthal at the dirty old Columbia gymnasium. I do not think I would promote a statute prohibiting students from doing things like that because I see so many of my own students and even my colleagues doing things so much worse.

After all you may be right about the C. To be rated as C by you is more of a compliment than to be rated as A by so many others I know. After all it does not represent what I am or what I was, but what you thought I was at one point of time. And now that you are convinced that I rate at least an A plus, I remain content.

---

1. As a student at Columbia, WOD had published an unsigned note on "Deprivation of 'Property' by Retroactive Legislation." Powell had evidently, as he put it, occasionally "cast animadversions" on the note, but on rereading had decided that it was a good piece of work.

March 27, 1934

Dear Reed:

When the spring gets a little further along, the Powell C Club will send you a formal communication inviting you and Henry Hart[1] to drink and sleep in the distinguished visitors' suite in the Sterling Law Building from Wednesday to Sunday, inclusive, of some week. Meanwhile I will see to it that the members of the Powell C Club do sufficient basking so as to be in proper form for the occasion.

Thurman [Arnold]'s habit of using my envelopes is expensive, but it has its compensatory features. Since a large percentage of his addresses are always wrong I have been in an enviable position of reading his mail without violating any standards of ethics or statutes of these United States.

Your reference to the instability of the Constitution shakes me not a little.[2] Is the reason why I got a C the fact that I thought the Constitution never changed but that it was a great flexible document and that the only problem in Constitutional Law was to find out what the forefathers really meant?. . .

---

1.   Henry Melvin Hart, Jr. (1904–1969) had just started his long tenure teaching at the Harvard Law School; he would become one of the nation's outstanding authorities on the federal courts system.

2.   Powell had written: "The situation of the Constitution is not the same as it was when last you were here, and this, perhaps, is something worthy of celebration. . . . I have been looking forward to the end of prohibition the way Jimmy Walker must have been looking forward to his marriage to Betty Compton. Now that the consummation is here I don't find things greatly different from what they were before, except they are more expensive."

November 12, 1938

Dear Reed:

The reunion of the Powell C Club was, so far as I was concerned, a complete success. I regretted very much that I had to leave comparatively sober which is, as I recall, a strong break with tradition. But if that turns out to be a reflection on that famous club, I promise to make amends at an early date. Aside from that matter of omission, I have one other regret and that is that I did not explain to the assembled multitudes the real significance of the Powell C Club, with an illustration of how even you might be wrong. But I refrained because of my feeling that if strong men were looking for confidence through certainty, I could justifiably transform for one occasion the SEC into the HUSH.

All of which is my C plus . . . manner of saying that it was swell to see you.

October 14, 1940

Dear Reed:

I was glad to get my report card. The delay made me a bit uneasy, for I feared that it meant I had fallen from a C to a D.

I am very happy to know that I am holding my own. That deduction was made as follows: Since I am better than "some", I probably stand seventh in the class. For "some" means at least two. That puts me in the bottom third of the class—where I was 15 years ago. But to be at the top of the bottom third cannot mean (even on the Harvard system of grading) that I got more than a C. . . .[1]

---

1. Powell had begun sending WOD a "report card," often in verse, on his performance on the bench the preceding term.

January 6, 1941

Report Card—1939 Term

The term was closed, opinions filed;
Though work was o'er for me,
My grades were yet to be received
From Harvard's T.R.P.

It seemed it always had been thus,
For in an earlier day
On constitutional quizzes, he,
Not I, had final say.

Of course it's now not quite the same,
For once he could correct
Conclusions as to voters' powers,
And those whom they elect.

But now, so far as I'm concerned,
He can't do more than grade;

Not even he plus four can change
A rule which I have made.

Yet still his power's not on the wane;
Suspense is in the air
As days go by and you don't know
If you are "poor" or "fair".

One eyes the mails and law reviews
For sign, or trace, or clue
Of what is working in his mind
And how he's grading you.

All this and more were my concern;
Each week was spoiled for me,
As months went by and wonder grew
If I had slipped to D.

At last I sent a friendly note,
Discreetly asking why
With such a little group to grade,
He still had passed me by.

More weeks went by and then one day
The postman brought the news:
The oracle of oracles
At last divulged his views.

He did not rate me "poor" or "fair",
"Feckless"[1] or "dull", or "dumb";
He merely said that I had done
A "better" job than "some".

I was elated with the news
Though of the group of nine,
It meant that there were five or six
With better grades than mine.

But I felt happy just the same,
For "some" to me meant "two";
That put me in the bottom third—
Now, do you get the clue?

That spot is where I always was,
Since first I got a C
For effort spent in writing down
What T.R.P. taught me.

The bottom third is still my rank;
I do not grieve or moan—
For those who mix with T.R.P.
Do well to hold their own.

---

1. WOD had written as a note here: "See *Puerto Rico* v. *Rubert Co.*, 309 U.S. 543, 549." On that page Frankfurter's majority opinion noted that the meaning of a word often depends on its context.

March 5, 1941

Dear Teacher:

Your report on our William was long overdue[1]
(Say we to his Teacher, say we)
And now that we have it we're bothered anew
(Say we to his Teacher, say we)
We thought all the others were doing just fine
With felixitous[2] phrases and logic sublime
And decisions that laid it right down on the line
(Say we to his Teacher, say we)

Cho. Mr. & Mrs. S.C. are we
      With our small happy family
      We ask your indulgence
      In grading each son
      We wanted some more
      But were told we were done

Till now you said William was worth but a C
(Say we to his Teacher, say we)
Though he worked very hard to get up to a B
(Say we to his Teacher, say we)
But the others were bright, so people did say
So ingenious, so agile, so quick and so gay
That with hardly no effort they would garner an A
(Say we to their Teacher, say we)

Cho. Mr. & Mrs. S.C. are we
      We're proud of our fraternity
      We notice with joy how
      Our boys knock 'em cold—
      How learned, how fervent
      How dashing, how bold!

Our worry was always the things that they did
(Say we to their Teacher, say we)
Poor reasons or logic we'd never forbid
(Say we to their Teacher, say we)
But now when their reasons appear to be weak
You say that their morals are starting to creak
Against which young William should STAND UP AND SPEAK
(Say we to his Teacher, say we)

Cho. Mr. & Mrs. s.c. are we
      Nine sons are all we'll ever see
      We ask your forbearance
      In rating our boys
      Their deeds give us pause
      Not their logic or noise

When there is a tax on the fuel in the tank
(Say we to the Maestro, say we)
And the tax must be paid, you have William to thank.
(Say we to the Maestro, say we)
For William won't wink at the extra big can
Which is added for mileage—a devious plan
To bring down the foreign and interstate ban
(Say we to the Maestro, say we)

Cho. Mr. & Mrs. s.c. are we
      We ask your generosity
      We hope you'll forgive us
      For "puffing" our sons
      Whatever you say
      They are our only ones

A brother who drafted an Act late at night
(Say we to his Teacher, say we)
Will probably know its true meaning at sight
(Say we to his Teacher, say we)
And so when the rest must divine the intent—
The law makers' purpose and all that was meant—
Must they look much further than their brother's tent?
(Ask we of their Teacher, say we)

Cho. Mr. & Mrs. s.c. are we
      Our boys deserve more than a D
      We tell all the brothers
      They'd better be right

Than rest on sheer logic
Like those who are bright

These brothers of course are not peas in a pod
(Say we to their Teacher, say we)
We never could make them agree with a rod
(Say we to their Teacher, say we)
Some put forth good reasons and some are quite rash.
They're slow to agree even under the lash
Though the thing that emerges is apt to be hash
(Say we to their Teacher, say we)

Cho.   Mr. & Mrs. S.C. are we
           We teach our boys integrity
           We say it's far better
           To do what is right
           Than search for good reasons
           For bad things to write

Now William is generous down to the bone
(Say we to his Teacher, say we)
His policy is to let others alone
(Say we to his Teacher, say we)
And so he is known to sign right on the line
Though words are employed which are fancy and fine
But whose meaning our Willie could never divine
(Say we to his Teacher, say we)

Cho.   Mr. & Mrs. S.C. are we
           We come to you with piety
           It seems so apparent
           That he who is meek
           Will hardly be bothered
           By blows on each cheek

When out on the field playing on the first team
(Say we to the Maestro, say we)
The boys say its tougher than books make it seem
(Say we to the Maestro, say we)
To make a few yards when a fumble is due
When fast stepping backs are converging on you
Say, just what in hell should our boy Willie do?
(Ask we of his Maestro, ask we)

Cho.   Mr. & Mrs. S.C. are we
           We don't go in for strategy
           We're glad for some progress

No matter how slow
If the ball keeps on moving
Our boys earn their dough

Your report we have read and perused carefully
(Say we to the Maestro, say we)
And we think we discern that which you failed to see
(Say we to the Maestro, say we)
Don't try to push William out over his head—
Except for his tolerance, it should be said
He rates not an A but a high C instead
(Say we to his Teacher, say we)

Cho. Mr. & Mrs. s.c. are we
      Our boys (in part) are fond of thee
      Since each is a scholar
      And not a mere dub
      Some more should be tapped
      For Powell's C Club.

---

1. Powell's "Report Card" had come in the form of a five-page single-spaced letter addressed to "Mr. and Mrs. Supreme Court," about their child "William," whose greatest fault seemed to be "his readiness to associate himself with some of his fellow pupils in joint responsibility for some really very bad things."

2. A deliberate misspelling following Powell's own usage, a reference to Felix Frankfurter's views of his own writing.

March 5, 1941

Dear Reed:

I understand that a script has been sent you from these parts. Though perhaps under common law principles I could not successfully assert a property interest in it, I thought I should nevertheless put you on notice that I would grieve should there be a public rendition at any cultural center (or at Columbia) in my absence.

February 11, 1944

Dear Reed:

Mark Childs[1] gave me a copy of your piece on Frankie.[2] I thought it was among your best, though I had the feeling that perhaps a more recent period had richer fields for you to explore. That is said, however, not to belittle your achievement but rather to suggest that there may be heights which you have not yet ascended.

I am still saving a bottle of scotch with the view that you might be able to put your feet under my table soon.

---

1. Marquis William Childs (1903–   ), the noted columnist and author.

2. Powell had written a two-page poem entitled "Since Frankie Spanked the Court," the gist of which was that since Roosevelt had attempted to "pack" the Court and succeeded in naming eight members, the Roosevelt appointees voted very carefully and always supported the New Deal.

October 11, 1944

Dear Reed:

I received this summer two Harvard Law productions—both of which interested me. One was by Powell who illustrated the statistical method as applied to Supreme Court decisions.[1] I thought it strange that Powell should embrace the Yale method at this late date. For I well remember how he once justly criticized others for pursuing the same course. And I assumed that he (and I) never forgot the lessons he taught. I was however glad to see that he did the counting himself. For I assume that if he did not, the article in good Harvard tradition would have appeared as written by "Powell and Whosis."[2]

The other Harvard production entailed quite a bit of counting also. But the author apparently had lots of help. So I do not suppose he should get too much credit for making no statistical errors. And I assume that at Harvard the more one makes the less such errors he is allowed. I am not sure that Powell had such a high score on the statistical side even when full weight is given the assumption that Vermont[3] teachings are easily forgotten, viz., that 5 plus 2 still makes 7 whether for the purpose of insurance or accounting. Of course, the question whether you start with 5 or 4 is an important one—as all students of Supreme Court history know. Many authors of opinions have made the same kind of error—although they are more apt to count 4 as 5 than vice versa. At times, as you know, it is even more important whether you end up with 5 or with 4. But that is a type of statistical worry which until recently I had assumed only those who were paid to worry worried about. Of course, if 4 assume to act as 5, different questions are raised. But before any such question is reached, a preliminary question may be raised. What is it that you are counting? At least the Yale counting school so held. For example, if only 4 out of 7 vote to affirm or reverse, it is hard to discover 5 in unison. But if the basic question was whether x equals commerce and 5 said it did, then I assume 5 equals 5 not 4—even though 1 of the 5 thinks some one else should clean up the mess—while 4 of the 5 think they should clean up their own mess.

And so I revert to my mid-summer query, "How do you count?" And since I once was a member in fair standing in the Yale counting school and since you are apparently slipping in that direction, I thought you should share the burden of my statistical worry.

My offer to furnish the stimulation if you furnish the transportation still holds.

---

1.   Powell wrote several pieces that summer critical of the Court, including a popular article in *The New York Times,* June 18, 1944, and in the *Harvard Law Review.*

2.   A less than flattering reference to Frankfurter's practice while at Harvard of cosigning his name to articles which students had researched and drafted under his direction, and which he then revised and polished.

3.   Powell was a Vermont native.

November 1, 1944

Dear Reed:

Is it really possible to be wrong seventy-one pages worth?[1]

Moreover, does not C[olumbia]. L[aw]. R[eview]. (now as formerly) equate H[arvard]. L[aw]. R[eview].?

---

1.   Powell had written a seventy-five-page article, "Insurance as Commerce in Constitution and Statute," 57 *H.L.R.* 937 (1944), criticizing the Court's decision in *U.S.* v. *South-Eastern Underwriters Assoc.,* 322 U.S. 533 (1944). WOD had been with the 4–3 majority in upholding the antitrust convictions of five insurance companies. Powell also had shorter articles in the *Columbia Law Review* attacking other opinions of the Court.

December 16, 1946

Dear Reed:

I have your "fungible" query.[1]

I have long thought you should have a dictionary. And the thought stirs in me at this time of year a generous impulse.

---

1. Powell had questioned woo's use of "fungible" in a case.

Part V

Final Things

Chapter 15

Impeachment

THE ELECTION of Richard Nixon in 1968 signaled the beginning of a new cycle in American politics, one marked by caution and conservatism rather than the liberalism which characterized American government from Roosevelt through Johnson. Given Douglas's outspoken liberalism both on and off the Court, his high public profile, his idiosyncratic life-style and his four wives, it was merely a matter of time before some conservative opponents decided to try to remove him from the bench.

The opening salvo involved Abe Fortas. When Lyndon Johnson named Fortas to succeed Earl Warren as Chief Justice in 1968, Republicans and conservative Democrats in the Senate stalled the nomination until Fortas finally asked to have his name withdrawn. Soon after the Nixon administration took over, new allegations of impropriety by Fortas led to demands that he resign; when Attorney General John Mitchell presented evidence to Fortas indicating that he might be indicted, the two struck a deal for the good of the country and the Court. Fortas would resign, and Mitchell would quash any further investigations.

Douglas knew his turn would be next, especially after the Senate turned down Nixon's first two nominees to take the Fortas seat, Clement Haynsworth and G. Harrold Carswell. The administration, determined to make the Court an instrument for the "peace forces" as Nixon had promised, wanted to appoint conservatives and get rid of the liberal members. Although Douglas never engaged in the questionable financial relationships which caused Fortas to leave the bench, the fact remained that in the sixties Douglas made more money from his extrajudicial activities than he drew in salary. The appearance of *Points of Rebellion* in 1970, which many misinterpreted as a justification for the wide-scale protest and social upheaval of the time, and publication of parts of it in *Evergreen*, a strange magazine combining pornographic material with expository essays on radical ideas, led to demands that Douglas either resign or be impeached.

On April 15, 1970, Congressman Gerald Ford (R-Mich) rose to demand an investigation of Associate Justice William O. Douglas on four specific charges:

1. Douglas had sold an article to *Fact* magazine and had received payment for it when the publisher, Ralph Ginzburg, was involved in litigation in federal courts which ultimately reached the Supreme Court. There Douglas dissented from the majority which upheld the lower court's libel judgment against Ginzburg.

2. Douglas had received substantial amounts of money from the Parvin Foundation, which he headed for nearly a decade. Although Ford did not claim that Douglas had himself associated with gangsters, he pointed out that Albert Parvin had significant interests in various gambling casinos and was often seen with known criminals.

3. Douglas had also "worked" for the Center for Democratic Institutions and had participated in various "leftist" events there, including meetings of New Leftists and leftist militants. Ford did not mention that Chief Justice Burger had appeared at some center functions and that in fact Douglas had not participated in the particular events involving the leftists.

4. *Points of Rebellion* constituted an un-American and inflammatory tract urging "militant hippies" on to further disorders.

Unspoken, but certainly in back of the charges, were Douglas's various marriages, including his latest to the very young Cathleen Heffernan, as well as the many rumors about his sexual exploits.

Did these constitute impeachable offenses? The Constitution is very vague on what grounds a federal judge may be impeached, but this did not bother Ford. "An impeachable offense," he declared, "is whatever a majority of the House of Representatives considers it to be at a given moment in history."

Ford wanted a special committee to look into these charges, but before he could act, Andrew Jacobs, Jr. (D-Ind) introduced a resolution to impeach Douglas. The liberal Jacobs had no desire to have Douglas impeached, but by his action he transferred the investigation from a select committee, which might have been packed, to the House Judiciary Committee, chaired by the liberal Emanuel Celler of New York.

Throughout the next several months, as a subcommittee looked into the charges, Douglas maintained an outward calm. But as these letters indicate, he took the threat seriously and provided his counsel with enormous data on what he had done, when, where, and for how much. In the end, the strategy planned by New York attorney and former judge Simon Rifkind worked; they met every one of Ford's vague charges with specific responses. The subcommittee, by a party vote, found no grounds for impeachment. Commentators throughout the hearings said they doubted if what Douglas had done would lead a Democratic Congress to remove him and give Richard Nixon another seat on the Court.

Douglas's actions, however, do raise serious questions about what should be the proper limits on a justice's extrajudicial activity. No one argues that a man or woman who goes onto the bench should forswear all previous interests and affiliations. Douglas himself took care to avoid situations in which he might have to disqualify himself from sitting in on cases. But should a sitting justice head a foundation, even a charitable one with noble purposes? Should a sitting justice engage in activities designed to produce an income larger than the generous salary Congress has appropriated in order to insulate the bench from outside pressures? Douglas traveled on Albert Parvin's money; should any justice be in that situation? Most commentators believe Douglas did not violate judicial canons of ethics but came very close to doing so. It is hard to judge exactly what he did because William Douglas was unique among the Brethren. Unfortunately, he saw himself that way as well and assumed that if he did it, it had to be right. It is questionable if in the future any sitting justice will act that way. Douglas's experience should serve as a warning, not an example.

To Martha Douglas Bost

May 24, 1969

Dear Martha:

. . . The word here went out from the High Command that the first to go would be Abe [Fortas], the second myself, and the third one Brennan.

I am very sorry that Abe resigned. But don't lie awake nights, as there is nothing to worry about.

There is nothing I have done of which I am ashamed, which I would not do again, or which is unethical or illegal. . . .

To Clark McAdams Clifford

October 23, 1969

Dear Clark:

Enclosed is a news item from yesterday's STAR.[1] It is, I think, a token that the campaign against me has started all over again.

The grossly unfair and malicious character of this particular item is that it relates to episodes that happened before I ever met Mr. Parvin.[2] He did, late in 1961 or early 1962, transfer a fractional interest in a mortgage on the hotel in question to the Parvin Foundation, an interest which the Foundation got rid of because it was on a Las Vegas property that had a gambling casino. But fractional interests in mortgages are always hard to liquidate. I mention this later item merely to orient you on the whole flow of events.

There is nothing that this article pertains to with which I had any connection whatsoever. But I thought perhaps I should be talking to you about it. . . .

---

1. The story, headlined "Mob-Linked Deal Aided Douglas' Foundation," alleged that much of the money in the Parvin Foundation came from a deal with Myer Lansky, described as "one of the nation's most notorious mobsters." Lansky served as middleman in selling the Flamingo Hotel in Las Vegas, of which Parvin was president and owner of 30% of the stock. The proceeds from the sale went in part to the foundation.

2. Albert Parvin (1900–   ) was a multimillionaire businessman who had befriended wod and had supported some of his causes. He had a passion for privacy, and much of the information about him is in the nature of "alleged" facts. He did own a number of properties in Las Vegas, and the Parvin Foundation's entire assets consisted of 31,291 shares of the Parvin Corporation.

To Stanley Norman Young[1]

November 11, 1969

Dear Stan:

. . . The ideological contest you refer to will go on and on. I think we are witnessing only noisy preliminaries.

The powers behind it all—Department of Justice—have incorrectly figured out how to get rid of me. . . .

---

1. Young (1923–   ), a New York lawyer, also taught at Pace University.

To Elon J. Gilbert

December 2, 1969

Dear Elon:

Thanks for your note. Politics is politics, and now there are those who think they can impeach me.

It promises to be a rough winter back here.

To Charles Horowitz

April 15, 1970

Dear Charlie:

I wrote you on February 6 that I was planning to retire this Summer. But now, I understand, there will be impeachment proceedings started against me. So I do not plan to retire. This, of course, is confidential.

To Ramsey Clark[1]

April 24, 1970

Dear Ramsey:

I have been fairly active *vis-a-vis* Soviet Jews. . . .

None of my activities have involved soliciting funds for the cause.

---

1. Clark (1927–) had first come to prominence as an assistant attorney general in the Kennedy administration involved in civil rights, a cause he later championed both as attorney general from 1967 to 1969 and as a private citizen. He would, as a member of Paul, Weiss, Rifkind, Wharton & Garrison, handle some of the strategy in WOD's defense against impeachment.

To Ramsey Clark

April 24, 1970

Dear Ramsey:

I have written numerous opinions expressing my views on:

(1) the First Amendment as it pertains to libel;

(2) the First Amendment as it pertains to obscenity.

I attach a list of the most important ones. In *Memoirs* v. *Massachusetts,* are my views as to the historical aspects of the problem.[1]

---

1. 383 U.S. 413 (1966), concurring opinion. WOD also listed his concurring opinion in *Garrison* v. *Louisiana,* 379 U.S. 64 (1964), for libel and his dissents in *Byrne* v. *Karalexis,* 396 U.S. 976 (1969), *Ginsberg* v. *New York,* 390 U.S. 620 (1968), *Ginsberg* v. *United States,* 383 U.S. 463 (1966), and *Roth* v. *United States,* 354 U.S. 476 (1957), for obscenity.

To Ramsey Clark

April 27, 1970

Dear Ramsey:

Yesterday, April 26th, Cathy and I were invited to the farm at 15000 River Road for a Greek Easter Feast. Mrs. Drew Pearson and Congressman Don Edwards[1] were the hosts and we were their guests. Tickets were about $20, I believe, but our tickets were complimentary.

Andreas Papandreou[2] and his wife were there and the four of us visited.

A hard-bitten lady reporter for the *Washington Post* came up and said, "I understand you are giving Andreas Papandreou legal advice."

I told her I had not practiced law since coming on the Court and was not giving Andreas Papandreou any legal advice.

"Why are you associating with him?'

"He's an old friend; and one of the great men in the world."

And so it went. The Committee pinned on me a button Democracy in Greece.

I mention this as it seemed at the time to be some kind of a "Plant" along the lines of the Ford charge.[3]

---

1. Edwards (1915–) represented the San Jose, California, district in Congress from 1963 to 1983.

2. Andreas George Papandreou (1919–), the former premier of Greece, had fled the country following a coup by the military and was then teaching economics at York University in Canada. He returned to Greece and again became premier following the ouster of the generals in October 1981.

3. Gerald Rudolph Ford, Jr. (1913–) represented Michigan in Congress from 1951 to 1973, when Nixon named him to replace Spiro Agnew as vice president; he became President the following year after Nixon's resignation. For the charges, see p. 390.

To Emanuel Celler

April 27, 1970

Dear Mr. Chairman:

I have retained The Honorable Simon Rifkind[1] of the New York Bar to represent me in the matter before your Committee.

I have instructed him to make anything in my files, which you deem relevant, available to you, whether it concerns Court records, correspondence files, financial matters, or otherwise.

---

1. Simon Hirsch Rifkind (1901–) had been a federal district judge from 1941 to 1950, when he returned to private practice. His firm has been one of the most powerful in New York for many years.

To Ramsey Clark

April 28, 1970

Dear Ramsey:

I gave Lectures in Baghdad in 1961, mostly on our Bill of Rights. They were put into Arabic and published.[1]

On my visit to Baghdad, I went to the University with my interpreter to see what books, if any, they had on our Constitution or Bill of Rights or Jefferson, Madison, democracy, etc.

That library was bare on those subjects. So when I returned, I prepared what I called the Douglas Eight Foot Shelf which I thought should be in every underdeveloped nation. I thought then— and still think—that those ideas are more important than military missions.

I got the Parvin Foundation to send out a set to Baghdad and to a few other places and interested Sargent Shriver[2] of the Peace Corps in sending out some sets.

I attach a copy of that List.

Out of this grew The International Law Book Exchange, Inc., 7 Church Lane, Baltimore, Maryland, headed by Carl A. Durkee, a strictly private agency.

---

1. *al-Hurriyah fi zill al-aqanun* (1961), a translation of "Three Lectures on American Law."

2. Robert Sargent Shriver, Jr. (1915–), a brother-in-law to the Kennedys, had been the first director of the Peace Corps (1961–1966) and of the Office of Economic Opportunity (1964–1968) and then ambassador to France. He ran unsuccessfully as the Democratic nominee for vice president in 1972.

To Ramsey Clark

April 28, 1970

Dear Ramsey:

My publications have at times raised conflicts of interest. I have written extensively for LOOK, mostly on foreign travels and experiences.

As a result, I have always recused myself in a Cowles Magazine case. See *Polizzi* v. *Cowles Magazine Inc.*, 344 U.S. 853, 345 U.S. 663 [1952].

For that reason, on April 27, 1970, I likewise withdrew from a motion in the case of No. 1985 Misc.—*Cowles Communications Inc.* v. *Alioto,* which the Court denied.

On April 27, 1970, I also withdrew from consideration of a motion in No. 905—*Grove Press Inc.* v. *Maryland State Board,* because I was told that Grove Press owned the Evergreen Magazine to which Random House sold, without my knowledge, excerpts from my book POINTS OF REBELLION.

To Ramsey Clark

April 29, 1970

Dear Ramsey:

I should add a word about the *Avant Garde* article.

It was written not for them but for my autobiography; and I was working on it when the magazine asked me to send them something.

The reason I decided to publish it then was that Cathy and I know Pete Seeger[1] and I wanted to pay him a tribute while he and I were both alive; also Joan Baez[2] whom we do not know but whom we admire.

I had never seen a copy of *Avant Garde* and did not realize it had any connection with the Ginsberg who had been before the courts on obscenity charges. Some of our young friends thought highly of the magazine and their response to my article was heart-warming.

Cathy and I decided that if a fee was paid we would return it and suggest that any fee be paid to some charity serving the needs of down-and-outers, such as the Salvation Army. To my surprise, I learned some weeks later that the check had arrived and had been deposited routinely in our checking account, contrary to my instructions and desires. That was a matter of misunderstanding and at the time did not seem important one way or the other.

---

1. Pete Seeger (1919–) is one of America's most popular folksingers, and he has been involved for more than six decades in a variety of liberal causes. This activity led to his blacklisting during the McCarthy Red Scare.

2.   Joan Baez (1941–   ), blessed with one of the most beautiful voices in the country, has also been involved with various liberal causes, including Amnesty International. She founded Humanitas/International Human Rights Committee.

To Ramsey Clark

May 5, 1970

Dear Ramsey:

Re: *Conflicts of Interest—Part I*

When I came on the Court, I had some long talks with Justice Brandeis whose place I took, about the disqualification of Justices to sit in cases coming here.

1.   Questions of a Justice's financial interest in one of the litigants. The custom has been for a judge not to sit if he or his wife or immediate family has any stock interest or bond interest or other security interest in one of the litigants. The amount of the interest, historically, does not seem important as a $1,000 interest in one litigant might be as important to one judge as a $500,000 interest would be to another. Brandeis told me that the one exception that had been historically agreed upon was the interest that a policy holder has in an insurance company. That is to say—a man whose life is insured or whose automobile or what not are insured—does not disqualify himself to sit in a case involving that insurance company. That kind of financial interest was thought to be remote and inconsequential in this present frame of reference.

Whether a member of the family who has an interest is close enough to the judge to disqualify him is sometimes a nice decision. It has been left to the judge himself; and my experience shows that if there is a doubt in the mind of the judge, he does not sit.

2.   Cases coming from a law firm in which a Justice was once a partner have presented perplexing questions. Stone was a member of Sullivan & Cromwell. He withdrew of course from any case that was in the office when he was a partner. But he also withdrew from cases that came to Sullivan & Cromwell, twelve years after he had left the firm. We have had other examples where some of us have felt that the lapse of time was so great as to make any idea of conflict of interest sheer nonsense. But here again the matter is for the conscience of the Justice alone.

In this connection, Justice Jackson soundly and vigorously denounced Justice Black for sitting in a case (*Jewel Ridge Coal Corporation* v. *Local No. 7167*, 325 U.S. 161 [1945]) that his old law partner argued. The statement of the account can be found in Frank, Mr. Justice Black—The Man and his Opinions, page 125, and the New York Times, June 11, 1946, p. 1, col. 8.

This charge was made at a time when Jackson was feuding a bit with Black and the charge did not make sense and no one on the Court took it seriously.

3. We usually withdraw from cases where someone approaches us on the matter that is in litigation.[1] In another letter to you (April 30, 1970), I indicated I withdrew from the *Waldron* case because Waldron had talked to me about his problem before litigation started. I now refer to cases where the litigation is before the Court and some eager lawyer or eager litigant corners one at a reception or party or on the street and puts in a special plea to the Justice for his side of the case. I think I have always withdrawn from a case under those circumstances. One such case was *Columbia Broadcasting System, Inc.* v. *Lowe's Inc.*, 356 U.S. 43 [1958], where I was approached prior to argument. The approach was not venal, merely indiscreet. There have been doubts as to the wisdom of withdrawing from cases under those circumstances. For example, former Chief Justice Warren used to say that if we all took that position, it would be easy for an unscrupulous person to drive a Justice out of a case merely by talking with him. Warren decided that was not going to happen to him. So what I am saying is not a generally accepted principle but it is one which I think I, myself, have always followed.

4. A Justice whose son, or other close relative argues a case does not sit. That was Hughes' practice when his son was Solicitor General and that is the reason, I think, why the son resigned as Solicitor General shortly after Hughes became Chief Justice. Moreover, Justice Black recuses himself from cases coming from his son's law office. So does Justice Brennan.

5. Even though a relative has no interest in one of the litigants, he may have one in an industry that may be directly affected by a case. A Justice then withdraws even though the particular company is not in the litigation. Such was my situation when the first CATV case reached here. *United States* v. *Southwestern Cable Co.*, 392 U.S.

157 (Cert. granted, 389 U.S. 911 [1968]). The reason I recused myself was that my son had a small CATV in the environs of Los Angeles and while it was not in litigation anywhere, the rulings on CATV might have an effect upon his investment.

6.   Partisanship is sometimes charged against a Justice. Most of the men serving here have led active lives—counsel for railroads and other corporations ([Stephen] Field and Butler); southerners conservative on economic issues (McReynolds); northerners conservative on economic issues (Roberts); southerners liberal on economic issues (Black); northerners liberal on economic issues (Murphy); men espousing racial equality (Warren and Marshall); men with racist leanings (Vinson and Byrnes); and so on.

Hughes ran for President and was identified with the burning issues of his day. [George] Sutherland and Black served in the Senate and were contenders *pro* and *con* for various causes.

The fact that a Justice has been identified with a cause does not disqualify him to sit in a case involving that cause. Justice Black properly sat in many cases construing labor laws which he sponsored or voted on in the Senate. I have sat in many cases involving the interpretation and application of the laws administered by the Securities and Exchange Commission when I was one of its members.

Knowledge of a problem, prior advocacy or promotion of one side or another of a cause, long identification with a particular program for legal or constitutional reform do not disqualify a Justice.

Partisanship, however, may at times give rise to a conflict of interest.

One may be so emotionally charged with views about a particular issue that he deems himself unfit to sit in judgment on a particular case. That was the view of Justice Frankfurter in the "captive audience" case—*Public Utilities Commission* v. *Pollak*, 343 U.S. 451, 466.[2] He said:

"The judicial process demands that a judge move within the framework of relevant legal rules and the covenanted modes of thought for ascertaining them. He must think dispassionately and submerge private feeling on every aspect of a case. There is a good deal of shallow talk that the judicial robe does not change the man within it. It does. The fact is that on the whole judges do lay aside private views in discharging their judicial functions. This is achieved through training, professional habits, self-discipline and that fortunate alchemy by which men are loyal to the obligation with which they are entrusted. But it is also true that reason cannot control the subconscious influence of feelings of which it is unaware. When there is ground for believing that such unconscious feelings may operate in the ultimate judgment, or may not unfairly lead others to believe they are operating, judges recuse themselves. They do not sit in judgment. They do this for a variety of reasons. The guiding consideration is that the administration of justice should reasonably appear to be disinterested as well as be so in fact.

"This case for me presents such a situation. My feelings are so strongly engaged as a victim of the practice in controversy that I had better not participate in judicial judgment upon it. I am explicit as to the reason for my non-participation in this case because I have for some time been of the view that it is desirable to state why one takes himself out of a case."

A second related reason concerns a Justice's views of a litigant before the Court. I recused myself from *National City Bank* v. *Republic of China*, 348 U.S. 356 [1955], because of my deep-seated antagonism to the Formosa regime on account of its corruption and its cruel suppression of civil rights. For like reasons I will recuse myself in the event that the *Sirhan* case reaches the Court.[3] Bobby Kennedy was too much my son or young brother to leave me fair judgment of the accused.

There are other extreme cases where a Justice's feelings run so high on a cause or against a litigant that in good conscience he should not sit. There is no measuring stick except the Justice's own conscience.

---

1. See p. 65.

2. The D.C. Public Utilities Commission allowed the bus and trolley company to receive and amplify radio programs on the cars, and the Court found no reason to overrule it. Frankfurter hated being forced to listen to something if he had no choice, and recused. WOD wrote the lone dissent in the 1952 case, claiming the inability to escape from the unwanted broadcast constituted an invasion of privacy.

3. Sirhan Sirhan, the man who killed Robert F. Kennedy, did appeal his conviction. The Court denied his petition for certiorari in *Sirhan* v. *California*, 410 U.S. 947 (1973); both WOD and Justice White took no part in either the deliberations or the decision.

To Ramsey Clark

May 7, 1970

Dear Ramsey:

Re: *Conflicts of Interest—Part II*

28 USC 455 provides:

"Any justice or judge of the United States shall disqualify himself in any case in which he has a substantial interest, has been of counsel, is or has been a material witness, or is so related to or connected with any party or his attorney as to render it improper, in his opinion, for him to sit on the trial, appeal, or other proceeding therein."

I have no "substantial interest" in LOOK Magazine or in the Cowles Company. I have indeed no interest at all.

I have, however, been over the years "connected" with it in such a way as to make it seem to me "improper" to sit in a Cowles case. I have known the Cowles Brothers for years; and LOOK sent me overseas on big missions, the first in 1952 when I went to Southeast Asia, wrote articles for them and published a book NORTH FROM MALAYA. LOOK paid all my expenses and paid large fees for my articles. There were other like assignments from LOOK, one being an extensive tour of Bolivia. My relationship with the Cowles Company and with LOOK has been so close that I have recused myself from all Cowles cases.

I have over the years done pieces for the *New York Times*, being paid at the going rate. I remember one article for the *New York Times Magazine* entitled *The Black Silence of Fear*[1] for which I was paid perhaps $150, perhaps $300—somewhere in that zone. But my relation to the *Times* has been so slight and so casual that I have not hesitated to sit in a *New York Times* case.

I had one article published in *Avant Garde* for a small fee—$350, I believe. This was a non-recurring item as they turned out to be so unethical in their tactics that I would never give them any other article of mine. The question of ethics arose when they misrepresented to the *New York Times* that I had agreed on an ad they wanted to run. I had not agreed and, learning of that matter from the *Times*, I stopped it.

I had nothing to do with placing a portion of my book POINTS OF REBELLION in *Evergreen*. That was done by my publisher without my knowledge and without consulting with me or my office. The fee I will get amounts, as I understand it, to $100. That too is a non-

recurring item as I would never give *Evergreen* any article. It too is
unethical. It acquired from my publisher permission to reprint provided it printed "Permission granted by Random House." Evergreen
merely printed "Permission granted," creating the impression that
I had granted the permission.

I would not hesitate to sit in an *Evergreen* case or in a case of
its owner Grove Press by reason of the article alone. Grove Press has
a case before the Court that will be argued in October. If there is
any litigation with *Evergreen* over the episode, I will not sit in the
Grove Press case. But absent some additional factor such as litigation, I would not hesitate to sit.

PLAYBOY is in a different category. I chose PLAYBOY for my
articles as I wanted to reach the young people, especially on conservation.[2] Since that time, so far as I am aware, PLAYBOY has had no
cases before the Court. If it has one, I would not sit. For, as in the
case of LOOK, I have been a frequent, if not regular contributor; and
while I do not know the owners, my connection with the magazine
is not casual and restricted to a small and solitary contribution.

My decision not to sit in the Cowles cases and in the PLAYBOY
cases but to sit in the others conforms, I think, to Canon 4 of the
ABA Canons of Judicial Ethics:

"A judge's official conduct should be free from impropriety and
the appearance of impropriety; he should avoid infractions of law;
and his personal behavior, not only upon the Bench and in the
performance of judicial duties, but also in his everyday life, should
be beyond reproach."

---

1. *New York Times*, January 13, 1952, vi: 7.

2. WOD published four articles in *Playboy:* "The Attack on the Right to
Privacy" (December 1967); "An Inquest on Our Lakes and Rivers" (June 1968);
"Civil Liberties: The Crucial Issue" (January 1969); and "The Public Be Damned"
(July 1969).

To Kay Kershaw & Isabelle Lynn

May 12, 1970

Dear Kay and Isabelle:
I wrote you last fall or winter that federal agents were in Yakima and
Goose Prairie looking me over at Goose Prairie. I thought they were
merely counting fence posts.

But I learned in New York City yesterday that they were planting marijuana with the prospect of a nice big TV-covered raid in July or August.

I forgot to tell you that this gang in power is not in search of truth. They are "search and destroy" people.

I do not know what the marijuana plant—growing or dried—looks like. I do not know if it would grow in Goose Prairie's harsh climate. Mint, white clover, and rhubarb do well there, as you know. But now that the snow is gone and summer is near, you might look to see if you can spot any marijuana. It would be ironic if they planted it in Ira's yard, not mine!

To Ramsey Clark

May 22, 1970

Dear Ramsey:

Conflicts of Interest—Part III

Either I or Mrs. Douglas and I have protested in speeches or by hikes or in writing, various anti-conservation measures. I am not sure the following list is complete, but it is representative:

1. A speech at a rally in 1964 at Norwell, Massachusetts over a proposal to dump sewage into the South River, an estuarine stream.

2. A hike in the North Cascades (and a speech) in 1967 to protest Kennecott Copper Company's plans to mine its deposits in the Glacier Peak Area.

3. A speech and a hike in Leonia, New Jersey in 1967 to protest a tract of wilderness in the city called Highwood Hills.

4. A hike in 1968 to preserve a section of the old Delaware Canal in Bristol, Pennsylvania.

5. A hike in 1967 to keep Sunfish Pond (along the Appalachian Trail in New Jersey) from being transformed into a huge reservoir servicing a power plant in the valley.

6. A hike and rally in Kentucky in 1967 to protest the Corps of Engineers' dam on the Red River.

7. A hike and rally in Allerton Park, Illinois in 1969 to protest the Corps of Engineers' dam on the Sangamon River.

8. A rally at Hanford, Washington in 1968 and a statement opposing the proposed Benjamin Franklin Dam on the Columbia River which was sponsored by the Corps.

9. Hikes along the Olympic Beach, State of Washington (one in 1958; another in 1964; and others earlier) to protest a highway proposed by the Park Service.

10. Running the Buffalo River in Arkansas in 1961 to protest a Corps' dam on that stream.

11. A 180-mile hike in 1954 down the C & O Canal to protest its conversion into a highway.

12. Annual hikes since 1954 (sponsored by the C & O Canal Association) to promote the conversion of the C & O Canal into a National Historic Park.

13. A rally in Saratoga, Texas in 1967 to protest the levelling of the Big Thicket and to promote its inclusion in a national park.

14. A rally in 1965 to preserve a playground in a park in the City of Los Angeles.

15. A 1966 raft trip on the Yakima River (sponsored by the Yakima River Conservancy) to promote clean water.

16. A hike and speech in 1961 in the Kettle Moraine State Forest to preserve the Ice Age Park, Wisconsin.

17. A hike and speech in Nyack (Rockland County), New York in 1966 to protest the erosion of natural beauty.

18. Speech January 11, 1966 at the Governor's Conference for California Beauty in Los Angeles—preserving the redwoods, etc.

If any of these projects—or others to which I have expressed protest or given promotion—reached the Court, I would of course be disqualified.

To Jim DeWitt Bowmer[1]

May 25, 1970

Dear Jim:

. . . The mail surveillance is very oppressive. We should, I suppose, not be too hard on the federal agents.

Think of all the unrest in the nation and all the student mail that must be read. Student mail is usually handwritten and often illegible. So the Bureau of Surveillance is doubtless swamped. I try to put all of mine in type to facilitate matters. Yet even so, processing is difficult. There are, I believe, review panels in the Bureau and at least some of the stuff from "big shots" must go up there.

The moral has something to do with Charity which 1 Corinthians 13 extols.[2] Moreover, it means that if you want to get any message to me by July first, you better get it off right soon. . . .

---

1. Bowmer (1919–   ) was a lawyer in Temple, Texas.
2. The chapter talks of faith, hope, and charity, of which the greatest is charity.

To Gerald Daniel Stern [1]

June 8, 1970

Dear Jerry:

Enclosed is a statement of my approximate assets and approximate liabilities as of June 1, 1970, in response to your letter of June 4.[2]

---

1. Stern (1933–   ) was a partner in the Rifkind firm.
2. WOD showed assets of $161,870, of which the largest items included the house on Hutchins Place with a purchase price of $35,000 (but which was worth far more), the Goose Prairie property, appraised at $40,000, and savings accounts of $37,000. His liabilities amounted to $60,048, most of it in the form of mortgages on the properties, giving him a net worth of $101,822.

To Simon Hirsch Rifkind

June 10, 1970

Dear Si:

This is not a word of advice, only an account of a conversation with Earl Warren who, by the way, you may want to see on your next visit here. (He plans a month in Cape Cod).

Yesterday he said it might be a good idea at some stage to take the deposition of Ford and Wyman[1], pinning them down to the emptiness of their charges.

I am not so sure. . . .

---

1. Louis Crosby Wyman (1917–   ), a Republican, then represented New Hampshire in the House of Representatives; he later became a state superior court judge.

To Ramsey Clark

June 25, 1970

Dear Ramsey:

I send you herewith my personal copy of Volume I of the Appel edition of the record in the *Sacco-Vanzetti* Case.[1] I am sending you this because this edition is rather hard to come by although it was finally printed only last year.

I did the Preface to it pursuant to a written agreement with Mr. Appel, which agreement is in the file of my papers now in your office, so you can find it there. As indicated in this volume which I am sending you, the prefatory essay was copyrighted by me in 1968.

I also enclose a xerox copy of a letter just received from Mr. Appel. As you can see, he wants to publish the Preface as a separate document. I think he is a wholly honorable man but his motive is obviously to try to make some additional money out of the present anti-Douglas or pro-Douglas sentiment in the country, and I think he should be stopped.

What I wrote was an account of the development of constitutional law in the last 40 or 50 years, the point being had the case been tried in the 1960's rather than in the 1920's it undoubtedly would have been reviewed here. With what result, of course, no one knows. I did the Preface with the hope that students of political science and law would be encouraged to mine the record so as better to understand what went on at that trial.

Either you or Judge Rifkind might tell Mr. Appel that you are handling this for me in my absence from the country and that I had expressed to you before I left that I did not think the Preface should be separated from the record of the trial. If a separate, detached pamphlet or book were to be done, it would have to be done differently and I do not have the time or inclination at this time to try my hand at it.

---

1. *The Sacco-Vanzetti Case; Transcript of* . . . with a prefatory essay by WOD; had been published by P.P. Appel in 1969.

To Simon Hirsch Rifkind

September 30, 1970

Dear Si:

I got back to Washington yesterday and I am here now for the duration. I will be calling you one of these days soon. I have nothing special in mind except that I gather from the Western press that the impeachment matter is going over until after the election. The story out there is that Congressman Ford wants a new crack at the thing and will renew his efforts after the election, trying to get the matter finally before the Senate for adjudication. . . .

To Betty B. Fletcher[1]

November 23, 1970

Dear Mrs. Fletcher:

I enclose a xerox copy of a column written by Allen and Goldsmith[2] which apparently appeared on November 15. A reader in Birmingham, Alabama first brought it to my attention.

The syndicate that publishes this is the Publishers-Hall Syndicate. Whether they circulate the column in the State of Washington, I do not know.

It is very difficult, as you can imagine, to be in public life and not be able to reply at all to much of the harsh and unfair and even malicious things that are said about you. It is almost impossible to stay silent when anything as scandalous and as false and as fabricated as this column is [published]. I do not suppose there is anything that a judge prizes more highly than his incorruptibility and the statement that I received money to release a man on bail is not only utterly false but it is appalling.

I cannot have a press conference and make statements. The matter that Congressman Ford started and that he apparently is going to pursue after the new Congress gets in, is my impeachment. Hopefully, the House Judiciary Committee will issue a report between now and the first of the year.

I have representing me, as you know, some outstanding lawyers headed by Judge Simon Rifkind of New York City. I have passed on to them my concern about this column and my question as to

whether I should bring a libel suit. As yet I have not had an opportunity to discuss and explore that matter with them.

I am, however, sending this on to you as you represent me in the
State of Washington—not to get a legal opinion from you at this
time nor advice as to what, if anything, I should do, but to see if
you have any way of finding out whether the Syndicate operates in
the State of Washington; and secondly, whether this column was
distributed in the State of Washington. If I do file a libel suit I would
bring it in the State Court and not the federal courts and since
Washington State is my home, I think the appropriate place would
be there if possible. . . .

---

1.   Fletcher (1923–   ) was then a Seattle lawyer and represented WOD in the
State of Washington; she would later be appointed to the Ninth Circuit Court of
Appeals.
2.   The column implied that WOD had misused his position for personal gain.

To John Parsons [1]

November 28, 1970

Dear Pat:

. . . Since talking with you, I learned that there probably will not be
any report from the full Committee of the Judiciary before Congress
adjourns. It is expected, however, there will be a report of the
Sub-Committee. I have no explanation as to the reason for the
change except shortness of time and the pressure of a multitude of
other things.

The Sub-Committee is composed of five and there is a rumor
now that its report may be four to one which means of course that
it will become a highly political document.[2]

---

1.   A New York lawyer and an old friend.
2.   The 924-page report of the subcommittee came out on December 3. The
three Democratic members concluded that no grounds existed for impeachment;
the two Republican members, while not calling for impeachment, criticized the
Democratic majority for evading the critical issue of whether WOD's activities "seem
so improper to merit congressional censure or other official criticism of the House."

To Simon Hirsch Rifkind

December 4, 1970
Dear Si:

. . . The report of the subcommittee is, as you anticipated, a political document. The only good thing I see coming out of it is that not one of the five said I should be impeached. Three exonerated me and the others in effect thought more should be done. It is the latter which is the ominous part because I am sure Nixon, Agnew,[1] Mitchell[2] and Ford put tremendous pressure on McCulloch[3] and Hutchinson[4] of the subcommittee to leave the matter open. The Administration has its eye on my seat. They want me off, and I am sure they are going to try very hard to get a new committee and get hearings going.

If I am not correct in my assumption, or if this does not come to pass, there will be no problem. If it does come to pass, then there are very large questions with which I will be confronted.

Assuming that the Ford committee will be disassociated from the Judiciary Committee and will be sort of a free-wheeling Un-American Activities Committee, they will try to have a Roman holiday. Then the first and most important question I will have to decide is whether I would appear as a witness if subpoenaed, or should I demand to be heard as a witness, or should I agree to testify only in executive session. These are large questions which no one can answer yet, but I wanted you to have them in your mind. You probably have them in your mind already. But in any event, I wanted you to know what I was thinking about and the concern which I have.

Perhaps when we get together about the first of the year we can talk about these things in more realistic terms.

The overshadowing political fact is that I am *persona non grata* to most, although not all, of the southern delegation, and also to Ford-like Republicans in the House. That means that those two groups probably command a majority and they can do what they want, which is to get their own definition of an impeachable offense and send me to trial before the Senate.

As I was thinking about these things this morning, Clark Clifford called. He said he had been listening to the early morning radio and that he had heard four or five radio announcements and that every one of them had said that I either had been cleared by the House subcommittee or that the House subcommittee had found no impeachable offenses.

He thought this added up to a good total and that the publicity of that kind would work against the designs of Ford. I am not so optimistic.

I have a feeling that once a person becomes a target of Nixon he continues to be a target no matter what he does or how many times a jury comes in with a verdict of Not Guilty.

I guess I forgot to tell you that he sent word to Walter Reed that they should not give medical attention to Earl Warren. I really don't know how more malicious someone can get than that. The old Chief Justice is eligible for assignment in the lower courts and is very active in judicial affairs, and under the statutes he has all the rights, privileges, and immunities of federal judges except the privilege of sitting on our court.

---

1. Vice President Spiro Theodore Agnew (1918–) had been governor of Maryland from 1957 to 1969; he resigned from the second highest elected office in the land when faced with possible indictment and conviction for bribery.

2. John Newton Mitchell (1913–), a Wall Street lawyer, became Nixon's attorney general. He resigned to run the 1972 presidential campaign and later went to jail for his role in the Watergate scandals.

3. William M. McCulloch (1901–1980) represented Ohio in the House of Representatives from 1947 to 1973.

4. Edward Hutchinson (1914–1985), a Republican from Michigan, sat in the House from 1965 to 1979. A member of the subcommittee, he complained that it had not sought to determine whether WOD's overall conduct was so "improper" as to warrant impeachment.

To Irving Brant

January 7, 1971

Dear Irving:

I thank you for the substitute pages of your little tract on impeachment.

It's too great a paper or manuscript to put out in a law review. . . .

Whether the impeachment matter is at an end I do not know. Wyman and a few other Congressmen have already circularized the new Congress asking support for a resolution that would set up a Special Investigating Committee. How that will fare no one knows.

Your little treatise is a signal contribution, and should be published as a book. . . .[1]

---

1. Brant did publish it as *Impeachment: Trial and Error* (New York: Knopf, 1972).

To Gerald Daniel Stern

March 17, 1971

Dear Jerry:

How about a letter to the Editor asking the question—suppose a Justice buys stocks or bonds and later learns that the company is before the Court in a case? He steps out of the case. Is the moral that no Justice should own securities?

To David Ginsburg [1]

June 8, 1971

Dear Dave:

You and your associates did an outstanding job in representing me in the impeachment proceedings.

The matter seems to be quiescent now, although it may not yet be completely terminated.

I am anxious, starting with the October 1971 Term, to get back into the full swing of Court work. That means participating in cases that may be brought by your own firm but on which I would not sit while you were actively representing me. That occasion has now passed, and so I am writing at this time to suggest a final settlement of our account.

If we could do it say by July 1st, it would expedite matters at this end very much indeed.

---

1. Ginsburg (1912–), had worked for WOD in the SEC from 1935 to 1939 and then was his law clerk that first year on the Supreme Court. After World War II, he entered private practice in the Washington office of the Rifkind firm.

To Emanuel Celler

December 1, 1971

Dear Manny:

It's been nearly a year since your Committee filed its historic Report. Hence I have concluded that it would comport with the proprieties for me to send you this note.

This is really not a note of thanks, as you only did your constitutional duty.

It is rather a note of great admiration and respect for one who has always held high our constitutional principles and has been alert to defend them.

Your career has brightened the conscience of America and made everyone within the radius of your actions and your word more mindful of the democratic ideal under our republican form of government.

The Douglases and all who live in the liberal tradition will always march to the cadence of your thoughts.

May God bless you and may this Holiday Season bring you joy and happiness.

———————————————————————————————

Chapter 16

The "Last Mile"

FOLLOWING HIS CLEARANCE by the House subcommittee, Douglas settled back to his work on the Court, challenging Warren Burger in the new Chief's efforts to streamline the Court's business and move it in a more conservative direction. He stuck to his absolutist position on the First Amendment and worried that the new appointees in their "moderation" would abandon civil rights and civil liberties. He became even more cantankerous than before in some ways, and yet observers noted a mellowing.

There were some victories as well, such as the abortion decision and the slapping down of Nixon's efforts to impose prior restraint on the press in the Pentagon Papers case. The Watergate scandal and the ignominious resignation of Nixon as President confirmed Douglas's earlier opinion of the man, but he took little comfort in Nixon's disgrace, aware of the enormous strain Watergate had put on the country. He began writing his memoirs, and friends observed that the marriage to Cathy seemed to be working better than anyone had expected. The two of them flew down to Nassau for a well-earned vacation in late December 1974.

There Douglas had a stroke; he was flown back to Washington so he could receive treatment at Walter Reed Army Hospital. He declared that he would be back on the Court within a few weeks, but it was not to be. He did not return to the bench until late March, and observers were shocked at his wasted appearance. Douglas did not want to resign and give his old enemy, Gerald Ford, the opportunity to name his replacement, but he really had little choice. He would suffer a number of ailments, all complicated by the stroke, and be in and out of hospitals for the less than five years remaining to him. He finally, and reluctantly, bowed to the inevitable and in November resigned from the Court with the longest tenure of any person in the Court's two centuries.

Douglas's last years proved difficult for him and for others as well. His colleagues on the Court tried to make his retirement as graceful as possible, and the Chief Justice went out of his way to be nice, bringing Douglas small gifts from time to time, gestures which Douglas greatly appreciated. But neither Burger nor the other Brethren could agree to Douglas's request to continue to participate in the business of the Court.

He finally desisted, finished his memoirs, and made his final arrangements. The man who had lived so independent a life did not intend to let others dictate his funeral arrangements.

To Edward Moore Kennedy

July 1, 1975

My dear Senator:

You were such a Prince to come all the way to New York to see me. Your presence was refreshing and invigorating. I have sent a note to Clark Clifford. Your interest and friendship mean much to me. I admire you greatly and know that you are our only hope.

Everyone at I[nstitute for] R[ehabilitative] M[edicine] was energized by your visit. The Kennedy tradition is a real force in American life and you can liven any group.

My best to you and your family as always.

To Sidney Davis

September 2, 1975

My dear Sid:

Goose Prairie is a great disappointment because the doctors won't let me do anything. Everything is "dangerous"—horses are dangerous; the woods are dangerous—"what happens if you meet a bear?" To enjoy Goose Prairie one must do all these things. . . .

To Joseph Freeman Paquet[1]

October 14, 1975

Dear Joe:

I went by Walter Reed and am starting there as an out patient.

The urology man fitted me to a catheter that promises hope. But the top therapy man says that my chances of improvement—arm and leg are nil.

That is a bleak and dreary outlook. I wish I could be in the environment of your clinic.

The pain persists as strong as ever. It is the only reason I should ever retire. Cathy, however, is pounding on me to resign. I think she's trying to produce another stroke and unhappily has medical advice as to how to manage it. My son is aligned with her in that cause.

---

1.   A Portland, Oregon, physician and an old friend of WOD.

To Gerald Rudolph Ford

November 12, 1975

Dear Mr. President:

It was my hope, when I returned to Washington in September, that I would be able to continue to participate in the work of the Supreme Court.

I have learned, however, after these last two months, that it would be inadvisable for me to attempt to carry on the duties required of a member of the Court. I have been bothered with incessant and demanding pain which depletes my energy to the extent that I have been unable to shoulder my full share of the burden.

Therefore, pursuant to the provisions of Title 28, U.S. Code, Section 371(b), I hereby retire at the close of this day from regular active service as an Associate Justice of the Supreme Court of the United States.

During the hours of oral argument last week pain made it necessary for me to leave the Bench several times. I have had to leave several times this week also. I shall continue to seek relief from this unabated pain but there is no bright prospect in view.

Chief Justice Burger and my other colleagues on the Bench have extended to me every courtesy and generous consideration. I have appreciated their thoughtfulness and I shall miss them sorely, but I know this is the right decision.

---

1. Ford, responding the same day, wrote:

> ... I want you to know first of all of my warm admiration for your valiant effort to carry on the duties of your high office, despite your recent illness, with the same courage and independent will that have characterized your long service to your country. . . .[M]ay I express on behalf of all our countrymen this nation's great gratitude for your more than 36 years as a Member of the Supreme Court. Your distinguished years of service are unequalled in all the history of the Court. . . . It is my sincere hope that your health will soon be restored so that you can enjoy your well-deserved retirement and relax among the natural beauties you love and have helped to preserve. Future generations of citizens will continue to benefit from your firm devotion to the fundamental rights of individual freedom and privacy under the Constitution. . . .

To The Chief Justice and Associate Justices

November 14, 1975

My dear Brethren:

Your message,[1] written on my retirement from the Court, filled my heart with overflowing emotion. You were kind and generous and made every hour, including the last one on our arduous journey, happy and relaxed.

I am reminded of many canoe trips I have taken in my lifetime. Those who start down a water course may be strangers at the beginning but almost invariably are close friends at the end. There were strong headwinds to overcome and there were rainy as well as sun drenched days to travel. The portages were long and many and some were very strenuous. But there were always a pleasant camp in a stand of white bark birch and water concerts held at night to the music of the loons; and inevitably there came the last camp fire, the last breakfast cooked over last night's fire, and the parting was always sad.

And yet, in fact, there was no parting because each happy memory of the choice parts of the journey—and of the whole journey—was of a harmonious united effort filled with fulfilling and beautiful hours as well as dull and dreary ones. The greatest such journey I've made has been with you, my Brethren, who were strangers at the start but warm and fast friends at the end.

The value of our achievements will be for others to appraise. Other like journeys will be made by those who follow us, and we trust that they will leave these wilderness water courses as pure and unpolluted as we left those which we traversed.

---

1. The letter of November 14, signed by all the justices, read:

Dear Bill:

Only when you made your decision known did we fully sense what that meant to us and to the Court. For us, as colleagues and friends, your absence from the Conference table and our deliberations will be deeply felt. Whether ultimately we agreed or not, as colleagues we valued highly your unparalleled knowledge of the multitude of decisions of the Court covering more than one-third of this century. It was a unique resource for the Court and one that may never again be present at our Conference table. We shall always remember your occasional verbal "footnotes" telling us intimate details as to how some opinion evolved. As friends we shall miss the daily contacts, which have varied in length and kind for each of us. Some have long been colleagues, some have argued before you, some have come here more recently, but all of us share great respect and affection for you.

The hope on our part is that, relieved of the burdens of Court work, your health will improve, and this eases our sense of loss. In the months since last January we have felt boundless admiration for your courageous fight to recover your strength and your placing duty above concern for your health.

So much has been and will be said on other occasions about your remarkable career that no more need be noted now than to recall that it is far more than a record of longevity, for it spanned a period in American history comparable to that of the formative period early in the 19th century when Marshall and then Taney were here.

We shall miss your vast reservoir of firsthand knowledge of the

Court's cases of the past 36 years and, as well, the warm daily contacts in Conference and on the Bench. It goes without saying that we shall expect you to share our table as usual, for you remain Senior Justice Emeritus.

To The Clerks[1]

November 14, 1975

Dear Clerks:

Keep the faith in the rule of law not only for our own people but for the people of the world.

Keep the faith in a unity of mankind irrespective of race, intellect, color, religion, or ideology.

Keep the faith in the informed citizenry who can govern wisely and justly.

Keep the faith in the system that allows a place for every man no matter how lowly or how great.

Keep the faith in a system which does not leave every issue of human rights to the ups and downs of the political campaigns.

I was deeply touched by your warm and generous letter of November 13, 1975. I wish you all happiness and success in every future endeavor.

Again my sincere thanks for your kindness.

---

1. The previous day the clerks of all the justices had written their own farewell letter to WOD:

Dear Mr. Justice Douglas:

We cannot adequately express our profound feelings for you at this time. All of us have been vividly aware of the courage you have quietly demonstrated for the past month and a half. Now, we feel a very deep sense of personal loss. That feeling, in and of itself, is testimony to the immeasurable influence that you have had on us by your vigorous example of faith—in justice, in principle and in the individual. Our loss, and the Court's loss, could not be greater. We wish you the very best.

With admiration and respect,

To the Conference

December 17, 1975

I enclose herewith a xerox copy of a memorandum I wrote the Chief Justice on November 15th. Recent discussions of this memorandum have indicated to me that some members of the Court feel that by it I chose to revert to the practice that I adhered to for years—having just one law clerk and two secretaries.

The precise issue as I recall was not brought up by either the Chief Justice or by myself and I do not endorse it at the present time. The regime of one law clerk and two secretaries seemed in earlier years better suited to the regime of work in this office than different sized staff. The situation in light of my retirement presents much different problems. The strictly legal work in the conventional sense of that term will now drop off considerably. I do not expect to do work on the cert list. It would be unusual for the list to contain a problem for a retired Justice. I need, however, the continuing services of a law clerk and I think two would meet my needs much better than one.

One of the reasons is that I have promised a member of the faculty of the Fairleigh-Dickinson College in New Jersey to write a 200 year history of this Court since 1787. The agreement has not been reduced to a contract and no arrangements for publication or publisher have been made but it is expected that in time it would become a public document. The recent publication of the Frankfurter Conference notes[1] is reminder enough that considerable research will be needed to untangle many of the cobwebs which he has spun over recent Supreme Court history. As a matter of fact I have used much of the time of two law clerks this term in the areas covered by Felix. I would need the help of at least two law clerks before this volume is finished. It is not a commercial project. No royalties have even been suggested and I'd be very happy to work out an arrangement with our library, the Library of Congress, or with the new Supreme Court Historical Society for one of those agencies to have the copyright.

As to the need for two secretaries, that question has in part been answered by what I said about the law clerks but beyond that the fact that I'm leaving public office after a long term of years, I have accumulated a huge amount of correspondence and the like. I shudder to think of the file cabinets on the second floor that are filled with letters and carbons of letters covering the span. Some of them in time may become important and I believe they should be classified, catalogued, and put in a condition for permanent caretaking. The task is way beyond the bounds of a secretary's normal activities and much beyond the capacity of any secretary I know to take on single handedly.[2]

---

1. Joseph P. Lash, ed., *From the Diaries of Felix Frankfurter* (New York: Norton, 1975), had appeared in August; it involved segments of Frankfurter's personal diary more than Conference notes.

2. This memo, as well as the earlier one (of which no copy was found in the Douglas Papers), dealt with WOD's views of his role as a retired justice. Traditionally, retired justices were given the courtesy of an office in the Court building and a clerk, and they could, at the discretion of the Chief Justice, be assigned to special sittings on the lower courts. WOD believed that he should be able to participate in the Conferences, a position supported neither by law nor custom. On December 22, the eight remaining members of the Court all signed a three-page memorandum to the effect that: (1) WOD would not be allowed to participate in deciding cases, pass on certiorari petitions and jurisdictional appeals, or attend conference meetings, but (2) he would be provided chambers, in fact could keep the ones he then occupied, and could have two secretaries (or a clerk and a secretary) and a messenger, but no more than a staff of three.

To Elizabeth Cuthbert[1]

February 6, 1976

Dear Elizabeth:

I appreciate all your letters and I apologize for not answering them sooner. I've been swamped with correspondence and working on another volume of my autobiography.

I retired from the Court because of the pain that seemed to get no better. It was impossible to sit on the bench for longer than an hour or so and follow the arguments. Intense mental concentration and intense pain are not compatible.

I've about given up all hope. I'm very depressed and while the pain is somewhat alleviated it still keeps me far below par. I have no plans for the future. I'm not sure what this coming summer will bring forth, whether I'll go to Goose Prairie or not I don't know.

I've been told that the Kaiser Foundation in your area has a wonderful therapy unit and that I should go there but I've been to so many hospitals and seen so many doctors that I've given up hope of any help from the medical profession.

---

1. A friend from Corona del Mar, California.

To Betty Fletcher

July 7, 1976

Dear Betty:

Here are some odds and ends touching on my will. In the 1940's after my Mother died my brother, Arthur, and I bought in our names a full cemetery lot at the Tohomish Cemetery in Yakima. We realized at the time that it was too large for the family's needs so we made a deal with the cemetery people that for perpetual care we would turn over every burial plot in that big lot to the cemetery company and as I understand that is the way the matter stands at the present time.

Mother and Father are buried there and there is one full plot that I've always reserved in my mind for my sister, Martha Douglas Bost . . . not for me. Arthur, who bought the big lot with me, died some years back so I should do something about this in my will and I thought the best thing to do was to leave all the interest in the plot Art and I had to my sister, Martha.

One of the last talks we had on the telephone dealt with the problem of the estate taxes and in thinking about it, it occurred to me that perhaps the best thing for me to do would be to sell the Hutchins Place property and the Goose Prairie property to have a fund large enough to pay the estate taxes. I think I could easily get $100,000 for the Goose Prairie property and $80,000 for the Hutchins Place property. At the present estate tax rates would those prices, if obtained, be adequate to take care of the state and federal death taxes?

To Thurgood Marshall

July 12, 1976

Dear Thurgood:

For a man who has lived so dangerously as you a hospital is a place to avoid and here you are in one.[1] I've been in and out of hospitals all year but that is no excuse for you to try to keep up with me. The remedy is simple: Heed more closely the advice of Cissie.

I've just finished a chapter on LBJ for my autobiography and I think you'll enjoy it not only because you play a prominent part in the chapter but because I think it stays pretty close to the facts of that important part of our history.

I'm off for Goose Prairie before long but we will keep in touch I hope. Meanwhile when in doubt of whether to grant or deny a cert always grant and then you'll never run out of business! Have a good summer, don't race your motor, and Keep the Faith.

---

1. Marshall had been hospitalized because of a minor heart attack on July 6; he recuperated over the summer and returned to the bench full-time at the October Term.

To Mildred Douglas Read

November 15, 1976

Dearest Millie:

Your letter of October 28th arrived today, November 15th. It was only yesterday that Cathy and I had a long talk, with both of us expressing the hope that you would be coming for a visit soon. Bill was here for several days and then returned to Portland where he is working, as you know, in a veterinary clinic.

I am very anxious to see you. I am still recovering from surgery. The left hip was broken so I made the mistake of allowing them to open it up. They found that the ball inside the socket was smashed and shattered so they took all those pieces out and replaced them with metallic. That didn't work out very well because the electrolysis of the metal was different from the body. They had to operate again and remove the metal which they did but that didn't help at all. I came out of the operating room feeling worse than ever. They decided they had done the wrong operation and so they took all the muscles in the hip and severed them thinking that I would be more comfortable. The result was to increase the pain and after the surgery I'm more of a cripple than ever.

Martha was here for about a week. She too was of the impression that you were coming for a visit. I'm not cross or angry—I'm only disappointed that you are not here now. Cathy said that what I need to turn the corner of good health is a visit from you. I think there is truth in that. I love you dearly and miss you greatly. I speak not only for myself but for Cathy to urge you if possible to come stay with us awhile. It is cold and bleak here as far as the weather goes. We had snow two days ago.

With love and affectionate regards.

To Warren Earl Burger

November 30, 1976

Dear Chief:

I want to thank you for the excellent bottle of wine and for your visit to my home on Thanksgiving Day. It was very kind of you to remember me and I greatly appreciate your kindness and generosity.

To Cathleen Heffernan Douglas

March 23, 1977

Dear Cathy:

I have taken out of my will all reference to the funeral and in that there is nothing affirmative or negative there are no instructions for you to do anything.

Betty [Fletcher] thought it would be better for me to write you a letter outlining my desires and this is the letter.

If you decide to go ahead with the original cremation plans the ashes could be placed in two urns and Mr. King would happily place them on the top of American Ridge near the lovely spot where we used to have lunch. If this is done, permission from the forest service should be obtained to erect a sign attached to a post saying that the ashes are there.

This may be too romantic an idea and perhaps should be dropped but I leave that up to you.

I'd like to be buried near you and perhaps the best place would be the dry high land just west of the little house that holds the generators. The drainage there is very good. Down on the lower part of the property where the monkey flowers are is very wet. The water table makes it unsuitable for a burial spot.

I thought you might at the last minute change your mind and decide to be buried next to your Father in Portland. That is something I leave to your own discretion.

To Cathleen Heffernan Douglas

June 28, 1977

Dear Cathy:

I've remembered that I would qualify for burial in the Arlington National Cemetery since I was in World War I. I wasn't very high—Private First Class—but I was honorably discharged.

Earl Warren and Hugo Black are buried there and if you want to pursue it Clark Clifford would be the one to talk to because he knows all the ropes. But don't push it or worry about it because Yakima or Goose Prairie would be fine with me.

To Edward L.R. Elson[1]

November 28, 1977

Dear Doctor Elson:

It was a great pleasure seeing you the other day at Walter Reed when I was in for a check-up.

I have been very despondent in recent weeks. I feel that I am walking the last mile and that I will not last much longer. So, I have been talking to members of my family about my will and funeral plans. I told Cathy if there was a funeral service, I wanted you to speak the words because you are my Pastor and I have enjoyed and appreciated our association during the last years. You came into my office during the impeachment proceedings and professed your confidence in me, and that meant a great deal to me in those dark times.

You have no physical resemblance to my father, but you and he think alike and approach the scriptures in much the same way. I hope to be buried next to my father in the church cemetery in Yakima, Washington. He would be thrilled to know that you were performing the last rites.

I would be honored if you could be in charge of the last rites.

---

1.   Chaplain of the Senate.

To Edward L.R. Elson

December 7, 1977

Dear Doctor Elson:
This is an addendum to the letter of November 28 which I wrote you concerning my funeral arrangements.

Years ago I knew a cowboy out West who used to sit rocking back and forth on a kitchen chair singing the Lord's Prayer. It was a beautiful rendition, and the last time I saw him I asked him if he would wash his blue jeans and polish his boots and come East to sing it at my funeral. I am sorry to report that he died before he was able to do this. Among the baritones you know from your church assignments, there should be one splendid vocalist who could do it.

And then from my hobo days, I knew the famous songwriter Woody Guthrie who wrote a song called, "This Land is Your Land, This Land is My Land". It reflects not a socialist dream of mine, but many of the freedoms that are explicit or implicit in the Constitution, such as the right to move from place to place to look for a job or establish a new home, and the right to move interstate without payment of a fee, as some states within the last thirty years have tried to impose. In other words, it expresses the vagrancy issue as I have expressed it and as it has become in-grained in the law. (See my opinion in *Papachristou et al* v. *City of Jacksonville,* 405 U.S. 156 [1972].)

Another song that goes way back to my boyhood was one that Mother and Father used to sing. Mother was a soprano vocalist in the church and Father was a singing evangelist at the beginning of his career. One song that they liked to sing was, "We Shall Gather at the River". If this is not the exact title, I am sure you will remember it, as this is an old and familiar song.

To The Wall Street Journal

October 16, 1978

To the Editors:
Notice of my demise has been emanating from several sources recently, not the least of which is your Journal.

Please be advised that I am today joining the ranks of citizens known as octogenarians and I assure you that I was never in a position to be resurrected in order to achieve such standing.

To Edward Moore Kennedy

March 13, 1979

Dear Ted:
The last time we saw each other, we talked of having lunch together, but didn't set a definite date.

This is to let you know that I could be available this week or next.

To William O. Douglas, Jr. and Mildred Douglas Read

July 3, 1979

I am dictating this to Rebecca because I am so weak I don't know if I will live long enough to tell either of you in person.

I just want to let you both know that with this memo comes all the love that I have for any human beings. I am mighty proud of both of you and I wish you great happiness.

William Orville Douglas entered Walter Reed Hospital on Christmas Eve 1979, suffering from pneumonia and kidney failure; he died on January 19, 1980, with his wife and children at his side.

Funeral services went as he had planned. On January 23, the

President and Vice President of the United States, many members of Congress, and his Brethren from the United States Supreme Court, gathered at the National Presbyterian Church in Washington. The Reverend Elson conducted the services along the lines Douglas had suggested. The United States Army Chorus sang "Shall We Gather at the River," Master Sergeant William F. Kugel sang "The Lord's Prayer," and the entire assemblage joined in "This Land Is Your Land." The Reverend Elson read portions of Douglas's letters to him to explain why certain songs had been included.

In his eulogy before the flag-draped coffin, Chief Justice Burger noted "There was a time when some who differed with him on issues mistakenly described him as an atheist and even questioned his belief in the American system. This shows how terribly wrong perceptions can be." Clark Clifford, Abe Fortas, Sidney Davis, and Eric Severeid rose to praise his contributions in protecting individual rights. "Each one of us is freer, safer, and stronger," declared Clifford, because of Douglas. "His person inhabited the beautiful places; so did his mind and spirit," said Severeid. Fortas, who had known Douglas since their days at Yale, recalled his friend's deep commitment to individual liberty, but he also recalled another side of the man, the one who had once induced the dean of the Yale Law School to board a train for Boston when he was supposed to be speaking in New York.

Douglas was interred later in the day with military honors at Arlington National Cemetery, only twenty feet from the resting place of another of the Court's great dissenters, Oliver Wendell Holmes.

Acknowledgments

Anumber of people made it possible for me to do this book. The Honorable Sheldon S. Cohen first told me about the Douglas Papers, then sealed in a warehouse outside of Washington. A friend of the Justice and one of the financial executors of his estate, Cohen spoke confidently of a "gold mine" of fascinating material buried in hundreds of stacked storage boxes.

With his assistance, I contacted the Justice's widow, Mrs. Cathleen Heffernan Douglas. She agreed to allow me into the papers on a "fishing expedition," and my son Philip and I spent a day in the Library of Congress warehouse in suburban Maryland. If anything, Sheldon Cohen's description of the papers as a "gold mine" proved an understatement. Douglas had kept meticulous notes on his travels, the cases he heard before the Court, his finances, and anything that interested him, while his secretaries—who enjoyed an amazing longevity in his employ—had kept thorough files of his correspondence.

After several months of negotiations, delayed by Mrs. Douglas's remarriage and her moving from Washington to Boston to establish a law practice, I received permission from her and from another of the estate's literary executors, Professor Vern Countryman of the Harvard Law School, to enter the Douglas Papers for the purpose of selecting letters for this volume. They placed no limits on what I could see, nor did they impose any restraints on what I could publish.

In July 1985, Philip and I spent several weeks working our way through the uncataloged materials. David Wigoder, the twentieth-century specialist in the Manuscripts Division, and the staff of the Manuscript Reading Room made our work not only productive but, as they always do, pleasant as well.

My agent, Audrey Wolf, has been a booster of this work from the beginning, and she brought author and publisher together. George Walsh, then chief editor, worked with me in the early stages of this book, and after he left, Jim and Esthy Adler themselves saw it through to completion. Their idea of creating a public-affairs press based in the nation's capital made this work and their publishing house a natural match, and it has been a pleasure working with them. Howard Cady gave the manuscript a careful reading and made a number of suggestions which greatly improved it; Madelyn Larsen's fine eye for detail saved me from numerous errors and gave the manuscript an added gloss. Others at Adler & Adler who contributed to the book were Jean Bernard, Lorrie Castaneda, Kathy Stafford, and Elizabeth Sweeney.

I also owe thanks to friends such as Miriam and Howard Netter of Albany, New York, who introduced me to Audrey, and to Jay Weinberg of Richmond, Virginia, whose advice on some legal matters proved very reassuring. Wanda Clary typed the various bits and pieces of paper I assembled into a proper manuscript with her usual efficiency. My wife, Susan, and son Robert tolerated our absence with a mixture of good humor and relief and showed extraordinary patience (most of the time) when it seemed Philip and I went on interminably about our work.

To Philip, now in his third year at the University of Virginia Law School, I owe a special debt. He had been my research assistant on several previous projects. During those years he picked up an astonishingly wide knowledge of things historical, political, and legal, as well as a marvelous facility for research. In this work he really became more of a collaborator than an assistant, and it seems only right that he be recognized as such.

Ronne and Cecil Jacobs and Sylvia and David Fine play a very important part in our lives. They are more than just friends; they have become family to Susan and to me. The six of us have enjoyed wonderful times and have helped each other through some bad moments as well. The dedication is but a token of the love and esteem we have for them.

Richmond, Virginia

FOR FURTHER READING

Persons interested in learning more about Douglas's life can start with the three volumes which constitute an autobiography, *Of Men and Mountains* (1950), *Go East, Young Man* (1974), and *The Court Years, 1939–1975* (1980). An excellent biography is James Simon, *Independent Journey: Life of William O. Douglas* (1980). Legal Realism is explained in Laura Kalman, *Legal Realism at Yale, 1927–1960* (1986), while the SEC is detailed in Michael E. Parrish, *Securities Regulation and the New Deal* (1970). Most of Douglas's more important opinions are in Vern Countryman, ed., *The Douglas Opinions* (1977), while his views on free expression can be found in Haig A. Bosmajian, ed., *Justice Douglas and Freedom of Speech* (1980). Bernard Wolfman et al. have attacked Douglas's taxation views in *Dissent Without Opinion* (1975).

Index

ABOUT THE MAKING OF THIS BOOK

The text of *The Douglas Letters* was set
in Avanta by ComCom, a division of
The Haddon Craftsmen of Allentown,
Pennsylvania. The book was printed and
bound by Maple Vail. The typography
and binding were designed by Tom
Suzuki of Falls Church, Virginia.